The Study of Social Problems

Seven Perspectives

SIXTH EDITION

Edited by
Earl Rubington
Martin S. Weinberg

New York   Oxford
OXFORD UNIVERSITY PRESS
2003

Oxford University Press

Auckland Bangkok Buenos Aires Cape Town Chennai
Dar es Salaam Delhi Hong Kong Istanbul Karachi Kolkata
Kuala Lumpur Madrid Melbourne Mexico City Mumbai Nairobi
São Paulo Shanghai Singapore Taipei Tokyo Toronto
and an associated company in Berlin

Copyright © 1971, 1977, 1981, 1989, 1995, 2003
by Oxford University Press, Inc.

Published by Oxford University Press, Inc.
198 Madison Avenue, New York, New York 10016

Oxford is a registered trademark of Oxford University Press

Library of Congress Cataloging-in-Publication Data

The study of social problems : seven perspectives / edited by Earl Rubington, Martin S.
Weinberg—6th ed.
   p. cm.
  Includes bibliographical references.
  ISBN-13 978-0-19-514219-8 (alk. paper)
  ISBN 0-19-514219-5 (alk. paper)
   1. Social problems. 2. Sociology—United States. I. Rubington, Earl. II. Weinberg,
Martin S.

HN17.5 .S837 2003
361.1—dc21

                                         2002070906

9 8 7 6 5 4 3

Printed in the United States
on acid-free paper

Dedicated to the memory of
Rose L. Rubington
and Herman H. Rubington,
Edith L. Weinberg,
and Fred C. Weinberg

CONTENTS

6. Labeling   172

7. Critical Perspective   221

8. Social Constructionism   279

PREFACE

Sociologists have long felt a need for a book that places social problems in a sociological perspective. In addition, instructors of social problems courses have been looking for sociological explanations for, rather than mere descriptions of, various social problems. We planned the first edition of *The Study of Social Problems* to give instructors the backdrop, perspectives, and explanations they sought. In that edition, we examined the five major theoretical sociological perspectives on social problems: Social Pathology, Social Disorganization, Value Conflict, Deviant Behavior, and Labeling. For each perspective, an introductory essay dealt with the people and the works that had fashioned it, the circumstances and stage of American sociology during which it arose, and its essential characteristics. Reprinted readings that exemplified the perspective followed each introductory essay, along with a critique of the perspective. Each chapter ended with questions for discussion and an annotated reference list for further study and exploration. This was the framework with which we hoped to provide a brief but comprehensive survey of social problems theory.

The second and third editions, which took into account some of the criticisms from students and instructors regarding the complexity of some of the introductory essays and reprinted readings, were made clearer and more readable. Sue Kiefer Hammersmith played a major role in editing the introductions so that undergraduates could understand them more readily.

In the fourth edition, we added an increasingly popular sixth perspective, the Critical Perspective. In so doing, we acknowledged the fertility of a variety of holistic perspectives on culture and society that draw from the tradition established by Karl Marx more than a hundred years ago. We thank David Zaret for his helpful comments on a draft of this chapter.

In the fifth edition we added a seventh perspective, Social Constructionism. This perspective, a synthesis of some earlier ones, has captured the imagination of a whole network of sociologists who study social problems.

In this edition, the sixth, we have updated the text, readings, and annotated references. Our thanks to Elizabeth Arnott for her help in obtaining permissions and taking care of the administrative tasks for this new edition.

The Study of Social Problems has always been intended for instructors who want to lay a sound theoretical foundation for their courses in social problems. We hope that this new edition will continue to be helpful in this enterprise.

Boston   E.R.
Bloomington   M.S.W.

I / THE PROBLEM

1 / SOCIAL PROBLEMS AND SOCIOLOGY

The morning paper reports a variety of social problems: war, pollution, traffic jams, and crimes. It also reports a decrease in automobile sales, rising prices, violence in high schools, an increase in drug use and cigarette smoking, and so on. After reading the news, readers find themselves upset about some of these reports, and, wanting to do something about them, they have mixed feelings about other news stories and are neutral or indifferent to many of the stories. On occasion, readers even experience secret or open delight at the misfortunes of others. The variety and inconsistency of these responses point to the complexities that surround the idea of social problems.

In addition, those who analyze social problems often differ among themselves. Some analysts say that modern society produces more social problems than do simpler societies; others disagree. Some say that modern society produces more problems than solutions, but others argue that the real difficulty lies in the overproduction of so-called solutions.

Trying to make sense of all this can easily result in confusion. Yet people continue to study social problems in an effort to understand how they occur and how they can be controlled. And more often than not the people studying social problems have been sociologists.

Sociologists have dominated the study of social problems for two reasons. First, sociology developed about a century ago, just when industrialization and urbanization seemed to be shaking the foundations of traditional society. At that time, there was a special interest in the problems people saw resulting from industrialization and urbanization, and sociologists, sharing this interest, took up the study of social problems as a relevant and challenging topic.

Second, sociology as a discipline lends itself especially well to the study of social problems. Sociology deals with social relations, those situations in which two or more people adapt their conduct to each other's. Most social problems arise in the course of, or as a result of, social relations. Few other disciplines in the late nineteenth century dealt with matters of this kind. Thus, partly by choice and partly by default, sociology arose to deal simultaneously with social problems and with social relations.

In this book, we look at how American sociologists have organized the study of social problems. We focus on the ideas and assumptions that have guided, and continue to guide, that study, and we examine the different perspectives on social problems that sociologists have developed. First, however, we examine just what sociologists mean by the term "social problem," how they came to study social problems, and how sociologists have differed in their treatment of social problems from time to time.

THE DEFINITION OF A SOCIAL PROBLEM

Some of the conditions we consider to be social problems were not so considered in earlier times. And some of the things our grandparents saw as social problems are accepted without question today. Some of the conditions we now ignore will undoubtedly come to be seen as social problems in the future. And there are probably some things that, regardless of their troublesome nature, never have been and never will be considered to be social problems.

What, then, makes a social problem? Sociologists usually consider a social problem to be *an alleged situation that is incompatible with the values of a significant number of people who agree that action is needed to alter the situation.* Let us consider this definition more closely.

An Alleged Situation.   This means that the situation is said to exist. People talk about it, and it may receive coverage on radio, on TV, and in the press. The allegation, however, need not actually be true. For example, a fear commonly expressed by white homeowners has been that desegregation of their neighborhoods would decrease the property values of their homes. Yet often the opposite is actually the case. There has been substantial demand for middle-class housing among blacks, and blacks have systematically been overcharged for such housing. As a result, after an initial period of panic selling by white homeowners, the same homes often sell for more after desegregation than before.[1]

Incompatible with Values.[2]   A situation is defined by people as a social problem in terms of certain values they hold. For example, pollution is considered to be a problem in light of the values people place on health and on preserving the natural environment. Traffic jams are considered to be a social problem in light of the value people place on their time. Communism is considered to be a social problem in light of the values people place on a capitalist economy and on certain types of personal freedom.

People are diverse and complex, however. Different people hold different values, and the same person may hold conflicting values. For these reasons, different people consider different things to be social problems. For example, while the environmentalist focuses on the problem of pollution, the auto manufacturer may be focusing on matters of profit and the economy. Thus, the auto manufacturer may see the government's requiring pollution control devices on cars as the real problem. Likewise, the driver who lives in a rural area where pollution is not apparent may value clean air, but he or she may also value good gas mileage. This driver, then, might agree with the auto manufacturer that the government's requiring pollution control devices, which cut gas mileage, is the problem.

Thus, what comes to be considered a social problem and the values that are involved are a complex matter. This is one of the most controversial aspects of the study of social problems, and it will be dealt with in more detail throughout this book.

1. See, for example, the description of blockbusting in Leonard Downie, Jr., *Mortgage on America* (New York: Praeger, 1974), pp. 14–22.

2. Note that many sociologists now emphasize "interests" rather than values. We recognize these types of considerations and consider "interests" to be subsumed under the term "values."

A Significant Number of People. How many people are "a significant number"? This question has no clearcut answer. And, of course, some people are more "significant" than others. The President of the United States, for example, is more powerful than an ordinary citizen in determining whether or not a particular situation is defined as a social problem. Likewise, adults are more "significant" than children are in defining social problems, and middle-class people are more "significant" than are lower-class people.

Sociologists would agree that in general the more "significant" people for defining social problems are those who are more organized, are in positions of leadership, and/or are more powerful in economic, social, or political affairs. So it is not just a matter of numbers. The important point for the study of social problems, however, is this: when sociologists study social problems, they usually look at what other people in the society consider to be social problems. Thus, in studying social problems sociologists usually deal only with socially troublesome or deleterious situations that are recognized as problems by the public.[3]

Action Is Needed. Hand in hand with the definition of a situation as a social problem is the call for action to remedy the situation. People say among themselves that something must be done. They may write letters to the editor, circulate petitions, or hold rallies. Laws or ordinances may be passed and regulations enacted. And organizations may be formed to deal with the situation. Thus, sociologists generally regard social problems as situations that are not just troublesome but that, in addition, people want corrected and/or are trying to correct.

If there is no call for action, then, most sociologists would not conceptualize the situation as a social problem even though it may be troublesome to a large number of people. For example, the sociologist may see the doctor's waiting room as one of the more aggravating situations in our society. Patients often have to sit for hours in a small room with nothing to do. Many patients would rather be home in bed, and some dislike being exposed to the infections of other patients in the waiting room. Yet we hear no call for action. Complaints are numerous, but no demand is made that the situation be changed. Thus, the sociologist is not likely to consider the doctor's waiting room as one of our social problems.

THE DEVELOPMENT OF AMERICAN SOCIOLOGY

The study of social problems has been inextricably intertwined with the field of sociology as a whole. Changes in the study of social problems have been closely related to more general developments in the field of sociology, and the different perspectives on social problems reflect different perspectives on society in general. Before turning to these different perspectives, then, let us take a more general look at the field of sociology.

3. It has been argued that the practice of studying what the public recognizes as social problems leads sociologists to neglect problems that are serious but unrecognized. Moreover, this approach is said to contain an implicit class bias in that troublesome conditions are more likely to be regarded as social problems when upper-class people label them as such. See, for example, Jerome G. Manis, "Assessing the Seriousness of Social Problems," *Social Problems* 22 (October 1974): 1–15; Alex Thio, "Class Bias in the Sociology of Deviance," *The American Sociologist* 8 (February 1973): 1–12; Alexander Liazos, "The Poverty of the Sociology of Deviance: Nuts, Sluts, and Preverts [sic]," *Social Problems* 20 (Summer 1972): 103–20; and Kenneth Westhues, "Social Problems as Systematic Costs," *Social Problems* 20 (Spring 1973): 419–31. An excerpt of Westhues' article is included in Chapter 4 of this book.

For centuries, people have thought about and studied their lives in society. But it remained for Auguste Comte in 1838 to give that activity a name. He coined the term "sociology," which means the scientific study of society.[4] Comte's interests, like those of Saint-Simon, Marx, Tocqueville, Spencer, and other early European sociologists, arose from the crises of industrialism. Accordingly, the big questions for these early European sociologists involved issues of social order and integration, on the one hand, and social development and change, on the other. The first of these questions asked, What holds a society together and makes it work? The second asked, Where is the society going, and how is it going there?

In the same way, the post-Civil War upheaval and the rise of industrialism in the United States spawned an interest in studying this society. In the two decades after the Civil War, books had begun to appear on the subject. By the middle of the 1890s, sociology courses were being taught in a number of American colleges. The first Ph.D. in sociology was granted in 1895, and the American Sociological Society was formed in 1905.

In the years that followed, American sociology continued to develop as an academic discipline, and it continued to deal with social problems. The ways in which sociologists dealt with such problems, however, changed from time to time. These changes reflect a succession of traditions in the development of sociology.

A "tradition" refers to beliefs, values, and customs. As new ideas are developed and as conditions change, these beliefs, values, and customs also change. In order to understand the study of social problems, and how it has changed over time, we must understand the changing traditions in the development of sociology.

The various traditions in the development of American sociology can be arbitrarily grouped into five stages: establishing a base (1905 to 1918); forming a scientific policy (1918 to 1935); integrating theory, research, and application (1935 to 1954); cultivating specialties (1954 to 1970); the reemergence of macro theory (1970 to 1985); and the ascendency of constructionism (1985 on).[5] The changing perspectives on social problems outlined in this book reflect these basic changes in the development of sociology.

1. Establishing a Base (1905 to 1918).   During the years between 1905 and 1918, a hardy band of pioneers established the study of sociology in a number of American colleges. At that time, most of the leading American sociologists were ministers' sons who had moved from small towns to the rapidly growing cities and who had witnessed the changes resulting from America's recent conversion from a farm to a factory economy. Their primary emphasis was on the problems of society, and they saw urbanism as the main source of social problems.

These early American sociologists were guided in their thinking by the philosophy of moral progress—that is, the notion that in the long run, societies improve in quality. Thus, they were more or less convinced that progress and moral uplift would occur. At the same time, they wanted to take a hand in solving some of the problems they saw around them in their rapidly changing society. These early American sociologists tried very hard to eliminate these problems. Their conservative way of thinking, however, led them to advocate social reform rather than revolution.

---

4. Auguste Comte, *Positive Philosophy,* trans. Harriet Martineau (London: George Bell & Sons, 1896).

5. This discussion uses all the dates for the first three stages, some but not all the arguments, and none of the titles that appear in Roscoe C. Hinkle and Gisela J. Hinkle, *The Development of Modern Sociology: Its Nature and Growth in the United States* (New York: Doubleday, 1954).

2. Forming a Scientific Policy (1918 to 1935). During this period, I dampened the optimism that had characterized the first period of Amer ology. Increasingly, sociologists began to realize that if they were ever going social action, they first had to develop a body of sociological knowledge. scientific method, rather than the values of small-town society, seemed mo. ..ly to produce such knowledge. Accordingly, during this period attention turned from solving the problems of society to developing sociology as a scientific discipline. The conviction grew among sociologists that science should be value-free, and working to solve social problems came to be regarded as somehow "unscientific."

3. Integrating Theory, Research, and Application (1935 to 1954). If the first period might be called an era of preaching, and the second period an era of retreat, then this period could be called an era of scientific contribution. During this period, sociologists became more professionalized, and they began to see theory, research, and applications as integrally related. As they did so, they began again to accept social reform as part of the sociological endeavor. Basic research and applied sociology came to be seen as two sides of the same coin, and the predominant attitude was that a scientific approach would both solve social problems and develop sociology as a science.

4. Cultivating Specialties (1954 to 1970). In the mid-1950s, sociology came of age. Both the number of sociologists and the number of sociology courses multiplied. For example, from 1926 to 1946, a total of 1,094 Ph.D.s in sociology were granted in the United States (an average of 55 per year); in the ten-year period from 1954 to 1964, 1,729 were granted (an average of 173 per year). At the same time, the sophistication of sociological work increased tremendously. Sociology became specialized, and within the various specialties sociologists began to develop bodies of theory and findings.

After 1954, however, rumblings began to be heard. Many sociologists began to feel that, in their race to answer basic theoretical questions, they had ignored the problems of society. These sociologists began to feel that sociology had neglected its social responsibility and become an instrument of the status quo. This attack was echoed by the next generation of college students. Thus, the recurrent tension between social problems and sociological problems became relevant to the students of sociology as well as to sociologists.

5. The Reemergence of Macro Theory (1970 to 1985). The attack on sociology as a theoretical discipline, which reached its peak in the early 1970s, and Gouldner's *Coming Crisis of Western Sociology,* which was published in 1970, heralded the most recent stage in sociology's development. Gouldner argued that sociology had reached a dead end in its usefulness to a society increasingly in crisis. A critical point of view was seen to be necessary in order to grapple with the problems of both sociology and society. Gouldner himself, in a series of books, extended and deepened a critical Marxist approach. He also helped found the journal *Theory and Society,* which was to become the main scholarly voice of this view of society.

Such concerns as these were evident not only in the United States, but also in Europe, in particular in England and Germany. And, in some ways, this most recent synthesis of Marxist cultural and economic analyses has provided powerful resistance to the Americanization of sociology throughout the academic world and provided a strong push to return sociology to its European roots. In so doing, it has restored a macrosociological, rather than microsociological, view of social problems.

6. The Ascendancy of Constructionism (1985 on).   Multiplication of perspectives, a characteristic feature of society in general during the latter part of the twentieth century, was also reflected in academic settings. Establishment of specialized programs in African American Studies, Latino Studies, Women's Studies, and Gay and Lesbian Studies increased the entrance of women and other minorities into faculties and student bodies, and it also increased the diversity of perspectives on many college campuses. As sociology itself became less socially and culturally homogeneous, its practitioners became aware of diverse perspectives, both in everyday life and with regard to its own conceptual traditions.

While traditional approaches to studying sociology continued to dominate, the profusion of symbols, languages, knowledge, and vocal persons and groups that people increasingly came into frequent contact with helped to popularize a constructionist approach toward gaining an understanding of social life. This involved explicating the point of view of people in various social locations. How particular groups of people constructed the meaning of events and situations became a basic question of all the academic disciplines. The constructionist approach became a familiar one in anthropology, literary criticism, psychology, history, cultural studies, sexuality studies, and sociology, especially in the study of gender, science, and social problems.

SOCIOLOGICAL PERSPECTIVES ON SOCIAL PROBLEMS

A perspective, generally speaking, is a way of looking at things. A sociological perspective includes a basic orienting idea from which one's conceptualization and analysis follow, and it reflects a particular set of ideas and assumptions regarding the nature of people and society. There are, of course, different ways of looking at social problems, and in sociology seven perspectives have been popular. In large part, these perspectives reflect the tension that has existed since sociology first developed—the tension between concentrating on the problems of society, on the one hand, and on the development of sociology as a scientific discipline, on the other. As sociologists emphasized first one and then another of these goals, they developed the perspectives dealt with in this book. These perspectives resolved for their proponents the questions of what should be studied, how it should be studied, and how the study would contribute to reforming society and to basic sociological knowledge.

The seven perspectives are Social Pathology, Social Disorganization, Value Conflict, Deviant Behavior, Labeling, the Critical Perspective, and the Social Constructionist Perspective. Each perspective contains its own notion of the definition, causes, conditions, consequences, and solutions of social problems. In order to better understand these alternative ways of looking at social problems, in the chapters that follow we will analyze each perspective in terms of these five elements. Before proceeding, we clarify what each element involves.

Definition.   We have already presented one general definition of social problems (see page 4), and each of the seven perspectives does, implicitly, presuppose this definition. In addition, however, each perspective includes its own more specialized definition of social problems. These more specialized definitions vary in terms of which particular aspect of a socially troublesome phenomenon they focus on in defining that phenomenon as a social problem. For example, all social problems involve expectations, alleged violations of these expectations, and reactions to the violations. Nonetheless, the seven perspectives differ in terms of whether the definition of the social problem hinges on the expectations, the alleged violations, or the reactions.

Causes.   Each perspective includes its own causal imagery—that is, its own set of ideas about what types of factors produce social problems and how they do so.

Conditions.   Each perspective also has something to say, implicitly or explicitly, about the conditions under which social problems emerge and develop. These are not the immediate causes of social problems. Rather, they are the more general background features out of which the causes of social problems develop.

Consequences.   All seven perspectives view social problems as harmful. They differ, however, in terms of how the harmful effects of social problems are described.

Solutions.   Finally, each perspective includes its own implications about how we can solve social problems. The perspectives emerged at different points in the development of sociology. Thus, some are more explicitly concerned with social reform than are others. Nonetheless, all seven perspectives have some implications for the solution of social problems, and the characteristics of each perspective determine whether the solution focuses on expectations, violations, or reactions.[6]

PLAN OF THE BOOK

Each of the next seven chapters deals with one of the seven perspectives. Every chapter is organized along the following lines. First, there is a brief history of the perspective, including which sociologists contributed most to its development. Next, we give a summary of the perspective—its characteristics regarding the definition, causes, conditions, consequences, and solutions of social problems. Then we present readings that explicate and illustrate the perspective, followed by a selection that criticizes it. Questions for discussion and selected references complete the chapter.

As previously noted, these perspectives arose at different stages in the development of sociology. Thus, each has had periods of popularity and periods of relative neglect. Yet even today each is to some degree the basis for the thinking and writing of some sociologists. This, more than anything else, is the reason for this book.

SUMMARY AND CONCLUSION

Sociology began in the late 1800s with a dual mandate to study social relations, on the one hand, and social problems, on the other. Since then, there has been a recurrent tension in sociology over which of these should receive primary emphasis. In an effort to resolve this tension, sociologists have from time to time developed new perspectives for the study of social problems.

A perspective is basically a way of looking at things, and it clarifies for the sociologist the focus of his or her work. In the study of social problems, sociologists have fashioned seven popular perspectives: Social Pathology, Social Disorganization, Value Conflict, Deviant Behavior, Labeling, the Critical Perspective, and Social Constructionism. Each perspective has its own notion of the definition, causes, conditions, consequences, and solutions of social problems. Now, we look more closely at each of the perspectives.

---

6. The implications of each of the first five perspectives for the solution of social problems are more thoroughly examined, and illustrated by readings, in Martin S. Weinberg, Earl Rubington and Sue Kiefer Hammersmith, eds., *The Solution of Social Problems: Five Perspectives*, 2nd ed. (New York: Oxford University Press, 1981).

Selected References

Berger, Peter L., and Thomas Luckmann. *The Social Construction of Reality.* New York: Anchor Books, 1967.

The first book in English to introduce the concept of social construction. Social construction, for Berger and Luckmann, is the process by which people convert subjective meanings into what are accepted as objective fact. They note the paradox "that man is capable of producing a world that he then experiences as something other than a human product."

Bernard, Jessie. *Social Problems at Midcentury: Role, Status, and Stress in a Context of Abundance.* New York: Holt, Rinehart and Winston, 1957.

A text that is extremely useful for its discussion of how middle-class reformers first formulated the concept of social problems.

Denzin, Norman K. "Who Leads: Sociology or Society?" *The American Sociologist* 5 (May 1970): 125–27.

A concise argument that sociology should itself lead the society, rather than be led by it, in formulating problems for study.

Gusfield, Joseph R. "On the Side: Practical Action and Social Constructionism in Social Problems Theory." In *Studies in the Sociology of Social Problems,* ed. Joseph W. Schneider and John I. Kitsuse. Norwood, NJ: Ablex, 1984, pp. 31–51.

Recent discussions of social problems theory have argued that sociologists study social problems because they share the values of those offended by the existence of the problems and because they wish to solve these problems. Gusfield argues that the sociologist should only ascertain the conditions under which the situation came to be defined as a social problem. Such a position, he argues, ends up by clarifying values while remaining silent on the question of how to achieve them.

Hinkle, Roscoe C. *Founding Theory of American Sociology 1881–1915.* London: Routledge and Kegan Paul, 1980.

From its very inception as an academic discipline, sociologists were very concerned about solving the social problems that accompanied industrialization, immigration, and urbanization. But at the same time they were concerned about establishing sociology as a scientific discipline. Tension from this dual mandate continues to influence sociological work to this very day.

Hinkle, Roscoe, C. and Gisela J. Hinkle. *The Development of Modern Sociology: Its Nature and Growth in the United States.* New York: Doubleday, 1954.

One of the best discussions of the rise and development of American sociology. Admirable for the wealth of its scholarship and the brevity of its presentation.

Lazarsfeld, Paul F., William H. Sewell, and Harold L. Wilensky, eds. *The Uses of Sociology.* New York: Basic Books, 1967.

A collection of essays on the application of sociology for the solution of social problems.

Lynd, Robert S. *Knowledge for What? The Place of Social Science in American Culture.* Princeton, N.J.: Princeton University Press, 1939.

Perhaps the best argument to date for using scientific knowledge to help society.

Maines, David R. "The Social Construction of Meaning." *Contemporary Sociology* 29 (July 2000): 577–84.

The constructionist perspective, developed best in the area of social problems, "has clearly grown rapidly in the last 30 years and now is being used in nearly every area of sociology." Maines says that constructionists try to show that the interpretations people make of social conditions produce, maintain, and change those very conditions. He goes on to argue that some categorical constructions, such as religion and race, have much greater consequences than do others. He further notes that the meaning of any construction depends quite heavily on the situation in which people express it.

Mauss, Armand. "Social Problems." In *Encyclopedia of Sociology*, ed. Edgar F. Borgatta and Marie L. Borgatta. New York: Macmillan, 1992, Vol. 4, pp. 1916–21.

Mauss argues that there are currently two sociological orientations toward social problems, the objectivist and the subjectivist. Most undergraduate textbooks on social problems today are in the objectivist tradition. Most of the current research on social problems, on the other hand, is in the subjectivist tradition. For the most part, this is because most students understand the objectivist tradition but have considerable difficulty following subjectivist arguments.

Nisbet, Robert A. *The Social Bond.* New York: Knopf, 1970.

An introductory text that defines sociology as the study of social interaction and shows how sociological concepts are employed to analyze interaction. Contains a useful discussion of the distinction between sociological problems and social problems.

II / THE PERSPECTIVES

2/SOCIAL PATHOLOGY

The idea that there are social problems would appear to be as old as man. But actually, this is not the case at all. Though problems and suffering seem to be found in every society and every historical period, the notion that they are social problems about which something should be done is fairly recent.[1] Before examining the social pathology perspective, we consider briefly how the idea of social problems came into being.

THE CONCEPT OF SOCIAL PROBLEMS

Nineteenth-century America witnessed the ushering in of the urban-industrial order. People began to migrate from farms to cities, and emigration from Europe brought additional thousands to America's burgeoning cities. As the cities swelled, a number of troublesome conditions became more and more noticeable. Near the end of the Civil War, the notion arose that these conditions of suffering, pain, social disorder, institutional malfunctioning, and the like could be remedied. With this corrective attitude, the concept of social problems was born.

Primarily, it was middle-class reformers who perceived situations in the cities as social problems. Impressed with scientific ideology and imbued with the humanism of the Enlightenment, they felt that scientific study, which had solved the puzzles of the physical universe, could also solve the problems of society.

Around 1865, the American Social Science Association was formed. Social reform was the overall goal of the association, and the scientific study of social problems was its immediate objective.[2] In time, however, a number of schisms took place within the association. First, several groups split off and formed more specialized associations in their respective academic disciplines—economics, political science, and so on. Second, within the association itself, distinctions arose between theory, on the one hand, and application, on the other. Eventually the association was dis-

1. According to Arnold Green, a consciousness of social problems did not arise until the latter part of the eighteenth century. Four ideas—those of equality, humanitarianism, the goodness of human nature, and the modifiability of social conditions—made this consciousness possible. See Arnold Green, *Social Problems: Arena of Conflict* (New York: McGraw-Hill, 1975).

2. For a more detailed discussion of the notion of social problems and the rise and fall of the American Social Science Association, see Jessie Bernard, *Social Problems at Mid-century: Role, Status, and Stress in a Context of Abundance* (New York: Holt, Rinehart, and Winston, 1957), pp. 90–102.

banded. It left a legacy, however, of social problems courses, which were soon being given in American universities by a variety of disciplines. As sociology became better established, it took over more and more of these courses.

Very much a product of its times, early American sociology dove-tailed neatly with the objectives of the American Social Science Association, as well as with the attitudes of middle-class reformers. In particular, early American sociology was characterized by four popular beliefs of the late nineteenth century: natural law, progress, social reform, and individualism.[3] Thus, the founding fathers of American sociology believed that human behavior was governed by natural laws and that it was the task of sociology to discover these laws. Most early sociologists also believed in progress. In the course of social evolution, they thought, societies change from simple to complex, and people become freer, more rational, and happier. At the same time, however, these early sociologists saw industrialization and urbanization as the sources of some undesirable conditions, and they wanted to ameliorate those conditions. Thus, the early sociologists wanted to discover the natural laws of human behavior so that they could effect social reform. Finally, these early sociologists had an individualistic conception of social life. They assumed that, although a person belongs to groups, it is ultimately one's personal interests, motives, and characteristics that determine one's behavior.

ROOTS OF THE SOCIAL PATHOLOGY PERSPECTIVE

Essentially, the social pathology perspective is rooted in the organic analogy. Some early writers employed this analogy in a relatively primitive fashion; for example, some portrayed the government as the head of society, the postal service as the nervous system, the police as the "long arm of the law." Herbert Spencer, however, made a more sophisticated use of the organic analogy. In his view, society is like an organism in that it has mass, a complexity of structure that increases with its growth, interdependent parts, and a life that surpasses the life of any particular part.[4]

To the writers employing the organic analogy, persons or situations were considered to be social problems to the extent that they interfered with the "normal" workings of the social organism. In keeping with the organic analogy, such interference was viewed as a form of illness, or pathology.

The influence of the organic analogy on early American sociology can be seen in the following definition of social pathology, which appeared in an early and widely used sociology textbook.[5]

> Since society is made up of individuals bound together in social relationships, social pathology refers to the maladjustments in social relationships. The phrase is based on the analogy of bodily maladjustment of function in the organ. . . . If carefully guarded . . . the term "social pathology" may be used to denote the social conditions which result (1) from failure of individuals so to adjust themselves to social life that they function as independent self-supporting members of society, who contribute their fair share to its stability and progressive development; and (2) from the lack of ad-

3. See Roscoe C. Hinkle, Jr., and Gisela J. Hinkle, *The Development of Modern Sociology: Its Nature and Growth in the United States* (New York: Doubleday, 1954), pp. 7–17.

4. Robert L. Cameiro, ed., *The Evolution of Society: Selections from Herbert Spencer's "Principles of Sociology"* (Chicago: University of Chicago Press, 1967).

5. John L. Gillin and Frank W. Blackmar, *Outlines of Sociology* (New York: Macmillan, 1930), p. 527.

justment of social structure, including ways of doing things and institutions, to the development of social personality.

Pathological conditions in society may result from (1) natural lack of ability in individuals to keep pace with the changing ideals and institutions of society; or (2) from the failure of society to keep pace in its functional machinery with the changing conditions in the world in which it lives.

The early social pathologists, then, saw both individual maladjustments (such as economic dependency) and institutional malfunctioning (such as economic depression) as obstacles in the forward march of social progress. Thus, they thought that such maladjustments, whether individual or institutional, should be rooted out.

Two sociologists who helped to establish the basic outline of the social pathology perspective were Charles Henderson and Samuel Smith. Both wrote social pathology textbooks, and the line of reasoning set forth in these books dominated the field of sociology for at least a generation.[6] Central to the work of Henderson, Smith, and their many followers in the field of textbook writing was cultural borrowing. Because sociology was still a young and developing field, sociologists were inclined to borrow ideas and metaphors from disciplines that were already well established, such as medicine, philosophy, economics, and political science. The medical metaphors of pathology and the organic analogy as developed in social philosophy helped to shape this perspective. In addition, most of these writers employed popular values in their sociological writings, saturating their textbooks with the moral judgments of the day.

Most of the social pathology textbooks appeared during the first two stages of American sociology. These texts dominated the classroom for years, with revisions appearing only every seven or eight years or more. This slow, settled pace of revision, coupled with the fact that only a few textbooks were available, perpetuated and strengthened the social pathology perspective. Today, in contrast, there are numerous textbooks representing different perspectives. Also, revisions appear every three years or so, allowing more opportunity to modify perspectives.

In addition, the slow and rather steady pace of social change during the early twentieth century probably made the original social pathology perspective seem more viable to early American sociologists than it may seem to us today. At that time, the status quo was more accepted as the normal, natural state of affairs. In such an atmosphere, it was easy for people to see anyone who deviated from the status quo as "sick."[7]

---

6. Charles Henderson, *Introduction to the Study of Dependent, Defective, and Delinquent Classes, and of Their Social Treatment* (Boston: Heath, 1909); Samuel Smith, *Social Pathology* (New York: Macmillan, 1911).

7. From a contemporary point of view, "there is little disagreement about what constitutes a healthy state of the organism. But there is much less agreement when one uses the notion of pathology analogically, to describe kinds of behavior that are regarded as deviant. For people do not agree on what constitutes healthy behavior. It is difficult to find a definition that will satisfy even such a select and limited group as psychiatrists; it is impossible to find one that people generally accept as they accept criteria of health for the organism" (Howard S. Becker, *Outsiders: Studies in the Sociology of Deviance* [New York: Free Press, 1963], p. 5).

CHANGES IN THE SOCIAL PATHOLOGY PERSPECTIVE

In its early form, the social pathology perspective was based on the metaphor of society as an organism. The so-called normal functioning of society was assumed to be "healthy," and the social pathologists occupied themselves with classifying the "ills" of society.

This simplistic and conservative strand of social pathology had its heyday before World War I, especially between 1890 and 1910. After the war, it went into slow but steady decline. In the 1960s, however, there was a resurgence of the social pathology perspective, with some sociologists again writing about the "pathology" of our existence.[8] Also, many liberals and radicals were seeing the society as "sick." Ironically, the "counter-culture" people (e.g., "hippies") who labeled society as sick were themselves the kinds of people whom the early social pathologists would have labeled "sick." However, there has been a blurring of these contrasting points of view in an attempt to make the pathology perspective more "objective" (e.g., see the selection by Kavolis in this chapter).

CHARACTERISTICS OF THE SOCIAL PATHOLOGY PERSPECTIVE

The more specific characteristics of this perspective are as follows:

Definition.   Desirable social conditions and arrangements are seen as healthy, while persons or situations that diverge from moral expectations are regarded as "sick," therefore bad. Thus, from the social pathology perspective, a social problem is a violation of *moral* expectations.

Causes.   The ultimate cause of social problems is a failure in socialization. Society, through its socializing agents, has the responsibility of transmitting moral norms to each generation. Sometimes, however, the socialization effort is ineffective. An early classification of deviants from the social pathology perspective portrayed them as defective, dependent, or delinquent.[9] Defectives cannot be taught; dependents are handicapped in receiving instruction; and delinquents reject the teachings. For later pathologists, social problems are the result of wrong values being learned. In this perspective's "tender" mood, the people who contribute to the social problem are viewed as "sick"; in its "tough" mood, they are viewed as "criminal." Behind both moods, however, is the notion that the person or situation is, at heart, "immoral."

Conditions.   The early social pathologists considered some people to be inherently defective. And, for the most part, the "defective, dependent, and delinquent" classes tended to perpetuate themselves through inbreeding.[10] Later, however, social pathologists began to see the social environment as the important condition

---

8. See, for example, Bernard Rosenberg, Israel Gerver, and F. William Howton, eds., *Mass Society in Crisis: Social Problems and Social Pathology* (New York: Macmillan, 1964).

9. Henderson, *Introduction to the Study*.

10. Lombroso claimed there was a definite "criminal type" and that these people were born criminal. The early social pathologists were much influenced by Lombroso's work, and they generalized his position to cover a host of "problem people." These dependent, defective, and delinquent people were viewed as the source of the great bulk of social problems. A summary of Lombroso's work may be found in Marvin E. Wolfgang, "Pioneers in Criminology: Cesare Lombroso (1835–1909)," *Journal of Criminal Law, Criminology, and Police Science* 52 (November–December 1961): 361–91.

contributing to social pathology. Indeed, Smith himself wrote, "social disease so prevalent as to create a social problem is rarely found without a bad environment of some sort or other, and so the social student is compelled to study the causes of social disease."[11] Whereas earlier pathologists tended to focus on the immoral properties of individuals, contemporary pathologists have tended to focus on the immoral properties of societies and to see problems as developing from societal forces such as technology and population density.

Consequences. In the early pathology view, social disturbances increase the cost of maintaining a legitimate social order. The early pathologists did believe, however, that ultimately the healthiest would survive. The more recent pathologists, in contrast, are morally indignant about the defects of society and are less optimistic in their prognosis. The most indignant see societal pathology as total, spreading, and likely to dehumanize the entire population.

Solutions. Both the early and the recent versions of the social pathology perspective suggest what form solutions to social problems might take. The early sociologists who dwelt on the troubles caused by "genetically" defective individuals, for example, turned to the eugenics movement as a solution. Other sociologists thought the solution to social problems lay in educating the troublemakers in middle-class morality. The recent variant, which tends to regard the society rather than its nonconforming members as "sick," has its roots in the Rousseauean view of human nature. Individuals are good; their institutions, on the other hand, are bad. Yet, even the modern social pathologists see the remedy to "sick" institutions as a change in people's values. Thus, according to this perspective, the only real solution to social problems is moral education.[12]

SUMMARY AND CONCLUSION

The social pathology perspective organized the thinking of early American sociologists with regard to social problems, and it has continued—in at least some quarters—to be an influential point of view. It is rooted in the organic analogy, and its primary concern is with the ills, or pathologies, of society.

From this perspective, social problems are seen as violations of moral expectations. Their cause is thought to be socialization failure, which was attributed first to genetic inheritance and later to social environment. The result of such failure is moral erosion; the solution, moral education.

Social pathologists can be grouped according to their period, orientation, and politics. Earlier pathologists tended to be conservative in their orientation and politics. Later pathologists tended to be liberal or radical in their orientation and politics. A synthesis of these approaches has appeared, but it is difficult to say what direction this perspective will take or what its influence will be in the future.

---

11. Smith, *Social Pathology,* p. 8.

12. For an early statement of this view, see Charles A. Ellwood, *The Social Problem: A Reconstructive Analysis* (New York: Macmillan, 1919).

THE ORGANIC ANALOGY
Samuel Smith

This brief excerpt from Samuel Smith's Social Pathology *shows the considerable influence the organic analogy had on writers around the turn of the century. Like medical doctors who study physical illness, social pathologists undertook to study the "social diseases" of society. And Smith believed that just as medical doctors study disease to learn how to treat it, so social pathologists study social problems in order to learn how to "cure" them.*

Pathology in social science has a certain parallel to pathology in medical science. As the study of physical disease is essential to the maintenance of physical health, so social health can never be securely grounded without a wider and more definite knowledge of social disease. General pathology in medicine teaches that many diseases have much in common and there are morbid processes which may be discussed, as well as particular diseases.

In social pathology the interrelation of the abnormal classes is one of the most impressive facts. Paupers often beget criminals; the offspring of criminals become insane; and to such an extent is the kinship of the defective, dependent, and delinquent classes exhibited, that some have gone so far as to hold that under all the various forms of social pathology there is a common ground in the morbid nervous condition of individuals.

Medical science classifies diseases and is not content with a study of symptoms, but seeks to find out the causes of the maladies with which it deals. Social students are coming to see with increasing clearness that the study and treatment of mere symptoms in social disease have been among the great defects of philanthropists and reformers who in times past, despite the generosity of their motives and the self-sacrifice of their labors, have failed in their task because of a lack of accurate observation and definite knowledge, which are the only foundations of wise action. The social doctrine is becoming clear and convincing to many minds that the individual can only be dealt with in his relationships. The weakness of the individual mind or will, the lack of development and the lack of self-control, are all elements in the problem but social disease so prevalent as to create a social problem is rarely found without a bad environment of some sort or other, and so the social student is compelled to study the causes of social disease.

Medical science teaches that the study of disease is only a step in the process leading to therapeutics, or the cure of disease, and instead of being the road to

From Samuel Smith, *Social Pathology*, pp. 8–9, 1911. The Macmillan Company.

despair in the vast majority of physical ills, it is the only basis of hope. Nearly every disease can be cured if it is taken in time, but the crowning achievement of medical science is not in therapeutics, but in sanitation and in the prevention of disease.

Social pathology would be a gloomy study indeed if its accurate knowledge of facts and principles did not indicate pathways out of social difficulties leading to a discovery of the means by which the social causes of disease can be removed, the weak individual be socially reinforced so that finally, as an ideal at least, the social body shall exist in the minds of social workers, radiant with health, in which there is not a living being which does not share in the general glow of wholesomeness and power.

THE CRIMINAL AS A BORN CRIMINAL TYPE
Cesare Lombroso and William Ferrero

In this excerpt, Lombroso and Ferrero analyze the facial characteristics of twenty female criminals. In these twenty faces they note such irregularities as facial asymmetry, large jaws, overlapping teeth, canine incisors, cleft palate, and receding forehead. They present these observations in support of Lombroso's theory—formulated in the early part of his career—that there are "born criminals" who represent biologically primitive specimens of Homo sapiens. These "born criminals," Lombroso reasoned, resemble apes in their physical characteristics, and thus can be identified as "throwbacks"—reversions to an earlier evolutionary stage.

Among the most ridiculous of the prohibitions obtaining in Italy, or rather in the Italian bureaucracy, which is certainly not the first in Europe, is the absolute impossibility of measuring, studying, or photographing the worst criminals once they have been condemned.

So long as there is a presumption of innocence, so long as these persons are only suspected or accused, one can discredit them in every way, and hold them up to publicity by recording their answers to their judges.

But once it is admitted beyond question that they are reprobates, once the prison doors have closed for good upon them—oh, then they become sacred; and woe to him who touches, woe to him who studies them!

Consumptive patients, pregnant women, may be manipulated, even to their hurt, by thousands of students for the good of science; but criminals—Heaven forefend!

From *The Female Offender* by Cesare Lombroso and William Ferrero. T. Fisher Unwin, London, 1895, pp. 88–93.

When one of the writers wished to publish photographs of male criminals in his "Uomo Delinquente," he was driven to the German prison "album"; and the difficulties thrown in his way by the Italian authorities were doubled in the case of female offenders and prostitutes, whose sense of shame it was considered necessary to respect in every way.

In Russian prisons Madame Tarnowsky was afforded every facility, and after making a complete study of the body and mind of the delinquents, she forwarded us their photographs.

FEMALE CRIMINALS

We will first take five homicides, of whom the two first have the true type of their class.

The first, aged 40, killed her husband with reiterated blows of a hatchet, while he was skimming the milk, then threw his body into a recess under the stairs, and during the night fled with the family money and her own trinkets. She was arrested a week later and confessed her crime. This woman was re-markable for the asymmetry of her face; her nose was hollowed out, her ears projecting, her brows more fully developed than is usual in a woman, her jaw enormous with a lemurian appendix.

No. 2, aged 60. Was constantly ill-treated by her husband, whom she finally joined with her son in strangling, hanging him afterwards so as to favour the idea of suicide.

Here again we have asymmetry of the face, breadth of jaw, enormous frontal sinuses, numerous wrinkles, a hollowed-out nose, a very thin upper lip, with deep-set eyes wide apart, and wild in expression.

No. 3, aged 21. Was married against her will, ill-treated by her husband, whom she killed, after a night altercation, with a hatchet while he slept.

In her we find only a demi-type. Her ears stand out, she has big jaws and cheek-bones, and very black hair, besides other anomalies which do not show in the photograph, such as gigantic canine teeth and dwarf incisors.

No. 4, aged 44. Strangled her husband by agreement with her lover, and threw him into a ditch. She denied her crime. Hollowed-out nose, black hair, deep-set eyes, big jaw. Demi-type.

No. 5, aged 50. A peasant. She killed her brother at supper, so as to inherit from him. She denied her guilt persistently. Was condemned, together with her hired accomplices, to twenty years' penal servitude. She had black hair, grey eyes, diasthema of the teeth, a cleft palate, precocious and profound wrinkles, thin lips, and a crooked face. Demi-type.

Passing now to poisoners, we find the following to be the most remarkable out of twenty-three:

No. 6, aged 36. Of a rich family, with an epileptic mother, and a father addicted to alcohol. She poisoned her husband with arsenic after sixteen years of married life. Nose hollowed out and club-shaped, large jaws and ears, squint eyes, weak reflex action of left patella. She confessed nothing. Character resolute and devout. Type.

No. 7, aged 34. Also poisoned her husband with arsenic; also denied her guilt. An enormous under jaw. On close examination displayed gigantic incisors, and down so long as to resemble a beard. Demi-type.

No. 8, aged 64. Poisoned her son's wife and the mother of the same. Deep wrinkles, ears much higher than the level of the brows. A singularity is the size of the neck-muscles, exaggerated as in oxen. Thin lips, and a cleft palate. Demi-type.

No. 9, a peasant, aged 47. Poisoned her daughter-in-law because of inability to work. Fluent in speech, never confessed the crime. Asymmetrical face, oblique eyes (a feature, however, which might be ethnological), huge, unequal jaws, small ears, nose club-shaped and hollowed out. On a near view she displayed big canine teeth, and a great parieto-occipital depression. Her children like her grandfather were epileptic. Type.

No. 10, aged 20. Attempted to poison her husband, an old man, who treated her ill. Darwin's lobule was enormously developed in her ear, as may be seen even from the photograph. Hydrocephalic forehead, nose hollowed out and club-shaped, large, unequal jaws, eyes and hair black. Type.

No. 11, aged 35. Poisoned her daughter-in-law, for an unknown reason, with some medicine. Fair hair, asymmetrical face, overlapping teeth. Guilt confessed.

Now we come to the incendiaries, of whom there are 10, four of a striking type.

No. 12. Set fire to the village palisades to revenge herself on some malignant gossips. A large nose, thin lips, lowering expression, with incisors replaced by molars. Type.

No. 13, aged 63. Set fire to a neighbour's house because of a quarrel about money. Denied the offence. Defective teeth, big, feline eyes, very large ears, asymmetry of eyebrows. Demi-type.

No. 14, aged 25. Set fire, in concert with her husband, to a neighbour's house out of revenge. She accused her husband and denied her own complicity. Many wrinkles, projecting parietal bones, big ears and jaws, low forehead. Demi-type.

No. 15, aged 41. A peasant. Set fire to nine houses out of revenge; pretended to have done it while drunk. Very ferocious countenance, asymmetrical, with enormous ears and jaws. Sullen, very black eyes, fair hair, diasthema of the incisors, narrow arch of palate. Type.

No. 16, aged 45. Convicted more than once as a receiver, who had twice hidden convicts in her house. Crooked face and teeth, hollowed-out nose, large, prognathous face, enormous superciliary arches.

Out of 9 infanticides, 3 presented the salient type.

No. 17, aged 60. Killed a newborn babe to save her daughter's reputation. Cut the infant into pieces and hid it. Confessed nothing. A strong character. Many wrinkles, enormous cheek-bones, ears, and frontal sinuses. Right side of face higher than the left. Forehead receding as in savages. Canine teeth gigantic and badly placed. Sunken eyes, brownish-green in colour.

No. 18, aged 60. Assisted her daughter to drown the latter's newborn child; then afterwards accused the daughter, in consequence of a quarrel about a lover whom the two women shared.

Physiognomy relatively good, in spite of the subject's licentious tendencies which age could not eradicate. Nothing anomalous beyond the hollowed-out nose and very wrinkled skin. The face, however, though it does not appear so in the photograph, was really asymmetrical, and the woman had the cleft palate and fleshy lips which betray a luxurious disposition.

No. 19, aged 19, the domestic servant of a priest, had a child, of which the father was a stable-boy. Driven out of every house, she killed her child by beating it on the frozen ground. Crooked face, a hollowed-out nose, big ears and jaws, incisors overlapping.

Finally comes a female brigand—No. 20, aged 25. Was the companion in arms of a band of brigands, one of whom was her lover. A hollowed-out nose, large jaws and ears, a virile physiognomy; and in her also there is congenital division of the palate.

Many may find that after all these faces are not horrible, and I agree, so far, that they appear infinitely less repulsive when compared with corresponding classes among the men whose portraits were reproduced by us from the "Atlas de L'Homme Criminel." Among some of the females there is even a ray of beauty, as in Nos. 19 and 20; but when this beauty exists it is much more virile than feminine.

THE CHILD SAVERS

Anthony M. Platt

In this excerpt, Platt discusses the evolution of the social pathology perspective. Among other things, he discusses the sources of its ideas and how these ideas changed with the development of the pathology perspective. One important source is the concept of the criminal as less than a complete human being (whether by nature or by nurture). Other features in the development of this perspective include the growth of professionalism in correctional work and the acceptance of a medical model and a "rehabilitative ideal," particularly for the treatment of "delinquent" youth.

The . . . [social pathologists'] ideology was an amalgam of convictions and aspirations. From the medical profession, they borrowed the imagery of pathology, infection, immunization, and treatment; from the tenets of social Darwinism, they derived their pessimistic views about the intractability of human nature and the innate moral defects of the lower classes; finally, their ideas about the biological and environmental origins of crime can be attributed to the positivist tradition in European criminology and anti-urban sentiments associated with the Protestant, rural ethic.

American criminology in the last century was essentially a practical affair—a curious conglomeration of pseudo-scientific theory, Old World ideas, and religious humanitarianism. Theories of crime were imported from Europe and an indiscriminating eclecticism dominated the literature. Educated amateurs, physicians, clergymen, and scholar-technicians became the experts on crime. Before 1870, there were only a few American textbooks on crime, and even the various penal and philanthropic organizations lacked specialized journals. Departments of law and sociology in the universities were rarely concerned with more than the formal description and classification of crimes.[1]

American pioneers in criminology were either physicians, like Benjamin Rush or Isaac Ray, or at least guided by medical ideology. Their training was often based on European methods and some, like Rush, actually attended European universities. With the notable exception of Ray's work, the authoritative literature on medical jurisprudence was of English origin.[2] The social sciences were similarly imported from Europe, and American criminologists fitted their data within the theoretical framework of criminal anthropology. Herbert Spencer's writings had an enormous impact on American intellectuals and made him even more popular in the United States than he was in his own country.[3] Cesare Lombroso, perhaps the most significant figure in nineteenth-century criminology, also sought recognition in the United States when he felt that his experiments had been neglected in Italy.[4]

Spencer and Lombroso, with their emphasis on Darwinist and biological images of human behavior, provided the ideological premise for crime workers and reformers. Anthropological explanations of crime complemented social Darwinism, which, in its most simple form, suggested that life is a competitive struggle for existence whereby the fittest survive and thus elevate the whole human race. The doctrine of "natural selection" also refuted revolutionary change and characterized human progress as a slow, natural, and inevitable process of evolution.[5] As Richard Hofstadter has observed, this view of social life was "seized upon as a welcome addition, perhaps the most powerful of all, to the store of ideas to which solid and conservative men appealed when they wished to reconcile their fellows to some of the hardships of life and to prevail upon them not to support hasty and ill-considered reforms."[6]

Spokesmen for conservative Darwinsim opposed welfare legislation and organized state care of the "dependent classes" on the grounds that all men, whatever their ability and resources, should engage in the competition for survival. The care and support of criminals, idiots, cripples, and the like, merely prolongs suffering, impedes human progress, and contradicts the laws of nature. The Darwinists, however, did not approve class warfare or the total elimination of the "unfit" through eugenic techniques. Hofstadter has pointed out that Spencer, accused of inhumanity in his application of biological principles to social life, "was compelled to insist over and over again that he was not opposed to voluntary private charity to the unfit, since it had an elevating effect on the character of the donors and hastened the development of altruism. . . ."[7]

Although Lombroso's theoretical and experimental studies were not translated into English until 1911, his findings were known by American academics in the early 1890s, and their popularity, as that of Spencer's, was based on the fact that they confirmed popular assumptions about the character and existence of a "criminal class." Lombroso's original theory suggested the existence of a criminal type distinguishable from non-criminals by observable physical anomalies of a degenerative or atavistic nature. He proposed that the criminal was a morally inferior human species, one characterized by physical traits reminiscent of apes, lower primates, and savage tribes. The criminal was thought to be morally retarded and, like a small child, instinctively aggressive and precocious unless restrained.[8] It is not difficult to see the connection between biological determinism in criminological literature and the principles of "natural selection"; both of these theoretical positions, according to Leon Radzinowicz, automatically justified the "eradication of elements that constituted a permanent and serious danger."[9]

Lombroso and his colleagues recognized other types of criminal behavior and even acknowledged the influence of social as well as biological factors on criminals.[10] . . .

In England, the ideas and data of the so-called Italian school of criminology had already been summarized and publicized by Havelock Ellis.[11] A similar, though much more superficial and less endurable, service was provided by Robert Fletcher in an address before the Anthropological Society of Washington, D.C., in 1891. Fletcher told his audience that criminal anthropology consisted of the study of individuals who are compelled to commit crimes as a consequence of "physical conformation, hereditary taint, or surroundings of vice, poverty, and ill example." The modern view of the criminal depicts him as a "variety of human species who had degenerated physically and morally." . . .

American penologists supported this derogatory image of criminals and enthusiastically welcomed pseudo-scientific proposals for their containment.[12] A typical medical view was expressed by Nathan Allen at the National Conference of Charities and Correction, where he observed that criminals are usually incapable of overcoming their biological fate:

> All history proves that the criminal class as a body originates from a peculiar stratum or type in society—sometimes from the middle or common walks of life, but more generally from the lowest orders, especially from the ignorant, the shiftless, the indolent and dissipated. . . . If our object, then, is to prevent crime in a large scale, we must direct attention to its main sources—to the materials that make criminals; the springs must be dried up; the supplies must be cut off.

Allen further proposed that crime would be reduced if "certain classes of vicious persons could be hindered from propagation. What right have such individuals to bring upon the public so much misery, shame and cost?"[13] . . .

The organization of correctional workers—through their national representatives and their identification with the established professions, such as law and medicine—operated to neutralize the pessimistic implications of social Darwinism, because hereditary and fatalistic theories of crime inevitably frustrated the professional aspirations of correctional functionaries. At the same time, even though the job of guard requires minimal training, skill, or intelligence, crime workers did not wish to regard themselves as merely the custodians of a pariah class.[14]

The self-image of penal reformers as doctors rather than guards and the domination of criminological research in the United States by physicians, helped to encourage the acceptance of "therapeutic" strategies in prisons and reformatories. As Arthur Fink has observed, "the role of the physician in this ferment is unmistakable. Indeed, he was the dynamic agent. . . . Not only did he preserve and add to existing knowledge—for his field touched all borders of science—but he helped to maintain and extend the methodology of science."[15] Perhaps what is more significant is that physicians furnished the official rhetoric of penal reform. Admittedly, the criminal was "pathological" and "diseased," but medical science offered the possibility of miraculous cures. It was, therefore, the task of correctional agencies to make every individual self-supporting and independent by restraining "prodigality and extravagance of expenditure of human force and substance."[16] Although there was widespread belief in the existence of a "criminal class" separated from the rest of mankind by a "vague boundary line," there was no good reason why this class could not be identified, diagnosed, segregated, changed, and controlled. Crime, like disease, was revealed "in the face, the voice, the person and the carriage," so that a skillful and properly trained diagnostician could arrest criminal tendencies. . . .

Despite the wide acceptance of biological imagery, penal reformers stressed the possibility of redemption through religious and medical intervention. The desire to promote the "welfare of the community and future of the race," the stress on pseudo-scientific methods of eliminating criminality, and the ruthless, mechanistic classification of criminals had to be weighed against traditional Christian benevolence, the indulgence of the unfit, and the "optimism of Religion" (as compared with the "pessimism of Science").[17] Charles Henderson, professor of sociology at the University of Chicago and President of the National Conference of Charities and Correction for 1899, resolved this dilemma by observing that the laws of "natural selection" and the principles of educative reform were not antagonistic. To hurt the "defective classes," said Henderson, would be to hurt the social order itself; social progress must rest on the capacity of those persons who deal with this class to develop altruistic sentiments. . . .

Professional correctional workers and administrators gradually refuted monolithic explanations of crime based on biological imagery. . . . The superintendent of the Kentucky Industrial School of Reform, for example, was convinced by 1898 that hereditary theories of crime were over-fatalistic. "While I believe heredity, of both moral and physical traits, to be a fact," he told delegates to a national conference, "I think it is unjustifiably made a bugaboo to discourage efforts at rescue. We know that physical heredity tendencies can be neutralized and often nullified by proper counteracting precautions."[18] E.R.L. Gould, a sociologist at the University of Chicago, similarly objected to hereditary theories of crime, on the grounds that the empirical data was unconvincing. He criticized many so-called scientific studies for being unclear, morbid, and sentimental:

> There is great danger in emphasizing heredity, and by contrast minimizing the influence of environment and individual responsibility. Consequences doubly unfortunate must ensue. Individual stamina will be weakened, and society made to feel less keenly the duty of reforming environment. Is it not better to postulate freedom of choice than to preach the doctrine of the unfettered will, and so elevate criminality into a propitiary sacrifice?[19]

The problem confronting criminologists of "whether the man makes the circumstances or the circumstances make the man" was skillfully clarified by Charles Cooley in an address before the National Conference of Charities and Correction in 1896. He considered it unnecessary and pointless to create a dichotomy between "nature" and "nurture," inferring that there is a choice of alternatives.[20] "Like male and female, each is sterile without the other." Cooley took a dynamic and flexible position regarding the way in which social character is formed:

> The union of nature and nurture is not one of addition or mixture, but of growth, whereby the elements are altogether transformed into a new organic whole. One's nature acts selectively upon the environment, assimilating materials proper to itself; while at the same time the environment moulds the nature, and habits are formed which make the individual independent, in some degree, of changes in either. . . .

Cooley made the important observation that criminal behavior depended as much upon social experiences and economic circumstances as it did upon the inheritance of biological traits. The delinquent child is constrained by social rather than biological forces; in essence, however, he is normally constituted and the "criminal class is largely the result of society's bad workmanship upon fairly good material." Cooley criticized theories of crime based on physical peculiarities, noting that there was a "large and fairly trustworthy body of evidence" to support the fact that many so-called degenerates could be made "useful citizens by rational treatment."[21]

. . . [Thus], the concept of the natural criminal was modified with the rise of a professional class of correctional administrators and social servants who promoted a medical model of deviant behavior and suggested techniques of remedying "natural" imperfections. The pessimism of Darwinism was counterbalanced by the spirit of philanthropy, religious optimism, and a belief in the dignity of suffering. . . .

Another important influence on nineteenth-century images of crime was a disenchantment with urban life. The city was depicted as the main breeding ground of criminals: the impact of the physical horrors of urban ghettos on unskilled, poorly educated European immigrants "created" criminals. Immigrants were regarded as "unsocialized" and the city's impersonality compounded their isolation and degradation. "By some cruel alchemy," wrote Julia Lathrop, "we take the sturdiest of European peasantry and at once destroy in a large measure its power to rear to decent livelihood the first generation of offspring upon our soil."[22] . . .

Many penal and educational reformers considered that human nature operated in a radically different way in the city compared with the country. It was, therefore, the task of reformers to make city existence more like life on the farm, where social relationships were considered wholesome, honest, and free from depravity and corruption. Jenkin Lloyd Jones, in a speech before the Illinois Conference of Charities in 1898, expressed the hope that redistribution of the population would remedy some of the serious social problems associated with industrialism:

> The currents of industrial and commercial life have set in tremendously towards the city. Thither flows with awful precipitancy the best nerve, muscle and brain of

the country, and the equilibrium will be permanently destroyed if there cannot be a counter current established, whereby the less competent, the unprotected, the helpless and the innocent can be passed back, to be restored and reinvigorated.[23] . . .

Children living in the city slums were described as "intellectual dwarfs" and "physical and moral wrecks" whose characters were predominantly shaped by their physical surroundings. Beverley Warner told the National Prison Association in 1898 that philanthropic organizations all over the country were

> making efforts to get the children out of the slums, even if only once a week, into the radiance of better lives. Seeing the beauties of a better existence, these children may be led to choose the good rather than the evil. Good has been done by taking these children into places where they see ladies well dressed, and with their hands and faces clean, and it is only by leading the child out of sin and debauchery, in which it has lived, into a circle of life that is a repudiation of things that it sees in its daily life, that it can be influenced.[24] . . .

SUMMARY

Important developments in the imagery of crime at the end of the last century were (1) the concept of the criminal as less than a complete human being, whether by nature or nurture, (2) the growth of professionalism in corrections work, and (3) the acceptance of the medical model and the "rehabilitative ideal," particularly with regard to the correction of "delinquent" children and adolescents.

1. Although there was a wide difference of opinion as to the precipitating causes of crime, it was generally agreed among experts that criminals were *abnormally* conditioned by biological and environmental factors. Early theories stressed the permanent, irreversible, and inherited character of criminal behavior. To the image of natural depravity was added the image of urban corruption. Reformers emphasized the disorganized features of urban life and encouraged remedial programs which embodied rural and primary group concepts. Slum life was regarded as unregulated, vicious and lacking in social rules; its inhabitants were depicted as abnormal and maladjusted, living their lives in conflict and chaos.[25]

2. The element of fatalism in theories of crime was modified with the rise of a professional class of penal adminstrators and social servants who promoted a developmental view of human behavior. The pessimistic implications of Darwinist creeds were antagonistic not only to the Protestant ethic but also to crime workers who aspired to the professional status of doctors, lawyers, and other human service functionaries. It was fortunate, as John Higham has observed, that Darwinism was flexible enough to suit both philanthropic and misanthropic views of social life.[26]

3. There . . . [was] a shift . . . in official policies concerning crime. The warrant . . . shifted from one emphasizing the criminal nature of delinquency to the "new humanism," which speaks of disease, illness, contagion, and the like. The emergence of the medical warrant is of considerable significance, since it is a powerful rationale for organizing social action in the most diverse behavioral aspects of our society.

The "rehabilitative ideal"[27] presupposed that crime was a symptom of "pathology" and that criminals should be treated like irresponsible, sick patients. The older a criminal, the more chronic was his sickness; similarly, his chances of recovery were less than those of a young person. Adult criminals, particularly recidivists, were often characterized as nonhuman. Children, however, were less likely to be thought of as nonhuman since universalistic ethics, especially the ethic of Christianity, made it almost impossible to think of children as being entirely devoid of moral significance.

Social reformers emphasized the temporary and reversible nature of adolescent crime. As Charles Cooley observed, "when an individual actually enters upon a criminal career, let us try to catch him at a tender age, and subject him to rational social discipline, such as is already successful in enough cases to show that it might be greatly extended."[28] If, as the child savers believed, criminals are conditioned by biological heritage and brutish living conditions, then prophylactic measures must be taken early in life. Delinquent children—the criminals of the next generation—must be prevented from pursuing their criminal careers. "They are born to it," wrote the penologist Enoch Wines in 1880, "brought up for it. They must be saved."[29] Many new developments in penology took place at this time in the reformatory system where, it was hoped, delinquents would be saved and reconstituted.

Notes

1. Arthur E. Fink, *Causes of Crime: Biological Theories in the United States, 1800–1915* [(Philadelphia: University of Pennsylvania Press, 1938)]. Needless to say, histories of American criminological thought are hard to find. Fink's study makes a useful bibliographical contribution to the literature by assembling and condensing a vast amount of interesting primary sources. But he rarely attempts to interpret his data other than to make the occasional bow to the evolutionary perspective. There are of course numerous modern textbooks on the history of penology—such as H. E. Barnes and N. K. Teeters, *New Horizons in Criminology* ([New York: Prentice-Hall], 1943), Max Grünhut, *Penal Reform* ([Toronto: Oxford], 1948), and George B. Vold, *Theoretical Criminology* ([New York: Oxford], 1958)—but these are essentially compiled for undergraduate reading.

2. Isaac Ray, *A Treatise on the Medical Jurisprudence of Insanity* [(Cambridge: Belknap/ Harvard University Press, 1962)]. The influence of English medical jurisprudence on American physicians is cursorily examined by Anthony M. Platt and Bernard L. Diamond, "The Origins of the 'Right and Wrong' Test of Criminal Responsibility and Its Subsequent Development in the United States," *California Law Review* 54 (1966): 1227–60. See also, Seymour Halleck, "American Psychiatry and the Criminal: A Historical Review," *American Journal of Psychiatry* 121, no. 9 (March, 1965): i–xxi.

3. Richard Hofstadter, *Social Darwinism in American Thought* [(Boston: Beacon Press, 1960)], pp. 31–50.

4. See Lombroso's introduction to Arthur MacDonald, *Criminology* [(New York: Funk & Wagnalls, 1893)].

5. As Charles Cooley remarked, "most of the writers on eugenics have been biologists or

physicians who have never acquired the point of view which sees in society a psychological organism with a life process of its own. They have thought of human heredity as a tendency to definite modes of conduct, and of environment as something that may aid or hinder, not remembering what they might have learned even from Darwin, that heredity takes on a distinctively human character only by renouncing, as it were, the function of pre-determined adaptation and becoming plastic to the environment" (*Social Process* [(New York: Charles Scribner's Sons, 1918)], p. 206).

6. Hofstadter, *Social Darwinism*, p. 5.

7. *Ibid.*, p. 41.

8. An excellent critique of Lombroso's theories, findings and intellectual traditions is provided by Marvin E. Wolfgang, "Cesare Lombroso," in Hermann Mannheim, ed., *Pioneers in Criminology* [(Chicago: Quadrangle, 1960)], pp. 168–227.

9. *Ideology and Crime* ([New York: Columbia University Press, 1966]), p. 55.

10. This study is not the place to debate Lombroso's contributions to criminology or to measure his effect on European ideas; what I am concerned with here is how Lombroso was interpreted and simplified in the United States before 1900. It is well recognized that his later writings were more cautious and emphasized a multifactor approach.

11. Havelock Ellis, *The Criminal* [(London: Walter Scott, 1914)].

12. See, for example, Fink, *Causes of Crime*, pp. 188–210, on criminological attitudes toward sterilization.

13. Nathan Allen, "Prevention of Crime and Pauperism," *Proceedings of the Annual Conference of Charities* (PACC), 1878, pp. 111–24.

14. Analogous developments in the emergence of social work as a professional career are treated by [Roy] Lubove in *The Professional Altruist* [(Cambridge: Harvard University Press, 1965)].

15. Fink, *Causes of Crime*, p. 247.

16. *First Biennial Report of the Board of State Commissioners of Public Charities of the State of Illinois*, p. 18 (Springfield, Illinois: Illinois Journal Printing Office, 1871).

17. Charles Henderson, "Relation of Philanthropy to Social Order and Progress," [*Proceedings of the National Conference of Charities and Corrections (PNCCC)*], pp. 1–15. Cf. Charles E. Faulkner, "Twentieth Century Alignments for the Promotion of Social Order," with Frederick H. Wines, "The Healing Touch," *PNCCC, 1900*, pp. 1–9, 10–26.

18. Peter Caldwell, "The Duty of the State to Delinquent Children," *PNCCC, 1898*, pp. 404–10.

19. E.R.L. Gould, "The Statistical Study of Hereditary Criminality," *PNCCC, 1895*, pp. 134–43.

20. According to Hofstadter, "The new psychology . . . was a truly social psychology. . . . [I]nsistence upon the unreality of a personal psyche isolated from the social surroundings was a central tenet in the social theory of Charles H. Cooley. . . . The older psychology had been atomistic. . . . The new psychology, prepared to see the interdependence of the individual personality with the institutional structure of society, was destroying this one-way notion of social causation and criticizing its underlying individualism" (*Social Darwinism*, p. 150).

21. Charles H. Cooley, " 'Nature v. Nurture' in the Making of Social Careers," *PNCCC, 1896*, pp. 339–405.

22. Julia Lathrop, "The Development of the Probation System in a Large City," *Charities* 13 (January, 1905): 348.

23. "Who Are the Children of the State?" Illinois Conference of Charities (1898), *Fifteenth Biennial Report of the State Board of Commissioners of Public Charities of the State of Illinois,* pp. 286–87 (Springfield: Phillips Brothers, 1899).

24. Beverley Warner, "Child Saving," *Proceedings of the Annual Congress of the National Prison Association, Indianapolis, 1898,* pp. 377–78.

25. William Foote Whyte, "Social Disorganization in the Slums," *American Sociological Review* 8 (1943): 34–39.

26. ". . . the general climate of opinion in the early Darwinian era inhibited the pessimistic implications of the new naturalism. What stood out in the first instance, as the great social lesson of the theory of natural selection, was not the ravages of the struggle for survival but rather the idea of 'the survival of the fittest.' To a generation of intellectuals steeped in confidence, the laws of evolution seemed to guarantee that the 'fittest' races would most certainly triumph over inferior competitors. . . . Darwinism, therefore, easily ministered to Anglo-Saxon pride, but in the age of confidence it could hardly arouse Anglo-Saxon anxiety.

"Secondly, Darwinism gave the race-thinkers little concrete help in an essential prerequisite of racism—belief in the preponderance of heredity over environment. Certainly the biological vogue of the late nineteenth century stimulated speculation along these lines, but the evolutionary theory by no means disqualified a fundamentally environmentalist outlook. Darwin's species struggled and evolved through adaptation to those settings" ([John] Higham, *Strangers in the Land,* pp. 135–36).

27. This term is used by Francis A. Allen, *The Borderland of Criminal Justice* [(Chicago: University of Chicago Press, 1964)].

28. Cooley, " 'Nature v. Nurture,' " p. 405.

29. Enoch C. Wines, *The State of Prisons and of Child-Saving Institutions in the Civilized World* [(Cambridge: University Press, 1880)], p. 132.

A UNIVERSAL CRITERION OF PATHOLOGY

Vytautas Kavolis

C. Wright Mills criticized the social pathology approach for cloaking the small-town values of conservative reformers in seemingly objective medical terms. In this excerpt, Kavolis argues that social pathology, carefully defined, can be a relatively objective and useful conception. Destructiveness to self or others, Kavolis holds, can be objectively identified, and such destructiveness is the core of social pathology. Thus, Kavolis believes, the study of social pathology should concern itself with people's destructive behavior and the conditions that give rise to such behavior.

From Vytautas Kavolis (ed.), *Comparative Perspectives on Social Problems,* pp. 2–6. Copyright © 1969 by Little, Brown and Company (Inc.). Reprinted by permission.

The . . . [social pathology] conception of social problems . . . provides a universal criterion for evaluating social arrangements by their human costs. If it were possible to arrive at a cross-culturally valid definition of "destructive or self-destructive behavior," then conditions causally associated with such behavior could be identified as pathogenic (or having pathogenic aspects), regardless of whether they were institutionalized in a society and supported by its cultural traditions or not, and whether anyone in the society in which they occurred was aware of their pathogenic effects. With this perspective on social problems, no longer would the sociologist stand theoretically helpless—as the "deviationists" must—in relation to prejudice in South Africa, slavery in the pre-Civil War American South, Nazi concentration camps, genocide under Stalin, or the pathologies arising from conformity to "normal" middle-class values.[1]

I do not accept the view that to define pathology in terms of destructiveness is a culture-bound judgment. To regard *destruction of life, health, or sense of personal identity* (a definition with a hard core and stretchable boundaries) as the universal criterion of pathological behavior constitutes the most general extension of the implications of the major ethical systems of mankind. With respect to this criterion, exceptions have to be justified, not the criterion itself; but the criterion has been frequently held to apply only to members of one's own group. What we are doing is universalizing the criterion of pathology—applying it to all societies, including those that have not generalized their moral norms sufficiently to make them applicable to outsiders as much as to themselves.

Nor can it be legitimately assumed that the social-pathology approach necessarily incorporates a conservative bias in favor of preserving existing institutions.[2] What is pathological is not behavior which deviates from established custom or disrupts social stability but that which is destructive or self-destructive in its consequences. Whenever established institutions (or innovations) promote such behavior, they must be regarded as pathogenic. Conflict, in this theoretical perspective, is not in itself pathological (unless it generates violence). Lack of conflict may be pathogenic if it perpetuates a high incidence of self-destructive behavior.

The "field" of social pathology may be defined as the study of the destructive or self-destructive behavior of individuals (pathological behavior) and of the social and cultural conditions, or processes, which cause or contribute to such behavior (pathogenic conditions). If the goal is to understand how particular conditions have pathogenic effects on individuals, studying one type of pathological behavior in isolation from others is insufficient. It is only by investigating the overall effects of a social condition, on all types of pathological behavior, that the social pathologist can determine to what extent and in what manner the condition is pathogenic. A theoretical framework is needed within which any given social condition can be related to all types of pathological behaviors (if a relationship can be demonstrated to exist).

In organizing the data for such a framework, it is helpful to distinguish self-directed destructiveness from other-directed destructiveness, and spontaneous pathological behavior from organized pathologies. Self-destructiveness refers to all forms of behavior by which an individual destroys or damages his own life, health, or sense of personal identity. Such forms of behavior range from suicide at the highest level of intensity, through alcoholism and neurosis at intermediate levels, to various kinds of "inauthentic" actions, alien to the "true nature" of the personality, that the individual performs either because he is forced by external circumstances or because he does not "know" himself. Only the higher and intermediate levels of intensity will be considered systematically in this article, as little reliable cross-cultural research has been done on "inauthentic" behavior, except on alienation.

Other-directed destructiveness is another umbrella term referring to all activities by which an individual destroys or damages the life, health, or sense of personal identity of another person or persons. Such activities include, at one extreme, the various forms of murder (including socially sanctioned killing, as in warfare) and, at the other extreme, the withdrawal of social esteem from a specific person or group of persons. (This may be a rational action when it has been "earned" by the specific behavior of such a person or persons, but even then it is other-destructive.) I would classify racial discrimination and most forms of crime as other-directed destructive behavior of intermediate intensity. However, racial discrimination is easily intensified to the level of genocide; and the intensity of aggression inherent in crime varies from high to low. Some activities officially designated as crimes, such as school truancy, are purely self-destructive. Some crimes do not affect either the self or others destructively (e.g., the crime of offering a glass of wine to a seventeen-year-old in Pennsylvania). On the other hand, numerous other-destructive activities have historically not been regarded as crimes (war, economic exploitation of the easily victimized).

Spontaneous pathological behavior is exhibited when an individual "chooses," in part voluntarily, to engage in a destructive or self-destructive course of action, or when he unconsciously develops, without having the ability to choose, the symptoms of a self-destructive disease. Organized pathology exists when the individual is either "morally" obligated or "politically" coerced by the group or organization to whose authority or power he is subject to commit destructive or self-destructive acts (or to encourage others to commit such acts). The purest cases of organized pathology are found in concentration camps and the institution of slavery. While the victims of these institutions are coerced into self-destructive behavior, their masters, by accepting their position within these institutions, assume the obligation to engage in other-destructive behavior, essentially (though not wholly) regardless of their personal malevolence or lack thereof. Both the victims and the masters of pathological institutions are required, by the conditions of operation of such institutions, to engage in pathological behavior.

On a lower level of intensity, but with broadly comparable psychological effects, is the organized pathology of imperialism and colonialism, the most prominent representative of which, after the virtual demise of West European colonial empires, is the Soviet Union, with its at least fifteen nations held by force in the same relationship to the Great Russians as the natives of Mozambique are to the Portuguese—"crushed with their inessentiality."[3]

Organized pathology is not necessarily, at any given time, socially disreputable. Respected organizations may require their members to participate, or unintentionally promote, pathological behavior. The Catholic church does so when it requires its clerical members, against their growing opposition, to persuade its lay members not to use effective methods of fertility control. The rationale of this requirement is moral upgrading of the faithful. The socially relevant result is a sizable contribution to over-population, malnutrition of children, illegal abortions that damage the health or destroy the lives of pregnant women, and revolutionary political extremism, especially in Latin America. Some readers might find that the rats of Rajasthan constitute an emotionally more acceptable illustration of the point that is being made here.[4]

These examples suggest to what extent the deviance perspective may be irrelevant to understanding the causes of major social pathologies. Yet one of the measures of the rationality of a social order is the degree to which its definitions of socially unacceptable deviance correspond with what can be empirically shown to be pathological behavior. In a rational society, presumably, only the pathological would be regarded as seriously deviant, and the only socially consequential deviance would be that of demonstrably destructive or self-destructive behavior. However, since societies are not rationally organized, both the deviance and the pathology perspectives are necessary to understand their problems.

In studying social pathology, we aim at establishing the characteristics of social structure and process as well as those of cultural orientation which promote pathological behavior wherever they occur. To eliminate accidental patterns of findings that hold in a particular time and place but lack general validity, systematic cross-cultural study of the various forms of pathological behavior is necessary. Such studies should eventually lead to a theoretical integration of the knowledge of pathological behavior in preliterate, historical, and modern societies accumulated by half a dozen scholarly disciplines. It should be possible, on the basis of such a theoretical system, to predict how much of what types of pathology would be likely to occur if we constructed a society with certain specified characteristics.

Notes

1. Erich Fromm, *The Sane Society* (Greenwich, Conn.: Fawcett Publications, 1955).

2. An accusation that has been justly directed against an earlier generation of American social pathologists. C. Wright Mills, "The Professional Ideology of Social Pathologists," in his *Power, Politics and People*, ed. Irving Louis Horowitz (New York: Ballantine Books, 1963), pp. 525–552.

3. Frantz Fanon, *The Wretched of the Earth* (New York: Grove Press, 1966), p. 30.

4. "Food is scarce in this desert town, as it is in much of India. . . . But the rats in this desert state of Rajasthan face no food problem. They are considered to be holy creatures, and they are fed by faithful worshippers. The rodent population of Rajasthan is said to outnumber the human population: 25 million rats to 20.1 million people." *The New York Times*, August 21, 1968, p. 16.

THE PURSUIT OF LONELINESS
Philip Slater

American culture emphasizes individualism. According to Slater, this leads to competition, denial of interdependence with one's fellows, and a heightened need for privacy. Faced with these signs of social pathology, Americans respond with increased individualism, but this only makes them feel worse, because individualism cannot cure the pathologies it has itself produced.

We are so used to living in an individualistic society that we need to be reminded that collectivism has been the more usual lot of humans. Most people in most societies have lived and died in stable communities that took for granted the subordination of the individual to the welfare of the group. The aggrandizement of the individual at the expense of his neighbors was simply a crime.

This is not to say that competition is an American invention—all societies involve some mixture of cooperative and competitive institutions. But our society lies near the competitive extreme, and although it contains cooperative institutions, we suffer from their weakness and peripherality. Studies of business executives reveal a deep hunger for an atmosphere of trust and fraternity with their colleagues. The competitive life is a lonely one and its satisfactions short-lived, for each race leads only to a new one.

In the past our society had many oases in which one could take refuge from the frenzied invidiousness of our economic system—institutions such as the extended family and the stable local neighborhood in which people could take pleasure from something other than winning symbolic victories over their neighbors. But these have disappeared one by one, leaving us more and more in a situation in which we must try to satisfy our vanity and our needs for intimacy in the same place and at the same time. This has made the appeal of cooperative living more seductive, and the need to suppress our longing for it more acute.

The main vehicle for the expression of this longing has been the mass media. Popular songs and film comedies for fifty years have been engaged in a sentimental rejection of our dominant mores, maintaining that the best things in life are free, that love is more important than success, that keeping up with the Joneses is futile, that personal integrity should take precedence over winning, and so on. But these protestations must be understood for what they are: a safety valve. The same man who chuckles and sentimentalizes over a happy-go-lucky hero in a film would view his real-life counterpart as frivolous and irresponsible, and suburbanites who philosophized over the back fence with complete sincerity about their "dog-eat-dog-world," and "what-is-it-all-for," and "you-can't-take-it-with-you," and "success-doesn't-make-you-happy-it-just-gives-you-ulcers-and-a-heart-condition," were enraged in the sixties when their children began to pay serious attention to these ideas. To the young this seemed hypocritical, but if adults didn't feel these things they wouldn't have had to fight them so vigorously. The exaggerated hostility that young people aroused in the "flower child" era argues that the life they led was highly seductive to middle-aged Americans.

When a value is strongly held, as individualism is in America, the illnesses it produces tend to be treated in the same way an alcoholic treats a hangover or a drug addict his withdrawal symptoms. Technological change, mobility, and in-dividualistic ways of thinking all rupture the bonds that tie a man to a family, a community, a kinship network, a geographical location—bonds that give him a comfortable sense of himself. As this sense of himself erodes, he seeks ways of affirming it. Yet his efforts accelerate the very erosion he seeks to halt.

This loss of a sense of oneself, a sense of one's place in the scheme of things, produces a jungle of competing egos, each trying to *create* a place. Huge cor-porations are fueled on this energy—the stockholders trying to buy place with wealth, executives trying to grasp it through power and prestige, public relations departments and advertisers trying to persuade people that the corporation can confer a sense of place to those who believe in it or buy its products.

Americans love bigness, mostly because they feel so small. They feel small because they're unconnected, without a place. They try to overcome that small-ness by associating themselves with bigness—big projects, big organizations, big government, mass markets, mass media, "nationwide," "worldwide." But it's that very same bigness that rips away their sense of connectedness and place and makes them feel small. A vicious circle.

Notice the names of corporations: "Universal," "Continental," "International," "General," "National," "Trans-World"—the spirit of grandiosity and ego-inflation pervades our economic life. Corporations exist not to feed or supply the people, but to appease their own hungry egos. Advertising pays scant attention to price or quality and leans heavily on our needs for acceptance and respect. The eco-nomic structure of our society continually frustrates those needs, creating an artificial scarcity that in turn motivates the entire economy. This is why the qual-ity of life in America is so unsatisfying. Since our economy is built on inflated vanity, rather than being grounded in the real material needs of the people, it must eventually collapse, when these illusions can no longer be maintained.

Much of the unpleasantness, abrasiveness, and costliness of American life comes from the fact that we're always dealing with strangers. This is what bu-reaucracy is: a mechanism for carrying on transactions between strangers. Who would need all those offices, all that paperwork, all those lawyers, contracts, rules and regulations, if all economic transactions took place between lifelong neigh-bors? A huge and tedious machinery has evolved to cope with the fact that we prefer to carry on our activities among strangers. The preference is justified, as are most of the sicknesses in American society, by the alleged economic benefits of bigness, but like many economic arguments, it's a con.

On the surface, it seems convincing. Any big company can undersell a little one. Corporations keep getting bigger and bigger and fewer and fewer. Doesn't that prove it? Survival of the fittest? Yet for some reason, what should be providing economic benefits to the consumer has in fact produced nothing but chronic inflation. If bigness lowers the cost of production, why does everything cost more and break sooner? Management, of course, blames it on labor, and each industry cites the rising prices of its own suppliers. Isn't it obvious that a few big nationwide companies can produce things cheaper than many local ones?

It all depends on what you leave out of your analysis (which is why a chimp pressing buttons randomly could predict as well as our economic forecasters). The fewer the companies, the less influence supply and demand have on prices. A heavy investment in advertising and public relations is necessary to keep a national reputation alive. And what about the transportation costs involved when all firms are national? Not to mention the air pollution costs, which are also passed on to the consumer. Chronic inflation suggests that someone is leaving something vital out of his analysis. How does one measure in dollars the cost of economic mistrust? It may be subtle, but it's clearly enormous.

THE GREAT ILLUSION

It's easy to produce examples of the many ways in which Americans try to minimize, circumvent, or deny the interdependence upon which all human societies are based. We seek a private house, a private means of transportation, a private garden, a private laundry, self-service stores, and do-it-yourself skills of every kind. An enormous technology seems to have set itself the task of making it unnecessary for one human being ever to ask anything of another in the course of going about his or her daily business. Even within the family Americans are unique in their feeling that each member should have a separate room, and even a separate telephone, television, and car, when economically possible. We seek more and more privacy, and feel more and more alienated and lonely when we get it. And what accidental contacts we do have seem more intrusive, not only because they're unsought, but because they're not connected with any familiar pattern of interdependence.

Most important, our encounters with others tend increasingly to be competitive as we search for more privacy. We less and less often meet our fellow humans to share and exchange, and more and more often encounter them as an impediment or a nuisance: making the highway crowded when we're rushing somewhere, cluttering and littering the beach or park or wood, pushing in front of us at the supermarket, taking the last parking place, polluting our air and water, building a highway through our house, blocking our view, and so on. Because we've cut off so much communication with each other we keep bumping into each other, so that a higher and higher percentage of our interpersonal contacts are abrasive.

We seem unable to foresee that the gratification of a wish might turn out to be a monkey's paw if the wish were shared by many others. We cheer the new road that shaves ten minutes off the drive to our country retreat but ultimately transforms it into a crowded resort and increases both the traffic and the time. We're continually surprised to find, when we want something, that thousands or millions of others want it, too—that other human beings get hot in summer and cold in winter. The worst traffic jams occur when a mass of vacationing tourists start home early to "beat the traffic." We're too enamored of the individualistic fantasy that everyone is, or should be, different—that a man could somehow build his entire life around some single eccentricity without boring himself and everyone else to death. We all have our quirks, which provide surface variety, but aside from this, human beings have little basis for their persistent claim that they are not all members of the same species.

THE FREEDOM FIX

Since our contacts with others are increasingly competitive, unanticipated, and abrasive, we seek still more apartness and thus accelerate the trend. The desire to be somehow special sparks an even more competitive quest for progressively more rare and expensive symbols—a quest that is ultimately futile since it is individualism itself that produces uniformity.

This is poorly understood by Americans, who tend to confuse uniformity with "conformity," in the sense of compliance with group demands. Many societies exert far more pressure on the individual to mold herself to play a sharply defined role in a total group pattern, but there is variation among these circumscribed roles. Our society gives more leeway to the individual to pursue her own ends, but since the culture defines what is worthy and desirable, everyone tends, independently but monotonously, to pursue the same things in the same way. Thus cooperation tends to produce variety, while competition generates uniformity.

The problem with individualism is not that it is immoral but that it is incorrect. The universe does not consist of a lot of unrelated particles but is an interconnected whole. Pretending that our fortunes are independent of each other may be perfectly ethical, but it's also perfectly stupid. Individualistic thinking is unflagging in the production of false dichotomies, such as "conformity *vs.* independence," "altruism *vs.* egoism," "inner-directed *vs.* other-directed," and so on, all of which are built upon the absurd assumption that the individual can be considered separately from the environment of which he or she is a part.

A favorite delusion of individualism—one that it attempts, through education and propaganda, to make real—is that only egoistic responses are spontaneous. But this is not so: collective responses—helping behavior, nurturance, supportiveness, the assumption of specialized roles in group tasks, rituals, or games—these are natural, not trained, even among animals. People are more *self-consciously* oriented toward others in competitive, individualistic societies—their behavior is calculated. They accommodate to others because they want to look good, impress people, protect themselves from shame and guilt, and avoid confronting people directly. In more organic and cooperative communities people respond spontaneously to impulses that are neither selfish nor unselfish, but more directly from the heart. Sometimes they look generous, sometimes grasping, but what's important is that the behavior is to others, not an effort to produce some sort of *effect* on others. Cooperative societies are unassuming—it's the competitive ones that are concerned with appearances.

Individualism in the United States is exemplified by the flight to the suburb and the do-it-yourself movement. Both attempt to deny human interdependence and pursue unrealistic fantasies of self-sufficiency. The first tries to overlook our dependence upon the city for the maintenance of the level of culture we demand. "Civilized" means, literally, "citified," and the state of the city is an accurate index of the condition of the culture as a whole. We behave toward our cities like an irascible farmer who never feeds his cow and then kicks her when she fails to give enough milk. But the flight to the suburb was in any case self-defeating, its goals subverted by the mass quality of the exodus. The suburban dweller sought peace, privacy, nature, community, good schools, and a healthy child-rearing environment. Instead, he found neither the beauty and serenity of the countryside, nor the stimulation of the city, nor the stability and sense of community of the small town. A small town, after all, is a microcosm, while the suburb is merely a layer, narrowly segregated by age and social class. A minor irony of the suburban dream is that, for many Americans, reaching the pinnacle of their social ambitions (owning a house in the suburbs) forces them to perform all kinds of menial tasks (carrying garbage cans, mowing lawns, shoveling snow, and so on) that were performed for them when they occupied a less exalted status.

Some of this manual labor, however, is voluntary—an attempt to deny the division of labor required in a complex society. Many Americans seem quite willing to pay the price rather than engage in encounters with workers. This do-it-yourself trend has accompanied increasing specialization in occupations. As one's job narrows, perhaps, he or she seeks the challenge of new skill-acquisition in the home. But specialization also means that one's encounters with artisans in the home proliferate and become more impersonal. It's no longer a matter of a few well-known people—smiths and grocers—who perform many functions, and with whom contact may be a source of satisfaction. One finds instead a multiplicity of narrow specialists, each perhaps a stranger—the same type of repair may even be performed by a different person each time. Every relationship, such as it is, must start from scratch, and it's small wonder the householder turns away from such an unrewarding prospect in apathy and despair.

Americans thus find themselves in a vicious circle in which their community relationships are increasingly competitive, trivial, and irksome, in part as a result of their efforts to avoid or minimize potentially irksome relationships. As the few vestiges of stable community life erode, the desire for a simple, cooperative lifestyle grows in intensity. The most seductive appeal of radical ideologies for Americans consists in the fact that all in one way or another attack the competitive foundations of our society.

Now it may be objected that American society is less competitive than it once was, and that the appeal of radical ideologies should hence be diminished. Social critics in the fifties argued that the entrepreneurial individualist of the past has been replaced by a bureaucratic Organization Man. Much of this historical drama was created by comparing yesterday's owner-president with today's assistant sales manager; certainly these nostalgia-merchants never visited a nineteenth-century company town. Another distortion is introduced by the fact that it was only the most ruthlessly competitive robber barons who survived to tell us how it was. Little is written about the neighborhood store that extended credit to the poor, or the small town industry that refused to lay off local workers in hard times. They all went under together. The meek may be blessed but they don't write memoirs.

Even if we grant that the business world was more competitive in the nine-teenth century, the total environment was less so. The individual worked in a smaller firm with lower turnover in which his or her relationships were more enduring and more personal. The ideology of Adam Smith was tempered by the fact that the participants in economic struggles were neighbors and might have been childhood playmates. Even if the business world then was as "dog-eat-dog" as we imagine it, it occurred as a deviant episode in what was otherwise a more comfortable and familiar environment than the organization man can find today in or out of his office. The organization man is simply a carryover from the paternalistic environment of the family business and the company town; and the "other-directedness" of the suburban community just a desperate attempt to bring some old-fashioned small-town collectivism into the transient and imper-sonal lifestyle of the suburb. The social critics of the 1950s were so preoccupied with assailing these rather synthetic forms of human interdependence that they lost sight of the underlying sickness that produced them. Medical symptoms usually result from attempts made by the body to counteract disease, and at-tacking the symptoms often aggravates and prolongs the illness. This seems to be the case with the feeble and self-defeating efforts of twentieth-century Amer-icans to create a viable social environment.

THE MORAL PREMISES
OF SOCIAL PATHOLOGY

Carl M. Rosenquist

Those who employ the social pathology perspective take an attitude toward social problems like that of the physician toward physical problems. They assume that society, like the individual, is an organism, and that there are normal and ab-normal conditions for that organism.

Such an approach, Rosenquist argues, is untenable, for there is simply no way to define objectively states of social pathology. First of all, very often the "health" of one sector of society depends heavily on the "ill-health" of other sec-tors. In addition, since society is not an organism, there is no necessary set of relationships by which to define health (as there is, for example, between the nervous system and the digestive system). For these reasons, statements about what is "normal" or "healthy" for society reflect the ideals of the speaker, rather than any objective truth.

The most familiar explanation of social problems uses the analogy between the biological and social organisms. The study of pathology presupposes the existence of an organism in which the symptoms of disease may be observed. For the biologist the organism is a plant or an animal; for the social pathologist, a society.[1] The study of pathology further presupposes a condition of normality in the organism from which disease may be regarded as a deviation. As to the meaning of normality, it will suffice at this point to say that it ordinarily refers to the operation of the various organs in such a way as to secure or promote the welfare of the organism as a whole. Since the nature of the functions involved is dependent upon the structure of the organs, it follows that normality and, consequently, pathology, vary according to the kind of organism concerned. In the biological field, this means that each species of plant or animal has its own peculiar set of diseases; in sociology, it means that social ills differ from society to society and, since societies change, from time to time within the same society.

NORMAL SOCIETY

In the study of pathological manifestations, it is necessary first to know and recognize normality. . . . [It] may be assumed that society exists for its members and that they have certain ideas as to what society should provide. To the extent that these expectations are realized, society may be spoken of as normal or, for the purpose of the analogy, as healthy. This conception of normality does not necessarily find its expression in actual experience. Probably no society has ever provided complete satisfaction for all of its members. Yet the requirement remains as an ideal, from which we measure deviations, referred to as social ills.

When this concept of normality is compared with that of biology, a conspicuous difference is at once apparent. The animal organism is in health when as a whole it is functioning perfectly; the social organism is in health when all of its members are functioning perfectly. . . . It must be emphasized that the social organism exists for the benefit of the individuals who compose it, rather than for itself alone. Conceivably, a society might be healthy according to standards similar to those used in biology—this is, the group as a whole might be wealthy, successful in war, increasing in size, and long of life—but if the internal organization is based upon a system of exploitation in which some of the people make life miserable for the rest, the society is sick according to the usually accepted sociological viewpoint.

THE MEANING OF PATHOLOGY

. . . The discussion of pathology as ordinarily carried on makes it appear that disease is an enemy of the biological organism, existing outside the organism and always waiting for a favorable moment to launch an attack, just as a wolf prowls around a flock of sheep, waiting for the shepherd to relax his vigilance long enough to permit a raid on his charges. This notion has doubtless been strengthened by the discovery that micro-organisms are found in connection with many types of disease. To the human mind, with its strong predilection for personification, the minute organisms have appeared in the role of an attacking army bent on the destruction of its victims. Actually, the picture thus presented is far from the facts.

Diseases are not entities: the classification of diseases is purely a matter of convenience: what are known as diseases are the results of what happens when the organism comes in contact with inimical agents.[2]

The word disease, then, does not properly refer to an attacking force, but to the response of the organism to certain conditions threatening its safety. The response consists of a series of physiological changes, described as the symptoms of the disease. They are but the indications that the organism has suffered from an injury or infection and is attempting to repair the damage. The symptoms are beneficent in character in the sense that they show active resistance on the part of the organism. To attempt to remove them may harm the organism instead of benefiting it. Disease may be tentatively defined therefore as a process of readjustment. . . .

THE CONCEPT OF NORMALITY

Since biologists invariably define disease in terms of deviation from a state of health, it becomes imperative to define health also. The definition of health as freedom from disease, is, of course, of no value. Substitution of the word "normality" does not remove the difficulty, for normality has no more specific meaning than health. It cannot mean the average condition of the organism, for perfect health is rarely if ever observed. Since normality does not exist as an actual condition, it must obviously refer to an imaginary condition, found only in the observer's mind. A brief inquiry shows this to be the case. Health or normality is an ideal state unattained and probably unattainable, but regarded as eminently desirable. It is taken for granted that good health and, consequently, a long life, are among the chief objectives of man, and that anything which militates against [their] attainment is pathological. This points plainly to the subjective and hedonistic elements in the definition of normality. From his own experience, the individual comes to certain conclusions regarding his own welfare. Sympathetically transferring his personal feelings to others, he produces a general notion of the kind of physical condition he considers ideal. To this he gives the name of normality. Not satisfied with this, he extends his anthropomorphism to all other forms of life, postulating norms for them as well as for himself. With these norms established for a given species, he can proceed at once to a study of its pathology. This is not to say that normality thus determined is without value. On the contrary, the results have amply justified working from postulates of this sort, as the triumphs of pathologists have shown many times; but it can hardly be maintained that the procedure is scientific, if by scientific we mean objective. . . .

This fairly well describes the status of the "pathology" which sociology has borrowed from biology. . . . As a basis for the study of social pathology, a "healthy" society is set up as a norm, from which deviations are observed. Unhappily for the comfort of sociologists, it appears to be much more difficult to arrive at an agreement as to the health of societies than as to the health of individuals. In this connection society is, of course, contemplated in its organic aspects, that is, it is considered as a whole composed of interrelated parts. Yet it is impossible to overlook the fact that there can be no social "health" apart from the health of individual members of society, and the further fact that the nature of the organization of society is determined by the members themselves. For example, it is possible to find described in history societies which have proved themselves very able in conflict with other societies and with nature, so that they have flourished and endured over long periods. From the viewpoint of society as an organism such a group might well be considered "healthy" or normal, whereas its internal organization might be of such a sort as to keep the vast majority of the members in a state of social degradation. On the other hand, it is possible to find societies which, because of looser controls, are less efficient and less secure, but in which the individual members find life highly agreeable. There can be hardly a doubt as to which society the ordinary individual would prefer to live in, and probably we cannot consider that society diseased which is, from the individual's point of view, the most desirable of all. . . .

What then is the most desirable society? What are we to take as the norms or ideals from which we may diagnose our social ills? The answers offered us in the numerous utopias in our literature are by no means unanimous. Some have war and others have peace; some are capitalistic and others are communistic; some are religious and others are unreligious. All have forms of family and community life. Each of them reflects its author's ideas as to what was wrong with the society he lived in. The variety presented makes instantly clear the fact that even in the planning of a new society, in which the authors are limited only by the powers of their own imagination, no agreement in form is possible. And if we were to question all the people in the world as to which of the several existing societies they would prefer, we should probably find no conclusive vote for any. . . .

CONCLUSION

In view of all these difficulties, it may well be wondered how social problems can be studied at all. Obviously we have no norm, real or imaginary, upon which we can agree. Nor is it likely, in view of the constantly changing character of society, that a norm can be established. How can we know what in society is really pathological? The only answer is: we do not and cannot know.

There is, however, a way in which social problems may be studied without answering these questions. They may be treated, not as the study of variations from a norm, but as manifestations of society itself. From this viewpoint popular recognition of any social condition or process as bad, followed by an attempt to eliminate or cure it, serves as the criterion for its inclusion in a study of social problems. The writer merely accepts the judgment of public opinion. . . . The question to be answered is not, then, whether poverty or any other condition is bad for society, and if so what is to be done about it, but what are the conditions of society which large numbers of people regard as harmful and remediable. Is poverty found among them? If so, what are its manifestations? How does it affect the individual? What is being done to remedy it? To these matters we address ourselves. Social problems are nothing more nor less than those conditions or aspects of society which considerable numbers of people are trying to change.[3]

Notes

1. That society is not an organism in the biological sense need not concern us here, but society must be seen as a mechanism of interacting parts if the concept of pathology is to be applied to a study of its ills.

2. William A. White, *The Meaning of Disease,* p. 171. Baltimore: The Williams and Wilkins Company, 1926.

3. "A social problem . . . is determined by group sanction, being the judgment of a group concerning the efficiency of a type of social organization in its structure or function. It is within the realm of folkways, mores, and opinions." George A. Lundberg, Read Bain, and Nels Anderson, Editors, *Trends in American Sociology;* Harold A. Phelps, "Sociology and Social Work," p. 332. New York: Harper and Brothers, 1929. Reprinted by permission of the publishers.

Questions for Discussion

1. Smith's statement appeared in 1911; Slater's, in 1970. What are the major differences between their statements?

2. What role did correctional workers play in the development of the social pathology perspective?

3. How did the "child savers" respond to Lombroso's work?

4. Does Rosenquist's critique apply to the later social pathology approach exemplified by Slater and Kavolis? How about the approach described by Platt? How does it apply or not apply? In what ways do you agree or disagree with Rosenquist?

5. What are some of the implications of the social pathology perspective for sociology in general? What do you yourself think about the approach?

Selected References

Duster, Troy. *Backdoor to Eugenics.* New York: Routledge, 1990.
    Examines the resurgence of biological explanations for social problems and specifies the social conditions under which the social pathology perspective continues to flourish.

Fink, Arthur E. *Causes of Crime: Biological Theories in the United States, 1800–1915.* Philadelphia: University of Pennsylvania Press, 1938.
    A scholarly review of the work of thirty-five authors who attributed crime to various biological factors. This work demonstrates the influence of biocentric theorizing before World War I.

Gillin, John L. *Social Pathology.* 2nd ed. New York: Appleton-Century, 1939.
    Gillin's book represents the turning point in pathology texts. This was perhaps the first social pathology book to "attempt to treat social maladjustments in a framework of sociological theory." The middle-class bias is less pervasive in Gillin's book than in other texts, and the theory is more eclectic. (For an example of the prominence of the middle-class bias in some social pathology textbooks, see Stuart Alfred Queen and Jennette Rowe Gruener, *Social Pathology: Obstacles to Social Participation,* 2nd ed. New York: Crowell, 1940.)

Gove, Walter R. "The Effect of Age and Gender on Deviant Behavior: A Biopsychosocial Perspective." In *Gender and the Life Course,* ed. Alice Rossi. New York: Aldine, 1985, pp. 115–44.

Attributes the low rate of deviant behavior among females to their affiliative nature, their physique, and their lack of assertiveness, which also, according to him, have a biological base.

Henderson, Charles Richmond. *Introduction to the Study of the Dependent, Defective, and Delinquent Classes, and of Their Social Treatment.* Boston: Heath, 1909.

Henderson coined the expression "dependent, defective, and delinquent classes." The expression was quite popular in social pathology books for at least a generation. Henderson's book is typical of those that blame the characteristics of the individual for any violation of social rules.

Jeffery, C. Ray, ed. *Biology and Crime.* Beverly Hills, CA: Sage, 1979.

A collection of studies on the relationship between biology and crime. The editor, C. Ray Jeffery, himself a sociologist, says that sociologists have shied away from and denied the significance of biology as a cause or condition of crime. Reversing his earlier point of view, Jeffery now feels that while biology and society interact as causes of crime, biology is more often the cause while environment is one of its conditions.

Mednick, Sarnoff A., and Jan Volavka. "Biology and Crime." In *Crime and Justice: An Annual Review of Research,* ed. Norval Morris and Michael Tonry. Chicago: University of Chicago Press, 1980, pp. 85–158.

The authors review genetic, neurophysiological, biological, physiological, and biochemical studies. They conclude that biological and social factors combine to produce criminal behavior.

Mills, C. Wright. "The Professional Ideology of Social Pathologists." *American Journal of Sociology* 60 (September 1942): 165–80.

In this widely celebrated essay, Mills points out that most writers on social pathology came from small towns and were middle-class in their outlook, pragmatic in their approach, and conservative in their politics. He attacks their studies for being atheoretical and heavily biased.

Owen, D. R. "The 47-XYY Male: A Review." *Psychological Bulletin* 78 (September 1972): 209–33.

A review and assessment of the research that purports to show that males with an extra Y chromosome are more apt to commit crimes. The author's data suggest that despite the popularity of the XYY chromosome theory, the great majority of XYY males do not commit crimes and appear to lead normal lives.

Rafter, Nicole. *White Trash.* Boston: Northeastern University Press, 1988.

Rafter shows how early exponents of social pathology made the facts of defectiveness, dependency, and delinquency fit their beliefs about the causes of these problematic conditions.

Rosenberg, Bernard, Israel Gerver, and William Howton, eds. *Mass Society in Crisis: Social Problems and Social Pathology.* 2nd ed. New York: Macmillan, 1971.

A book of readings compiled in the framework of the later perspective on social pathology. Included is "A New Look at Mills' Critique," by Emil Bend and Martin Vogelfanger.

Wilson, James Q., and Richard J. Herrnstein. *Crime and Human Nature.* New York: Simon and Schuster, 1986.

An encyclopedic review of the sources of criminal behavior from the perspective of social pathology. The authors conclude that most criminals are mesomorphic, have low IQs, and poor impulse control. Criminality stems from defects in character, socialization, or both.

3/SOCIAL DISORGANIZATION

The social disorganization perspective arose after World War I in response to a particular set of circumstances in both the larger society and the field of sociology. In this chapter, we look at the circumstances that gave rise to the social disorganization perspective, the sociologists who formulated it, and the basic features of the perspective.

PROBLEMS OF SOCIETY

Migration, urban living, and factory work are certainly nothing new. The ancestors of the American Indians, for example, migrated from Siberia across the Bering Strait and down into the Americas. The ancient Greeks and Egyptians lived in cities. And the ancient Romans are said to have established some of the earliest factories.

After World War I, however, these processes—migration, urbanization, and industrialization—began to occur in the United States at an unprecedented pace. And as they did so, many previously recognized social problems, such as poverty, delinquency and crime, mental illness, and alcoholism, seemed to become more and more prevalent.

Migration, for example, produced considerable culture conflict both for European immigrants and for American in-migrants (e.g., people moving from the rural South to the northern cities). The European immigrants, for example, were likely to find considerable conflict between their native culture and the prevailing culture in their new home. Of course, many soon became "Americanized." Others, however, were less successful at the "Americanization process," and these people soon came to be seen as the source and substance of most American social problems. Urbanization also contributed to the sense of increasing social problems. The cities, for instance, included deviant subcultures that were not found in more rural areas—delinquent gangs, for example. Finally, industrialization brought with it many social problems. For example, working conditions were often poor, and technological advances put many people out of work.

Taken together, then, these three factors—migration, urbanization, and industrialization—established a broad social and cultural base for a host of undesirable conditions. Outgrowths of these conditions—such as crime, mental illness, alcoholism, drug addition, and juvenile delinquency—all came to be treated in the social problems textbooks of the day. When these problems had been smaller in scale, the social pathology perspective had seemed adequate. As they increased, however, the pathology perspective seemed less useful. Concomitantly, sociology was facing new problems as a discipline. In coping with these problems—both in society and in sociology—sociologists fashioned the social disorganization perspective.

PROBLEMS OF THE DISCIPLINE

Any fledgling discipline faces a number of difficulties. It has to state a rationale for its existence, it has to formulate what it will do that other disciplines do not do, and it has to make clear what its relationship to other disciplines will be. During its formative period (up to 1918), sociology had not yet resolved these issues.

When the Frenchman Auguste Comte coined the term "sociology," he envisioned it as the queen of the sciences, encompassing all the other scientific disciplines.[1] But Emile Durkheim, battling two generations later to establish sociology as a university discipline in France, took a quite different tack: he set out to make sociology a science with its own concepts and subject matter.[2]

Throughout its formative period, American sociology remained a hodgepodge of history, political science, economics, psychology, and social philosophy. It dealt with issues that overlapped these older disciplines or that they chose to ignore. Thus, some of the early critics called sociology a "science of leftovers." Throughout these years, sociology's concern with order, progress, and the philosophy of history ran strong.

As American sociology moved into its second period (1918 to 1935), it centered more and more on the formation of a scientific policy. Heavy emphasis was placed on the development of concepts and definitions, and much of this conceptual and definitional effort centered on showing how the subject matter of sociology differed from that of other disciplines.

The emergence of the social disorganization perspective during the 1920s reflects this effort to develop sociology as a scientific discipline. The very concept of social disorganization springs from a then-developing network of ideas centering on the concept of social organization. The notion of social organization implies, first of all, that there is a whole whose parts stand in some ordered relationship to one another. Second (and secondarily), it implies the concept of social disorganization— that is, that the various parts can get out of phase with one another.

Central to this entire conceptualization, implicitly or explicitly, is the notion of *rules*. Rules define not only the different parts of society, but also the way in which they interrelate. And by focusing on rules, sociologists succeeded in defining their subject matter as different from that of any other discipline.

The social disorganization perspective emerged from this developing sociological viewpoint, and in time it came to be the most popular way of studying social problems. To be more specific, sociologists began to see social problems as an index of social disorganization; as they developed a body of sociological concepts to deal with social organization, they also developed sister concepts to describe and explain social disorganization. In the end, sociology began to bloom as a discipline with its own subject matter, its own concepts, and its own way of describing reality.

---

1. Auguste Comte, *Positive Philosophy,* trans. Harriet Martineau (London: George Bell & Sons, 1896).

2. Emile Durkheim, *The Rules of Sociological Method,* trans. Sarah Solovay and John Mueller (Chicago: University of Chicago Press, 1938).

DIFFERENCES BETWEEN THE PATHOLOGY
AND THE DISORGANIZATION PERSPECTIVES

Compared with the earlier social pathology perspective, the social disorganization perspective is more complex, more intellectually distinct, and considerably more systematic—benefiting, of course, from the greater maturity of sociology as a discipline at the time it developed. It is instructive, at this point, to compare these two perspectives in terms of their subject matters, vocabularies, methods, and concerns with practical applications. The social pathologists, it will be recalled, studied social problems by looking at the failings of individuals and institutions. Their concepts and vocabularies, however, were borrowed from other disciplines, most notably medicine. Their methods were more philosophical than scientific. Finally, they wanted action; they wanted to apply their discoveries to the solution of social problems.

Writers using the social disorganization perspective, in contrast, studied social problems by examining social rules. They developed their own conceptualizations and vocabularies. They became more concerned with the development of theory and with precision in methodology. Finally, their emphasis on theory led them to be more concerned with acquiring knowledge than with finding practical solutions to social problems.

This comparison of the pathology and disorganization perspectives brings up the chronic division of opinion in sociology regarding whether sociologists should themselves make moral judgments or should merely study the moral judgments of others. Pathologists made moral judgments with regard to institutions and individuals alike. Disorganization writers, in contrast, chose to study moral judgments in a more detached, "objective" manner. (The social disorganization perspective, however, has since been criticized for not being objective. Critics have charged that nonconforming ways of life are often called disorganized when, in reality, they simply represent a different system of social organization. See, for example, the Clinard reading in this chapter.)

THE MAJOR SOCIAL DISORGANIZATION THEORISTS

The social disorganization perspective as we know it today stems largely from the writings of Charles H. Cooley, W. I. Thomas and Florian Znaniecki, and William F. Ogburn. To be sure, the idea of social disorganization has been considerably refined since these men first wrote about it. However, the major influences on current social disorganization writers can all be traced back to these four. All were primarily theorists, and all sought to explain why individuals sometimes fail to obey rules. And, as the following discussions show, they all pictured social problems as a function of social disorganization.

Cooley. A very early but still influential writer, Cooley made some important conceptual contributions to the social disorganization perspective. First, he formulated the distinction between primary and secondary group relations. Primary relations refer to personal and enduring face-to-face relationships.[3] Secondary relationships, on the other hand, are less frequent, impersonal contacts. Given this distinction, sociologists quickly saw that the movement from rural to urban areas was accompanied by a breakdown in primary group controls. Second, Cooley conceptualized

---

3. Charles Horton Cooley, *Human Nature and the Social Order* (New York: Scribner's, 1902).

social disorganization as the disintegration of traditions. He argued that the worst aspect of social disorganization is that "the absence of social standards is likely to lower . . . [a person's] plane of achievement and throw him back upon sensibility and other primitive impulses."[4]

Thomas and Znaniecki. In their major work on the Polish immigrant to America,[5] Thomas and Znaniecki defined social disorganization as the breakdown of the influence of rules on the individual. The bulk of their work consists of letters written by Polish immigrants to friends and relatives back home in Poland. The letters all give testimony to the conflict of cultures, ethnic as well as generational. According to Thomas and Znaniecki, the Polish immigrant faced either no rules or too many rules. In the case of a paucity of rules, the immigrant had no means of defining his or her situation. In the case of a plentitude of rules, the rules were either unclear or in conflict with one another. Thus, the immigrant often did not know how to behave in America and lacked mutual understanding with native-born Americans. In their study of Polish immigrants, Thomas and Znaniecki conceptualized the experiences of millions who immigrated to the United States. They also indicated that a variety of social problems (e.g., delinquency, crime, mental illness, and alcoholism) could be attributed in large part to the failure of the immigrant family to control its members.

Ogburn. Ogburn's contribution lies primarily in his notion of cultural lag.[6] The different parts of a culture are interdependent, Ogburn said, and when different parts change at different rates, one part can get out of phase with another and produce disorder. Usually, Ogburn observed, people accept new tools more readily than new ideas; thus, material culture changes much more quickly than does nonmaterial culture. Stated another way, changes in customs and rules tend to lag behind those in technology, which is what Ogburn means by "cultural lag." The principal source of social disorganization, according to Ogburn, is this uneven rate of cultural change.

CHARACTERISTICS OF THE SOCIAL DISORGANIZATION PERSPECTIVE

People who work with this perspective view society as a social system—a complex, dynamic whole whose parts are coordinated. When events change one part of the system, there is a corresponding need for adjustment in other parts. "Social disorganization" refers to lack of adjustment, or poor adjustment, between the parts. The major elements of the social disorganization perspective are as follows:

Definition. Social disorganization is conceived of as a failure of rules. Three major types of disorganization are *normlessness, culture conflict,* and *breakdown.* With normlessness, no rules exist on how to act. With culture conflict, at least two opposing sets of rules exist on how to act. In such situations, persons who act in terms of one set of expectations may in so doing violate another set of expectations. Break-

---

4. Charles Horton Cooley, *Social Organization: A Study of the Larger Mind* (New York: Scribner's, 1909), p. 348.
5. William I. Thomas and Florian Znaniecki, *The Polish Peasant in Europe and America,* 2 vols. (New York: Knopf, 1927).
6. William F. Ogburn, *Social Change with Respect to Culture and Original Nature* (New York: Huebsch, 1922), pp. 199–280.

down is a variation on this same theme. Here rules exist, but conformity to them either fails to produce the promised rewards or yields punishments instead.

Causes. The root cause of social disorganization is, broadly speaking, social change. As changes occur, the parts of the social system get out of tune with one another.

Conditions. The parts of a social system are never perfectly in tune. Nevertheless, there is usually a dynamic equilibrium. Any condition that upsets the equilibrium may precipitate social disorganization. Such conditions include technical, demographic, or cultural changes that generate social change (i.e., a change in social relationships).

Consequences. The social disorganization perspective predicts outcomes for the system and for persons in it. For persons, social disorganization produces stress, which in turn produces "personal disorganization"—for example, mental illness, alcoholism.[7] For the system, social disorganization may have three types of consequences. First, there can be change in the system (i.e., some response or adaptation may bring the various parts of the system back into equilibrium). Second, the system can continue to operate in a steady state (i.e., the disorganization may remain but the system continues to function anyway). Third, the system may break down (i.e., the disorganization may be so disruptive that it destroys the system).

Solutions. Attempts to reduce social disorganization can be put into effect once the proper diagnosis has been made. Thus, parts of the system that are out of phase can be brought back into equilibrium—for example, technical changes can be slowed down.

SUMMARY AND CONCLUSION

After World War I, American sociologists strove to establish sociology as an independent scientific discipline with its own concepts and subject matter. At the same time, migration, urban growth, and technological change seemed to be producing a number of social problems, and sociologists worked hard to devise a set of terms to describe and explain these problems.

Cooley taught a generation of sociologists to look for the signs of a breakdown of traditions, especially as reflected in the decreased hold of small, intimate groups on their members. Thomas and Znaniecki devised an important set of concepts and, in their study of Polish immigrants to America, showed how moving to a strange city in a foreign land disrupts families, sharpens generational conflict, and increases chances of criminality and mental illness. Ogburn examined the effects of technology on social organization, developed his influential theory of cultural lag, and fostered a whole school of technological determinists.

Briefly stated, social disorganization denotes a failure of rules. Social change is

7. See, for example, Robert E. L. Faris and H. Warren Dunham, *Mental Disorders in Urban Areas: An Ecological Study of Schizophrenia and Other Psychoses* (Chicago: University of Chicago Press, 1939).

usually viewed as the cause, and technological, demographic, and cultural changes are viewed as the precipitating conditions. Personal disorganization and disequilibrium of the social system are seen as consequences of social disorganization, and the solution for disorganization is to bring the features of the social system back into equilibrium.

SOCIAL CHANGE AND SOCIAL DISORGANIZATION

Robert E. Park

The basis of social organization, Park says, is tradition and custom. And during periods of stability, the family, neighborhood, and community combine to exercise control over people. Urbanization, industrialization, and immigration disrupt these stabilizing influences, thereby undermining the authority of traditional social systems. The trends of modern society induce rapid changes that, in turn, produce social disorganization. Examples of social disorganization are found among migrants, delinquents, and derelicts, and in the rootlessness of life in areas where these people are found.

In the family and in the neighborhood such organization as exists is based upon custom and tradition, and is fixed in what Sumner calls the folkways and the mores. At this stage, society is a purely natural product; a product of the spontaneous and unreflective responses of individuals living together in intimate, personal, and face-to-face relations. Under such circumstances conscious efforts to discipline the individual and enforce the social code are directed merely by intuition and common sense.

In the larger social unit, the community, where social relations are more formal and less intimate, the situation is different. It is in the community, rather than in the family or the neighborhood, that formal organizations like the church, the school, and the courts come into existence and get their separate functions defined. With the advent of these institutions, and through their mediation, the community is able to supplement, and to some extent supplant, the family and the neighborhood as a means for the discipline and control of the individual. However, neither the orphan asylum nor any other agency has thus far succeeded in providing a wholly satisfactory substitute for the home. The evidence of this is that they have no alumni associations. They create no memories and traditions that those who graduate from them are disposed to cherish and keep alive.

It is in this community with its various organizations and its rational, rather than traditional, schemes of control, and not elsewhere, that we have delinquency. Delinquency is, in fact, in some sense the measure of the failure of our community organizations to function.

Historically, the background of American life has been the village community. Until a few years ago the typical American was, and perhaps still is, an inhabitant

From Robert E. Park, Ernest W. Burgess, and Roderick D. McKenzie, *The City*, pp. 105–110. © 1967 by The University of Chicago Press. Reprinted by permission.

of a middle western village; such a village, perhaps, as Sinclair Lewis describes in *Main Street*. And still, today, the most characteristic trait of Homo Americanus is an inveterate individualism which may, to be sure, have been temperamental, but in this case temperament has certainly been considerably reinforced by the conditions of life on the frontier.

But with the growth of great cities, with the vast division of labor which has come in with machine industry, and with movement and change that have come about with the multiplication of the means of transportation and communication, the old forms of social control represented by the family, the neighborhood, and the local community have been undermined and their influence greatly diminished.

This process by which the authority and influence of an earlier culture and system of social control is undermined and eventually destroyed is described by Thomas—looking at it from the side of the individual—as a process of "individualization." But looking at it from the point of view of society and the community it is social disorganization.

We are living in such a period of individualization and social disorganization. Everything is in a state of agitation—everything seems to be undergoing a change. Society is, apparently, not much more than a congeries and constellation of social atoms. Habits can be formed only in a relatively stable environment, even if that stability consists merely—as, in fact, it invariably does, since there is nothing in the universe that is absolutely static—in a relatively constant form of change. Any form of change that brings any measurable alteration in the routine of social life tends to break up habits; and in breaking up the habits upon which the existing social organization rests, destroys that organization itself. Every new device that affects social life and the social routine is to that extent a disorganizing influence. Every new discovery, every new invention, every new idea, is disturbing. Even news has become at times so dangerous that governments have felt it wise to suppress its publication.

It is probable that the most deadly and the most demoralizing single instrumentality of present-day civilization is the automobile. The automobile bandit, operating in our great cities, is much more successful and more dangerous than the romantic stage robber of fifty years ago. The connection of the automobile with vice is notorious. "The automobile is connected with more seductions than happen otherwise in cities altogether."[1]

The newspaper and the motion picture show, while not so deadly, are almost as demoralizing. If I were to attempt to enumerate all the social forces that have contributed to the disorganization of modern society I should probably be compelled to make a catalogue of everything that has introduced any new and striking change into the otherwise dull routine of our daily life. Apparently anything that makes life interesting is dangerous to the existing order.

The mere movement of the population from one part of the country to another—the present migration of the Negroes northward, for example—is a disturbing influence. Such a movement may assume, from the point of view of the migrants themselves, the character of an emancipation, opening to them new economic and cultural opportunities, but it is none the less disorganizing to the communities they have left behind and to the communities into which they are now moving. It is at the same time demoralizing to the migrating people them-selves, and particularly, I might add, to the younger generation.

The enormous amount of delinquency, juvenile and adult, that exists today in the Negro communities in northern cities is due in part, though not entirely, to the fact that migrants are not able to accommodate themselves at once to a new and relatively strange environment. The same thing may be said of the immigrants from Europe, or of the younger generation of women who are just now entering in such large numbers into the newer occupations and the freer life which the great cities offer them.

"Progress," as I once heard William James remark, "is a terrible thing." It is a terrible thing in so far as it breaks up the routine upon which an existing social order rests, and thus destroys the cultural and the economic values, i.e., the habits of thrift, of skill, of industry, as well as the personal hopes, ambitions, and life-programs which are the content of that social order.

Our great cities, as those who have studied them have learned, are full of junk, much of it human, i.e., men and women who, for some reason or other, have fallen out of line in the march of industrial progress and have been scrapped by the industrial organization of which they were once a part.

A recent study by Nels Anderson of what he calls "Hobohemia," an area in Chicago just outside the "Loop," that is to say, the downtown business area, which is almost wholly inhabited by homeless men, is a study of such a human junk heap. In fact, the slum areas that invariably grow up just on the edge of the business areas of great cities, areas of deteriorated houses, of poverty, vice, and crime, are areas of social junk.

I might add, because of its immediate connection with the problems and interests of this association, that recent studies made in Chicago of boys' gangs seem to show that there are no playgrounds in the city in which a boy can find so much adventure, no place where he can find so much that may be called "real sport," as in these areas of general deterioration which we call the slums.

In order to meet and deal with the problems that have been created by the rapid changes of modern life, new organizations and agencies have sprung into existence. The older social agencies, the church, the school, and the courts, have not always been able to meet the problems which new conditions of life have created. The school, the church, and the courts have come down to us with their aims and methods defined under the influence of an older tradition. New agen-cies have been necessary to meet the new conditions. Among these new agencies are the juvenile courts, juvenile protective associations, parent-teachers' associ-ations, Boy Scouts, Young Men's Christian Associations settlements, boys' clubs of various sorts, and I presume, playgrounds and playground associations. These agencies have taken over to some extent the work which neither the home, the neighborhood, nor the other older communal institutions were able to carry on adequately.

These new institutions, perhaps because they are not to the same extent hampered by our earlier traditions, are frankly experimental and are trying to work out a rational technique for dealing with social problems, based not on sentiment and tradition, but on science.

Largely on the basis of the experiments which these new agencies are making, a new social science is coming into existence. Under the impetus which the social agencies have given to social investigation and social research, sociology is ceasing to be a mere philosophy and is assuming more and more the character of an empirical, if not an exact, science.

As to the present condition of our science and of the devices that we have invented for controlling conduct and social life, I can only repeat what I said at the very outset of our paper: "The thing of which we still know least is the business of carrying on an associated existence."

Note

1. W. I. Thomas, *The Unadjusted Girl—with Cases and Standpoint for Behavior Analysis,* Criminal Science Monograph No. 4, Boston, 1923, p. 71.

THE ECOLOGY OF URBAN DISORGANIZATION

Robert E. L. Faris and H. Warren Dunham

Although urbanism and social disorganization tend to go together, the incidence of social problems varies within the ecological structure of the city. In looking at different areas of the city, Park, Burgess, and McKenzie found that rates of social disorganization and social problems were greatest in what they called the "zone in transition"—a zone characterized by boarding houses and tenements, transitory businesses, and dilapidated buildings. Social problems associated with these indices of disorganization included vice, poverty, crime, alcoholism, mental illness, and broken families. Faris and Dunham believe that social disorganization leads to social problems by breaking down primary group controls. Hence, rates of social problems are highest in the center of the city, where social disorganization is also highest; conversely, on the periphery the indices of social disorganization are at their lowest and so is the incidence of social problems.

A relationship between urbanism and social disorganization has long been recognized and demonstrated. Crude rural-urban comparisons of rates of dependency, crime, divorce and desertion, suicide, and vice have shown these problems to be more severe in the cities, especially the large rapidly expanding industrial cities. But as the study of urban sociology advanced, even more striking com-

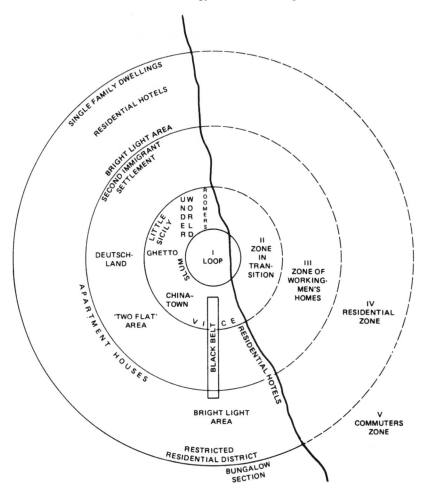

From Robert E. Park, Ernest W. Burgess and Roderick D. McKenzie, *The City*, Chart I, p. 42.
Reprint 1966. Reprinted by permission of the University of Chicago Press.

parisons between the different sections of a city were discovered. Some parts
were found to be as stable and peaceful as any well-organized rural neighborhood
while other parts were found to be in the extreme stages of social disorganization.
Extreme disorganization is confined to certain areas and is not characteristic of
all sections of the city.

Out of the interaction of social and economic forces that cause city growth a
pattern is formed in these large expanding American cities which is the same for
all the cities, with local variations due to topographical and other differences.
This pattern is not planned or intended, and to a certain extent resists control
by planning. The understanding of this order is necessary to the understanding
of the social disorganization that characterizes urban life.

THE NATURAL AREAS DEPICTED AS CIRCULAR ZONES

The most striking characteristics of this urban pattern, as described by Professor Burgess,[1] may be represented by a system of concentric zones, shown in Chart I. Zone I, at the center, is the central business district. The space is occupied by stores, business offices, places of amusement, light industry, and other business establishments. There are few residents in this area, except for transients inhabiting the large hotels, and the homeless men of the "hobohemia" section which is usually located on the fringe of the business district.

Zone II is called the zone in transition. This designation refers to the fact that the expanding industrial region encroaches on the inner edge. Land values are high because of the expectation of sale for industrial purposes, and since residential buildings are not expected to occupy the land permanently, they are not kept in an improved state. Therefore, residential buildings are in a deteriorated state and rents are low. These slums are inhabited largely by unskilled laborers and their families. All the settlements of foreign populations as well as the rooming-house areas are located in this zone.

Zone III, the zone of workingmen's homes, is inhabited by a somewhat more stable population with a higher percentage of skilled laborers and fewer foreign-born and unskilled. It is intermediate in many respects between the slum areas and the residential areas. In it is located the "Deutschlands," or second immigrant settlement colonies, representing the second generation of those families who have migrated from Zone II.

Zone IV and V, the apartment-house and commuters' zones, are inhabited principally by upper-middle-class families. A high percentage own their homes and reside for long periods at the same address. In these areas stability is the rule and social disorganization exceptional or absent.

The characteristics of the populations in these zones appear to be produced by the nature of the life within the zones rather than the reverse. This is shown by the striking fact that the zones retain all their characteristics as different populations flow through them. The large part of the population migration into the city consists of the influx of unskilled labor into the second zone, the zone in transition. These new arrivals displace the populations already there, forcing them to move farther out into the next zone. In general, the flow of population in the city is of this character, from the inner zones toward the outer ones. Each zone, however, retains its characteristics whether its inhabitants be native-born white, foreign-born, or Negro. Also each racial or national group changes its character as it moves from one zone to the next.

Within this system of zones, there is further sifting and sorting of economic and social institutions and of populations. In the competition for land values at the center of the city, each type of business finds the place in which it can survive. The finding of the place is not infrequently by trial and error, those locating in the wrong place failing. There emerge from this competition financial sections, retail department store sections, theater sections, sections for physicians' and dentists' offices, for specialized shops, for light industry, for warehouses, etc.

Similarly, there are specialized regions for homeless men, for rooming-houses, for apartment hotels, and for single homes. The location of each of these is determined ecologically and the characteristics also result from the interaction of unplanned forces. They maintain their characteristics in spite of the flow of various racial and national groups through them and invariably impress their effects on each of these groups. These have been called "natural areas" by Professor Park,[2] because they result from the interactions of natural forces and are not the result of human intentions.

Fortunately, the city of Chicago has been studied somewhat more intensively than most cities of its size. Certain of these areas are significant in relation to social disorganization. It is possible to define and describe these areas with certain kinds of objective data. The major divisions of the city can be seen in Map I. Extending outward from the central business district are the principal industrial and railroad properties. The rooming-house sections extend along three arms radiating from the center to the north, west, and south. The slum areas are roughly defined by the regions containing over 50 per cent foreign-born and native-born of foreign parentage and over 50 per cent Negro. Beyond these areas is the residential section. In the Lake Calumet section at the southeastern corner of the city is another industrial region inhabited by a foreign-born population.

Too small to be shown on this map are the areas of homeless men—the "hobohemia" areas.[3] These are located on three main radial streets and are just outside the central business district. Their inhabitants are the most unstable in the city. The mobility and anonymity of their existence produces a lack of sociability and in many cases deterioration of the personality. Although spending their time in the most crowded parts of the city, these homeless men are actually extremely isolated. For the most part they represent persons unable to obtain an economic foothold in society, and so they maintain themselves by occasional labor, by petty thievery, by begging, and by receiving charity. As they have no opportunity for normal married life, their sexual activities are limited to relations with the lowest type of prostitutes and to homosexuals. The rate of venereal infection is high among these men. Chronic alcoholism is also a common characteristic of the members of this group. Their lives are without goal or plan, and they drift aimlessly and alone, always farther from the conventional and normal ways of living.

Another area of importance is the rooming-house area. This is usually located along main arteries of transportation and a little farther from the center of the city. In Chicago there are several rooming-house sections, the three largest consisting of arms radiating to the north, west, and south, just beyond the hobohemia areas, each extending for something over two miles in length and from a half-mile to over a mile in width. The populations of these areas are principally young, unmarried white-collar workers, who are employed in the central business district during the day and live in low-priced rented rooms within walking distance or a short ride from their work.[4] Within the area the population is constantly shifting, turning over entirely about once each four months. Anonymity and isolation also characterize the social relations in this area; no one knows his neighbors and no one cares what they might think or say. Consequently the social control of primary group relations is absent, and the result is a breakdown of standards of personal behavior and a drifting into unconventionality and into dissipations and excesses of various sorts. The rates of venereal diseases and of alcoholism are high in this area, and the suicide rate is higher than for any other area of the city.[5]

Types of Cultural and Economic Areas

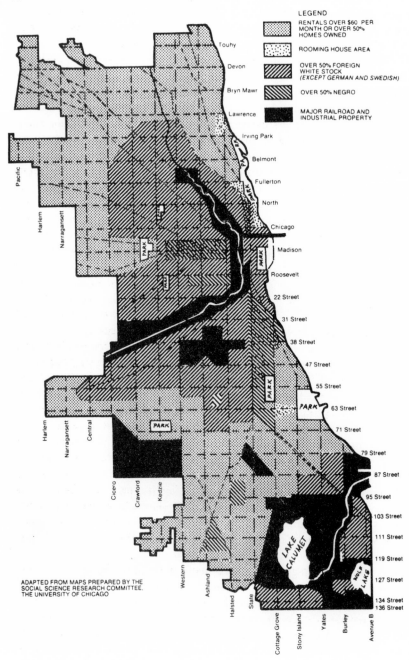

LEGEND

RENTALS OVER $60 PER MONTH OR OVER 50% HOMES OWNED

ROOMING HOUSE AREA

OVER 50% FOREIGN WHITE STOCK *(EXCEPT GERMAN AND SWEDISH)*

OVER 50% NEGRO

MAJOR RAILROAD AND INDUSTRIAL PROPERTY

ADAPTED FROM MAPS PREPARED BY THE SOCIAL SCIENCE RESEARCH COMMITTEE. THE UNIVERSITY OF CHICAGO

From Robert E. Park, Ernest W. Burgess and Roderick D. McKenzie, *The City*, Map I, p. 44. Reprint 1966. Reprinted by permission of the University of Chicago Press.

The foreign-born slum areas occupy a large zone surrounding the central business and industrial area. Within this zone there are a number of segregated ethnic communities, such as the Italian, Polish, Jewish, Russian, and Mexican districts. The newly arrived immigrants of any nationality settle in these communities with their fellow-countrymen. In these groups the language, customs, and many institutions of their former culture are at least partly preserved. In some of the most successfully isolated of these, such as the Russian-Jewish "ghetto," the Old-World cultures are preserved almost intact. Where this is the case, there may be a very successful social control and little social disorganization, especially in the first generation. But as soon as the isolation of these first-settlement communities begins to break down, the disorganization is severe. Extreme poverty is the rule; high rates of juvenile delinquency, family disorganization, and alcoholism reflect the various stresses in the lives of these populations.

Two distinct types of disorganizing factors can be seen in the foreign-born slum areas. The first is the isolation of the older generation, the foreign-born who speak English with difficulty or not all and who are never quite able to become assimilated to the point of establishing intimate friendships with anyone other than their native countrymen. Within the segregated ethnic communities these persons are well adapted to their surroundings, but as soon as they move away or are deserted by their neighbors, they suffer from social isolation.[6] The second type of disorganizing factor operates among the members of the second and third generations. The very high delinquency rate among the second-generation children has been shown by Shaw.[7] This disorganization can be shown to develop from the nature of the child's social situation. Also growing out of the peculiar social situation of the second generation is the mental conflict of the person who is in process of transition between two cultures—the culture of his ancestors and the culture of the new world in which he lives. As he attends American schools and plays with children of other than his own nationality, the child soon finds himself separated from the world of his parents. He loses respect for their customs and traditions and in many cases becomes ashamed of his own nationality, while at the same time he often fails to gain complete acceptance into the American group of his own generation. This is particularly true if he is distinguished by color or by features which betray his racial or national origin. This person is then a "man without a culture," for though he participates to some extent in two cultures, he rejects the one and is not entirely accepted by the other.[8]

The Negro areas are, in general, similar in character to the foreign-born slum areas. The principal Negro district in Chicago extends for several miles southward from the business district. Two smaller Negro districts are located on the Near West Side, as well as one on the Near North Side. In the larger area on the South Side, the social disorganization is extreme only at the part nearest the business district.[9] In the parts farther to the south live the Negroes who have resided longer in the city and who have become more successful economically. These communities have much the same character as the nearby apartment-house areas inhabited by native-born whites.

For some miles along the Lake Front in Chicago a long strip of apartment-hotel districts has grown up. These districts occupy a very pleasant and favorable location and attract residents who are able to pay high rentals. The rates of various indices of social disorganization are in general low in these sections.

The outlying residential districts of middle-class and upper-middle-class native-born white population live in apartments, two-flat homes, and single homes. In these districts, and especially the single home areas in which there is a large percentage of homes owned by the inhabitants, the population is stable and there is little or no social disorganization in comparison with those areas near the center of the city. . . .   Not only are such statistical facts as population composition, literacy, dependency rates, and disease rates known to vary greatly in the different sections of the city, but also mental life and behavior. In one of the most conclusive of these studies, the study of juvenile delinquency by Clifford R. Shaw and his associates,[10] sufficient control was obtained to establish with reasonable certainty that the high rates of delinquency were products not of the biological inferiority of the population stocks that inhabit the slum areas, nor of any racial or national peculiarity, but rather of the nature of the social life in the areas themselves. The delinquency rates remained constantly high in certain urban areas which were inhabited by as many as six different national groups in succession. Each nationality suffered from the same disorganization in these areas and each nationality alike improved after moving away from the deteriorated areas.

As has been shown, the natural areas which have been defined above can be identified by the use of certain mathematical indices for different types of social phenomena. Such indices as the percentage of foreign-born, the percentage of homes owned, the sex ratio, the median rentals paid, the density of population, the rate of mobility, the educational rate, the percentage of rooming-houses and hotels, and the percentage of condemned buildings, roughly tend to identify these areas and to differentiate between them. These indices might be regarded as ones which measure the extent of social disorganization between the different communities and the natural areas of the city. Other types of objective data, representing such social problems as juvenile delinquency, illegitimacy, suicide, crime, and family disorganization, might be considered as indices representing effects or results of certain types of social processes. As in the research of Clifford Shaw which has been described above, the rates for these different social problems tend to fit rather closely into the ecological structure of the city as described by Park, Burgess, and others. In other words, in all of these social problems there is the concentration of high rates close to the center of the city, with the rates declining in magnitude as one travels in any direction toward the city's periphery. Shaw's study of juvenile delinquency gives one of the most complete pictures of this pattern. The other studies, in general, show the same pattern with certain variations which develop because of the location of certain ethnic groups in certain parts of the city.

The problem of mental disorder has been for the first time approached by the utilizing of this ecological technique. It is the attempt to examine the spatial character of the relations between persons who have different kinds of mental breakdowns. While this type of approach is used in this study, the authors wish to emphasize that they regard it as having definite limitations in understanding the entire problem of mental disorder. It can be looked upon as a purely cultural approach and as such does not tend to conflict with any understanding of this problem which may come from biological, physiological, or psychological approaches. However, in the light of these previous studies of social problems utilizing this method it does seem particularly desirable to study the distribution of the different types of mental disorders.

Notes

1. R. E. Park and E. W. Burgess, *The City* (Chicago: University of Chicago Press, 1925).

2. R. E. Park, "Sociology," in *Research in the Social Sciences,* ed. Wilson Gee (New York: Macmillan Co., 1929), pp. 28–29.

3. Nels Anderson, *The Hobo* (Chicago: University of Chicago Press, 1923).

4. H. W. Zorbaugh, *The Gold Coast and the Slum* (Chicago: University of Chicago Press, 1929).

5. R. S. Cavan, *Suicide* (Chicago: University of Chicago Press, 1928).

6. Louis Wirth, *The Ghetto* (Chicago: University of Chicago Press, 1928).

7. C. R. Shaw *et al., Delinquency Areas* (Chicago: University of Chicago Press, 1929).

8. Everett Stonequist, *The Marginal Man* (New York: Charles Scribner's Sons, 1937).

9. E. Franklin Frazier, *The Negro Family in Chicago* (Chicago: University of Chicago Press, 1932).

10. C. R. Shaw and H. D. McKay, *Report on the Causes of Crime,* National Commission on Law Observance and Enforcement (Washington, D.C.: U.S. Government Printing Office, 1931).

FAMILY DISORGANIZATION

W. I. Thomas and Florian Znaniecki

The rules for defining situations in traditional society require people to focus on what is best for the group, or the "we" attitude, as Thomas and Znaniecki call it. Immigration exposes people, especially children, to a new set of rules for defining situations in more modern society. Here, people are expected to focus more on what is best for them personally, or what Thomas and Znaniecki call the "I" attitude. The conflict of these two attitudes results in competing definitions and rules. And once groups are able to distinguish between the "I" and the "we" attitude, the ability of either set of rules to influence conduct is weakened immeasurably. This is the essence of family disorganization as Thomas and Znaniecki see it.

From W. I. Thomas and Florian Znaniecki, *The Polish Peasant in Europe and America* (2 vols.), New York Dover Publications, 1927, pp. 1167–1170.

We can now draw certain general conclusions from our data which we shall hypothetically propose as sociological laws, to be verified by the observation of other societies.

1. The real cause of all phenomena of family disorganization is to be sought in the influence of certain new values—new for the subject—such as: new sources of hedonistic satisfaction, new vanity values, new (individualistic) types of economic organization, new forms of sexual appeal. This influence presupposes, of course, not only a contact between the individual and the outside world but also the existence in the individual's personality of certain attitudes which make him respond to these new values—hedonistic aspirations, desire for social recognition, desire for economic security and advance, sexual instinct. The specific phenomenon of family disorganization consists in a definite modification of those preexisting attitudes under the influence of the new values, resulting in the appearance of new, more or less different attitudes. The nature of this modification can be generally characterized in such a way that, while the attitudes which existed under the family system were essentially "we"-attitudes (the individual did not dissociate his hedonistic tendencies, his desires for recognition or economic security, his sexual needs from the tendencies and aspirations of his family group), the new attitudes, produced by the new values acting upon those old attitudes, are essentially "I"-attitudes—the individual's wishes are separated in his consciousness from those of other members of his family. Such an evolution implies that the new values with which the individual gets in touch are individualistic in their meaning, appeal to the individual, not to the group as a whole; and this is precisely the character of most modern hedonistic, sexual, economic, vanity values. Disorganization of the family as primary group is thus an unavoidable consequence of modern civilization.

2. The appearance of the new individualistic attitudes may be counteracted, like every effect of a given cause, by the effects of other causes; the result is a combination of effects which takes the form of a suppression of the new attitude; the latter is not allowed to remain in full consciousness or to manifest itself in action, but is pushed back into the subconscious. Causes that counteract individualization within the family are chiefly influences of the primary community of which the family is a part. If social opinion favors family solidarity and reacts against any individualistic tendencies, and if the individual keeps in touch with the community, his desire for recognition compels him to accept the standards of the group and to look upon his individualistic tendencies as wrong. But if the community has lost its coherence, if the individual is isolated from it, or if his touch with the outside world makes him more or less independent of the opinion of his immediate milieu, there are no social checks important enough to counterbalance disorganization.

3. The *manifestations* of family disorganization in individual behavior are the effects of the subject's attitudes and of the social conditions; these social conditions must be taken, of course, with the meaning which they have for the acting individual himself, not for the outside observer. If the individual finds no obstacles in his family to his new individualistic tendencies, he will express the latter in a normal way; disorganization will consist merely in a loss of family interests, in a

social, not anti-social action. If there are obstacles, but disorganization of the primary-group attitudes has gone far enough in the individual to make him feel independent of his family and community, the effect will probably be a break of relations through isolation or emigration. If, however, the individual meets strong opposition and is not sufficiently free from the traditional system to ignore it, hostility and anti-social behavior are bound to follow. In the measure that the struggle progresses, the new attitude of revolt becomes a center around which the entire personality of the individual becomes reorganized, and this includes those of his traditional values which are not dropped, but reinterpreted to fit the new tendency and to give a certain measure of justification to his behavior. In the relatively rare cases where both the new attitude is very strong and the obstacles from the old system are powerfully resented and seem insuperable because the individual is still too much dependent on this system to find some new way out of the situation, the struggle leads to an internal conflict which may find its solution in an attempt to remove the persons by whom the old system is represented in this situation rather than in a complete rejection of the system itself.

4. It is evidently impossible to revive the original family psychology after it has been disintegrated, for the individual who has learned consciously to distinguish and to oppose to one another his own wishes and those of other members of his family group and to consider these wishes as merely personal cannot unlearn it and return to the primary "we"-attitudes. Reorganization of the family is then possible, but on an entirely new basis—that of a moral, reflective coordination and harmonization of individual attitudes for the pursuit of common purposes.

THE DECLINE OF A BLACK COMMUNITY
Elijah Anderson

What are the social conditions under which a community begins to lose control over its members? Anderson suggests two: (1) out-movement of leaders and (2) decreasing social contact with the few role models remaining. Before changes in civil rights, Northton's leaders, both middle class and upper class, maintained frequent contact with all segments of Northton's population. As leaders and keepers of a tradition, they espoused an ethic of hard work and were powerful agents of social control. After civil rights victories opened opportunities for them in the white world, both their numbers in the community and their contacts with it dropped markedly. Absence of leaders who espoused both work norms and their enforcement in everyday life led to the breakdown of primary group controls on

From Elijah Anderson, *Streetwise*, Chapter 2: "The Northton Community," pp. 56–76. Copyright © 1990 by University of Chicago Press. Reprinted by permission of the author and publisher.

conduct. In due course, what followed were increases in some of the typical indices of social disorganization: delinquency, drug use, teenage pregnancy, and perhaps most striking of all, black-on-black crime.

Northton was first settled before the turn of the century by well-to-do industrialists and working-class Irish and Germans, who wanted to be close to their workplaces. Because of the important social and territorial link between the traditional ethnic neighborhood and the factory, residents took a proprietary interest in both living and working spaces, often physically defending them against outsiders. Protecting such territorial interests gave rise to intense feelings of group solidarity that were readily expressed as racial prejudice, particularly toward invading black migrants from the South.

The first blacks began arriving around World War I, when workers were needed for the railroad and the small factories of the area. But the most impressive migration occurred during World War II, when great numbers left the South in search of social and economic opportunities in northern cities. Because of a labor shortage and ongoing strikes by white unions that excluded black members, the companies were able to use blacks as strikebreakers.

These developments enabled blacks to penetrate the industrial workplaces. To be close to their jobs, they looked to nearby white working-class neighborhoods and settled in areas that began as enclaves but soon turned into ghettos. Racial conflict ensued, resulting in the gradual but steady flight of the whites. The ghettos spread until blacks succeeded whites in virtually all areas of Northton, not only in homes, but also in the schools, churches, and small businesses. For instance, throughout the Village and Northton, formerly white churches began ministering to black congregations as the growing black community was able to support these institutions. Over the years of neighborhood change, many middle-class blacks have moved out but remain connected to their old churches, commuting back for Sunday services, sometimes from many miles away.

Black social life in the Northton of the 1940s and 1950s appears to have been highly cohesive compared with the present situation. Some of the changes may be viewed as indirect consequences of the civil rights movement, the urban riots of the 1960s, and various government remedies for racial exclusion, including the civil rights legislation of the 1960s and 1970s. Fair housing, affirmative action, and various "set asides" for blacks and other minorities have made a tremendous difference in the lives of great numbers of black Americans. These programs have affected Northton, but mainly by expanding opportunities for housing and status for a minority of residents who were poised to take advantage of such "openings" in the wider society's occupational and class structure. Some of them have in fact risen socially and economically, approaching upper-middle-class status.

But as members of this group move socially and economically, they also tend to move geographically, becoming more distant from the ghetto and leaving it without the leadership from which it has traditionally benefited. If those who are better off do remain in Northton, they tend to become socially disengaged, thinking their efforts as instructive agents of social control are futile and may in fact bring them trouble. Consistent with this, current high rates of teenage pregnancy, rampant drug use, a lack of motivation to work in certain jobs when they are available, a desire by some to "get over" on fellow residents, and a prevalence of black-on-black crime may reflect the increasing absence of the black middle class as a stabilizing social force within such ghetto communities.

At the same time, opportunities for poorer blacks to participate in the regular economy are limited, as evidenced by recurrent high levels of black unemployment and underemployment. With severely limited education and skills, numerous Northton blacks are caught in an employment bind. Low-skill Eastern City manufacturing jobs have declined, and jobs in the emerging service economy that are available to young blacks are low paying or far from the inner city, constraining many to a life of poverty.

To many young inner-city blacks the underground economy of drugs and vice appears attractive (see Anderson 1980). This economy pervades Northton, in many instances augmenting or replacing the regular one. As it expands, it undermines the interpersonal trust and moral cohesion that once prevailed. Young men without legitimate job opportunities become especially vulnerable. And law-abiding people who remain in or near the neighborhood, particularly the elderly, fear crime and personal injury. An atmosphere of distrust, alienation, and crime pervades the community, segmenting its residents. These changes, indirectly effected by wider social and economic forces, alter the social organization of Northton (see Wilson 1980, 1985, 1987).

CHANGES IN THE BLACK COMMUNITY

In the past, blacks of various social classes lived side by side in segregated Northton, a "Negro" section of the city. They shared racially separate neighborhood institutions, including churches, schools, barber shops, and even liquor stores and taverns (see Drake and Cayton 1962; Lewis 1955; Clark 1965). For instance, on a visit to a local barbershop, it would not have been unusual to see a black doctor, dressed in coat and tie, follow a black factory worker, still in his overalls, into the chair. Living close together, the children of working-class blacks attended school with the children of black lawyers, doctors, and small businessmen; the black churches often worked to help such disparate individuals coalesce into a single congregation.

Successful people in Northton carried local reputations as big shots and were treated as pillars of the community. Their behavior, mannerisms, and habits were studied, discussed, and imitated; young people paid especially close attention. For instance, people knew all about Dr. Davis: where he lived, what car he drove, how he walked; they knew the same things about the lawyer, Mr. Willis. They knew Mr. and Mrs. Jones, the proprietors of the corner grocery store, who "raised" so many children of the community; highly respected, they served as stand-ins when parents were not around, chastising and disciplining those who needed it, and Mrs. J was an usher at church. Residents also knew Reverend James, a moral force and human institution of the community; he was always ready with a word of advice to those who sought it—and often to those who didn't. He could be counted on to help people, particularly young men in trouble with the law. Until recently, these leaders had to live in areas like Northton because of widespread residential segregation, but they served the black community well as visible, concrete symbols of success and moral value, living examples of the fruits of hard work, perseverance, decency, and propriety. Because of their presence and the honor accorded them, there was more cohesion among individuals and the various classes of the black community than is generally seen today. They were effective, meaningful role models, lending the community a certain moral integrity.

But it was not solely black professionals and small businessmen who led the community. There were also construction workers, factory workers, and others who had "slaves"—jobs that required hard physical labor. Some men would hold two jobs or have a "hustle" on the side, in the form of odd jobs or handyman work, in order to get ahead. Not only did such men set an example for others, who at times would compete with them, they actively encouraged the young to follow their lead. Imbued with a strong commitment to the work ethic, they generally viewed working hard for a living as a positive value. Their wives often worked as domestics, hairdressers, nurse's aides, or storekeepers, setting an important example for young women. In those days people generally regarded having children out of wedlock as serious deviance. To be single and pregnant was generally frowned upon and considered a sign of being "messed up." Moreover, being "on welfare" was a stigma in many circles.

Because of recent openings in the opportunity structure of the wider society, as well as a widespread belief that the local community has changed for the worse, Northton has experienced an outflow of middle- and upper-income people such as Dr. Davis and Mr. Willis, as well as some church leaders. Many have died, and others have moved away; their children have been educated and have joined the professional class of blacks away from their original community. With legally enforced "fair housing," for the first time blacks are theoretically able to move into any housing they can afford. In this social climate, even some of the construction and factory workers have moved to "better" neighborhoods, though some still meet strong resistance in entrenched white areas of the city. Many of their children, too, are becoming better educated and hoping to join the middle and professional classes.

When students used to leave segregated communities like Northton for college, they would often go to institutions such as Howard, Spelman, Fisk, Wilberforce, Central State, Southern University, or Virginia Union, the traditionally black colleges and universities. After graduation many returned to the black community, perhaps to work as schoolteachers, social workers, dentists, doctors, or undertakers. They did this not so much because they preferred to as because of widespread discrimination and the fact that social rewards and economic opportunities for educated blacks were in the black community.

But today, when many black students are educated in major, formerly all-white universities and colleges, they tend not to return to urban black communities like Northton. In pursuit of bright futures in big corporations, law firms, and universities, these young educated blacks gravitate to suburbia or to trendy areas of the city. As they move into leadership positions in the wider society, they leave the poorer, uneducated blacks without tangible role models or instructive agents of social control. As it was described by a black minister who is a part-time taxi driver:

> The [black] community needs these people. I know, they've worked hard for what they got. [Black] people don't resent them for it. They worked for what they got, and they're still working to keep it. They're well qualified for their jobs. But people, black children, need them. They need to be around them. How many of these kids have met a Mayor Johnson, you know? They see him, you know, just sometimes. How many of these kids get close to a black businessman? Or a black lawyer, or somebody? None. They need these people right around them who will guide them and show them how to take hold of life. To teach them how to behave themselves and to teach them that they care. That's the big thing, too. People don't care. See, time was when the big people had distinguishing features about them, and they made you feel like "here's someone who is a leader of the community" and "I want to be like him" or "I want to be like her."

To be sure, newly mobile members of the black middle class may have close kin in Northton. In a unique manner, they serve as culture brokers, linking the new black middle class with the ghetto and, more generally, the black community with the wider society. Occasionally there are family reunions that may include relatives from diverse backgrounds, ranging from members of the lower class to successful medical doctors and business executives. Such reunions may be related to trouble of some sort, such as sickness or death in the family or legal difficulties. During such occasions, when old ties are renewed, those in need may make outright requests for financial help, and the successful members of the family may feel some obligation to render at least token assistance. But repeated requests can discourage intimacy between well-off and poorer relatives, or at least strain the relationship. The successful members of these families may also feel a duty to serve as role models for younger sisters, brothers, cousins, and other kin. It is at this family level that the new black middle class may have an effective social connection with the Northton ghetto.

But in general the newly educated groups appear increasingly distant and formal in their relations with ghetto residents. Involved in careers ranging from doctor to investment banker to lawyer, this new middle class appears much less a merchant and service class, financially dependent upon the black community, than the middle class traditionally has been (see Frazier 1957; Landry 1987). Members do not aspire to own a restaurant, tavern, or barbershop, and they seldom operate the local grocery, clothing, and furniture stores. In Eastern City other ethnic groups, including Jews and Koreans, tend to dominate in these commercial areas of Northton.

On the streets of Northton, race-conscious blacks at times complain bitterly about the recent incursion of Asians and wonder aloud "who helped them out." Some fail to distinguish among the Asian groups, assuming they are all "boat people who just got here." A common view is that the federal government has made loans readily available to Asians, helping them to establish businesses in Northton. Yet Jews, who have long run similar businesses there, provoke little hostility; the community is used to Jewish merchants. The hostile reception the Asians get has to do with the way residents perceive them as a new competitive group bent on taking opportunities from blacks and establishing itself within

Northton. But generally the working class does not have the capital or the inclination to take over local businesses, and the upwardly mobile blacks have their sights set on careers far beyond Northton. The following narrative by the middle-aged proprietor of a barbershop in Northton illustrates these points:

> Yeah, look like the black man always gets the raw deal. Now the Vietnamese are coming in. Course, I can't tell 'em from the Koreans, ha-ha. One time I called a Korean lady a Vietnamese to her face, and she like to had a fit. She said, "No! No! I'm Korean." I guess it's kinda like the blacks and the Puerto Ricans. The blacks don't want to be mixed up with the Puerto Ricans. But the Koreans are moving in strong. They taking over businesses left and right, and they move the blacks out and bring in they own people. Now take what happened up on the corner. That big cleaners was just taken over by a Korean. It had been owned by a Jew . . . Well, the Jew first offered it to a black man who had been working there for many years. He knew the business well, too. He could run it himself, knew how to mix all the chemicals himself. Well, he was gonna get it, but his family got together and discouraged him, told him it was too much responsibility, and he listened to them. Well, then the Koreans came along, and the Jew sold it to them. The Koreans invited this black man over to their home and treated him real nice and everything. And he then continued to work for them and taught them everything he knew. Showed them how to mix the chemicals, how to do everything. Then after they learned it from him and had the business moving along, the black fella found his paycheck short a hundred dollars. He say, "There's some mistake here." And they say, "No, there ain't no mistake. That's all you worth, now." Boy, was he ever mad. It took him a while to get straight over that. He started drinking a lot. Man, he was mad. He wanted to do something [violence] to them, but I talked to him. I told him how he had his whole life in front of him, that he should just try to forget it. It took him a long time, but he finally settled down. Then he went on and got himself another job, and tried to forget about it, but I know he never will forget that.

But it must be pointed out that not all black residents feel hostility to the Asian newcomers. Some working people admire them, comparing their apparent successes with the financial "failings" of local blacks. As one sixty-seven-year-old, now retired, formerly "hardworking" (twenty-eight years as a welder) black man said:

> See, I have no objection to them people. They hardworking people. See, the blacks have that same opportunity. See, look here. See this man's car. [He walks me over to the recently broken-into car of one of his friends.] See here, this is all they wanta do. See here. See this man's car. They went in there, right where my car parked at right now [he points across the street to his car]. They went there night before last and ripped that man's radio out of his car. Now, you would never hear tell of a Vietnamese [tendency is not to distinguish among Asians] doin' that. What they make, they make their money honestly. Now you see how they ripped that man's car up. See, today, everybody is prejudiced against everybody. But see, I don't have no objection to them people. If they hardworking people, come over here and build a foundation for themselves, God bless them. Understand what I'm saying? These niggers have the same opportunity, but that's all they wanta do. Ripped the man's radio out, and he caught him doing it! He run him down and tried to catch him, and he outrun his shoes. The man come back and throwed his shoes in the trash. See, that's all they wanta do. About an hour later, he caught him with the radio. But I noticed these people have come over here, and stores have been empty for twenty years and they get together, and two or three months later, they got that whole place stocked off. Colored folks got the same opportunity to do

that, if they want to. The don't wanta do that, though. Onliest thing they wanta do is sell crack, stand on the corner, sell ten bags.

On "the avenue," the central business street of Northton, Asian shops proliferate, filling a void left by the Jewish merchants who owned family businesses in Northton for many years; they are now prepared to move on, but generally they seem to prefer to sell their businesses rather than pass them on to family members. The Asians run family businesses as well, but with a somewhat different twist. They seemed somewhat crude at first, but they are now catching on to the art of doing business in Northton. In any number of instances a Korean, for example, would buy out the owner of a particular store and set up for business with all his family, relatives, or friends in his employ. The common picture, then, in grocery, clothing, fish, produce, or hoagie shops, was of two teams of different ethnicities: the proprietor and his staff were conspicuously Asian, and the customers were exclusively black. Initially these changes caused some black people to grumble and threaten to boycott the stores. No effective boycott ever materialized, but certain militant and race-conscious blacks expressed resentment toward the storeowners, at times physically harassing them. To deal with this, Korean businessmen began to hire more blacks. Now the common picture of the Asian-owned establishment is of a number of trusted blacks performing certain functions, from armed guard to grillman at the hoagie shops, being supervised by an Asian, usually male, who invariably stands at the cash register and takes the money:

> At one of the primary intersections of Northton there sits a large old brick structure with a newly remodeled facade and eating area that serves hoagies and other fast foods as well as providing check cashing and other financial services. Until two years ago, it was simply one more crumbling and unused building. Today it is a true market center, drawing customers in search of both legal and illegal items from many parts of Northton and even from the Village.
>
> Out in front is a newsstand run by an elderly black man "who's been here for twenty years and knows the community like the back of his hand." Black people pass by freely or stop to chat with the news vendor or other friends. It is the site of much camaraderie and heavy foot and vehicle traffic. A large bright yellow sign proclaiming Hoagies invites the hungry to step inside, where there is almost always a line of black people standing at the long counter, waiting to be served cheese steaks, hoagies, fried chicken, french fries, and various sandwiches.
>
> Off to the left is a Plexiglas booth with the sign Check Cashing above it. A stern, no-nonsense black woman cashes checks, sells lottery tickets, and transacts business for Western Union. The place is packed with middle-aged black men, young men, little girls and boys, and young women with babies in their arms. After getting their food, they go over to the booths along the back wall or out on the street. In the booths may sit one or two intoxicated men.
>
> Behind the counter taking orders are Sammy, Joe, R. D., and two other black men. "Hey, baby, what can I do for you," is the usual question from Sammy. Someone opens the front door and hollers in, "What's up, Joe?" Everyone turns toward the door. The person is acknowledged, "Yo, baby, see you tonight!" The workers are clearly from the neighborhood. Sammy resumes his work, in view of the black clientele. Sitting at the cash register at the end of the counter is a small Korean man, busily taking money.

A black minister who was unfamiliar with the changed community had the following reaction:

Yeah, I visited a variety store, you know, where they sell all this junk and sandals and stuff. Well, I bought comb and umbrella and hair products. I bought me a pair of sandals, for a dollar, from China, you know. Ha-ha. I bought a little scarf for a dollar, you know. Nothing over two dollars—hats, umbrellas, and they had a kinda built-up counter with a glass booth. And there stood two Asians back there taking the money. Then they had two black male employees waiting on folks and watching them. Like one Asian kinda floated back and forth. And the brother [black man] would say, "Now what's the price on this?" And he would answer, "Chie chei dit che che," you know, so and so. But they were very much in charge, using blacks ironically as fronts. It was so shocking, because I had never seen this in the area before, you know, close up.

Members of the emerging black middle class, people who might have the business and organizational skills, and also the financial resources, for small business enterprise, tend to be uninterested in such pursuits in Northton. Such people find their futures in the private and public professional sectors of the wider society. The new middle class tends to gravitate to residential areas of second and third settlement, as did the upwardly mobile Irish, Italians, and Jews who preceded them (see Wirth 1928; Shaw and McKay 1942). Ostensibly they are motivated by concern about crime, drugs, poor public schools, run-down and crowded housing, and social status. They are attracted by the prospect of good schools, "crime-free" suburban neighborhoods, good real estate investments, and the status requirements of their professional and corporate careers. A few find their way into the Village, but for many there may be a deep emotional desire to get as far as possible from poorer blacks. The black middle classes increasingly send their children to private schools. Although their black peers sometimes chide them about remembering where they came from, they generally offer no apologies for leaving the ghetto, believing it is their right to enjoy success.

Advanced education and connections with professional and corporate America thus contribute to gradual social, economic, and perhaps political estrangement between the black middle and upper classes and the poor urban black communities. As these processes mature, the socially mobile group is likely to be slowly transformed from separate individuals ambivalent about their connection with places like Northton into a class increasingly concerned with itself.

The prospect is for the lower-income residents of Northton to become increasingly isolated, sharing neighborhood institutions with the financially desperate and the criminal element. Great numbers of Northton residents appear mired in poverty and second-class citizenship reminiscent of the castelike system of racial exclusion described by Drake and Cayton (1962), Myrdal et al. (1944), and Clark (1965) more than a generation ago. In this situation crime, drugs, and general antisocial behavior serve as social forces that underscore status lines drawn within the community. With the massive introduction of drugs and the correspondingly high incidence of black-on-black crime, fear and distrust abound, particularly toward young males. It is this feature of the present situation that has such fateful implications for the way the community is related to its erstwhile leadership class. Many of the better-off people simply want to get as far away as they can. And what they do not achieve by moving physically, they work to accomplish socially: they distance themselves from others who do not meet their standards of behavior. Yet through such conduct they in fact contribute, however unintentionally, to the construction of a local underclass.

THE UNDERCLASS

This underclass of Northton is made up of people who have failed to keep up with their brethren, both in employment and in sociability. Essentially they can be seen as victims of the economic and social system. They make up the unemployed, the underskilled, and the poorly educated, even though some hold high-school diplomas. Many are intelligent, but they are demoralized by racism and the wall of social resistance facing them. In this context they lose perspective and lack an outlook and sensibility that would allow them to negotiate the wider system of employment and society in general.

Emerging from the ghetto's crippling educational experience, often lacking even rudimentary skills but scorning subsistence jobs, they also tend to be discriminated against by prospective employers, who find it difficult to trust them. In part this is because of their inability or unwillingness to follow basic rules of middle-class propriety with respect to dress and comportment, but it is also because of their skin color and what this has come to symbolize.

Though one may argue that the institutions of both the wider society and the local community have failed members of the black underclass, local working-class and middle-class residents often hold the people themselves to blame. Such a stance allows those who are better-off to maintain faith in the wider institutions, particularly the work ethic, thus helping to legitimate their own position in the local system of stratification. Hence, by many employed and law-abiding blacks who live in the inner city, members of the underclass are viewed, and treated, as convenient objects of scorn, fear, and embarrassment.

In this way the underclass serves as an important social yardstick that allows working-class blacks to compare themselves favorably with others they judge to be worse off, a social category stigmatized within the community. Included in this category are the local residents who threaten the financially more successful blacks who remain in Northton and thus incur their wrath or condescension.

To the stable working class remaining in Northton, those fitting the stereotype of the underclass symbolize "how low a black person can fall from decency." On the streets, the members of this class are viewed as "trouble" and are avoided, but residents often have difficulty accomplishing this, for the conditions and cultural manifestations of poverty and blight are all around. For example:

> Walking the streets of Northton at midday on a Saturday in April, one gets a striking impression of the neighborhood. Back streets are lined with small three-story, crumbling brick houses. The old buildings have not been well maintained, and cracks often line the bricks to the foundations. Signs of past fires are everywhere. The third floor of a building is windowless, and another nearby has its windows covered with galvanized iron. Another building looks on the verge of toppling over, as it seems to totter in the wind. Now and again an intact structure shows definite signs of life, for people come and go and children play nearby. At one house white-painted automobile tires are used as planters for geraniums, and a bright green-and-red awning shades the front porch, where ancient but recently

used metal porch furniture sits undisturbed. On other occasions I have noticed residents sitting out on the stoops or porches, watching the traffic pass. They generally watch carefully over the street, at times attempting to quash bad conduct before it goes too far.

Most automobiles are at least ten years old, but now and again late-model cars turn up, including BMWs and Mercedes and Lincoln Town Cars driven, though rarely, by boys of nineteen and twenty. The young men drive with their stereos booming, and the windshields vibrate to the beat. They nod in time to the music, as though they were in another world.

On the sidewalk little girls run, laugh, and jump rope. Little boys play cops and robbers or basketball; some ride makeshift scooters. In this block the streets are alive with noise and life, with familiar eyes noticing everything.

A middle-aged man dressed in blue jeans, a jacket, and a baseball cap, his hands dug into his pockets, makes his way with a demonstrative style and walk. Two women follow, undisturbed, unafraid; they moved with aplomb, for they know the neighborhood and it knows them; they know where they're going, and everyone else knows it too.

Down an alley, teenage "young boys," eight or ten of them, are shooting dice, gambling in broad daylight. An expensive portable radio sits nearby, blaring a "rap" song; a couple of the boys nod with the beat, which sounds almost military. They are dressed in bright-colored athletic suits of green or red or gold, their bodies accentuated by the white stripes down the arms and legs. Some wear baseball caps, and others proudly "go bareheaded," sporting waves or close-cropped hair with two or three lines shaved into it. It is the latest style in "cuts." A few of the boys wear gold chains and rings, testifying to their worth and lending a measure of self-esteem. The group is abuzz with talk back and forth, getting the dice game right and awaiting the next throw.

All eyes are on the dice. Some of the boys work at local businesses, including the recently opened Korean-owned hoagie shop up on the avenue. Another works at McDonald's. But some of these boys are known drug dealers and can make, some say, hundreds of dollars in a single day.

This element of the local community is often perceived as having a "street" orientation, generally known—and feared—as "slick" and dangerous, with few moral compunctions against engaging in "wrongdoing" and "mistreating" others. In the minds of the law-abiding, decent residents these young men have a claim to "hipness," and they are believed to sell drugs and commit most of the local street crime to support their habits. Those who are trying hard to achieve a more conventional life readily lump such people with the pimps, hustlers, prostitutes, destitute single mothers, and anonymous street corner men. The easy stereotype is that they "think nothing of making two or three babies with no way to care for them. They don't want to work, and have no get up about themselves." People who develop this street orientation are thought to begin their careers in early childhood, and if they are not controlled and "trained," the parents and families are believed to run a good chance of losing them to "the streets."

In Northton, the homeless and others who are very poor are seen to be "out there." They live on the streets or in abandoned houses and automobiles and from time to time may be seen rummaging through refuse, thus fueling the community's negative conception of them. But they usually draw little sympathy from the stable working class. Ghetto residents themselves seldom use the term "underclass" when referring to the poor and others who have trouble surviving by conventional means. The category referred to by that term is in effect socially constructed through public observations of relatively better-off residents concerned with their own status and identity. The local underclass is a highly stigmatized group, and residents refer to them by terms of derision, working socially to distinguish such people from themselves. Common terms are "lowlife," "street niggers," "tacks," "zombies," or "pipers."

OF "OLD HEADS" AND YOUNG BOYS

The relationship between "old heads" and young boys represents an important institution of the traditional black community. It has always been a central aspect of the social organization of Northton, assisting the transition of young men from boyhood to manhood, from idle youth to stable employment and participation in the regular manufacturing economy. The old head's acknowledged role was to teach, support, encourage, and in effect socialize young men to meet their responsibilities with regard to the work ethic, family life, the law, and decency. But as meaningful employment has become increasingly scarce, drugs more accessible, and crime a way of life for many young black men, this institution has undergone stress and significant change.

An old head was a man of stable means who was strongly committed to family life, to church, and, most important, to passing on his philosophy, developed through his own rewarding experience with work, to young boys he found worthy. He personified the work ethic and equated it with value and high standards of morality; in his eyes a workingman was a good, decent individual.

The old head/young boy relationship was essentially one of mentor and protégé. The old head might be only two years older than the young boy or as much as thirty or forty years older; the boy was usually at least ten. The young boy readily deferred to the old head's chronological age and worldly experience. The nature of the relationship was that of junior/senior, based on the junior's confidence in the senior's ability to impart useful wisdom and practical advice for getting on in the world and living well.

The old head was a kind of guidance counselor and moral cheerleader who preached anticrime and antitrouble messages to his charges. Encouraging boys to work and make something of themselves, he would try to set a good example by living, as best he could, a stable, decent, worry-free life. His constant refrain was "Get yourself a trade, son," or "Do something with your life," or "Make something out of yourself." Displaying initiative, diligence, and pride, as a prime role model of the community, he lived "to have something," usually something material, though an intact nuclear family counted for much in the picture he painted. On the corners and in the alleys of Northton, he would point to others as examples of how hard work and decency could pay off. He might advise young boys to "pattern yourself after him." In these conversations and lectures, he would express great pride in his own outstanding work record, punctuality, good credit rating, and anything else reflecting his commitment to honesty, independence, hard work, and family values.

The old head could be a minister, a deacon in the church, a local policeman, a favorite teacher, an athletic coach, or a street corner man. He could be the uncle or even the father of a member of the local group of young boys. Very often the old head acted as surrogate father for those he considered in need of such attention. A youth in trouble would sometimes discuss his problem with an old head before going to his own father, if he had one, and the old head would be ready with a helping hand, sometimes a loan for a worthy purpose. The following interview with a twenty-nine-year-old Northton man gives a glimpse of the relationship between an old head and a young boy:

> Yeah, I got three of my boys in the service right now, and another is on the way. Just the other day, a young boy come up to me in the neighborhood and say he need twenty-five dollars to get some underwear and toiletries so he can get ready to leave for the army. We talked for a while, and then I reached into my pocket and came up with two tens and a five and handed it to him. He said "Thanks." And I said, "I'm gettin' ready to go downtown; you want to come along? We can pick up that stuff you need." He said, "OK." We got the trolley and went on downtown. We got his stuff and come on back home. I was glad I could do that for him, help him out. Now he gone to the army. He's one of my young boys. I been knowin' him since he was very young, and now he's nineteen. I don't worry 'bout my money. He'll pay me. I don't worry 'bout it.

Through this kind of extension of himself, the old head gained moral affirmation that would be his reward, an important if subtle incentive for helping other young boys.

It may be that such rewards are related to what Drake and Cayton (1962) called the "race man." In the days of the traditional segregated black community, the race man was one who felt an intense responsibility to "the race," to the point of viewing most events, especially public ones involving white society, as having definite implications for the well-being of blacks. To such men it was important to present their race in a positive light, particularly to whites. The traditional old head in the present-day black community embodies a significant amount of the race-man ideology. His attempt to help young boys is also a way to help the black community. It demonstrates to whites that black people are decent, law-abiding, and respectable.

In the old days young boys would gather around an old head on a street corner or after Sunday school to listen to his witty conversation and moral tales on hard work and decency. They truly felt they were learning something worthwhile from someone they could look up to and respect. One of the primary messages of the old head was about good manners and the value of hard work: how to dress for a job interview and deal with a prospective employer, how to work, and how to keep the job. Through stories, jokes, and conversation, the old head would convey his conception of the "tricks of the trade."

On occasion he might be seen walking through the streets with one or two of his boys, showing them how to "hustle"—to make money by doing legal odd jobs. An old head might bring some of his boys over to the Village to help him with yard work, snow shoveling, or general household chores for white residents. The boys then might attempt such jobs on their own, meeting strangers at the supermarket door and offering to carry groceries to the car for money, or standing around the self-service gas station and offering to pump gasoline for a small fee. There was often an old head in the background, encouraging the boys to earn spending money through honest work. If the old head owned his own business, in auto repair, general hauling, cleaning services, or yard work, the boys might serve as his apprentices.

The old head sometimes affectionately referred to his recruits as "my boys." Some would become runners, taking the lead in being publicly responsible for the neighborhood, but under the control or direction of an old head. Whenever the old head needed a favor done or an errand run, one of his protégés would be eager to carry out his wishes. And he would keep an informal record of how well they had learned their lessons—which ones had gone on to college, to successful employment, to the military, or to jail.

Within the traditional black community, the old head served as an important link to the more privileged classes. Often he could be seen pointing out the big shots and speaking about them in glowing terms. Through his example, he offered support to both the local and the wider systems of social stratification and inspired his boys to negotiate them through legitimate means.

Today, as the economic and social circumstances of the urban ghetto have changed, the traditional old head has been losing prestige and credibility as a role model. One of the most important factors in this loss is the glaring lack of access to meaningful employment in the regular economy, resulting in more and more unemployed and demoralized black young people. When gainful employment and its rewards are not forthcoming, boys easily conclude that the moral lessons of the old head concerning the work ethic, punctuality, and honesty do not fit their own circumstances. (For the provocative "social capital" position, which may be applicable to the situation here, see Coleman 1988; Bourdieu 1986; and Wacquant and Wilson 1989.)

In turn, the old heads' attitudes toward young people have been modified to reflect current employment realities, particularly the youths' adaptation to them. For instance, Harry Hamilton, a seventy-year-old wallpaper hanger who has taken on young black men as apprentices over the years, laments the way things have changed with the young boy/old head relationship and says that he cannot find honest, hardworking young men the way he used to. He begins his day at about 6:30 in the morning, arriving at his job promptly at 7:30. He wears a brown work uniform spotted with paint and stains and a beat-up white hat, and he carries his lunch pail. He works steadily until lunchtime, rests for about thirty minutes, then goes right back to work. Some nights it is 6:30 before he has cleaned up and is ready to go home, and he follows this schedule every day, regardless of the weather. At times he makes as much as $100 a room, and he has more than enough work. He fails to understand why there is a youth employment problem, saying simply:

> These young boys today just don't want to work. They could work if they wanted to. There's plenty of work to do. Today they just want somethin' give to them, wanta get on welfare, I think. I did it [made a living], and they can too.

The following interview with a forty-year-old black man who works two jobs to make ends meet follows the same lines:

> This used to be a heavily industrialized nation, but now all that's done changed. Now it's technology. There's a lot of unemployment, but the statistics just give one picture. I think that's overblown, 'cause there are a lot o' guys out here who just

don't wanta work. There are cats who can barely read and write, and they wanta come in and take over. There's a lot o' young men doing the dope thing. They sell it, get high on it. But I'd rather work hard on a grind; the money's better. That dope money is fast, quick money. And you know, easy come, easy go. Can't depend on it. When they doing good, they doing real good, but when they doing bad, they doing real bad. I still try to talk to the youngsters that I run into, but it's hard to talk to these young boys. I tell them to go and try to learn something, but they don't wanta listen. There's a different kind of black man today. And I'll tell you something, as quiet as it's kept [between you and me]. There are some old heads out here selling that dope, and they know better. They sho' know better.

FEMALE OLD HEADS

If old heads were important for boys, they were also important for girls, in similar ways. The female old heads were seen as mature and wise figures in the community, not only by women and girls, but also by many young men. The term "old head" usually refers to males; their female counterparts were and are often called "Mama," "Big Mama," "Moms," "Mis' Lu," or "Mis' Dawson," to show deference and respect.

An important source of social control and organization for the community, such a woman operated through bonds of kinship and friendship. She might have been someone's aunt or grandmother, but if not, she played the grandmother role. Like the male old head, she was someone others could "talk to" or "lean on." But unlike the male, she was and still is capable of meting out advice, discipline, and at times corporal punishment to both boys and girls. With this role as her warrant, she takes such actions and offers guidance without condemnation, all with a sensitive appreciation of the child's situation and needs as she interprets them, filling an important fictive kinship role of extra parent or surrogate mother.

Like the male old head, her role is often played out in public places. Supportive of the family, she serves as a third party to publicly augment the relationship between parent and child. Needing a good deal of wisdom, sensitivity, candor, and trust, she is an important source of instruction and social sanction within the community. To play the old head role effectively, a woman must possess what blacks call "mother wit," an earthy wisdom that is readily apparent through her actions, material possessions, and relationships, all of which make up her public biography.

Though declining in influence and authority, these women still serve the community as beauticians, church ladies, and more recently community organizers. They are usually very popular and well respected, and they know everyone. At the same time, they are viewed as successful in a way that makes others defer to them in their presence and say complimentary things about them when they are not around. They might have a number of other women working with them, and together they make up a core group in the neighborhood.

One of the main credentials for serving effectively as such a role model is having lived a "good life." The visible expression of this is involvement "in church" or with "the Lord." The female old head attends church regularly and displays in her home pictures of Jesus and other symbols attesting to her moral worth. She is generally known as a "good" and decent person.

Although these women tend to be rather proper, they also form a social group that "talks about" others, imposing social sanctions through gossip. Taking the lead in the community, some also act as psychologists and advisers for other women.

In Northton the female old head usually has been quite serious about taking care of young girls, attempting to protect them from abuse at the hands of males, but also trying to help them achieve a better material life. Such is the nature of her traditional role, and to some extent it is a role many continue to play, though, with the proliferation of so many "street kids," less and less effectively.

As is shown in the following interview with an elderly black woman, the primary ingredients of the female old head role are motherly love, concern, and wisdom:

> They call her just a mother, a real mother, not a mother who don't care for children from the bottom. The way I feel about it, the way I tell these children, is "I love all children: If you don't love somebody else children, you really don't love yo' own."
>
> This is when you see any child out there doing wrong, you goes to him and you corrects him, just like he is yo' child. And that's what I do. I don't care what I'm doing, if I see somebody fighting, arguing, or whatever. I have taken care of all the kids in this street going backwards and forwards to school. They come through here, get in a fight, I get out there and stop it.
>
> And if they wanta be strong with me, I get stronger. I let them know that they not gon' outdo me. I tell 'em, "If you want me to take you in the house and give you a good spankin', I will do it."
>
> And they listen. A lot of kids come back and visit me. There was one boy. About twenty years ago. He went up on the fire escape, way up on the third-floor fire escape, and he almost fell. And I told him, I say, "If I catch you again, I'm gon' take you in my house and I'm gon' tear you up good." He said, "Alright, Mis' Porter." He came down. But then another day, he went back up. And I was just lucky enough to catch him. The wind was blowin' so hard. And he got on top of the rail and he sat there, rocked, he almost fell.
>
> And I say, "OK, Eddie, come on, come on." He walked on in the house and sat down. I said, "You know what I promised you for that." I said, "I promised you a whuppin'. Now, I'm gon' whup you." So I said, "Take off the coat." So he took off the coat. And he said, "You gon' tell my mother that you beat me?" I said, "Yes, I am. Soon as she get home, I'm gon' have your mother and father to come up here, and let them know what I done to you, and let them know why." So I whupped him. So, when they came home, I had 'em to come in and sit down and talk with 'em. And they said, "Well, he gets another whuppin'." It was so funny. When I got finished whuppin' him, and he finished crying, and all, he said, "Mis' Porter, now you already whupped me and all, can I have some of them collard greens and cornbread you cookin'?"
>
> I said, "Yeah, you can have some. You can have all you want." I say, "I don't mind doin' or givin' you anything that I have." I say, "But you must not do wrong things to hurt yourself. I say, "When somebody tell you not to go up such steps as those, way up there, and you are only eight years old, you shouldn't go." I say, "You should listen. Yo' mother and father are both gone to work." I say, "I don't know them that well. And it doesn't matter if I don't know them. Long as I save they child. You just get down and remember to do what I tell you to do. And I'll always look out for you."
>
> So one day I went out to the doctor's here. And I guess I hadn't seen him in about twenty years. I was sick. And this tall boy reached and grabbed me round my waist and he hugged me and he hugged me. He say, "Mis' Porter, you can't

forget me." He say, "You don't know who I am, do you?" I said, "Yes I do!" We called him Eddie spaghetti for a funny name. And he say, "Mis' Porter, like you whupped my behind; you made a man out of me! I've been to the army, and everybody in the army knows that you whupped me. I told 'em. Ha-ha." He reached down and he just hugged me. He said, "I will never forget you. You gave me a good start, that I had to listen. And I'm listening right on. And I'll never forget to do that for my kids." And I said, "OK, fine."

To gain greater appreciation of this narrative, I interviewed various residents of the ghetto. Many of those I canvassed said the woman's behavior is not so likely to occur on the streets today. Their responses suggest a breakdown in feelings of community. Residents say people tend to keep more to themselves now, that they no longer involve themselves in their neighbors' lives as they did as recently as ten years ago. As one middle-aged mother pointed out,

> A grown person takes a real risk when she corrects someone else's child. And if she puts her hands on another's child, that's asking for trouble, unless she knows the family real well.

While a spanking might once have been generally approved of, and perhaps welcomed as an affirmation of love and caring, today the issue of child abuse looms, and the authorities might be called. Possible legal action or out-and-out verbal and physical retaliation constrains many from actively playing such old head roles.

But there are other constraining influences as well. The old head often exercises authority in public places. As the community has experienced the coming and going of so many residents, social life has become less stable. But the really important factors complicating public life are drugs, community perceptions of increased crime in the streets, and the virtual abandonment of the neighborhood by the middle class. In a word, the area is experiencing segmentation, and residents feel especially distant and wary around strangers. Public spaces have become increasingly complicated and dangerous, or at least they are perceived that way.

These developments make the roles of male and female old heads, in part because of their public nature, all the more difficult to enact. Declining in influence and authority, the would-be old heads tend to disengage. And the community becomes even more vulnerable to a variety of social ills, from teenage pregnancy to rampant drug use.

References

Anderson, Elijah. 1980. Some observations on black youth employment. In *Youth Employment and public policy*, ed. Bernard E. Anderson and Isabel V. Sawhill, 64–87. Englewood Cliffs, NJ: Prentice-Hall.

Bourdieu, Pierre. 1986. The forms of capital. In *Handbook of theory and research for the sociology of education*, ed. J. G. Richardson. New York: Greenwood Press.

Clark, Kenneth B. 1965. *Dark ghetto*. New York: Harper and Row.

Coleman, James. 1988. Social capital in the creation of human capital. *American Journal of Sociology* 94:S95–S120.

Drake, St. Clair, and Horace Cayton. 1962. *Black metropolis*. New York: Harper and Row.

Frazier, E. Franklin. 1957. *Black bourgeoisie*. New York: Free Press.

Landry, Bart. 1987. *The new black middle class*. Berkeley: University of California Press.

Lewis, Hylan. 1955. *Blackways of Kent*. Chapel Hill: University of North Carolina Press.

Myrdal, Gunner, et al. 1944. *An American dilemma: The Negro problem in America*. New York: Harper and Row.

Shaw, Clifford, and Henry McKay. 1942. *Juvenile delinquency and urban areas*. Chicago: University of Chicago Press.

Wacquant, Loic J. D., and William J. Wilson. 1989. The cost of racial and class exclusion in the inner city. *Annals of the American Academy of Political and Social Science* 501 (January): 8–25.

Wilson, William J. 1980. *The declining significance of race*, 2nd edition. Chicago: University of Chicago Press.

Wilson, William J. 1985. Cycles of deprivation and the underclass debate. *Social Service Review* 59 (December): 541–59.

Wilson, William J. 1987. *The truly disadvantaged*. Chicago: University of Chicago Press.

Wirth, Louis. 1928. *The ghetto*. Chicago: University of Chicago Press.

A DISORGANIZING CONCEPT

Marshall B. Clinard

Social disorganization started out as a sensitizing concept for sociologists, and those of the first generation who used the concept were able to understand a changing society better by means of the notion. The next generation of sociologists, however, often found the idea baseless and confusing. In this excerpt, Clinard summarizes the problems with the concept. Subjectively, writers tended to be unclear, whimsical, or biased when using the idea. Objectively, they tended to confuse change, deviant behavior, subcultures, and human variation with social disorganization.

. . . A state of disorganization is often thought of as one in which there is a "breakdown of social controls over the behavior of the individual" and a decline in the unity of the group because former patterns of behavior and social control no longer are effective.[1] There are a number of objections to this frame of ref-

From Marshall B. Clinard, *Sociology of Deviant Behavior*, third edition, pp. 41–42. Copyright © 1957 by Marshall B. Clinard. Copyright © 1963, 1968 by Holt, Rinehart and Winston, Inc. Reprinted by permission of Holt, Rinehart and Winston, Inc.

erence. (1) Disorganization is too subjective and vague a concept for analyzing a general society. Effective use of the concept, however, may be made in the study of specific groups and institutions. (2) Social disorganization implies the disruption of a previously existing condition of organization, a situation which generally cannot be established. Social change is often confused with social disorganization without indicating why some social changes are disorganizing and others not. (3) Social disorganization is usually thought of as something "bad," and what is bad is often the value judgment of the observer and the members of his social class or other social groups. For example, the practice of gambling, the patronage of taverns, greater freedom in sex relations, and other behavior do not mean that these conditions are naturally "bad" or "disorganized." (4) The existence of forms of deviant behavior does not necessarily constitute a major threat to the central values of a society. The presence of suicide, crime, or alcoholism may not be serious if other values are being achieved. American society, for example, has a high degree of unity and integration despite high rates of deviant behavior if one considers such values as nationalism, a highly developed industrial production, and goals of material comfort. (5) What seems like disorganization actually may often be highly organized systems of competing norms. Many subcultures of deviant behavior, such as delinquent gangs, organized crime, homosexuality, prostitution, and white-collar crime, including political corruption, may be highly organized. The slum sex code may be as highly organized and normative regarding premarital relations in one direction as the middle-class sex code is in the other.[2] The norms and values of the slums are highly organized, as Whyte has shown in his *Street Corner Society*.[3] (6) Finally, as several sociologists have suggested, it is possible that a variety of subcultures may contribute, through their diversity, to the unity or integration of a society rather than weaken it by constituting a situation of social disorganization.[4]

Notes

1. Contemporary use of the concept "social disorganization" comes largely from W. I. Thomas and Florian Znaniecki, *The Polish Peasant in Europe and America* (New York: Alfred A. Knopf, Inc., 1927). For criticisms of this concept see John F. Cuber, Robert A. Harper, and William Kenkel, *Problems of American Society* (New York: Holt, Rinehart and Winston, Inc., 1956), Chap. 22; [Edwin M.] Lemert, *Social Pathology* (New York: McGraw-Hill, 1951), Chap. 1; and [Frank E.] Hartung, "Common and Discrete Values," *Journal of Social Psychology*, 38:3–22 (1953).

2. William F. Whyte, "A Slum Sex Code," *American Journal of Sociology*, 49:24–32 (1943).

3. William F. Whyte, *Street Corner Society* (Chicago: University of Chicago Press, 1943). Also see Marshall B. Clinard, *Slums and Community Development: Experiments in Self-Help* (New York: The Free Press, 1967).

4. See Robin Williams, Jr., "Unity and Diversity in Modern America," *Social Forces*, 36: 1–8 (1957).

Questions for Discussion

1. What does Park see as the basic features of social disorganization?

2. Apply Park's conception of social disorganization (a) to Northton (b) to the inner areas of cities, and (c) to Thomas and Znaniecki's description of family disorganization.

3. How does rapid social change precipitate social disorganization? Discuss the articles in this chapter in this light.

4. Do you agree with Clinard's critique of the social disorganization perspective? Is there any way a social disorganization analysis can avoid Clinard's criticisms? How so or why not?

Selected References

Bursik, Robert J., Jr. "Social Disorganization and Theories of Crime and Delinquency: Problems and Prospects." *Criminology* 26 (November 1988): 519–51.

In this study, Bursik shows how the Shaw-McKay perspective on social disorganization, as derived from Thomas and Znaniecki, can still help to account for reported variations in urban juvenile delinquency rates.

Carey, James T. *Sociology and Public Affairs: The Chicago School.* Beverly Hills, CA: Sage, 1975.

Chapter 4 ("The Social Disorganization Paradigm") tells how Thomas and Znaniecki first developed the social disorganization perspective, how students of theirs and their followers applied it to a variety of studies on social problems, and how the perspective came under critical attack in later years.

Cohen, Albert K. "The Study of Social Disorganization and Deviant Behavior." In *Sociology Today,* ed. Robert K. Merton, Leonard Broom, and Leonard S. Cottrell, Jr. New York: Basic Books, 1959, pp. 474–83.

According to Cohen, in order to understand social disorganization one must first examine the components of social organization. The basic conditions of social organization are the existence of rules to define events and the motivation of people to follow the rules. With regard to the first condition, social disorganization results from no rules, vague rules, or conflicting rules. With regard to the second condition, social disorganization may result from inadequate socialization or a failure in social control.

Coleman, James S. "Community Disorganization and Urban Problems." In *Contemporary Social Problems,* 4th ed., ed. Robert K. Merton and Robert Nisbet. New York: Harcourt Brace Jovanovich, 1976, pp. 557–601.

A description of the social processes leading to community organization or disorganization, as well as of the connection between social disorganization and urban problems.

Cooley, Charles Horton. *Social Organization: A Study of the Larger Mind.* New York: Scribner's, 1927, pp. 342ff.

Discusses the effects of disorganization—namely, chaos and lack of discipline in the lives of individuals.

Cottrell, W. F. "Death by Dieselization: A Case Study in the Reaction to Technological Change." *American Sociological Review* 16 (June 1951): 358–65.

A useful study of how changes in railroad technology disorganized a whole town centered around railroading.

Elliott, Mabel A., and Francis E. Merrill. *Social Disorganization,* 4th ed. New York: Harper, 1961.

An encyclopedic text on the interrelationship of personal and cultural problems in society. The authors make a vigorous effort to include all types of deviant behavior under the rubric of social disorganization.

Faris, Robert E. L., and H. Warren Dunham. *Mental Disorders in Urban Areas: An Ecological Study of Schizophrenia and Other Psychoses.* Chicago: University of Chicago Press, 1939.

An application of Burgess's concentric zone theory of the city. Near the heart of the city is the most socially disorganized area—the "zone of transition." Faris and Dunham show that, for certain mental illnesses, the rates are highest in this zone.

Homans, George C. *The Human Group.* New York: Harcourt, Brace, 1950.

In Chapter 13 ("Social Disintegration: Hilltown"), Homans shows how the enforcement of moral norms broke down in a small New England town. Economic and technological changes drastically reduced the frequency of activities and interaction among town members. These reductions in the social contacts of everyday life reduced consensus on traditional moral norms. The result was normlessness. Violation of moral norms, formally met by such sanctions as gossip, disapproval, or avoidance, went unpunished. Moral norms without enforcement are for Homans a major index of the breakdown of social control.

Linsky, Arnold S., and Murray A. Straus. *Social Stress in the United States: Links to Regional Patterns in Crime and Illness.* Dover, MA: Auburn House, 1986.

A study of crime, maladaptive behavior, and stress-related diseases as related to social conditions that reflect change, loss of stable relationships, and loss of secure normative guidelines. The authors discuss their findings in the framework of social disorganization theory.

Martindale, Don. "Social Disorganization: The Conflict of Normative and Empirical Approaches." In *Modern Sociological Theory,* ed. Howard Becker and Alvin Boskoff. New York: Holt, Rinehart and Winston, 1957, pp. 340–68.

In this chapter, Martindale gives perhaps the first detailed critical analysis of the concept of social disorganization as used by sociologists. He points out that the very notion of social disorganization is rooted in the society's values and has no real status as an objective scientific concept.

Obgurn, William F. *Social Change with Respect to Culture and Original Nature.* New York: Huebsch, 1922.

Ogburn presents his theory of cultural lag. Social disorganization arises out of a failure of groups to adapt to technological change.

Skogan, Wesley G. *Disorder and Decline.* New York: The Free Press, 1990.

Skogan examines some of the consequences of the breakdown of social control in several urban areas. He finds that persons living in neighborhoods with the highest crime rates are the most alienated and the least likely to join a neighborhood crime watch program. This is yet another study attesting to the rebirth of social disorganization theory.

Thomas, William I., and Florian Znaniecki. *The Polish Peasant in Europe and America.* 2 vols. New York: Knopf, 1927.

In the introduction to this famous book, Thomas and Znaniecki state that social disorganization consists of a breakdown in social rules. They then present letters written by recent immigrants from Poland to America, piling up abundant evidence of the anomalous situation they face in America.

Wirth, Louis. "Ideological Aspects of Social Disorganization." *American Sociological Review* 5 (August 1940): 472–82.

A distinguished American sociologist indicates that the term "social disorganization" frequently conceals a set of vested interests or special pleading.

4/VALUE CONFLICT

During the first two stages of American sociology's development (1905 to 1935), a number of theorists pointed to the prominence of conflict in society.[1] In addition, these early theorists were social critics. They found much that was wrong with American society, and they argued for basic changes in its structure.[2] Since American sociology was only in its infancy, however, all these writers addressed a reform-minded audience that was outside the academic setting.

During the 1930s and throughout the third period (1935 to 1954), American sociologists were to fashion a different role for themselves and were to begin addressing a different kind of audience. They became more concerned with developing sociology as a scientific discipline, and other academics became their audience. Instead of espousing social reform on behalf of an explicit set of values, they became more "objective" and detached in their analyses of social problems. And because the social disorganization perspective seemed the most congenial to the development of sociology as a scientific discipline, most sociologists subscribed to that perspective. Nonetheless, the conflict perspective was not forgotten, and during the third period in the development of American sociology the value conflict perspective was resurrected.

CONFLICT THEORISTS AND THE FORMULATION OF THE VALUE CONFLICT PERSPECTIVE

The value conflict perspective grew out of a synthesis of European and American theories of conflict. Among early European sociologists, conflict theorists abounded.[3] Karl Marx, for example, described history in terms of a struggle between the classes, and Georg Simmel analyzed conflict as a form of social interaction.[4] Americans had studied European masters such as these and developed their own notions about

1. Early American conflict theorists included Albion Small, Edward Ross, Lester Ward, Thorstein Veblen, and Robert Park.

2. Lewis A. Coser, *The Functions of Social Conflict* (New York: Free Press, 1956).

3. For example, Ludwig Gumplowicz, Karl Marx and Friedrich Engels, Gustav Ratzenhofer, and Georg Simmel.

4. See, for example, Karl Marx and Friedrich Engels, *Selected Works*, 2 vols. (Moscow; Foreign Languages Publishing House, 1965), and Georg Simmel, "The Sociology of Conflict," trans. Albion Small, *American Journal of Sociology* 9 (1903–04): 490–525, 672–89, 798–811.

social conflict,[5] but until the 1920s and 1930s, they did not apply the conflict perspective to the study of social problems. In 1925, Lawrence K. Frank advocated the value conflict approach to the study of social problems; applying this perspective to housing problems, Frank showed how a variety of social interests were entangled in housing questions and how changes introduced to solve the problems of the urban slum would involve a host of groups in endless conflicts of interests.[6]

The major formulation of the value conflict approach to social problems, however, was accomplished more than a decade later by Richard C. Fuller and Richard R. Myers. In two seminal papers published in 1941[7] (and reprinted in this chapter), Fuller and Myers held that conflicts of values usually figure in all phases of most social problems, regardless of the specific issues involved. They argued that all problems have a natural history with three stages—awareness, policy determination, and reform—and that at each of these stages, the values and interests of different groups clash.

The formulation of the value conflict perspective reflected the times. Fuller began to develop the approach during the Depression,[8] and his and Myers's papers were published during World War II.[9] The Depression and the war revived interest in conflict theory. In contrast to the disorganization perspective, conflict theory assumed that there is nothing wrong (or "disorganized") about people upholding their own interests and values against the competing interests and values of other groups.

In addition, when the nation went to war, sociologists found a patriotic rationale for injecting social values into their sociology. In the early 1940s, two articles criticized the social disorganization perspective in a way that indirectly supported this school of thought. In these articles, the term "disorganization," like "pathology," was criticized for violating the norm of value neutrality.[10] More recently, as mentioned in the preceding chapter, what was labeled "disorganization" was said to reflect simply the sociologist's failure to recognize organization among people who did not have middle-class lifestyles.[11] Thus, it was suggested that sociologists using the disor-

---

5. In America, the most important early conflict theorists were Albion Small and Robert Park. Small is largely responsible for introducing Simmel's writings to American sociologists. In addition, Small treated conflict as an important social process in his own writings. Park was also greatly influenced by Simmel. He treated conflict as one of the basic forms of interaction, and he used the notion of conflict at great length in his writings on community, city, and race relations. See Albion W. Small and George E. Vincent, *An Introduction to the Study of Society* (New York: American Book Company, 1894), and Robert E. Park and Ernest W. Burgess, *Introduction to the Science of Sociology* (Chicago: University of Chicago Press, 1921).

6. Lawrence K. Frank, "Social Problems," *American Journal of Sociology* 30 (January 1925): 463–75.

7. Richard C. Fuller and Richard R. Myers, "Some Aspects of a Theory of Social Problems," *American Sociological Review* 6 (February 1941): 24–32; Richard C. Fuller and Richard R. Myers, "The Natural History of a Social Problem," *American Sociological Review* 6 (June 1941): 320–28.

8. Richard C. Fuller, "Sociological Theory and Social Problems," *Social Forces* 15 (May 1937): 496–502; Richard C. Fuller, "The Problem of Teaching Social Problems," *American Journal of Sociology* 44 (November 1938): 415–28; Richard C. Fuller, "Social Problems," Part I, in *New Outline of the Principles of Sociology,* ed. R. E. Park (New York: Barnes & Noble, 1939), pp. 3–61.

9. Fuller and Myers, "Some Aspects of Theory," Fuller and Myers, "Natural History."

10. Louis Wirth, "Ideological Aspects of Social Disorganization," *American Sociological Review* 5 (August 1940): 472–82; C. Wright Mills, "The Professional Ideology of Social Pathologists," *American Journal of Sociology* 49 (September 1942): 165–80.

11. See, for example, Marshall B. Clinard, *Sociology of Deviant Behavior,* 2nd ed. (New York: Holt, Rinehart and Winston, 1968), pp. 41–42, and Albert K. Cohen, "The Study of Social Disorganization and Deviant Behavior," in *Sociology Today: Problems and Prospects,* ed. Robert K. Merton, Leonard Broom, and Leonard S. Cottrell, Jr. (New York: Basic Books, 1959), p. 474. Two classic field studies

ganization approach were only deluding themselves when they claimed to deal with social problems in a value-free and "objective" manner. By pointing out that value judgments are implicit even when sociologists try to avoid them, these critiques gave solace to those sociologists who believed that they *should* inject their values into their sociology.

Consequently, the formulation of the value conflict perspective included the notion that sociologists' concern should be with service to society rather than scientific appearances. Fuller, for example, pointed out that the social problems course is a "service" course.[12] Most students who take it do not intend to go on to graduate work in sociology; thus what they need is a textbook and a point of view that will help them as citizens to understand, analyze, and take action regarding the social problems they are bound to face after graduation. (Fuller himself was planning a textbook along these lines when he died.) The notion of applied sociology was also echoed in another work of the period, a famous study of race relations that argued, among other things, that social scientists should labor explicitly in the service of their society.[13]

The first social problems textbook to be organized around the value conflict perspective appeared in 1948.[14] This book built on the papers by Fuller and Myers and by sociologists of the early 1940s. The authors differed from Fuller and Myers and others regarding the value conflict perspective, however, by seeking to make the sociologist a detached analyst (and not, in addition, a therapist) of social problems. Thus, even within a perspective, there can be dissension regarding how sociology should fulfill its dual mandate.

CHARACTERISTICS OF THE VALUE CONFLICT PERSPECTIVE

Value conflict, as a perspective, is considerably sharper in focus than the social pathology perspective, yet less complex than the social disorganization perspective. Its essential characteristics are as follows:

Definition. Social problems are social conditions that are incompatible with the values of some group whose members succeed in publicizing a call for action.

Causes. The root causes of social problems are conflicts of values or interests. Various groups, because they have different interests, find themselves in opposition. Once opposition crystallizes into conflict, a social problem is born.

Conditions. Background conditions affecting the appearance, frequency, duration, and outcome of social problems are competition and contact among groups. When two or more groups are in competition and in particular types of contact with one another, a conflict cannot be avoided. A number of kinds of social problems

refute the claim that slums are examples of social disorganization. See William Foote Whyte, *Street Corner Society: The Social Structure of an Italian Slum,* 2nd ed. (Chicago: University of Chicago Press, 1955), and Gerald D. Suttles, *The Social Order of the Slum: Ethnicity and Territory in the Inner City* (Chicago: University of Chicago Press, 1968).

12. Fuller, "Problem of Teaching."

13. Gunnar Myrdal, *An American Dilemma: The Negro Problem and Modern Democracy* (New York: Harper, 1944).

14. John F. Cuber and Robert A. Harper, *Problems of American Society: Values in Conflict* (New York: Henry Holt, 1948).

have arisen under these conditions. And once the problem has arisen, the competing groups can also be in conflict over how to resolve the problem.

Numerous writers have pointed out that social problems consist of an objective condition and a subjective definition. The objective condition is contact and competition; the subjective definition reflects different ways of defining and evaluating contact, competition, and the distribution of goods and rights. The social problem, then, emerges out of the volatile mixture of objective condition and subjective definition.

Consequences.   Conflicts can be abrasive and costly. Sometimes they result in the sacrifice of higher values on behalf of lesser-ranked values. More often, they result in abortive stalemates or in loss by the weaker party in the conflict. They also produce a tradition of "bad feeling" between the groups. In addition, however, as more liberal observers point out, conflicts can have the positive effect of helping groups clarify their values.

Solutions.   The value conflict perspective suggests three ways in which social problems arising out of clashing interests and values may be resolved: consensus, trading, and naked power. If the parties can resolve the conflict on behalf of a set of higher values shared by both parties, then consensus wins the day. If the parties can bargain, then a trade of values—all in the spirit of democratic process—can take place. If neither consensus nor trading works, then the group with the most power gains control.

SUMMARY AND CONCLUSION

Conflict has always figured in the thinking of important European and American sociologists. But as American sociologists sought to develop sociology as a science, they began to focus on social order and seemed to forget about conflict as a basic fact of social life and a major component of many social problems.[15] The Depression years, together with World War II, rekindled interest in conflict theory and in making sociology more "relevant" to society. Fuller and Myers produced the outstanding formulation of this view, which continues to be popular among sociologists.

From this perspective, social problems are seen as arising from conflicts of values. Competition and particular types of contact among groups are the conditions under which such conflicts develop. Value conflicts frequently lead to the polarization of groups and a clarification of their values. "Solutions" take the form of exerting power, bargaining, or reaching a consensus.

15. John Horton, "Order and Conflict Theories of Social Problems," *American Journal of Sociology* 71 (May 1966): 701–13.

THE CONFLICT OF VALUES

Richard C. Fuller and Richard R. Myers

Fuller and Myers, the two main theorists of the value conflict perspective, posit three kinds of social problems: the physical, the ameliorative, and the moral. The distinctions revolve around whether or not people agree on the undesirability of the condition and on what actions should be taken. With physical problems (such as tornadoes or hurricanes), people agree that the condition is undesirable and that nothing can be done about the physical cause of the problem. (They may disagree, however, about how to deal with the consequences of the event.) With ameliorative problems (such as crime or poverty), people agree that the condition is undesirable and that the condition can be corrected, but they disagree about what action should be taken. With moral problems (such as abortion or gambling), people do not agree about whether the condition is undesirable or about what action, if any, should be taken. As society changes, problems can shift from one category to another. Nonetheless, Fuller and Myers maintain, central to all social problems are "conflicts in the value scheme of the culture."

Social problems courses have too often fallen into disrepute because sociologists have had no clear understanding of the nature of the social phenomena out of which problems arise. Because of this lack of understanding, courses have been "informational" in character, the teaching lopsided and incomplete, and the textbooks primarily compendia of unrelated facts.

"Social Problems" has been a convenient heading under which a mass of data pertaining to crime, divorce, immigration, insanity, and the like, has been assembled and presented to the student in unsystematic and undigested form. In this lumping together, the contribution of the sociologist as such has been negligible. He has borrowed from the fields of history, economics, medicine, psychiatry, penology, and social work and has condensed findings from these various disciplines into a series of separate courses in miniature, but has added to the totality very little distinctly sociological analysis.

What justification is there for preserving in the sociology curriculum a course which surveys differentiated and discrete problems, catch-as-catch-can, without a unifying and systematic sociological interpretation? It may be that there is some place in the college curriculum for a survey course which considers a variety of social problems from a variety of viewpoints—biological, medical, economic, po-

From Richard C. Fuller and Richard Myers. "Some Aspects of a Theory of Social Problems," *American Sociological Review*, 6, February 1941, quotes from pp. 24–25, 27–32. Copyright 1941 by the American Sociological Association. Reprinted by permission.

litical—but a course of that type should be presented in collaboration by a number of different specialists. There is no reason why a sociologist should have any special competence to handle so many varied kinds of data with so many different scientific analyses.

Some may object that social problems do not have enough in common to be dealt with by one central thread of sociological theory. If such be the case, then each separate problem must be interpreted with a different set of sociological concepts and the only excuse for considering a number of problems together would be that of practical expediency—to satisfy students who desire a survey course because they have not the time or interest for more specialized study.

It seems worthwhile, therefore, to inquire whether sociology can work out a common orientation for the treatment of diverse social problems as "sociological phenomena," and whether this central thread of analysis can be maintained consistently throughout a course or textbook.

Attempts to achieve such common orientation have been made by certain textbook writers. The most popular climate of theory has been the application of cultural lag and social disorganization analyses to social problems.[1] We find this theory set up in skeleton form in first and last chapters of textbooks, but rarely, if ever, consistently applied throughout the book to all the problems with regard to which the author presents factual data. The result is that the theoretical discussion of the concept "social problem" is of little practical use to the student and is relegated to a minor role in the introduction or conclusion of the course.

The failure of sociologists to develop a workable sociological orientation stems from their inability to free themselves from the traditional concept "social problem" which is unrealistic because it is incomplete. Traditionally, sociologists have dealt with social problems as "givens," rather than as phenomena to be demonstrated. They have assumed certain conditions as inevitable social problems, either to suit their own scheme of values, or because such conditions have historically been discussed as problems in the textbooks.

A social problem is a condition which is an actual or imagined deviation from some social norm cherished by a considerable number of persons. But who is to say whether a condition is such deviation? The sociologist may say so, but that does not make the condition a social problem from the point of view of the layman. Sociologists, nonetheless, have been content to take deviations for granted, without bothering to consult the definitions of conditions which laymen make. . . .

A common sociological orientation for the analysis of all social problems may thus be found in the conflict of values which characterizes every social problem. These conflicts are mirrored in the failure of people to agree that a given condition is a social problem, or assuming such agreement, failure to reach an accord as to what should be done about it. It is exactly this disagreement in value-judgments that is the root cause of all social problems, both in the original definition of the condition as a problem and in subsequent efforts to solve it. May we suggest, tentatively, a threefold classification of social problems on the principle of different levels of relationship to the value-scheme?[2]

At the first level, we have what we may call the *physical* problem. The physical problem represents a condition which practically all people regard as a threat to their welfare, but value-judgments cannot be said to cause the condition itself. This is perhaps best demonstrated by such catastrophic problems as earthquakes, hurricanes, floods, droughts, locust plagues, and so forth. That these are "serious" problems from the standpoint of the people which they affect, we can have no doubt. However, we may raise the question whether or not they are "social" problems, since they do not usually occur because of conflicts in the value-scheme of the culture. We find no public forums debating the question of what to do about preventing earthquakes and hurricanes. There is no controversy over how to stop volcanic eruptions and cloudbursts. The causation is thought of as nonhuman, resting in natural forces outside the control of man. Perhaps we may call such causation noncultural or precultural.

Here, we must distinguish between the condition itself and the effects of the condition. While the earthquake itself may involve no value-judgments, its consequences inevitably will call for moral judgments and decisions of policy. People will not agree on how much should be spent in reconstruction, how it should be spent, or how the funds should be raised. There may be serious questions as to whether people in other unaffected areas of the same society should come to the aid of the stricken area. However, the earthquake itself is not a social problem in the same sense as illegitimacy and unemployment. The latter have cultural elements in their causation.

In the case of the physical problem, there is scientific ignorance of causation and control, and we cannot say that the value-judgments of the people are obstructing the solution of the problem. There is no social disorganization involved, no clash of social values, no lag between public opinion and scientific opinion. If scientific knowledge has ascertained the causes of the condition and for some reason the value-judgments of the people interfere with the acceptance and application of this knowledge, then we can say that value-judgments are a part of the causal pattern of the problem and that the problem is truly "social" and no longer belongs at our first level. Thus, if we may anticipate the time when scientists can tell us how to prevent earthquakes, control hurricanes, and make rain for drought-stricken areas, we may imagine some elements of the population who will oppose the application of scientific techniques on the ground that they are too costly and threaten budget-balancing, or that they interfere with nature and God's will, or for some other reason. At this point in the evolution of the culture, we do have a man-made problem, since the will of certain groups is a causal element in the occurrence of the condition itself.

Most diseases have at one time or another constituted physical or medical problems rather than social problems. Many years ago, the bubonic plague, small-pox, and syphilis were far beyond medical knowledge of prevention and control. Today, if the bubonic plague and small-pox should again sweep the world, they would not be essentially "medical" problems since medicine now knows how to deal with them. They would be "social problems" since their recurrence could be traced to the breakdown of our educational techniques, popular resistance against vaccination, confusion as to public policy in public health matters, or some other man-made situation. Likewise, the control of syphilis is now definitely a social problem. Medical knowledge of prevention and control is very nearly per-fected, but the problem of changing social attitudes and removing social inertia is very much with us. . . .

As for locust plagues and floods, it is perhaps debatable whether or not they belong at this first level of the physical problem. To the degree that we know how to check boll weevil and grasshopper invasions and avoid floods, these things are social problems. To the degree that we lack such knowledge, they are merely technical, engineering, or physical problems.

At the second level, we have the *ameliorative* problem. Problems of this type represent conditions which people generally agree are undesirable in any in-stance, but they are unable to agree on programs for the amelioration of the condition. The essence of the ameliorative problem is one of solution and the administration of reform rather than original agreement that the condition con-stitutes a social problem which must be eradicated. Crime and delinquency fall in this category. Though there are individuals who offend the dominant com-munity mores by robbing, murdering, raping, and petty thieving, there are no interest groups who openly in forum and legislature seek to perpetuate the in-terests which these individuals represent. All "right-thinking" people, regardless of race, nationality, religion, or economic status, look upon the ameliorative prob-lem as intolerable. Among other problems which we may place in this class are most physical diseases, mental deficiency and insanity, and industrial and auto-mobile accidents.

In contrast to the physical problem at the first level, the ameliorative problem is truly "social" in the sense that it is a man-made condition. By this we mean that value-judgments not only help to create the condition, but to prevent its solution. In the case of crime, certain moral judgments of our culture are to a large extent responsible for the criminal act in the first place. To the degree that our mores of conspicuous consumption enter into the motivation of crimes for pecuniary gain, there is a cultural responsibility for such criminal acts. Or again, traditional prison policies based on our belief in severity of punishment may become part of the causal pattern of further criminal behavior in the prisoner after his liberation. These same cherished notions of retribution in punishment of criminals operate to dissuade legislatures from adequately financing probation and parole systems, juvenile delinquency clinics, and the schools for problem children.

At this level, also, we have those physical and mental diseases where tradi-tional beliefs obstruct the application of medical and psychiatric knowledge to the prevention and treatment of individual deficiencies. Certainly illness, disease, and industrial accidents among the low income groups reflect the failure of our culture both in preventing high incidences of risk to these people and in ade-quately insuring them against the costs of such risks. Specifically, the uneven distribution of wealth and income throughout our various social classes serves both to expose wage-earners and their families to malnutrition, disease, and ac-cident, and to deprive them of the means to meet the economic costs of such disasters. . . .

It is true that all our ameliorative problems have their technical, medical, or engineering aspects similar to those involved in the physical problem. Venereal disease, tuberculosis, insanity, and automobile accidents all necessitate investigation by scientific specialists. The point is, of course, that in the case of such problems, even when the specialists have isolated the cause and are agreed upon programs of control, laymen still are hopelessly divided over questions of policy.

At the third level we have what we will call the *moral* problem. The moral problem represents a condition on which there is no unanimity of opinion throughout the society that the condition is undesirable in every instance. There is no general agreement that the condition is a problem and thus many people do not feel that anything should be done about it. With the moral problem, we have a basic and primary confusion in social values which goes much deeper than the questions of solution which trouble us in the ameliorative problem.[3] Of course, the ameliorative problem reflects confusion in the value-scheme and thus contains real elements of moral conflict, but such conflict centers more around techniques and means of reform than around fundamental agreement on objectives and ultimate values. Hence, though all "right-thinking" people regard such conditions as crime, insanity, and disease as bad, there are interest groups openly defending and perpetuating the conditions classified as moral problems. Witness the problems of child labor and low wage and hour standards. We have only to read the record of newspaper and Congressional debate on the recently enacted Fair Labor Standards Act to learn that many individuals and groups not only objected to the specific solution attempted in the legislation, but also refused to admit that the conditions themselves were problems over which we should be concerned. In one of the first cases heard under the child labor legislation, one Michigan judge defended the labor of a newsboy on the ground that when he was a boy such work was regarded as excellent character development and training in individual qualities of initiative and self-discipline. Certainly employers in the beet sugar fields of the middle-western states who rely heavily on the labor of children do not define the condition, insofar as it pertains to them, in terms of a social problem. In those families where the labor of children is considered necessary to the maintenance of the family budget, parents and children alike have a stake in the continuance of the condition so abhorred by others. Religious groups have even frowned on government control of child labor as an unjustifiable invasion of the home and a threat to the prerogatives of the church. As to long hours and low wages, the opposition of some dominant groups in the southern states to the enactment of the federal legislation indicated no "problem-conscious" attitude on their part. Classical economists and employers have been known to look upon unemployment and low wage and hours standards as the inevitable, if not the necessary, mechanics of competition in the labor market. . . .

The utility of this classification is in its relativity. The purpose is not to pigeonhole the different problems with finality at any one level, but rather to give us a working basis for observing the position of each problem relative to other problems, and to the value-scheme as a whole. Note that problems will move from one category to another with changes in the state of scientific knowledge and with shifts in the value-scheme. When the physical problems cease to be essentially problems of engineering and medical knowledge, and come to involve questions of social policy, they will move over into alignment with the ameliorative problems at the second level. As indicated, venereal disease has seemingly made this transition though infantile paralysis has not. When problems now classed as moral come to have wide disapproval throughout our culture as conditions which must in every instance be done away with, they will become essentially problems of solution rather than agreement on basic values and will be dealt with as ameliorative problems. Someday child labor may be looked upon as criminal in the same sense that robbery and murder are now regarded as criminal. Conceivably, war may sometime be defined as wrong as venereal disease.

Nor is there any finality about the problems tentatively classified as ameliorative. Many crimes, such as political corruption, gambling, liquor offenses, and traffic violations are condoned, tolerated, and even participated in by respected and otherwise responsible members of the community. White-collar crimes are conspicuous in this category. Crimes of this sort reflect the same fundamental confusion of values as the problems which we discussed as moral. Before such offenses can be said to be merely problems of police detection and judicial enforcement, the citizens of the community must get together and agree that something should be done.

It may well be that there are very few contemporary problems which can be said to be purely ameliorative in nature, since most of them reflect no underlying clarity of definition and moral evaluation. If such be the case, it is a revealing commentary on the absence of any firm tissue of cultural integration in the value-scheme. Cultural integration itself is a matter of degree. There is always more or less, but never complete integration. A complete homogeneity of social values would mean we would have no social problems at all unless we include only the purely physical problems discussed at the first level.

Notes

1. For a discussion of some of the limitations of the social disorganization theory in the analysis of social problems, see Richard C. Fuller, "The Problem of Teaching Social Problems," *Amer. J. Sociol.*, Nov. 1938, 415–25.

2. The elements of this classification were stated by Richard C. Fuller in the article, "The Problem of Teaching Social Problems," 419–20.

3. The term "moral problem" is used by Stuart A. Queen and Jennette R. Gruener in their *Social Pathology*, 38–42, New York, 1940. The moral problem, as they define it, pertains to questions of fundamental right and wrong.

THE STAGES OF A SOCIAL PROBLEM
Richard C. Fuller and Richard R. Myers

Social problems, according to Fuller and Myers, follow an orderly "career." The authors argue that all social problems go through the three stages of awareness, policy determination, and reform. In the first stage, groups begin to see a particular situation as a threat to important values. In the second stage, people choose sides, redefine values, and offer proposals for action. In the third stage, some group or groups succeed in rallying action on behalf of their values. Thus, Fuller and Myers argue, values are clearly involved in all phases of the history of a social problem.

It is our thesis that every social problem has a natural history and that the natural history approach is a promising conceptual framework within which to study specific social problems.

Let us first clarify our usage of the terms "social problem" and "natural history." The concept "social problem" as used in this paper can be stated in a series of propositions.

1. A social problem is a condition which is defined by a considerable number of persons as a deviation from some social norm which they cherish. Every social problem thus consists of an objective condition and a subjective definition. The objective condition is a verifiable situation which can be checked as to existence and magnitude (proportions) by impartial and trained observers, e.g., the state of our national defense, trends in the birth rate, unemployment, etc. The subjective definition is the awareness of certain individuals that the condition is a threat to certain cherished values.

2. The objective condition is necessary but not in itself sufficient to constitute a social problem. Although the objective condition may be the same in two different localities, it may be a social problem in only one of these areas, e.g., discrimination against Negroes in the South as contrasted with discrimination in the North; divorce in Reno as contrasted with divorce in a Catholic community. *Social problems are what people think they are* and if conditions are not defined as social problems by the people involved in them, they are not problems to those people, although they may be problems to outsiders or to scientists, e.g., the condition of poor southern sharecroppers is a social problem to the brain-trusters of the New Deal but not to many southern landowners.

From Richard C. Fuller and Richard Myers. "The Natural History of a Social Problem," *American Sociological Review*, 6, June 1941, pp. 320–328. Copyright 1941 by the American Sociological Association. Reprinted by permission.

3. Cultural values play an important causal role in the objective condition which is defined as a problem, e.g., the objective conditions of unemployment, race prejudice, illegitimacy, crime, divorce, and war come into being, in part at least, because people cherish certain beliefs and maintain certain social institutions which give rise to these conditions.

4. Cultural values obstruct solutions to conditions defined as social problems because people are unwilling to endorse programs of amelioration which prejudice or require abandonment of their cherished beliefs and institutions, e.g., one possible "solution" to illegitimacy would be social acceptance of contraception and abortion, practices which in themselves are now defined as violations of the mores.

5. Social problems thus involve a dual conflict of values: first, with regard to some conditions, people disagree as to whether the condition is a threat to fundamental values, e.g., race prejudice, divorce, child labor, war, unorganized labor; second, with regard to other conditions, although there is a basic agreement that the condition is a threat to fundamental values, because of a disparity of other values relative to means or policy, people disagree over programs of reform, e.g., crime, mental and physical disease, motor car accidents.

6. In the last analysis, social problems arise and are sustained because people do not share the same common values and objectives.

7. Sociologists must, therefore, study not only the objective condition phase of a social problem but also the value-judgments of the people involved in it which cause them to define the same condition and means to its solution in different ways.[1]

The specific analytical frame which we have called the "natural history" is derived from the above conception of what constitutes a social problem. In our concept "social problem," we have attributed to all social problems certain common characteristics. These common characteristics imply a common order of development through which all social problems pass, consisting of certain temporal sequences in their emergence and maturation. The "natural history" as we use the term is therefore simply a conceptual tool for the examination of the data which constitute social problems.

Social problems do not arise full-blown, commanding community attention and evoking adequate policies and machinery for their solution. On the contrary, we believe that social problems exhibit a temporal course of development in which different phases or stages may be distinguished. Each stage anticipates its successor in time and each succeeding stage contains new elements which mark it off from its predecessor. A social problem thus conceived as always being in a dynamic state of "becoming" passes through the natural history stages of awareness, policy determination, and reform. As we proceed to discuss the qualitative differences between these stages, we will refer by way of illustration to data gathered by graduate students on the residence-trailer problem in Detroit.

AWARENESS

The genesis of every social problem lies in the awakening of people in a given locality to a realization that certain cherished values are threatened by conditions which have become acute. Definitions of alarm emerge only as these group values are thought to be involved. Without awareness or "problem consciousness" in certain groups of people, be they scientists, administrators, or likeminded neighbors, no identifiable problem can be said to exist. Before a social problem can be identified, there must be awareness on the part of people who express their concern in some communicable or observable form.[2] The outstanding characteristic of this initial phase of awareness inheres in the constantly recurrent statements of people involved in a challenging situation that "something ought to be done." As yet, these people have not crystallized their definition sufficiently to suggest or debate exact measures for amelioration or eradication of the undesirable condition. Instead, there is unsynchronized random behavior, with protest expressed in general terms.

The objective condition aspect of the residence-trailer problem is the residence-trailer camp or community. The earliest record of such a community in Detroit goes back to the spring of 1920. This was a small camp of eight or ten families located on the periphery of the city; the residents were industrial workers living in homemade trailers. At this time, no discernible residence-trailer problem existed in Detroit. The three Detroit newspapers contain no reference to the situation and the records of the police, health department, and social work agencies are equally silent. Although neighbors remember the camp, they insist it was "no trouble at all." However, the objective condition grew rapidly in proportions. By 1930, there were four well-established camps within the city limits and by 1935 the number had increased to nine. In five of these nine communities, the inhabitants made no pretense of temporary camping, but removed the wheels from their trailers, mounted them on saw horses and two-by-fours, and settled down to a semipermanent existence. As the visibility of trailers and trailerites increased, there came the dawn of a social problem awareness as measured by newspaper items, gossip of neighbors, formal complaints of neighbors to the press and to civic authorities, and the official utterances of these civic authorities.

A sampling of the three Detroit newspapers reveals no comment on the situation either in the form of news or editorials until January, 1925, when we have an item in one paper noting a "brawl" which occurred in one of the camps. During the next decade, 1925–35, there was a steadily increasing number of items and in the two-year period 1936–37, the items reached their greatest frequency. If a qualitative interpretation of these items is permissible, we can say that up to 1930 their tone was one of curiosity and amusement rather than alarm. Before 1930, the editorial columns and "letters to the editor" section gave very little attention to the situation. After 1930, the editorial departments of all three papers made frequent comment and "letters to the editor" became quite common. In both straight news reporting and in editorial page comment, the tone of the items rapidly took on a note of concern and alarm. In 1936–37, over one half of the items were editorials or letters to the editor; the remainder were news items concerned with crime, disease, fires, accidents, and humorous incidents in the camps. The letters to the editor were principally from people living in the neighborhoods close to the trailer communities, from school authorities, from real estate dealers, and from social workers.

Complaints of neighbors were articulated on the grounds of the unsightliness of the camps, noises, odors, immorality, crime, and property depreciation in the surrounding districts. The response of neighborhood groups to the condition was measured not only by formal complaints to police, health officials, and newspapers, but also by the participant observations of students living in local areas near trailer camps. One student reported:

> At first, none of us paid much attention when a number of families moved into the big open lot on the next corner below us. They were poor factory workers and the depression was pretty tough in 1932. They did not have to pay much rent. Most of us thought they would only stay a month or two and then be on their way. But after a year there were more trailers there than ever and neighbors began to say, "Well, it looks as if they were here to stay." But no one seemed to think that the camps were hurting any of us. Then we all began to miss certain small articles around the house. Newspapers, milk bottles, and tools began to disappear. We laid it to the trailer kids and blamed their parents for letting them run wild. Then someone said, "Why aren't these kids in school? That will keep them out of trouble." A neighbor wrote a letter to the truant officer about it but nothing came of it at first.
>
> [Another typical comment] Dad said Mother thought the trailer children were a bunch of sex perverted brats, but Dad said he did not worry half so much about that as how he would ever sell his house unless they got the campers out of the district. And Dad was always saying that he had nothing against the trailerites themselves. They could not help being poor, he said, but it was a "hell of a note why that should mean we all must be poor." [This statement referred to the situation in 1932.]

Awareness was registered in the official statements of organized civic authorities, such as health agencies, the police, and school functionaries, almost as soon as protests were being registered by local neighborhood groups. The health authorities were the first governmental unit to show concern in public statements and their information was given them first by social workers called into the camps to administer relief. The chief complaints of health inspectors to the Common Council were: families averaged two to each trailer and accommodations were scarcely large enough for one; several of the camps had no toilet accommodations and there was little or no privacy in such matters; water supply was low and residents were often dependent on sources outside the camp; in winter, the heating accommodations were deficient, small gas stoves serving most trailers and others had no heating whatsoever; garbage disposal was indiscriminate and dumping on nearby vacant lots was the usual expedient.

The police, as another organized official group, came to view trailer camps as potential danger spots, presenting a new challenge to the preservation of law and order. This awareness definition reflected in official police reports emerged as the police were increasingly called in to quell brawls, apprehend delinquents, and investigate reports of indignant neighbors.

School authorities became aware of the residence-trailer problem because the stability and routine of the school were affected. Some schools did not have the accommodations for the incoming trailer children, day to day attendance of the newcomers was extremely irregular, and, because of the impermanence of the trailer community, many children would depart before the school year was completed.

Thus, the stage of progressive awareness for Detroit's residence-trailer problem covered the approximate period of 1925–35, and is measurable by newspaper indexes as well as by the definitions of citizens and government officials who felt that group values of health, education, private property, and morals were threatened by the existence of the objective condition.

POLICY DETERMINATION

Very soon after the emergence of awareness comes debate over policies involved in alternative solutions. Ends and means are discussed and the conflict of social interests becomes intense. People who propose solutions soon find that these solutions are not acceptable to others. Even when they can get others to agree on solutions, they find agreement as to means a further difficulty. The stage of policy determination differs significantly from the stage of awareness in that interest groups are now concerned primarily with "what ought to be done" and people are proposing that "this and that should be done."[3] Specific programs occupy the focus of attention. The multi-sided protests have become organized and channelized.

Policy determination on the residence-trailer problem in Detroit indicated discussion on at least three interrelated levels: first, discussion by neighbors and other interested but unorganized groups; second, discussion by organized interest or pressure groups such as taxpayers, trailer manufacturers, real estate organizations, parent-teacher associations, women's clubs, and men's clubs; third, discussion among specialists and administrators in government or quasi governmental units—the police, health officials, Common Council, social workers, and school boards. The interinfluence and cross-fertilization of debate among and between these three levels of participating discussants represent the dynamics of policy determination.

Policy determination was preoccupied both with broad questions as to ends and with narrow, more specialized questions as to means. As to ends, should the trailer camps be prohibited entirely and expelled from the community, should they only be licensed, taxed, or otherwise restricted in growth, or should they be let alone in the hope that the situation would right itself? As to narrower questions of means, the more established, organized, and official the group, the more likely it was to agree on ends but to disagree on means. For instance, health officials debated periodic inspection, which would be costly but more efficient, as against sporadic inspection on complaints received, which would be less costly but involve more risk to the health of the community at large. Similarly, school officials debated the pros and cons of expansion, the pros and cons of vigorous truant officer activity, the pros and cons of a special class for trailer children. Police had to decide whether or not special details and augmented forces were necessary for trailer camp areas and whether a tough or lenient policy of arrest should be applied to trailer inhabitants.

Conflicts over policy determination can best be observed by charting the alignments of different interest groups who have various stakes in the solution of the difficulty. These groups represent certain institutional values, many of which appear incompatible with each other, all of which must be reconciled or compromised before the community can go ahead on a collective policy of reform. The official groups (police, health, school, social workers) can be said to be perpetuating basic organizational mores pertaining to the protection of private property, public health, education, and relief of the distressed. Then there are the special interest groups such as the real estate operators, hotel owners, and neighborhood taxpayers who want elimination or restriction of the homes on wheels because their pecuniary values of survival and status are threatened.

Lined up on the other side is the Coach Trailer Manufacturers' Association, a pressure group seeking the protection of the interests of trailerites, also motivated by self-interest and the profit mores. Then there are the interests of those who live in trailers. Though these trailer communities consist of low-income groups of migrant and transient workers, the casually employed, the chronic unemployable, factory wage earners, and the like, some of them are identified with an interest group of their own—The Mobile Home Owners' Association of America. This organization contends that trailer homes are the solution to the housing problems of the low-income family. With property and rental values held beyond their means, what is left for these people but the trailer house? There are citizens who are in sympathy with the position of trailer-residents, and although they favor some public control, they oppose abolition of these communities. Labor unions, civil rights groups, and other liberal organizations also are on record as championing the survival of trailer communities.

It seems, then, that the dynamics of policy determination on the residence-trailer problem, which became intensified during the approximate period of 1935–37, can be represented as an alignment of certain humanitarian interests with certain organizational interests to combat other humanitarian interests aligned with other organizational interests.

REFORM

The final stage in the natural history of a social problem is that of reform. Here we find administrative units engaged in putting formulated policy into action. General policies have been debated and defined by the general public, by special interest groups, and by experts. It is now the task of administrative experts specially trained in their jobs to administer reform. This is the stage of action, both public and private. The emphasis is no longer on the idea that "something ought to be done" or that "this or that should be done" but on the fact that "this and that are being done." Public action is represented in the machinery of government bodies, legislative, executive, and judicial; and in the delegated authority of administrative tribunals, special supervisory officers and boards. This is the institutionalized phase of the social problem in the sense that we have established policies carried out by publicly authorized policy-enforcing agencies. Reform may also be private in character, as witnessed by the activities of private clubs and organizations, private charities and other benevolent associations, and church groups.

Decisions of policy remain necessary at the reform stage, but such decisions usually involve quite technical matters pertaining to means and fall within the special bailiwick of the experts concerned with such questions. Of course, such policy questions may be taken out of the hands of the administrators whenever the general public exercises its powers of censorship, veto, or referendum. The already established public agencies may prove sufficient for the administration of reform in connection with a new community problem or it may be necessary to establish new agencies of administration.

The residence-trailer problem in Detroit is just beginning to enter the reform stage in its natural history. Although police and sanitation officials had sporadic contacts with the camps prior to 1937, their activities were not concerned with carrying out any special policies established for trailer communities. They were merely acting on community policies already established pertaining to crime and public health, wherever and whenever conditions called for bringing such old policies into action. Beginning about 1937, however, the Common Council enacted legislation which placed the trailer camps within the city under certain prohibitions and restrictions. These camps were absolutely prohibited from certain areas and allowed to survive only in specially designated areas. Also, special requirements as to licensing, inspection, and supervision of the camps were enforced on owners and/or leasees of the real estate where the camps were located. The health officials and sanitation inspectors were ordered to establish special rules of public health for the trailer communities. Reform has only begun, and many knotty legal problems remain to be ironed out before collective action can proceed further. There is no indication that the school authorities have taken any official action. The problem seems to be on the border of transition from policy determination to reform.

It should be fairly obvious from the statement of the residence-trailer problem that the stages in the natural history are not mutually exclusive and that they tend to overlap. For conceptual purposes, however, the three general phases may be set off from each other; in practical reality, the state of development of a problem at any one time usually contains elements of all three stages.

Is the natural history technique equally adaptable to all types of social problems? The residence-trailer problem is a situation which can be observed on a local and emergent basis in specific neighborhoods and communities. The factors of localism and emergence offer the investigator a delimited area and a timeliness of observation which permit a current, intimate focus on the items of awareness, policy determination, and reform. The data are fresh and immediate and the participant observer technique is available. Such problems are often transitory— that is, awareness, discussion, and conflict cease permanently with some arrangement for compromise or removal of the difficulty; or the abatement of conflict may be only momentary and the issue flares up again and again.

What of the traditional, older, more pervasive problems which have occupied the attention of teacher and student in social problems texts for the past fifty years or more? What of crime, poverty, insanity, war, family disorganization, prostitution, illegitimacy, and race prejudice? Obviously, we cannot go back into antiquity to record the first awareness of social groups defining such conditions as problems. We cannot trace the earliest conflicts over policy and the first attempts at solution. Anthropological, historical, and contemporary data may be used to demonstrate to the student the universal aspects of these problems in space and in time. Such materials, however, are inadequate in that they do not bring the student face to face with the dynamics of the problem. If the student is to understand why these old established problems persist and defy solution, he must examine the values of our social organization which bring the undesirable conditions into existence and which obstruct efforts to remove them. His laboratory for the study of these realities is the local community where the cross-sectional conflicts at the core of the problem can be observed most intimately.

The important fact which the textbooks overlook is that the old traditional problems are given relative emphases in the local community. At the awareness stage, a problem such as crime may be receiving very little attention in community A, whereas in the neighboring community B it is the all-absorbing focus of interest. Similarly, there may be no discussion of policies relative to race discrimination in B, whereas the people of A are intensely occupied with such discussion. The administration of relief for unemployment may be in an advanced stage in B, whereas little if anything is being done in A. Thus, even these problems which are persistently national in scope do not blanket the country with the same stage of development. Such conditions are only latent, dormant, or potential problems in the local area, and before they rise to local consciousness, debate, and control, a local issue is essential to set the natural history going. Although the conflicts of social values which make up the problem, once it has evolved, are much the same in all communities, the natural history technique provides a specific focus on these conflicts as they function in the concrete reality of a local situation.

CONCLUSION

We have presented the "natural history" interpretation of social problems as a broad conceptual frame for the examination of the dynamics of specific social problems. Obviously, before the natural history technique can be made a precise tool of research, the many implications of our statement must be refined and explored by further analysis.

Within our experience as teachers, the natural history approach has proved most valuable in bringing students to grips with the realities of social problems. These realities, as we see them, are the cross purposes at which people find themselves because they cherish incompatible and inconsistent objectives. The very norms of organization which give the community a working routine tend to produce conflicts of cultural values which create and sustain conditions defined as social problems.

In the search for temporal sequences in the "becoming" of a social problem, the student does not take problem conditions for granted, as objective "evils" caused by "evils." He seeks to explain social problems as emergents of the cultural organization of the community, as complements of the approved values of the society, not as pathological and abnormal departures from what is assumed to be proper and normal. As such, the natural history technique is a sociological orientation rather than a social welfare orientation. If social problems theory is to come of age, it must cease being a poor relation of sociological theory and become sociological theory in its own right.

Notes

1. The basic idea that the social problem is a conflict of values is not a new one. See Lawrence K. Frank, "Social Problems," *Amer. J. Sociol.*, 1925, 30:463–473, page 468 for Frank's definition; Harold A. Phelps, *Contemporary Social Problems,* rev. ed., 737, New York, 1938; Willard Waller, "Social Problems and the Mores," *Amer. Sociol. Rev.,* 1936, 1:922–933; Kingsley Davis, "The Sociology of Prostitution," *Amer. Socio. Rev.,* 1937, 2: 749–755, and "Illegitimacy and the Social Structure," *Amer. J. Sociol.,* 1939, 45:215–233; Richard C. Fuller, "The Problem of Teaching Social Problems," *Amer. J. Sociol.,* 1938, 44:415–425, and [with Richard R. Myers], "Some Aspects of a Theory of Social Problems," *Amer. Sociol. Rev.,* 1941, 6:24–32; Stuart A. Queen and Jennette R. Gruener, *Social Pathology,* 38–42, New York, 1940; Louis Wirth, "Ideological Aspects of Social Disorganization," *Amer. Sociol. Rev.,* 1940, 5:472–482. Talcott Parsons, *The Structure of Social Action, passim,* New York, 1937, and "The Role of Ideas in Social Action," *Amer. Sociol. Rev.,* 1938, 3:652–664, and Robert K. Merton, "Social Structure and Anomie," *Amer. Sociol. Rev.,* 1938, 3:672–682, have also analyzed the concepts of social problem and social disorganization from a general sociological point of view.

2. As yet, we have not perfected research techniques which can penetrate covert mental states very satisfactorily.

3. Newspaper comment on the residence-trailer problem subsequent to 1935 reveals this transition in emphasis from simple alarm to concrete proposals.

VALUES, POLITICS, AND SOCIAL PROBLEMS

Joseph R. Gusfield

The political process has a symbolic as well as an instrumental dimension. Gusfield shows that groups sometimes pass laws that reflect credit on their values while discrediting other groups with divergent values. Prohibition, for example, expressed rural, middle-class, Protestant values and fostered conflict with immigrant, urban, lower-class, Catholic values. Thus, laws that serve as social symbols foster value conflict and the emergence of a long-standing social struggle.

An action of a governmental agent takes on symbolic import as it affects the designation of public norms. A courtroom decision or a legislative act is a gesture which often glorifies the values of one group and demeans those of another. In their representational character, governmental actions can be seen as ceremonial and ritual performances, designating the content of public morality. They are the

From Joseph R. Gusfield, "Moral Passage," *Social Problems* 15:2 (Fall 1967), pp. 175–178. Reprinted by permission of The Society for the Study of Social Problems and the author.

statement of what is acceptable in the public interest. Law can thus be seen as symbolizing the public affirmation of social ideals and norms as well as a means of direct social control. This symbolic dimension is given in the statement, promulgation, or announcement of law unrelated to its function in influencing behavior through enforcement.

. . . The fact of affirmation through acts of law and government expresses the public worth of one set of norms of one sub-culture vis-à-vis those of others. It demonstrates which cultures have legitimacy and public domination, and which do not. Accordingly it enhances the social status of groups carrying the affirmed culture and degrades groups carrying that which is condemned as deviant. We have argued elsewhere that the significance of Prohibition in the United States lay less in its enforcement than in the fact that it occurred.[1] Analysis of the enforcement of Prohibition law indicates that it was often limited by the unwillingness of Dry forces to utilize all their political strength for fear of stirring intensive opposition. Great satisfaction was gained from the passage and maintenance of the legislation itself.[2]

Irrespective of . . . [enforcement,] public designation of morality is itself an issue generative of deep conflict. The designating gestures are dramatistic events, "since it invites one to consider the matter of motives in a perspective that, being developed in the analysis of drama, treats language and thought primarily as modes of action."[3] For this reason the designation of a way of behavior as violating public norms confers status and honor on those groups whose cultures are followed as the standard of conventionality, and derogates those whose cultures are considered deviant. My analysis of the American Temperance movement has shown how the issue of drinking and abstinence became a politically significant focus for the conflicts between Protestant and Catholic, rural and urban, native and immigrant, middle class and lower class in American society. The political conflict lay in the efforts of an abstinent Protestant middle class to control the public affirmation of morality in drinking. Victory or defeat were consequently symbolic of the status and power of the cultures opposing each other.[4] Legal affirmation or rejection is thus important in what it symbolizes as well or instead of what it controls. Even if the law was broken, it was clear whose law it was.

Notes

1. Joseph R. Gusfield, *Symbolic Crusade: Status Politics and the American Temperance Movement,* Urbana: University of Illinois Press, 1963, pp. 117–126.

2. Gusfield, "Prohibition: The Impact of Political Utopianism," in John Braeman, editor, *The 1920's Revisited,* Columbus: Ohio State University Press, forthcoming; Andrew Sinclair, *The Era of Excess,* New York: Harper Colophon Books, 1964, Chap. 10, pp. 13–14.

3. Kenneth Burke, *A Grammar of Motives,* New York: Prentice-Hall, 1945, p. 393. Burke's writings have been the strongest influence on the mode of analysis presented here. Two other writers, whose works have been influential, themselves influenced by Burke, are Erving Goffman and Hugh D. Duncan.

4. Gusfield, *Symbolic Crusade, op. cit.,* Chap. 5.

WORDS WITHOUT DEEDS
Willard Waller

In this classic statement on the role of values in social problems, Waller discusses the basic tension between humanitarian and organizational mores. People make value judgments on the basis of humanitarian mores. But, at the same time, they are often constrained in eliminating the problematic conditions because of the costs that would result vis-à-vis institutions that are important to them. Hence, many people can object to a situation without wanting to do what is necessary to change it. In terms of Fuller's and Myers's scheme, awareness and policy determination can exist without necessarily leading to reform. Thus, Waller claims, "social problems are not solved because people do not want to solve them."

If we are to treat social problems scientifically, we must try to understand why we consider them problems. We must subject to analysis our judgments of value as well as the social phenomena upon which these judgments are passed. We may do this by applying the concept of the mores to the problem of social problems as we have defined it. Social problems exist within a definite moral universe. Once we step out of our circle of accustomed moralities, social problems cease to exist for us. Likewise, if we consider the possibility of revolutionary change, social problems lose most of their complexity. A simple formulation of our standpoint, which we advance as roughly accurate for most social problems, rests upon the assumption of two conflicting sets of mores. Social problems result from the interaction of these two groups of mores, which we may call the *organizational* and the *humanitarian* mores.[1]

The organizational, or basic, mores, are those upon which the social order is founded, the mores of private property and individualism, the mores of the monogamous family, Christianity, and nationalism. Conditions of human life which we regard as social problems emanate from the organizational mores as effective causes. Indeed, the fact that a certain condition is in some sense humanly caused is an unrecognized but essential criterion of the social problem. We are all, as Galsworthy remarked, under sentence of death, but death is not a social problem; death becomes a social problem only when men die, as we think, unnecessarily, as in war or by accident or preventable disease. Not all the miseries of mankind are social problems. Every condition which we regard as a social problem is in some sense a result of our institutions or we do not concern ourselves with it.

From Willard Waller, "Social Problems and the Mores," *American Sociological Review*, 1, December 1936, 924–33. Copyright 1936 by the American Sociological Association. Reprinted by permission.

Alongside the organizational mores there exists a set of humanitarian mores; those who follow the humanitarian mores feel an urge to make the world better or to remedy the misfortunes of others.[2] Probably the humanitarian impulse has always existed, but it has apparently attained group-wide expression at a relatively late period in our history, following the breakdown of primary group society. Social problems in the modern sense did not exist when every primary group cared for its own helpless and unfortunate. Social problems as we know them are a phenomenon of secondary group society, in which the primary group is no longer willing and able to take care of its members. It was this breakdown which called group-wide humanitarianism into existence; it was this situation which brought it about that we were asked to feel sympathy for those whom we had never seen. Humanitarian mores are frequently expressed, for they are highly verbal, and they command the instant assent of almost any group.

The formula which crystallizes in our minds as we approach social problems from the angle of the mores is this: Social problems are social conditions of which some of the causes are felt to be human and moral. Value judgments define these conditions as social problems. Value judgments are the formal causes of social problems, just as the law is the formal cause of crime. Value judgments originate from the humanitarian mores, which are somewhat in conflict with the organizational mores. Social problems are moral problems; they are like the problems of a problem play. The existence of some sort of moral problem is the single thread that binds all social problems together. Any important social problem is marked by moral conflict in the individual and social conflict in the group. It is thus that the strain for consistency in the mores expresses itself.[3]

When someone has expressed a value judgment upon some condition of human life which originates from the organizational mores, and begins to reflect upon possible courses of action, he is at last in a position to understand the sense in which social problems are complex. For the same mores from which the deplored conditions originate continue to operate to limit any action which one takes in order to remedy them. Frank illustrates this limiting action of the organizational mores by showing how difficult it would be to explain our housing problem to a man from Mars.

> We should have to delegate an economist, a lawyer, a political scientist, a sociologist, and a historian to explain about the system of private property, the price system, popular government, congestion of population, transportation, and so on. And when they had severally and jointly expounded the complexities of the situation, pointing out that we cannot just build houses, but must rely upon individual initiative and private enterprise to enter the field of building construction, that we must use the "price system" to obtain the needed land which is someone's private property, to buy the necessary materials and to hire the skilled labor, that we must borrow capital on mortgages to finance these expenditures, paying a bonus to induce someone to lend that capital and also pay interest on the loan, together with amortization quotas and then we must contrive to rent these dwellings in accordance with a multiplicity of rules and regulations about leases and so on—after all these sundry explanations showing that to get houses built we must not infringe anyone's rights of private property or freedom to make a profit, and that what we want is to find a way of getting houses without interfering with anyone's customary activities, our visitor would suddenly exclaim, "Yes, I begin to see; have you any other such difficult problems, for this is exceedingly interesting?"[4]

In every social problem seek the moral problem; try to discover the complex processes of conflict, supplementation, and interference in our own moral imperatives. That is the principle which should guide the sociologist as he seeks to study social problems scientifically. Let us attempt to sketch the outlines of this conflict of mores with regard to a few typical social problems. Poverty is a social problem, when it exists in the midst of plenty, or in a world in which universal plenty is a technological possibility. The value judgment passed on poverty defines it as at least in part socially caused and as something which ought to be remedied. A simpleton would suggest that the remedy for poverty in the midst of plenty is to redistribute income. We reject this solution at once because it would interfere with the institution of private property, would destroy the incentive for thrift and hard work and disjoint the entire economic system. What is done to alleviate poverty must be done within the limits set by the organizational mores.

A slightly different type of conflict appears when a value judgment is passed, not upon the conditions of someone's life, but upon his behavior. An unmarried girl has a baby; her family and community take harsh and unreasoned action against her. The humanitarian comes in to save the pieces, but he cannot make things too easy for the girl or try to convince her family and community that she is not guilty of moral turpitude for fear of encouraging illegitimacy and injuring the morality upon which the monogamous family is founded. Likewise, venereal disease becomes a social problem in that it arises from our family institutions and also in that the medical means which could be used to prevent it, which would unquestionably be fairly effective, cannot be employed for fear of altering the mores of chastity. The situation is similar when it is a question of adjusting family relationships; Kingsley Davis has supplied a penetrating analysis of the "family clinic" as an agency operating within a circle of conflicting moral demands.[5]

Confusing conflicts of mores appear in those situations, frequent enough in unemployment relief, in which human misery and misbehavior are intermingled. When people suffer privation, the humanitarian mores dictate relief. If these people are willing to work, if the old live in strict monogamy and the young do not contract marriage until they are off the relief rolls, if they obey the law, if they do not conceal any assets, if they spend absolutely nothing for luxuries, if they are grateful and not demanding, if the level of relief does not approach the income of the employed, relatively few objections are raised to the giving of relief. But let any of the above violations of the organizational mores defining the situation of the recipient of charity arise, and the untrained investigator will quite possibly cut off relief in a storm of moral indignation. Herein he is in agreement with the moral sense of the greater part of the community. The trained social worker attempts at this point to bring the investigator over to a more broadly humanitarian point of view.[6]

It is necessary to remember that in all this the humanitarian is simply following his own mores, which he has received irrationally and which he obeys without reflection, being supported in this by the concurrence of his own group. When the social worker says, "One must not make moral judgments," she means that one must not make moral judgments of the conventional sort, but that it is perfectly all right to pass a moral judgment on the cruel judge or to hate the man who hates the Negro. Often the humanitarian has all the prejudices of his society upside down, and one who talks to him is reminded that there is still "a superstition in avoiding superstition, when men think to do best when they go furthest from the superstition formerly received." Among the sociologists, those who teach so-called "attitudes courses" are particularly likely to fall into this type of confusion.

A few further complications may be noted. The humanitarian often argues for his reforms on the basis of considerations which are consonant with the organizational mores but alien to the spirit of humanitarianism; he advocates a new system of poor relief, saying that it will be cheaper, while really he is hoping that it will prove more humane. As all of us must do sometimes, in order to communicate truth he has to lie a little. Great confusion is caused in the field of criminology by shuttling back and forth between practical and humanitarian universes of discourse. Orthodox economists have recognized the humanitarian impulse in an almost perverted manner; they owlishly assure us that prevalent economic practices are not what they seem to be, but are in the long run ultra-humanitarian.

Certain implications of this interpretation of social problems on the basis of conflict in the mores seem very clear. I should venture to suggest the following point:

The notion of conflict of mores enables us to understand why progress in dealing with social problems is so slow. Social problems are not solved because people do not want to solve them. From a thousand scattered sources the evidence converges upon this apparently unavoidable conclusion, from the history of reform movements, from the biographies and autobiographies of reformers, from politics, from the records of peace conferences, from the field of social work, from private discussions, and even from the debates of so-called radical groups. Even those who are most concerned about social problems are not quite at one with themselves in their desire to solve them. Solving social problems would necessitate a change in the organizational mores from which they arise. The humanitarian, for all his allegiance to the humanitarian mores, is yet a member of our society and as such is under the sway of its organizational mores. He wishes to improve the condition of the poor, but not to interfere with private property. Until the humanitarian is willing to give up his allegiance to the organizational mores, and in some cases to run squarely against them, he must continue to treat symptoms without removing their causes.[7]

Frequently the liberal humanitarian is brought squarely up against the fact that he does not really want what he says he wants. The difficulty which he faces is that the human misery which he deplores is a necessary part of a social order which seems to him good. A cruel person may amuse himself at the expense of humanitarians by suggesting simple and effective means to secure the ends which they believe they value above all others, or a cynical person may use this device to block reform. The means suggested, if adequate to the ends, are certain to involve deep changes in our society, and their cost terrifies the humanitarian so that he feels compelled to make excuses. The pacifist is sincerely concerned about war, and he will even assent to the general proposition that permanent peace requires, among other things, a redistribution of world population. But suggest that the United States should make a start by ceding the Philippines and Hawaii to Japan and opening its doors to Oriental immigration, and the pacifist usually loses heart! Indeed, one wonders whether there are many pacifists whose pacifism would not be shattered by a Japanese invasion of Mexico or Canada. The pacifist does not really want peace at its necessary price; he wants peace with the continuation of things in the present order which necessitate war. He wants a miracle. Lincoln Steffens tells how the shrewd but illiberal Clemenceau defeated Wilson by showing him the costs of peace; the incident is valuable, at any rate, as showing how the two men might have behaved.[8] Professing to be completely in sympathy with Wilson's ideals, Clemenceau stated that peace would involve giving up empire and the thought of empire; for England it would involve the loss of colonies; the French would have to come out of Morocco; the United States would have to surrender island possessions, give up spheres of influence, abrogate the Monroe doctrine, and so on. When Wilson replied that America was not ready to go quite so far, all at once, Clemenceau retorted that in that case the conference did not want peace, but war, and that the best time for France to make war was when she had one of her enemies down. One is reminded of Bacon's saying, "For it is the solecism of power to think to command the end, and yet not to endure the mean."

When one considers the conditions under which the humanitarian impulse comes to expression, he must realize that the urge to do something for others is not a very important determinant of change in our society, for any translation of humanitarianism into behavior is fenced in by restrictions which usually limit it to trivialities. The expression of humanitarian sentiments must remain almost wholly verbal, and because of this situation which is inherent in our acquisitive and possessive society: No one loses by giving verbal expression to humanitarianism or by the merely verbal expression of another, but many would lose by putting humanitarianism into practice, and someone would certainly lose by any conceivable reform. From the powerful someone who is certain to lose comes opposition to reform.

Notes

1. I have limited the present paper to discussion of the interaction of these mores at the present time. A lengthier treatment of the subject would have to pay considerable attention to the historical interrelations of these sets of mores.

2. While an explanation in terms of psychopathology would account for the fact that certain persons rather than certain others are the ones to pass value judgments, we must assume humanitarian mores in order to account for the fact that anyone passes them.

3. I should not like to be understood as making a claim for the originality of this conception of social problems. My interpretation is apparently not very far from Sumner's. L. K. Frank, in the paper quoted and in some other writings, appears to have anticipated my statement almost completely. Burgess makes use of a similar conception in one of his papers. (See E. W. Burgess, "Social Planning and the Mores," *Pub. Amer. Sociol. Soc.*, 29,

No. 3, 1–18.) In numerous writings Woodard has attacked the same problem by means of a different type of analysis; I have in fact borrowed some terminology and certain interpretations from him. The Marxian conception of dialectic seems closely related to my interpretation; so, I am informed, are certain passages of Bergson. It appears, then, that a great many thinkers have converged upon what is essentially the same interpretation, a fact which should serve, at any rate, to give the interpretation a certain added cogency.

4. L. K. Frank, "Social Problems," *Amer. J. Sociol.,* 30, Jan., 1925, 465–466.

5. Kingsley Davis, "The Application of Science to Personal Relations, A Critique of the Family Clinic Idea," *Amer. Sociol. Rev.,* 1, April, 1936, 236–247.

6. For a delightful discussion of a number of these situations, see the column, *Miss Bailey Says,* edited by Gertrude Springer, in *The Survey.*

7. Frank makes his intelligent Martian say: "If it is not indelicate of me to remark, every social problem you describe seems to have the same characteristics as every other social problem, namely, the crux of the problem is to find some way of avoiding the undesirable consequences of your established laws, institutions, and social practices, without changing those established laws, etc. In other words, you appear to be seeking a way to cultivate the flower without the fruit, which, in a world of cause and effect is somewhat difficult, to say the least." (*Op. cit.,* p. 467.)

8. Lincoln Steffens, *The Autobiography of Lincoln Steffens,* pp. 780–781.

A CRITIQUE OF THE VALUE CONFLICT PERSPECTIVE

Kenneth Westhues

Westhues makes three major criticisms of the value conflict perspective. First, it is class-biased, for it simply accepts the judgments of the more powerful social classes in defining what conditions are social problems. Second, the value conflict perspective does not contribute to a theoretical understanding of society; it tells us nothing about the structure of a society, how it works, and what it produces in the way of social problems. Third, Westhues claims that the perspective does not tell us how to resolve social problems. Westhues does suggest, however, that the sociologist can overcome these three shortcomings by studying cross-culturally the systemic costs of different forms of social organization.

PLEBISCITARY APPROACHES

Even when social pathology was still a respectable name for the social disorganization approach, various sociologists were discontented with it. The organic model of society on which it was based and its obvious bias toward the existing

From Kenneth Westhues, "Social Problems as Systemic Costs," *Social Problems* 20:4 (Spring 1973), quotations from pp. 419, 422–426, 428–429. Reprinted by permission of The Society for the Study of Social Problems and the author.

order led to a search for alternative approaches. Virtually all of those that have resulted choose "public opinion," "significant groups," or "a majority of people" as the actor with respect to whom the social problem is defined. The expert analysis of the sociologist is rejected as the criterion of what is or is not a social problem; instead the sociologist studies what others say are social problems. He then applies the tools of social science to the particular problems he is given; and the sociology of social problems proceeds in the same way as if its object were education, religion, the family, or any other facet of the given society.

Fuller, both alone (1937, 1938) and with Myers (1941a, 1941b), developed one early alternative to the social disorganization approach. In his "natural history" approach, the problem is defined by "a considerable number of persons." Then the job of the sociologist is to bring sociological theory to bear on the social problem and to study the stages through which the social problem passes, from initial formulation to eventual solution. Related to Fuller's approach is Blumer's (1970) portrayal of social problems as collective behavior; he argues (in contrast to the social disorganization proponents) that social problems are not objective phenomena but rather the result of subjective definition by some collectivity.

For Fuller and Blumer, the study of social problems becomes the study of *problematization,* the processes by which various publics define and solve problems; it is a field close to that of social movements. This orientation has the effect of insulating the sociologist from the kind of political implications with which the social disorganization approach is necessarily involved. It enhances the sociologist's claim that as sociologist he is free of evaluative biases and instead only an objective student of society. The study of social problems becomes another substantive course in the curriculum. . . .

Three problems of the plebiscitary approaches may be pointed out. First is that they are without a sophisticated theory of society or of history. This is not to say that a large number of logically-interrelated and empirically-supported hypotheses have not been accumulated. It is to say only that the theory has been mostly on the micro or social psychological level. There is no theoretically and empirically sound portrayal of what kind of society the United States (or any other society) is, as compared to alternatives. For this reason the plebiscitary approaches remain within the walls of the given society and do not result in policy-relevant theory.[1]

A second problem with plebiscitary approaches is that the definition of social problems is still largely dictated by the given society (this criticism has been developed at length by Liazos, 1972). If "significant groups" are relied upon to define what the social problems are, it is most likely that these are also the powerful groups who sit in central positions of the *status quo.* If—in order to become more democratic (see Finnigan, 1971)—representative samples of the population at large are asked to decide what the social problems are, the answers obtained are largely determined by the current whims of the mass media, which are in turn greatly influenced by the public opinion makers, namely those in power. In either case, as Liazos points out, the problems studied in the sociology of social problems are those given to the field by the existing order. As a result, plebiscitary approaches share at root the same biases as the social disorganization approach.

The third problem of approaches of this kind is that students are seldom satisfied to see the social problems course redefined as a substantive area, whether collective behavior or deviance. Students expect that the social problems course will be geared toward policy-relevant or applied sociology; they want to come out of the social problems course with knowledge they can use. . . .

SYSTEMIC COSTS

[An alternative] approach to the sociology of social problems can be termed the systemic costs approach, in which problems are defined as costs of the particular form of sociocultural organization a given society manifests. This approach, like the social disorganization approach, conceptualizes the given society as an ordered structure or system. Instead, however, of defining as problems those phenomena which do not fit into or satisfy the given order, problems are defined as those qualities or aspects of the given order that do not satisfy some outside criterion. Such a criterion is the actor with respect to which the problems are defined. The question raised in this approach is fundamentally, out of all possible gratifications, what does it cost members of a given society to be gratified according to the structure of their society. What this approach calls into question is not the behavior of deviants or dysfunctional sectors of the society; rather it calls into question the society itself, and asks what one has to forego in order to live in it, and why.

This approach is suggested to some extent in the social problems text of Bredemeier and Toby (1960:x), in which they "emphasize those aspects of American society which (we believe) produce problems, and necessarily, we ignore aspects of American society which (we believe) are achievements of the human spirit." The costs (their term) which they study are withdrawal from, submission to, relentless self-reliance upon, or rejection of what Bredemeier and Toby define as the four governing principles of American society. Congruity between these governing principles and people's behavior appears as the criterion or yardstick against which American society is evaluated. Thus, even while their approach is critical of the existing order, the perceptive student using the book cannot help but conclude that if only people were not frustrated there would be no problems. Even while they adopt a critical approach, Bredemeier and Toby's yardstick is not external to American society. Hence, their analysis of social problems remains trapped within the boundaries of American society.

Another example of a systemic costs approach is Mishan's (1967) *The Costs of Economic Growth.* He calls into question the compulsion for growth and the cult of efficiency which are integral to the workings of industrial societies and points out their undesirable effects. Although an economist, he does not limit himself to studying costs that can be quantified monetarily. The costs (or problems) he reviews are "the ways in which the organized pursuit and realization of technological progress themselves act to destroy the chief ingredients that contribute to man's well-being" (1969:165). The yardstick by which Mishan evaluates industrial society is a humanistic model of man. Unfortunately, his book does not systematically describe what that model of man is.

In a similar vein is Lindenfeld's (1968:3) collection of readings, *Radical Per-*

spectives on Social Problems. This reader is grounded in the notion that "the sociologist's biases show through precisely in *what he takes for granted.*" Lindenfeld is determined not to take the existing order for granted. The criterion by which the readings evaluate it varies from the Marxist model to other utopian ideals; in some articles the criterion appears simply as moral man, who is expected to be incensed at a portrayal of the United States as a garrison society or at the existence of an "Other America." While Lindenfeld's reader does take a critical approach, it risks being perceived as a collection of potshots at America, some of them hardly social scientific, that appeal to readers who already believe America is bad.

The most useful and policy relevant form of a systemic costs approach, it seems to me, is one in which the yardstick for assessing costs (and defining problems) is another existing society, or at least one that has existed at some point in time. Careful and systematic comparative analysis of alternative societies calls one's own society into question and at the same time prevents unrealistic utopian criticisms by forcing empirical thinking.

Comparative approaches to social problems are not unknown. Eisenstadt (1964:v) has produced a reader of this kind, prefaced with a statement of the utility of a comparative approach:

> Second, the recognition that social problems are inherent in any social system, in any social organization, necessarily increases the importance of studying their manifestations and incidence in a variety of societies—be they primitive, historical, modernizing, or modern—and analyzing them in terms of these social structures.

Unfortunately, Eisenstadt limits his comparative approach largely to the conventional list of popularly regarded social problems: suicide, alcoholism, mental illness, family stability, etc. While a reader cannot be expected to offer a theoretically integrated framework, Eisenstadt's book does suggest the need for such frameworks for comparative analysis. The same can be said for Gerson's (1969) reader in social problems; while it takes a cross-cultural approach, its list of problems is quite conventional.

A good, albeit limited, example of a systemic costs approach is Faunce's (1968) *Problems of an Industrial Society.* The principal cost of industrial society on which Faunce concentrates is worker alienation. In the beginning of his book he analyzes the social structure of a Guatemalan peasant society, and later on he systematically compares craft production systems with mechanized and automated production systems. In this way he uses empirically observable alternative societies to evaluate the structure of work and production in modern industrial societies.

The matter of which problems should be chosen for study in a social problems class or for research priority outside the classroom is up to the sociologist himself in the systemic costs approach. Depending on which alternative society he might choose as the yardstick by which to measure costs, virtually any aspect of the given society can be regarded as a cost or problem. In choosing which costs or problems to examine, the sociologist may be aware of what the major problems are according to public opinion, but he may also decide upon problems not currently in the public vocabulary. He may, as it were, make students and readers aware of what they are missing and then explain with careful analytic techniques why they, in this particular society, are missing it.

The political implication of the systemic costs approach is social change. Through a theoretically integrated comparative analysis of his own and other societies, the students come to understand how variation in culture and social structure accounts for variation in the social problems experienced. Such a theory, provided it has an empirical basis, lends itself to effective social action in the manipulation of the cultural and structural variables which govern the particular area studied.[2] To the extent that students are given such a theory they are given power. Even if, by virtue of their social position, they lack the power to manipulate the variables that cause the particular social problem, at least they know that the problems are not inevitable or solvable only by the manipulation of personality variables. Such knowledge is itself a form of power, just as ignorance of social process is a form of powerlessness. . . .

CONCLUSION

A month or two before the beginning of each semester, literally thousands of sociologists have to choose what they will teach in their social problems classes. . . .

The choice is made to a great extent according to how one views the given society at present and the sociologist's role within it. If the given society is seen as good, and if the sociologist sees himself like Nisbet (1966:16) as one "interested in making the protection of society his first responsibility," then the social disorganization approach (or one of its surrogates) will be chosen. If, whatever the evaluation of the given society, the role of sociologist is seen as one removed from the arena of public policy, then one of the plebiscitary approaches can be taken. If, finally, society is seen as in need of structural change, and the sociologist as one whose professional expertise can be used for that purpose, then the systemic costs approach is appropriate.

It is true that many critical sociologists, especially in the United States, have little interest in comparative research. Cannot their evaluation of given structures by the yardstick of utopian models or native deviant subcultures or the given society's stated ideology result in progressive and change-oriented thinking? The answer is certainly yes. The question, however, is whether this means is most effective. Utopian models risk on the one hand being too visionary to put into practice; on the other hand, utopian models which find their way into practice tend to be rather nasty and oppressive. With regard to the deviant subcultures, the problem is that they have been born out of reaction to the dominant order and are likely to be greatly conditioned by its way of doing things. To rely on deviant reactions for new ideas may result in ideas which appear much newer than they are. Evaluation of the given society by the yardstick of its own ideology may indeed disclose grievous problems, but why should the sociologist restrict his yardstick to a single society when he has a worldful to choose from? . . .

The reason why American sociologists in particular, and others in general, tend to limit themselves to their own society is that sociologists, like everybody else, internalize the values of their society and learn to take them for granted.

The task of unlearning is not only the demand of personal growth but of good sociology and particularly of sociology that would lead to structural change. In the case of American sociologists, this is an even greater problem, since the careers of almost all American sociologists have been developed during the period of ascendancy of the United States in the international community. American culture, of which American sociologists are a part, has grown to take for granted the contention of *Fortune* magazine in 1940, "less by definition than by achievement, the United States is the greatest nation on earth." Given such a belief, American sociologists could scarcely need cross-cultural analyses of the kind that would call their own system into question: what could possibly be learned? Now that the knowledge has become more common, even within the United States, that this country is not in a class apart from all others, but rather lags behind on a range of indices, perhaps a comparative, systemic costs approach to the study of social problems will gain in popularity.[3] . . .

Notes

1. This criticism has been developed at length against Gouldner's moralism by Bredemeier (1971). The point is only that liberal values cannot substitute for careful societal theory. Becker (1963), for example, attributes American anti-marijuana legislation largely to the "moral entrepreneurship" of Harry Anslinger, one-time head of the Federal Narcotics Bureau. Becker's social-psychological explanation is happily biased toward the pot-smoker, but the sympathetic reader is left with no policy conclusion except to try to get rid of Harry Anslinger. Dickson (1968), on the other hand, has offered an organizational analysis to explain the anti-marijuana legislation. Not only is his analysis more convincing, it is grounded in macro-level theory. The reader is left with some insight into how bureaucratic societies function; he learns something about the *structure* of his society, not just about personalities within it.

2. This is not to say that the systemic costs approach limits its analysis to variables that are manipulable—to applied sociology in the sense in which Gouldner (1957) has used the term. A comprehensive theory includes variables of both kinds, theoretical or pure, manipulable or applied. The role of the social problems teacher, as I see it, is to present comprehensive theory, realizing at the same time that not all the variables in the theory will be relevant for political action.

3. It is interesting that two prominent "left-wing" sociologists, Howard Becker and Irving L. Horowitz, in a 1972 article on the differences between radical political positions and radical sociological research, still fail to suggest the need for comparative analysis of the United States with other sociocultural systems. Again and again they write of "society" as if the United States were the only one or as if all societies were alike. They propose, for example, studying communal living groups from a sympathetic point of view, while they seem unaware that other societies have produced forms of family and kinship which the United States might possibly find instructive, perhaps even more instructive than the deviant life-styles of its own sons and daughters. The fact that Horowitz has himself done considerable research outside the United States, it may also be noted, illustrates the fact that cross-cultural research does not necessarily lead to comparative frameworks that question the structure of one's own society.

References

Becker, Howard. 1963. *Outsiders: Studies in the Sociology of Deviance.* Glencoe: Free Press.

Blumer, Herbert. 1970. "Social problems as collective behavior." *Social Problems* 18 (Winter): 298–306.

Bredemeier, Harry C. 1971. "Banfield, Gouldner, and 'Social Problems'." *Social Problems* 18 (Spring): 554–568.

———— and Jackson Toby. 1960. *Social Problems in America.* New York: John Wiley and Sons.

Dickson, Donald. 1968. "Bureaucracy and morality: An organizational perspective on a moral crusade." *Social Problems* 16 (Fall): 143–156.

Eisenstadt, S. N. (ed.). 1964. *Comparative Social Problems.* New York: Free Press.

Faunce, William A. 1968. *Problems of an Industrial Society.* New York: McGraw-Hill.

Finnigan, B. W. 1971. "The relevance of sociological theory to Canadian social problems," paper presented at the Annual Meeting of the Western Association for Sociology and Anthropology, Calgary.

Fuller, Richard C. 1937. "Sociological theory and social problems." *Social Forces* 15 (May): 496–502.

———— 1938. "The problem of teaching social problems." *American Journal of Sociology* 44 (November): 415–435.

Fuller, Richard C. and Richard R. Myers. 1941a. "The natural history of a social problem." *American Sociological Review* 6 (June): 320–328.

———— 1941b. "Some aspects of a theory of social problems." *American Sociological Review* 6 (February): 24–32.

Gerson, Walter M. (ed.). 1969. *Social Problems in a Changing World.* New York: Thomas Y. Crowell.

Gouldner, Alvin W. 1957. "Theoretical requirements of the applied social sciences." *American Sociological Review* 22 (February): 92–102.

Liazos, Alexander. 1972. "The poverty of the sociology of deviance: Nuts, sluts and preverts." *Social Problems* 20 (Summer): 103–120.

Lindenfeld, Frank (ed.). 1968. *Radical Perspectives on Social Problems.* New York: Macmillan.

Mishan, E. J. 1967. *The Costs of Economic Growth.* Middlesex: Penguin.

Nisbet, Robert A. 1966. "The study of social problems," pp. 1–25 in R. K. Merton and R. A. Nisbet (eds.), *Contemporary Social Problems.* New York: Harcourt Brace and World.

Questions for Discussion

1. What type of social problem would Fuller and Myers consider the issue of equal opportunity for women to be? Why? Discuss the natural history of this problem.

2. What are the similarities between the natural history of the contemporary women's rights issue and the natural history of present-day racial problems? Discuss whether "symbolic struggles" play a role in these social problems?

3. What are the "organizational mores" involved in the problems of equal opportunity for women and for African-Americans? How do organizational mores contribute to these problems? How do humanitarian mores "cause" these social problems?

4. Westhues presents three basic criticisms of the value conflict approach. Do you agree that these features are necessarily characteristic of the value conflict approach? Why or why not? Do you think these features are necessarily weaknesses? Why or why not? What perspective does Westhues employ? Do you question anything he has to say about the superiority of the systemic approach?

Selected References

Becker, Howard S., ed. *Social Problems: A Modern Approach.* New York: Wiley, 1966, pp. 1–31.

A useful statement that succinctly presents the Fuller–Myers approach in terms of symbolic interaction. Most useful for people who subscribe to the value conflict approach.

Bernard, Thomas J. *The Cycle of Juvenile Justice.* New York: Oxford University Press, 1992.

Throughout U.S. history, according to Bernard, official responses to juvenile delinquency have cycled between harsh punishment and lenient treatment. The value conflict between justice and treatment personnel, Bernard says, accounts for the cycle.

Chambliss, William J., ed., *Problems of Industrial Society.* Reading, MA: Addison-Wesley, 1973.

A collection of social problems readings organized around the value conflict perspective.

Collins, Randall. *Conflict Sociology: Toward an Explanatory Science.* New York: Academic Press, 1974.

An important theoretical work that spells out the general conditions under which conflicts among groups with divergent interests and values produce social conditions that later give rise to serious social problems.

Cuber, John F., William F. Kenkel, and Robert A. Harper. *Problems of American Society: Values in Conflict.* 4th ed. New York: Holt, Rinehart and Winston, 1964.

This textbook first states the Fuller–Myers position, and then goes on to examine a series of social problems from this point of view.

Dahrendorf, Ralf. *Class and Class Conflict in Industrial Society.* Stanford, CA: Stanford University Press, 1959.

An important statement of conflict theory.

Green, Arnold W. *Social Problems: Arena of Conflict.* New York: McGraw-Hill, 1975.

A textbook that examines several different types of social problems from the value conflict perspective.

Kobrin, Solomon. "The Conflict of Values in Delinquency Areas." *American Sociological Review* 16 (1951): 653–61.

As Fuller originally conceived of the value-conflict perspective, it was conflict between different interest groups that gave rise to social problems. However, Kobrin advances the argument that the most aggressive and persistent juvenile delinquents are those who have internalized both middle-class values and delinquent values. The degree of their delinquency turns out to be proportional to their adoption of middle-class values and their frustration at not achieving legitimate middle-class status.

Lemert, Edwin M. "Is There a Natural History of Social Problems?" *American Sociological Review* 16 (April 1951): 217–23.

An empirical test of Fuller's and Myers's three stages in the natural history of social problems—awareness, policy formation, and reform. Based on case histories of California trailer camps, interviews with public officials, and newspaper items and Letters-to-the-

Editor regarding trailer camps, Lemert concludes that the Fuller–Meyers formulation is not applicable to the trailer-camp situation in California cities.

Lemert, Edwin M. "Social Problems." In *International Encyclopedia of Social Sciences*, ed. David L. Sills. New York: Macmillan and The Free Press, 1968, vol. 14, pp. 452–59.

A scholarly review of the various strands of thought that have been interwoven in the sociological analysis of social problems. Lemert concludes that analysis of such problems can be objective only if the analysts are aware of their values and make them explicit. He also concludes that values are central to the development and resolution of problems.

McCaghy, Charles H. *Deviant Behavior: Crime, Conflict, and Interest Groups.* New York: Macmillan, 1982.

McCaghy analyzes various forms of deviance by means of the interest group conflict perspective; these include crimes against persons and property, assaults against children and spouses, deviance with regard to organizations, drug use, mental disorders, prostitution, and homosexuality.

Schur, Edwin M. "Recent Social Problems Texts: An Essay-Review." *Social Problems* 10 (Winter 1963): 287–93.

With Mills's criticisms in mind, Schur examines eleven recent textbooks. He shows that a distinctively sociological approach to social problems has emerged since the publication of Mills's article. More general sociological theory has been applied to analyzing social problems, and most social problems textbooks combine theory and data in a sophisticated manner. Schur argues, though, that sociologists should take a value position on social problems, drawing on their own discipline for factual support.

5/DEVIANT BEHAVIOR

From World War I until 1954, the social disorganization perspective dominated sociological thought regarding social problems. And during these years, sociology, like the larger society, underwent a number of changes, becoming increasingly complex. Departments of sociology expanded, concepts multiplied, theoretical systems matured, and research became a prime objective. Yet despite overall conceptual developments, social disorganization remained the dominant perspective for the study of social problems. Competitors emerged only to be defeated or incorporated into the framework of social disorganization, and the disorganization perspective continued to dominate the textbooks on social problems.[1]

Why did the social disorganization perspective enjoy such long-lived popularity? First, certain features of the perspective helped to sustain it. It was systematic; it represented the best attempt at that time to determine a special subject matter for sociology; and it appeared to be faithful to the developing norms of science. Another reason was textbook lag. The textbook is one vehicle for the transmission of a discipline's ideas and findings. Sifting through and organizing them into a comprehensible and useful book is a lengthy process, especially in the early stages of a discipline's development. Then, once in print, a textbook and a perspective can have a long life.

Eventually, however, other factors undermined the popularity of the social disorganization perspective. As sociology became a channel for social mobility, the number of sociologists greatly increased.[2] And as the society became more affluent,

---

1. Fuller argued in 1937 that textbooks on social problems usually took one of two approaches—to be conceptual or to be community-oriented. Conceptual textbooks either used a battery of sociological concepts or tried to fit all problems under just one concept. Community-oriented textbooks showed how different kinds of problems affected the community. Conceptual textbooks labored more on behalf of sociology, while community-oriented textbooks sought to perform a service for society. Yet, in both approaches, the disorganization perspective remained dominant. Thus, conceptual textbooks—whether eclectic or monistic—made social disorganization the key concept, usually explicitly. Disorganization was also the key concept in community-oriented textbooks, though this was more often implicit than explicit.

Perhaps the most influential textbook during these years was Mabel Elliott and Francis Merrill, *Social Disorganization* (New York: Harper, 1931). This book began as a single-concept book, but later editions were revised to include a developing battery of sociological concepts.

2. In 1935, for example, the American Sociological Association began with a membership of 1,169. By 1945, membership had grown only slightly to 1,309. In the next decade, however, membership

it could afford more support for research. These factors were important in promoting an increase in social research that, in turn, was important in prompting a reformulation of the social disorganization perspective. This is discussed in more detail below.

THE REFOCUSING OF SOCIOLOGICAL THOUGHT

As more and more sociologists were trained, two schools of sociological thought developed. One school, centered at Harvard University, focused primarily on social structure. The other school, centered at the University of Chicago, emphasized social process. Both the Harvard and the Chicago sociologists recognized the importance of studying social problems in order to develop mature and systematic sociological theory. Controversy arose, however, over the correct approach to the study of social problems. The deviant behavior perspective has roots in both these sociological traditions. In order to understand how it developed, let us briefly review the character of sociology in each of these great universities.

Sociology at Harvard had a strongly theoretical bent. The work of classic European sociologists, such as Emile Durkheim, Max Weber, and Vilfredo Pareto, were studied. In addition, Talcott Parsons and some of his students developed a broad theoretical perspective that later came to be known as structural-functionalism, a theoretical orientation that, according to many, dominated the next three decades of American sociology.[3]

At Chicago, by contrast, more sociologists emphasized description than grand theory. Throughout the 1920s and early 1930s, Chicago faculty and students treated the city of Chicago as a natural laboratory for their studies.[4] Books on the hobo, the Gold Coast and the slum, the ghetto, the taxi dance hall, the hotel, mental disorders, and juvenile delinquency appeared in rapid succession.

Although the Chicago sociologists were more concerned with describing the facts than with developing broader theories, this department did develop the concentric zone theory of urban development, a theory that predicted different rates of social disorganization in different sectors of the city.[5] Empirical studies found rates of juvenile delinquency and certain mental disorders to be consistent with this theory,[6] and numerous sociologists conducted other studies correlating various rates of deviance with census tracts or other ecological properties.

In 1950, however, a famous article pointed out that just because the rates of several characteristics are higher in some geographic areas than in others, one cannot conclude from this that the same people always manifest these various char-

increased by 240 percent—reaching 4,454 in 1955. (Since then, the association has continued to grow, with 8,892 members in 1965, 12,300 members in 1988, and approximately 13,000 members in 2001.)

3. For one important example, see Talcott Parsons, *The Social System* (Glencoe, IL: Free Press, 1951).

4. For an informal history of the Chicago department, see Robert E. L. Faris, *Chicago Sociology 1920–1932* (San Francisco: Chandler, 1967).

5. Robert E. Park, Ernest W. Burgess, and Roderick D. McKenzie, *The City* (Chicago: University of Chicago Press, 1925).

6. Clifford R. Shaw, with the collaboration of Harvey Zorbaugh, Henry D. McKay, and Leonard S. Cottrell, *Delinquency Areas: A Study of the Geographical Distribution of School Truants, Juvenile Delinquents, and Adult Offenders in Chicago* (Chicago: University of Chicago Press, 1929); Robert E. L. Faris and H. Warren Dunham, *Mental Disorders in Urban Areas: An Ecological Study of Schizophrenia and Other Psychoses* (Chicago: University of Chicago Press, 1939).

acteristics.[7] (For example, a census tract may have a large proportion of immigrants and a high rate of crime, but it does not necessarily follow that immigrants are more likely to be committing these crimes.) Recognition of the fact that individual correlations cannot be deduced from collective correlations helped to foster the deviant behavior perspective. Finding the conceptualizations of the disorganization perspective too broad for research on individuals, sociologists developed the deviant behavior perspective to discover why some people undertake a deviant line of conduct while others do not. As the deviant behavior perspective developed, the social disorganization approach became confined more to the discussion of social units than to the analysis of the behavior of individual persons.[8]

ROOTS IN CLASSICAL THEORY

Before examining the development of the deviant behavior perspective from these two traditions, a few words about its theoretical roots are in order. As numerous scholars in the history of science have pointed out, theory is often years ahead of its time. Theory must sometimes wait several decades before anyone develops the methodology and/or technology necessary to test its implications. Testing must sometimes await translation of the theory into another language, or the development of a scientific point of view with which later generations can grasp the essentials of the theory and formulate ways of testing, revising, extending, and generalizing it.

All this is true for the concept of anomie, which first appeared in Emile Durkheim's study of suicide, published in France in 1897. This classic work was not translated into English until 1951.[9] Thus, more than fifty years passed before several variations on this theory began to produce an impressive and growing list of empirical studies testing it in a number of problem areas.

Durkheim formulated a typology of suicide that concentrated on the nature of the social bond. He called one type of suicide egoistic suicide. When people have weak social integration, there is little to deter them from taking their lives when stress arises. For example, responsibility to his family may deter a married man from committing suicide, while an unmarried man does not have this bond to restrain him. He called a second type of suicide altruistic suicide. When people have something positive to die for because of intense attachments to primary groups and strong social integration, they can be induced to sacrifice their lives—for example, suicide bombers. Egoistic and altruistic suicides reflect the two poles of extremely weak social integration and attachment, and extremely strong social integration and attachment, respectively. A third type of suicide—anomic suicide—reflects something else. This type of suicide occurs in response to sudden changes—for example, sudden wealth or sudden poverty. Others had noticed that suicide rates increase during times of economic hardship, but Durkheim found that suicide rates also increase during pe-

7. The article that first pointed out the "fallacy" of ecological correlations was W. S. Robinson, "Ecological Correlations and the Behavior of Individuals," *American Sociological Review* 15 (June 1950): 351–57.

8. See, for example, Robert K. Merton and Robert Nisbet, eds., *Contemporary Social Problems: An Introduction to the Sociology of Deviant Behavior and Social Disorganization,* 3rd ed. (New York: Harcourt Brace Jovanovich, 1971); Albert K. Cohen, "The Study of Social Disorganization and Deviant Behavior," in *Sociology Today,* ed. Robert K. Merton, Leonard Broom, and Leonard S. Coltrell, Jr. (New York: Basic Books, 1959).

9. Emile Durkheim, *Le Suicide: Etude de Sociologie* (Paris: Felix Alcan, 1897). The American edition is Emile Durkheim, *Suicide: A Study in Sociology,* trans. John A. Spaulding and George Simpson (Glencoe, IL: Free Press, 1951).

riods of increasing prosperity. Durkheim saw these suicides as a sign of anomie (that is, normlessness). During sudden prosperity, Durkheim reasoned, the traditional rules that ordinarily limit people break down, and people find it hard to put limits on themselves. They do not know what limits to accept; they want more and more and are never satisfied. The result is frustration that may lead to suicide. During sudden poverty, on the contrary, people can feel demoralized if they do not accept such changes as just, and this may also lead to suicide.

THE DEVELOPMENT OF ANOMIE THEORY

In 1938, Robert K. Merton (a Harvard student of Parsons) published an extremely important paper entitled "Social Structure and Anomie."[10] Developing one line of Durkheim's theory, Merton argued that anomie could be the normal state of affairs for persons in certain segments of society when cultural goals (for example, financial success) are overemphasized and legitimate opportunities to achieve those goals are blocked. Merton then theorized that this disjunction between legitimate means and cultural goals produces four types of deviance: *innovation,* where new, usually illicit means are adopted to achieve the goals; *ritualism,* where people renounce the goals, only to overemphasize the means; *retreatism,* where they renounce both cultural goals and institutionalized norms; and *rebellion,* where they wish to replace the established system of goals and means with another system.

Several points are important here. First, this is a general theory applicable to many different social problems. For instance, white-collar crime, organized rackets, vice, cheating on exams, or doping horses or athletes can reflect innovation; psychosis, drug addiction, and Skid Row can reflect retreatism.

Second, given Americans' emphasis on the goal of success, anomie and some forms of deviant behavior may be construed as *normal* responses to abnormal situations (rather than as abnormal or "sick" responses). As such, no assumptions about biological or psychological abnormalities are required to explain the behavior.

Third, different segments of the population (America's lower classes, Merton suggested) have higher rates of deviance, presumably because the goals of success are held out for all to strive for, but the legitimate means of attaining them are not available to everyone. Thus, if people want things they cannot afford, they may steal.

Merton's anomie theory has become one of the two most powerful influences on the development of the deviant behavior perspective, and its influence grew as American sociologists began cultivating specialties. Merton's paper inspired ten pieces of empirical research between 1940 and 1944; and between 1955 and 1964, no fewer than sixty-four studies based on Merton's theory appeared in the sociological literature.[11]

THE DEVELOPMENT OF DIFFERENTIAL ASSOCIATION THEORY

The other profound influence on the development of the deviant behavior perspective was that of Edwin H. Sutherland, of the University of Chicago. Sutherland first published his deceptively simple theory of differential association in 1939.[12] Following

10. Robert K. Merton, "Social Structure and Anomie," *American Sociological Review* 3 (October 1938): 672–82.

11. See Robert K. Merton, "Anomie, Anomia, and Social Interaction," in *Anomie and Deviant Behavior: A Discussion and Critique,* ed. Marshall B. Clinard (New York: Free Press, 1964), p. 216.

12. Edwin H. Sutherland, *Principles of Criminology* (Philadelphia: Lippincott, 1939), pp. 4–9.

Thomas and Znaniecki, he thought social disorganization played an important role in the production of deviance. In his work, however, Sutherland gave greater attention to the social process by which a person becomes deviant than to the social structural conditions that promote deviance. In his theory of differential association, Sutherland maintained that people learn deviant behavior(s) in primary groups. He identified four dimensions of contact with deviant and nondeviant patterns (frequency, duration, priority, and intensity), and he set forth seven propositions regarding such learning.

Later sociologists came to see that the differential association theory could be considered to be a complement to the anomie theory. Both theories extended Durkheim's axiom that deviant behavior is to be expected as a natural part of social life.[13] Merton's theory could explain why rates of deviant behavior are higher in some sectors of the society than in others; it could not, however, explain why some persons in these sectors engage in such acts, while others do not. Sutherland's theory, because it is essentially a theory based on social interaction, is silent on the question of rates but can explain why some people, but not others, commit deviant acts.

The first publication to synthesize anomie theory and differential association theory was by Albert Cohen in 1955.[14] In his theory of the development of the delinquent subculture, Cohen maintained that working-class boys faced a situation of anomie in middle-class school systems. As a result, they came together and devised a culture that was antithetical to middle-class values. Through the process of differential association, Cohen argued, they transmitted a set of norms that required the violation of legitimate codes, if only to achieve and maintain status in the gang.

In 1960, Richard Cloward and Lloyd Ohlin provided another synthesis of anomie theory and differential association theory.[15] They suggested that *illegitimate* opportunity structures must also be considered, and that different types of delinquent subcultures arise in response to the presence or absence of illegitimate as well as legitimate opportunities. This formulation is exceedingly important for devising solutions to social problems. Opportunity theory was the basis for the War on Poverty and most of the community action programs that appeared in the 1960s.

The first textbook written from the deviant behavior perspective appeared in 1957.[16] This book, *Sociology of Deviant Behavior* by Marshall Clinard, provided the first codification of the deviant behavior perspective. It called attention to the array of factors involved in the social production of deviant behavior, and while it drew heavily on Merton's and Sutherland's theories, other points of view were not neglected. Soon after this book appeared, social problems courses began to be redefined. Numerous courses, once called either "Social Problems" or "Social Disorganization," were renamed "Sociology of Deviant Behavior." This renaming presented a new question: Does the term "deviant behavior" denote all social problems or only some of them? For example, Clinard's book includes chapters on family maladjustment, old age, minority groups, and discrimination and prejudice. Not everyone would agree that these problems fall under the rubric "deviant behavior."

Another question that arose was this: If deviant behavior does not include all

---

13. For the contributions of both structural-functional theory and the Chicago school to naturalism in American sociology, see David Matza, *Becoming Deviant* (Englewood Cliffs, N.J.: Prentice-Hall, 1969).

14. Albert K. Cohen, *Delinquent Boys: The Culture of the Gang* (Glencoe, IL.: Free Press, 1955).

15. Richard A. Cloward and Lloyd E. Ohlin, *Delinquency and Opportunity: A Theory of Delinquent Gangs* (New York: Free Press, 1960).

16. Marshall B. Clinard, *Sociology of Deviant Behavior* (New York: Holt, Rinehart and Winston, 1957).

social problems, then what *is* its relationship to other types of problems—for example, problems of social disorganization? To Merton, Sutherland, and their followers, deviant behavior and social disorganization were separate and distinct; nonetheless, they tended to see each as causing the other.

Finally, since the deviant behavior perspective came into its own, sociologists have become aware of the difficulty of researching the causes of deviant behavior. As a result, this perspective has turned increasingly away from the study of etiology and toward the study of deviant behavior systems (which describe the characteristic social features of the particular deviant activity) and of social control (see the "Solutions" section below).

CHARACTERISTICS OF THE DEVIANT BEHAVIOR PERSPECTIVE

The key characteristics of the deviant behavior perspective are as follows:

Definition.   Social problems reflect violations of normative expectations. Behavior or situations that depart from norms are deviant.

Causes.   The cause of deviant behavior lies in inappropriate socialization—for example, when the learning of deviant ways is not outweighed by the learning of nondeviant ways. This socialization is viewed as taking place within the context of primary group relations.

Conditions.   Restricted opportunities for learning so-called conventional ways, increased opportunities for learning deviant ways, restricted opportunities for achieving legitimate goals, a feeling of stress, and access to a deviant mode of relief are all important background conditions for the evolution of deviant patterns of behavior.

Consequences.   The deviant behavior perspective postulates a variety of consequences. Many kinds of deviant behavior are costly to society. One outcome, for example, is the firm establishment of illegitimate social worlds. In addition, however, some observable deviant behavior is useful, if only because it establishes negative role models showing the kinds of behavior that will be punished.

Solutions.   The principal solution for deviant behavior is resocialization, and the best way to resocialize is to increase meaningful primary group contact with legitimate patterns of behavior and reduce meaningful primary group contact with illegitimate patterns of behavior. At the same time, the opportunity structure must be opened in order to alleviate the strains that motivate people to behave in unacceptable ways. As legitimate opportunities increase, socially problematic behavior should decrease.

SUMMARY AND CONCLUSION

The social disorganization perspective dominated sociological thought on social problems during the second and third periods of American sociology—that is, from the end of World War I until the mid-1950s. During the third period, however, more and more sociologists were trained in scientific analysis, more and more research was conducted, and sociologists became increasingly concerned with integrating theory and research.

Some sociologists focused on social structure, while others concentrated on social process, and two traditions of sociological thought developed around this cleavage. The Harvard school centered on structure; the Chicago school, on process. From the former came Merton's anomie theory as a way of explaining rates of deviant behavior. From the latter came Sutherland's theory of differential association as a way of explaining how people learn deviant patterns. When these two conceptions were fused, the perspective of deviant behavior emerged.

The main postulate in this perspective is that the propensity for deviant behavior is socially learned within the context of the primary group. Its cause, broadly speaking, is inappropriate socialization. Its conditions are blocked opportunities, stress, access to a deviant mode of relief, and deviant role models. Its consequences are sometimes beneficial to society. And its solutions lie in redistributed access to opportunity, increased primary relations with legitimate role models, and reduction (if not complete elimination) of opportunities and contacts with deviant role models.

ROBERT MERTON: ANOMIE AND SOCIAL STRUCTURE

Marshall B. Clinard

In this excerpt, Clinard reviews Merton's anomie theory and discusses how it links deviant behavior to social structure. Material success is a highly valued goal in America, but the legitimate avenues for attaining this goal are unavailable to lower-class people. This discrepancy places lower-class people in a frustrating position that may lead psychologically normal people to engage in deviant behavior. Clinard reviews the several ways in which Merton says people may adapt to this disjunction between cultural goals and social structural opportunities. These adaptations are conformity, ritualism, rebellion, innovation, and retreatism.

. . . In the essay "Social Structure and Anomie," which first appeared in 1938, was revised in 1949, and was further extended eight years later, Robert Merton set forth his now well known social and cultural explanation of deviant behavior in terms of anomie.[1] The significance for sociology of this formulation has been great, one writer stating: "Without any doubt, this body of ideas, which has come to be known as 'anomic' theory, has been the most influential single formulation in the sociology of deviance in the last 25 years, and Merton's paper, in its original and revised versions, is possibly the most frequently quoted single paper in modern sociology."[2]

While derived from Durkheim's concept of anomie, Merton's formulation was at the same time both broader in orientation and more specific in application. Durkheim's view that a situation of normlessness may arise from a clash of aspirations and a breakdown of regulatory norms was reformulated into a general principle that "social structures exert a definite pressure upon certain persons in the society to engage in nonconforming rather than conforming conduct."[3] Merton emphasized normative structures and, like Durkheim, viewed behavior such as crime as a "normal" response to given social situations: pressures toward deviation in a society could be such that forms of deviant behavior were psychologically as normal as conformist behavior.

While Durkheim confined his application of anomie chiefly to suicide, Merton sought to explain not only suicide but crime, delinquency, mental disorder, alcoholism, drug addiction, and many other phenomena.[4]

Merton's definition of deviant behavior was never very clear in his two basic

From Marshall B. Clinard, *Anomie and Deviant Behavior*, pp. 10–21. Copyright © 1964 by The Free Press of Glencoe, a division of The Macmillan Company. Reprinted by permission of the publisher.

essays. In a later writing he said that it "refers to conduct that departs significantly from the norms set for people in their social statuses . . . [and] must be related to the norms that are socially defined as appropriate and morally binding for people occupying various statuses."[5]

Unlike Durkheim, Merton did not consider man's biological nature to be important in explaining deviation: what Durkheim considered the innate desires of man, such as ambition to achieve unattainable objectives, Merton felt were induced by the social structure. With an eye to the Freudians, he pointed out that man is not contending with society "in an unceasing war between biological impulse and social restraint. The image of man as an untamed bundle of impulses begins to look more like a caricature than a portrait."[6] Even if one were to grant some role to biological impulses, there still remained the question of "why it is that the frequency of deviant behavior varies within different social structures and how it happens that the deviations have different shapes and patterns in different social structures."[7]

In explaining anomie and deviant behavior, Merton therefore concentrated not on the individual but on the social order. He set what he admitted to be an arbitrary dichotomy between cultural goals and the institutional means to achieve these goals. For analytical purposes he first divided social reality into cultural structures, or culture, and social structure, or society. The cultural structure is "that organized set of normative values governing behavior which is common to members of a designated society or group."[8] The other element, the social structure, consists of institutional norms which define and regulate the acceptable mode of reaching these goals. This represents an "organized set of social relationships in which members of the society or social groups are variously implicated."[9]

Cultural goals and institutionalized norms do not bear a constant relation to one another, for "the cultural emphasis placed upon certain goals varies independently of the degree of emphasis upon institutionalized means."[10] There can be many dominant success goals—accumulation of wealth, scientific productivity, religious orthodoxy, and others—which may clash with the means open to those who are socially disadvantaged in the competitive race for achievement.[11] In fact, any cultural goal which is greatly emphasized in a society is likely to affect institutionalized means. Goals may take precedence at one time over the institutionally prescribed means to achieve them. On the other hand, one can have situations where sheer conformity becomes a central value; the original purpose of the cultural goals becomes forgotten and the institutional means become a ritual to be observed.[12] Actually, an effective equilibrium between these two phases of a society is usually maintained as long as individuals secure satisfactions from conforming to both cultural goals and institutional means.

The emphasis on a disequilibrium between cultural goals and institutional norms in a society is clear in Merton's definition. Anomie is "conceived as a breakdown in the cultural structure, occurring particularly when there is an acute disjunction between cultural norms and goals and the social structured capacities of members of the group to act in accord with them."[13] He goes on to add that "cultural values may help to produce behavior which is at odds with the mandates of the values themselves."[14] The malintegration of culture and social structure, one preventing what the other encourages, can lead to a breakdown of the norms and the development of a situation of normlessness.[15]

Merton assumes that rates of deviant behavior within a given society vary by social class, ethnic or racial status, and other characteristics. His explanation of deviant behavior hinges, then, on the validity of the proposition that the *strain toward anomie,* i.e., the inability to achieve the goals of society by available means, will be differentially distributed through a social system, and that different modes of deviant adaptation will be concentrated in varying social strata. The distribution of deviant behavior will depend on the accessibility of legitimate means to secure the goals and the degree of assimilation of goals and norms by the different social strata of society. Not all of those subject to pressures to achieve goals become deviant. "The theory only holds that those located in places in the social structure which are particularly exposed to such stresses are more likely than others to exhibit deviant behavior."[16] Those who conform despite stresses do so because alternative cultural goals are available to provide a basis for stabilizing the social and cultural systems. Schematically the relation of anomie to social structure can be summarized in this way:

1. *Exposure* to the cultural goal and norms regulating behavior oriented toward the goal.
2. *Acceptance* of the goal or norms as moral mandates and internalized values.
3. *Relative accessibility to the goal:* life chances in the opportunity structure.
4. *The degree of discrepancy* between the accepted goal and its accessibility.
5. *The degree of anomie.*
6. *The rates of deviant behavior* of the various types set out in the typology of modes of adaptation.[17]

In his writings, he confined his analysis of deviant behavior to those societies like the American, where certain goals tend to be stressed without a corresponding emphasis on institutional procedures to obtain them. American culture is characterized by great emphasis on the accumulation of wealth as a success symbol without a corresponding emphasis on using legitimate means to march toward this goal.[18] "The culture may be such as to lead individuals to center their emotional convictions upon the complex of culturally acclaimed ends, with far less emotional support for prescribed methods of reaching out for these ends. . . . In this context, the sole significant question becomes 'Which of the available procedures is most efficient in netting the culturally approved value?' "[19]

At the other extreme from American society on the continuum are those societies where the emphasis is on goals which have been largely subordinated to institutional means and lack their original meaning, and where conformity has become an end in itself. Other, more integrated societies fall between these two types of "malintegrated cultures" where goals and means to achieve them are in some sort of rough balance.

It is important to recognize from Merton's analysis that the high frequency of deviant behavior among certain classes in American society cannot be explained by a lack of opportunity alone or by an exaggerated emphasis on a pecuniary value nexus. A more rigid class structure, such as a caste system, might restrict opportunities to achieve such goals even more, without resultant deviant behavior. It is the set of equalitarian beliefs in American society, stressing the opportunity for economic affluence and social ascent for all of its members, which makes for the difference.

As Merton points out, however, these are idealized goals: the same proportion of persons in all social classes does not internalize them. Since the number of persons in each of the social classes varies considerably, it is important to distinguish between absolute numbers and relative proportion. Only a substantial number or "a number sufficiently large to result in a more frequent *disjunction* between goals and opportunity among the lower-class strata than among the upper-class strata" need to be goal-oriented.[20] It is the restriction on the use of approved means for a considerable part of the population that is crucial to the discussion of adaptations which follows.

> It is only when a system of cultural values extols, virtually above all else, certain *common* success-goals *for the population at large* while the social structure rigorously restricts or completely closes access to approved modes of reaching these goals *for a considerable part of the same population,* that deviant behavior ensues on a large scale.[21]

The discussion so far has dealt, in general, with anomie: it has not explained the origin of particular forms of deviant behavior. This brings us to one of the perhaps most important and certainly most intriguing parts of Merton's theory, the ways in which a person can adapt to a situation where *legitimate* means to reach a goal are not available to him.

ADAPTATIONS

There are five types of individual adaptations to achieve culturally prescribed goals of success open to those who occupy different positions in the social structure. One is conformity; the other are the deviant adaptations of ritualism, rebellion, innovation, and retreatism. None of these adaptations, as Merton points out, is deliberately selected by the individual or is utilitarian, but rather, since all arise from strains in the social system, they can be assumed to have a degree of spontaneity behind them. The paradigm is the following.

A Typology of Modes of Individual Adaptation[22]

Modes of adaptation	Cultural goals	Institutionalized means
I Conformity	+	+
II Innovation	+	−
III Ritualism	−	+
IV Retreatism	−	−
V Rebellion	±	±

+ = acceptance; − = rejection; ± = rejection of prevailing values and substitution of new values.

Conformity. Conformity to both cultural goals and institutional means is the most common adaptation, but can be passed in this discussion which deals with non-conformity, although Merton claims that all five forms of adaptation relate to deviant behavior. Conformity of commitment to goals and institutional norms on the part of a large proportion of people, however, makes human society possible. It is not in focusing on conforming or normal behavior that it is possible to find out about the basic stresses of a society but rather by directing attention to deviant behavior.

Ritualism.   The abandoning or scaling down of the lofty goals of pecuniary success and rapid social mobility to the point where our aspirations can be satisfied is ritualism. "But though one rejects the cultural obligation to attempt 'to get ahead in the world,' though one draws in one's horizons, one continues to abide almost compulsively by institutional norms."[23] Actually this adaptation seems also to have little direct relationship to deviation, except perhaps to some forms of compulsive neuroses, and Merton himself says that the behavior exhibited by the ritualist is not generally considered deviant. Still, he feels that those who "play it safe," who become "bureaucratic virtuosos," who avoid high ambitions and consequent frustration, clearly represent a departure from the cultural model in which men are obliged to strive actively, preferably through institutionalized procedures, to move onward and upward in the social hierarchy.

Rebellion.   In this form of adaptation persons turn away from the conventional social structure and seek to establish a new or greatly modified social structure. This form of adaptation arises when "the institutional system is regarded as a barrier to the satisfaction of legitimized goals. . . ."[24] If it goes on to organized political action, the allegiance of persons such as the radical or revolutionary must be withdrawn from the existing social structure and transferred to new groups with new ideologies. The adaptation through rebellion requires little further discussion; in fact, the radical seldom is treated in conventional texts on deviant behavior.[25] In a sense Merton recognizes this for he points out that rebellion is an adaptation which is on a clearly different plane from the others. "It represents a transitional response seeking to *institutionalize* new goals and new procedures to be shared by other members of the society. It thus refers to efforts to *change* the existing cultural and social structure rather than to accommodate efforts *within* this structure."[26]

Merton, in a later paper, modified his view that rebellion was deviation in the same sense as were the other adaptations. Using different terms, he distinguished between rebellion, on the one hand, and innovation, ritualism, and retreatism, on the other.[27] In this paper he divided deviant behavior into two types, non-conforming and aberrant behavior, on the basis of social structure and consequences for the social system. Non-conformity is quite different from aberrant behavior such as crime and delinquency. The non-conformist announces his dissent publicly; the aberrant hides behind his departure from norms. The non-conformist challenges the legitimacy of social norms he rejects; the aberrant acknowledges the legitimacy of the norms he violates. The non-conformist tries to change the norms and may appeal to a higher morality; the aberrant merely wishes to escape the sanctioning force of present society. The non-conformist is often acknowledged by conventional society as departing from norms for disinterested purposes; the aberrant deviates to serve his own interests. Finally, the non-conformist draws upon the ultimate basic values of society for his goals, as distinguished from the aberrant whose interests are private, self-centered, and definitely antisocial.

Innovation.   Societies where the culture emphasizes pecuniary success and the social structure places undue limitations on approved means provide numerous situations for the development of socially disapproved departures from institutional norms, in the form of innovative practices. The use of such illegitimate means as crime to achieve culturally prescribed goals of success, power, and wealth, therefore, has become common in our society. Such a form of adaptation presupposes that individuals have been inadequately socialized with respect to cultural goals emphasizing success-aspirations. As evidence Merton maintains that unlawful behavior such as delinquency and crime appears to be most common in the lower strata of our society and this is "a 'normal' response to a situation where the cultural emphasis upon pecuniary success has been absorbed, but where there is little access to conventional and legitimate means for becoming successful."[28] These pressures tend to result in the gradual reduction in efforts to use legitimate means and an increase in the use of more or less expedient illegitimate means. The opportunities of the lower class are largely restricted to manual labor, and this is often stigmatized. Consequently, "the status of unskilled labor and the consequent low income cannot readily compete *in terms of established standards of worth* with the promise of power and high income from organized vice, rackets and crime."[29]

Illegitimate innovations are not restricted to crime among the lower socioeconomic classes. Similar pressures for ever greater monetary status symbols are exerted on the upper socioeconomic groups and give rise to unethical business practices and what has been termed white collar crime. "On the top economic levels, the pressure toward innovation not infrequently erases the distinction between business-like striving this side of the mores and sharp practices beyond the mores."[30] He points out, however, that "whatever the differential rates of deviant behavior in several social strata . . . the greatest pressures toward deviation are exerted on the lower social strata."[31]

In his second basic essay on anomie, Merton attempted to qualify his earlier all-embracing explanation of delinquency and crime as a form of anomie. He recognized that various types of behavior are included in the legal rubrics of delinquency and crime, and therefore that "the foregoing theory of anomie is designed to account for some, not all, forms of deviant behavior customarily described as criminal or delinquent."[32] Except, however, for specifically indicating that a theory of anomie does not account for much of the non-utilitarian character of behavior occurring in delinquent groups, he is vague as to which behavior is covered by his explanation and which is not.

The effect of innovative adaptation such as delinquency can be dynamic. Some individuals, because of their disadvantaged positions or personality patterns, are subjected more than others to the strains of the discrepancy between cultural goals and institutional means. They are, consequently, more vulnerable to deviant behavior. This "successful" adjustment tends to affect others and to lessen the legitimacy of the institutional norms for others. Others who did not respond to the original, rather slight anomie now do so. "This, in turn, creates a more acutely anomic situation for still other and initially less vulnerable individuals in the social system. In this way anomie and mounting rates of deviant behavior can be conceived as interacting in a process of social and cultural dynamics, with cumulatively disruptive consequences for the normative structure, unless counteracting mechanisms of control are called into play."[33]

Not all deviations in the form of innovation are dysfunctional for society.[34] Some may form the basis for new institutions better equipped to function than older ones. In any event, innovation, even of a deviant nature, is likely to be dynamic. "Social dysfunction is not a latter-day terminological substitute for 'immorality' or 'unethical practice.' "[35] In some cases it may even be "the norms of the group which are at fault, and not the innovator who rejects them." Although the extent is unknown, some deviation from current norms is probably functional for the basic goals of a group.[36] As Merton has written later:

> In the history of every society, one supposes, some of its culture heroes eventually come to be regarded as heroic in part because they are held to have had the courage and the vision to challenge the beliefs and routines of their society. The rebel, revolutionary, non-conformist, heretic or renegade of an earlier day is often the culture hero of today. Moreover, the accumulation of dysfunctions in a social system is often the prelude to concerted social change that may bring the system closer to the values that enjoy the respect of members of the society.[37]

Retreatism.   The adaptation to disjunctive means and goals through retreatism is significant in understanding certain specific forms of deviant behavior. In a sense one might say this is not so much an adaptation but a rejection of both cultural goals and institutional means. "The retreatist pattern consists of substantial abandoning both of the once-esteemed cultural goals and of institutionalized practices directed toward those goals."[38] The individual has internalized fully the cultural goals of success but finds inaccessible the institutionalized means to obtain them. Under internalized pressure not to obtain the goal by illegitimate means such as innovation provides, the individual finds himself frustrated and handicapped. He [thus] . . . adopts escape mechanisms such as "defeatism, quietism and retreatism."

Retreatism constitutes some of the adaptive activities of "psychotics, autists, pariahs, outcasts, vagrants, tramps, chronic drunkards and drug addicts."[39] Their mode of adaptation in many cases is derived from the social structure which, in a sense, they have sought to repudiate. The retreatist form of adaptation is particularly condemned by conventional society because it is nonproductive, nonstriving, attaches no value to the success-goal of a society and does not use institutional means. The conformist keeps the wheels of society running; the innovator is at least "smart" and actively striving; the retreatist at least conforms to the mores.[40]

Retreatism is a private rather than a collectivized form of adaptation. "Although people exhibiting this deviant behavior may gravitate toward centers where they come into contact with other deviants and although they may come to share in the sub-culture of these deviant groups, their adaptations are largely private and isolated rather than unified under the aegis of a new cultural code."[41]

Notes

1. See Robert K. Merton, "Social Structure and Anomie: Revisions and Extensions," in Ruth Nanda Anshen, *The Family: Its Function and Destiny* (New York: Harper & Row, 1949), 275–312; "Social Structure and Anomie," 131–60, and "Continuities in the Theory of Social Structure and Anomie," 161–94, in Robert K. Merton, *Social Theory and Social Structure* [(Glencoe: The Free Press, 1957)]. The original essay was reprinted in the first edition (1949, rev. 1957) as "Social Structure and Anomie."

2. Albert K. Cohen, "Towards a Theory of Deviant Behavior: Continuities Continued," paper presented to session on deviant behavior, American Sociological Association meeting, August 28, 1963.

3. Merton, *Social Theory and Social Structure, op. cit.,* 132.

4. In this volume we are concentrating arbitrarily on behavior accompanied by a strong, negative societal reaction. Such deviant behavior includes delinquency and crime, mental disorder, alcoholism, and drug addiction. While Merton explained all as anomic adaptations, it should be emphasized that his analysis includes other behavior. It is, as he says, a theory "that distinguishes forms of deviant behavior which may be far removed from those which represent violations of law." To him deviant behavior includes, for example, the over-conformist with norms, the radical and the revolutionary, the "bureaucratic virtuosos," the person caught in the net of conformity, widows and aged persons who retreat into the past, and workers who develop passivity in response to anomic situations.

5. Robert K. Merton, "Social Problems and Sociological Theory," in Robert K. Merton and Robert A. Nisbet, *Contemporary Social Problems* [(New York: Harcourt, Brace & World, 1961)], 723–24.

6. Merton, *Social Theory and Social Structure, op. cit.,* 131.

7. *Ibid.*

8. *Ibid.,* 162.

9. *Ibid.*

10. *Ibid.,* 133.

11. *Ibid.,* 181.

12. *Ibid.,* 134.

13. *Ibid.,* 162. Robert Bierstedt, in his review of the original 1949 edition of *Social Theory and Social Structure,* questioned the applicability of the word "anomie" in Merton's sense to situations which exhibit opposing norms rather than no norms. *Amer. Sociological Rev.,* 15 (February, 1950), 140–41. In another connection Merton has suggested three other potential sources of anomie but they have never been incorporated into his basic theoretical position. Anomie may arise (1) in a situation where there is a system of contradictory norms, (2) where there are many values but individuals are not afforded any way of determining which is appropriate, (3) where norms are insufficiently defined in relation to others so that this ambiguity may result in difficulties in predicting environmental responses. "The Social-Cultural Environment and Anomie," in Helen L. Witmer and Ruth Kotinsky, Eds., *New Perspectives for Research in Juvenile Delinquency* (Washington, D.C.: U.S. Government Printing Office, 1956), 63–67.

14. Merton, *Social Theory and Social Structure, op. cit.,* 162.

15. The existence of a situation of anomie resulting from a conflict between important cultural values and sanctioned institutional means is not the same, however, as "value conflict." The conflict between goals and institutional means is the source of anomie. In

fact, conflicts between members of various subgroups, rather than resulting in anomie, may cause the members of each group to comply more fully with their own norms.

16. Merton, *Social Theory and Social Structure, op. cit.,* 183.

17. *Ibid.,* adapted from 175.

18. *Ibid.,* 135. This emphasis on wealth is not peculiar to an economic system. As Max Weber has pointed out, the impulse to gain money has nothing to do with capitalism. "This impulse exists and has existed among waiters, physicians, coachmen, artists, prostitutes, dishonest officials, soldiers, nobles, crusaders, gamblers, and beggars. One may say that it has been common to all sorts and conditions of men at all times and in all countries of the earth, wherever the objective possibility of it is or has been given." Max Weber, *The Protestant Ethic and the Spirit of Capitalism,* tr. Talcott Parsons (New York: Charles Scribner's Sons, 1930), 17.

19. As a simple illustration of an anomic situation, Merton cites instances where winning the game may become the paramount goal. Rather than follow the rules of the game, universities may resort to illegitimate means, such as "surreptitiously slugging the star of the opposing team." The university alumni may "covertly subsidize 'students' whose talents are confined to the athletic field." Merton, *Social Theory and Social Structure, op. cit.,* 134–35.

20. *Ibid.,* 174.

21. *Ibid.,* 146.

22. *Ibid.,* 140.

23. *Ibid.,* 150.

24. *Ibid.,* 156.

25. An exception is Edwin M. Lemert's *Social Pathology* (New York: McGraw-Hill Book Co., 1951), which contains the chapter "Radicalism and Radicals."

26. Merton, *Social Theory and Social Structure, op. cit.,* 140.

27. "The foregoing account of non-conforming behavior develops somewhat the pattern of behavior identified as 'rebellion' in the typology set forth in 'Social Structure and Anomie.' In that same typology, innovation, ritualism, and retreatism would comprise forms of aberrant behavior." Robert K. Merton, "Social Problems and Sociological Theory," *op. cit.,* 727.

28. Merton, *Social Theory and Social Structure, op. cit.,* 145.

29. *Ibid.*

30. *Ibid.,* 144.

31. *Ibid.,* 141.

32. *Ibid.,* 178.

33. *Ibid.,* 180.

34. There are a number of theoretical problems inherent in the terms "functional" and "dysfunctional," but since the terms are used by Merton and currently used extensively in sociological literature, we have employed them in this paper. See, for example, "Functionalism in Social Science," in Ernest Nagel, *The Structure of Science: Problems in the Logic of Scientific Explanation* (New York: Harcourt, Brace & World, 1961), 530–35, and Llewellyn Gross, Ed., *Symposium on Sociological Theory* (New York: Harper & Row, 1959).

35. *Ibid.,* 182.

36. The latent positive functions of deviance, such as innovation, have been developed by Lewis Coser, who has pointed out that the deviant helps to arouse the community to the consequences of the breach of norms, and that deviance from this point of view may have the aspects of "normalcy." Lewis A. Coser, "Some Functions of Deviant Behavior and Normative Flexibility," *Amer. J. Sociology,* 68 (September, 1962), 172–81.

37. Merton, "Social Problems and Sociological Theory," *op. cit.,* 736.

38. Merton, *Social Theory and Social Structure, op. cit.,* 187.

39. *Ibid.,* 153.

40. *Ibid.,* 154. Merton later included in this adaptive response those whose social relations and norms had become seriously disturbed. Examples of this include widows and persons forced into retirement, and those experiencing the anomie of prosperity and depression, where disruptions in status may occur with great rapidity.

41. *Ibid.,* 155.

LEARNING TO BE DEVIANT

Edwin H. Sutherland and Donald R. Cressey

Although Durkheim had maintained that crime is normal in any society, many sociologists continued to regard deviant behavior as the result of individual pathology. Merton and Sutherland, however, helped to revive the Durkheimian notion of deviant behavior as a normal occurrence. On the level of social structure, Merton showed that deviant behavior can be seen as a normal response to an abnormal social situation. On the level of social interaction, Sutherland argued that people learn to be criminal in the same way that they learn to be law-abiding. Thus, Sutherland concluded, deviant behavior is best explained by the principles of social learning rather than the principles of abnormal psychology.

If criminology is to be scientific, the heterogeneous collection of "multiple factors" known to be associated with crime and criminality should be organized and integrated by means of an explanatory theory which has the same characteristics as the scientific explanations in other fields of study. That is, the conditions which are said to cause crime should always be present when crime is present, and they should always be absent when crime is absent. Such a theory would stimulate, simplify, and give direction to criminological research, and it would provide a framework for understanding the significance of much of the knowledge acquired about crime and criminality in the past. Furthermore, it would be useful in control of crime, providing it could be "applied" in much the same way that the engineer "applies" the scientific theories of the physicist.

There are two complementary procedures which may be used to put order into criminological knowledge, to develop a causal theory of criminal behavior. The first is logical abstraction. Negroes, urban-dwellers, and young adults all have comparatively high crime rates. What do they have in common that results in these high crime rates? Research studies have shown that criminal behavior is associated in greater or less degree with the social and personal pathologies, such as poverty, bad housing, slum-residence, lack of recreational facilities, inadequate and demoralized families, feeble-mindedness, emotional instability, and other traits and conditions. What do these conditions have in common which apparently produces excessive criminality? Research studies have also demonstrated that many persons with those pathological traits and conditions do not commit crimes and that persons in the upper socio-economic class frequently violate the law, although they are not in poverty, do not lack recreational facilities, and are not feeble-minded or emotionally unstable. Obviously, it is not the conditions or traits themselves which cause crime, for the conditions are sometimes present when criminality does not occur, and they also are sometimes absent when criminality does occur. A causal explanation of criminal behavior can be reached by abstracting, logically, the mechanisms and processes which are common to the rich and the poor, Negroes and whites, urban and rural dwellers, young adults and old adults, and the emotionally stable and the emotionally unstable who commit crimes.

In arriving at these abstract mechanisms and processes, criminal behavior must be precisely defined and carefully distinguished from non-criminal behavior. The problem in criminology is to explain the criminality of behavior, not behavior as such. The abstract mechanisms and processes common to the classes of criminals indicated above should not also be common to non-criminals. Criminal behavior is human behavior, has much in common with non-criminal behavior, and must be explained within the same general framework used to explain other human behavior. However, an explanation of criminal behavior should be a specific part of a general theory of behavior. Its specific task should be to differentiate criminal from non-criminal behavior. Many things which are necessary for behavior are not for that reason important to the criminality of behavior. Respiration, for instance, is necessary for any behavior, but the respiratory process cannot be used in an explanation of criminal behavior, for it does not differentiate criminal behavior from non-criminal behavior.

The second procedure for putting order into criminological knowledge is differentiation of levels of analysis. This means that the problem is limited to a particular part of the whole situation, largely in terms of chronology. The causal analysis must be held at a particular level. For example, when physicists stated the law of falling bodies they were not concerned with the reasons why a body began to fall except as this might affect the initial momentum. It made no difference to the physicist whether a body began to fall because it was dropped from the hand of an experimental physicist or rolled off the edge of a bridge because of vibration caused by a passing vehicle. Also, a round object would have rolled off the bridge more readily than a square object, but this fact was not significant for the law of falling bodies. Such facts were considered as existing on a different level of explanation and were irrelevant to the problem with which the physicists were concerned. Much of the confusion regarding criminal behavior is due to a failure to define and hold constant the level of explanation. By analogy, many criminologists would attribute some degree of causal power to the "roundness" of the object in the illustration above. However, consideration of time sequences among the factors associated with crime and criminality may lead to simplicity of statement. In the heterogeneous collection of factors associated with criminal behavior, one factor often occurs prior to another factor (in much the way that "roundness" occurs prior to "vibration," and "vibration" occurs prior to "rolling off a bridge"), but a theoretical statement about criminal behavior can be made without referring to those early factors. By holding the analysis at one level, the early factors are combined with or differentiated from later factors or conditions, thus reducing the number of variables which must be considered in a theory.

A motion picture several years ago showed two boys engaged in a minor theft; they ran when they were discovered; one boy had longer legs, escaped, and became a priest; the other had shorter legs, was caught, committed to a reformatory, and became a gangster. In this comparison, the boy who became a criminal was differentiated from the one who did not become a criminal by the length of his legs. But "length of legs" need not be considered in a criminological theory for, in general, no significant relationship has been found between criminality and length of legs and certainly many persons with short legs are law-abiding and many persons with long legs are criminals. The length of the legs does not determine criminality and has no necessary relation to criminality. In the illustration, the differential in the length of the boys' legs may be observed to be significant to subsequent criminality or non-criminality only to the degree that it determined the subsequent experiences and associations of the two boys. It is in these experiences and associations, then, that the mechanisms and processes which are important to criminality or non-criminality are to be found. A "one-level" theoretical explanation of crime would be concerned solely with these mechanisms and processes, not with the earlier factor "length of legs."

TWO TYPES OF EXPLANATIONS OF CRIMINAL BEHAVIOR

Scientific explanations of criminal behavior may be stated either in terms of the process which are operating at the moment of the occurrence of crime or in terms of the processes operating in the earlier history of the criminal. In the first case, the explanation may be called "mechanistic," "situational," or "dynamic"; in the second, "historical" or "genetic." Both types of explanation are desirable. The mechanistic type of explanation has been favored by physical and biological scientists, and it probably could be the more efficient type of explanation of criminal behavior. However, criminological explanations of the mechanistic type have thus far been notably unsuccessful, perhaps largely because they have been formulated in connection with the attempt to isolate personal and social pathologies among criminals. Work from this point of view has, at least, resulted in the conclusion that the immediate determinants of criminal behavior lie in the person-situation complex.

The objective situation is important to criminality largely to the extent that it provides an opportunity for a criminal act. A thief may steal from a fruit stand when the owner is not in sight but refrain when the owner is in sight; a bank burglar may attack a bank which is poorly protected but refrain from attacking a bank protected by watchmen and burglar alarms. A corporation which manufactures automobiles seldom or never violates the Pure Food and Drug Law, but a meat-packing corporation might violate this law with great frequency. But in another sense, a psychological or sociological sense, the situation is not exclusive of the person, for the situation which is important is the situation as defined by the person who is involved. That is, some persons define a situation in which a fruit-stand owner is out of sight as a "crime-committing" situation, while others do not so define it. Furthermore, the events in the person-situation complex at the time a crime occurs cannot be separated from the prior life experiences of the criminal. This means that the situation is defined by the person in terms of the inclinations and abilities which the person has acquired up to date. For example, while a person could define a situation in such a manner that criminal behavior would be the inevitable result, his past experiences would for the most part determine the way in which he defined the situation. An explanation of criminal behavior made in terms of these past experiences is an historical or genetic explanation.

The following paragraphs state such a genetic theory of criminal behavior on the assumption that a criminal act occurs when a situation appropriate for it, as defined by the person, is present. The theory should be regarded as tentative. . . .

GENETIC EXPLANATION OF CRIMINAL BEHAVIOR

The following statement refers to the process by which a particular person comes to engage in criminal behavior.

1. *Criminal behavior is learned.* Negatively, this means that criminal behavior is not inherited, as such; also, the person who is not already trained in crime does not invent criminal behavior, just as a person does not make mechanical inventions unless he has had training in mechanics.

2. *Criminal behavior is learned in interaction with other persons in a process of communication.* This communication is verbal in many respects but includes also "the communication of gestures."

3. *The principal part of the learning of criminal behavior occurs within intimate personal groups.* Negatively, this means that the impersonal agencies of communication, such as movies and newspapers, play a relatively unimportant part in the genesis of criminal behavior.

4. *When criminal behavior is learned, the learning includes (a) techniques of committing the crime, which are sometimes very complicated, sometimes very simple; (b) the specific direction of motives, drives, rationalizations, and attitudes.*

5. *The specific direction of motives and drives is learned from definitions of the legal codes as favorable or unfavorable.* In some societies an individual is surrounded by persons who invariably define the legal codes as rules to be observed, while in others he is surrounded by persons whose definitions are favorable to the violation of the legal codes. In our American society these definitions

are almost always mixed, with the consequence that we have culture conflict in relation to the legal codes.

6. *A person becomes delinquent because of an excess of definitions favorable to violation of law over definitions unfavorable to violation of law.* This is the principle of differential association. It refers to both criminal and anti-criminal associations and has to do with counteracting forces. When persons become criminal, they do so because of contacts with criminal patterns and also because of isolation from anti-criminal patterns. Any person inevitably assimilates the surrounding culture unless other patterns are in conflict; a Southerner does not pronounce "r" because other Southerners do not pronounce "r." Negatively, this proposition of differential association means that associations which are neutral so far as crime is concerned have little or no effect on the genesis of criminal behavior. Much of the experience of a person is neutral in this sense, e.g., learning to brush one's teeth. This behavior has no negative or positive effect on criminal behavior except as it may be related to associations which are concerned with the legal codes. This neutral behavior is important especially as an occupier of the time of a child so that he is not in contact with criminal behavior during the time he is so engaged in the neutral behavior.

7. *Differential associations may vary in frequency, duration, priority, and intensity.* This means that associations with criminal behavior and also associations with anti-criminal behavior vary in those respects. "Frequency" and "duration" as modalities of associations are obvious and need no explanation. "Priority" is assumed to be important in the sense that lawful behavior developed in early childhood may persist throughout life, and also that delinquent behavior developed in early childhood may persist throughout life. This tendency, however, has not been adequately demonstrated, and priority seems to be important principally through its selective influence. "Intensity" is not precisely defined but it has to do with such things as the prestige of the source of a criminal or anti-criminal pattern and with emotional reactions related to the associations. In a precise description of the criminal behavior of a person these modalities would be stated in quantitative form and a mathematical ratio be reached. A formula in this sense has not been developed, and the development of such a formula would be extremely difficult.

8. *The process of learning criminal behavior by association with criminal and anti-criminal patterns involves all of the mechanisms that are involved in any other learning.* Negatively, this means that the learning of criminal behavior is not restricted to the process of imitation. A person who is seduced, for instance, learns criminal behavior by association, but this process would not ordinarily be described as imitation.

9. *While criminal behavior is an expression of general needs and values, it is not explained by those general needs and values since noncriminal behavior is an expression of the same needs and values.* Thieves generally steal in order to secure money, but likewise honest laborers work in order to secure money. The attempts by many scholars to explain criminal behavior by general drives and values, such as the happiness principle, striving for social status, the money motive, or frustration, have been and must continue to be futile since they explain

lawful behavior as completely as they explain criminal behavior. They are similar to respiration, which is necessary for any behavior but which does not differentiate criminal from noncriminal behavior.

It is not necessary, at this level of explanation, to explain why a person has the associations which he has; this certainly involves a complex of many things. In an area where the delinquency rate is high, a boy who is sociable, gregarious, active, and athletic is very likely to come in contact with the other boys in the neighborhood, learn delinquent behavior from them, and become a gangster; in the same neighborhood the psychopathic boy who is isolated, introverted, and inert may remain at home, not become acquainted with the other boys in the neighborhood, and not become delinquent. In another situation, the sociable, athletic, aggressive boy may become a member of a scout troop and not become involved in delinquent behavior. The person's associations are determined in a general context of social organization. A child is ordinarily reared in a family; the place of residence of the family is determined largely by family income; and the delinquency rate is in many respects related to the rental value of the houses. Many other aspects of social organization affect the kinds of associations a person has.

The preceding explanation of criminal behavior purports to explain the criminal and noncriminal behavior of individual persons. As indicated earlier, it is possible to state sociological theories of criminal behavior which explain the criminality of a community, nation, or other group. The problem, when thus stated, is to account for variations in crime rates and involves a comparison of the crime rates of various groups or the crime rates of a particular group at different times. The explanation of a crime rate must be consistent with the explanation of the criminal behavior of the person, since the crime rate is a summary statement of the number of persons in the group who commit crimes and the frequency with which they commit crimes. One of the best explanations of crime rates from this point of view is that a high crime rate is due to social disorganization. The term "social disorganization" is not entirely satisfactory and it seems preferable to substitute for it the term "differential social organization." The postulate on which this theory is based, regardless of the name, is that crime is rooted in the social organization and is an expression of that social organization. A group may be organized for criminal behavior or organized against criminal behavior. Most communities are organized both for criminal and anti-criminal behavior and in that sense the crime rate is an expression of the differential group organization. Differential group organization as an explanation of variations in crime rates is consistent with the differential association theory of the processes by which persons become criminals.

A THEORY OF WHITE COLLAR CRIME
Edwin H. Sutherland

Sutherland proposed that people learn criminal behavior in the same way that they learn any other kind of behavior—namely, through interaction in primary groups. When the definitions favorable to criminal behavior that are learned exceed those favorable to legal behavior, people in these situations are much more likely to take on attitudes conducive to breaking the criminal law. This constitutes Sutherland's famous principle of differential association. He developed this theory in subsequent editions of his classic text Criminology *and in his 1937 life-history of Chic Conwell,* The Professional Thief. *He coined the term "white collar crime" in his 1937 presidential address to the American Sociological Society ("White Collar Criminality."* American Sociological Review 5 (1940) 1–12). *In 1949 he published the book* White Collar Crime *(New York: Dryden Press) in which he broadened the concept of crime with his study of numerous law violations by corporations. (In the 1983 "uncut versions" of this book, he included the names of all those corporations whose names had been deleted in the 1949 version.) He succeeded in broadening the definition of crime by including those committed in the course of doing business. He extended the principle of differential association to violations of law in everyday business life. His chapter on a theory of white collar crime is excerpted below.*

A complete explanation of white collar crime cannot be derived from the available data. The data which are at hand suggest that white collar crime has its genesis in the same general process as other criminal behavior, namely, differential association. The hypothesis of differential association is that criminal behavior is learned in association with those who define such behavior favorably and in isolation from those who define it unfavorably, and that a person in an appropriate situation engages in such criminal behavior if, and only if, the weight of the favorable definitions exceeds the weight of the unfavorable definitions. This hypothesis is certainly not a complete or universal explanation of white collar crime or of other crime, but it perhaps fits the data of both types of crimes better than any other general hypothesis.

This hypothesis or other hypotheses can be tested adequately only by research studies organized specifically for this purpose and by first-hand acquaintance with the careers of businessmen. In the absence of such studies, it is necessary for the present to fall back upon data now available. The data at hand provide two

From Edwin H. Sutherland, "A Theory of White Collar Crime," *White Collar Crime: The Uncut Versions* (New Haven: Yale University Press, 1983), pp. 240–257.

types of documentary evidence, namely, biographical or autobiographical descriptions of the careers of businessmen and descriptions of the diffusion of criminal practices from one situation to another. These two types of evidence will be illustrated in the following paragraphs.

PERSONAL DOCUMENTS

A young businessman in the used-car business in Chicago described the process by which he was inducted into illegal behavior.

When I graduated from college I had plenty of ideals of honesty, fair play, and cooperation which I had acquired at home, in school, and from literature. My first job after graduation was selling typewriters. During the first day I learned that these machines were not sold at a uniform price but that a person who higgled and waited could get a machine at about half the list price. I felt that this was unfair to the customer who paid the list price. The other salesmen laughed at me and could not understand my silly attitude. They told me to forget the things I had learned in school, and that you couldn't earn a pile of money by being strictly honest. When I replied that money wasn't everything they mocked at me: "Oh! No? Well, it helps." I had ideals and I resigned.

My next job was selling sewing machines. I was informed that one machine, which cost the company $18, was to be sold for $40 and another machine, which cost the company $19, was to be sold for $70, and that I was to sell the de luxe model whenever possible in preference to the cheaper model, and was given a list of the reasons why it was a better buy. When I told the sales manager that the business was dishonest and that I was quitting right then, he looked at me as if he thought I was crazy and said angrily: "There's not a cleaner business in the country."

It was quite a time before I could find another job. During this time I occasionally met some of my classmates and they related experiences similar to mine. They said they would starve if they were rigidly honest. All of them had girls and were looking forward to marriage and a comfortable standard of living, and they said they did not see how they could afford to be rigidly honest. My own feelings became less determined than they had been when I quit my first job.

Then I got an opportunity in the used-car business. I learned that this business had more tricks for fleecing customers than either of those I had tried previously. Cars with cracked cylinders, with half the teeth missing from the fly wheel, with everything wrong, were sold as "guaranteed." When the customer returned and demanded his guarantee, he had to sue to get it and very few went to that trouble and expense: the boss said you could depend on human nature. If hot cars could be taken in and sold safely, the boss did not hesitate. When I learned these things I did not quit as I had previously. I sometimes felt disgusted and wanted to quit, but I argued that I did not have much chance to find a legitimate firm. I knew that the game was rotten but it had to be played—the law of the jungle and that sort of thing. I knew that I was dishonest and to that extent felt that I was more honest than my fellows. The thing that struck me as strange was that all these people were proud of their ability to fleece customers. They boasted of their crookedness and were admired by their friends and enemies in proportion to their ability to get away with a crooked deal: it was called shrewdness. Another thing was that these people were unanimous in their denunciation of gangsters, robbers, burglars, and petty thieves. They never regarded themselves as in the same class and were bitterly indignant if accused of dishonesty: it was just good business.

Once in a while, as the years have passed, I have thought of myself as I was in college—idealistic, honest, and thoughtful of others—and have been momentarily ashamed of myself. Before long such memories became less and less frequent and it became difficult to distinguish me from my fellows. If you had accused me of dishonesty I would have denied the charge, but with slightly less vehemence than my fellow businessmen, for after all I had learned a different code of behavior.

A graduate student in an urban university, in order to supplement his income, took a job as an extra salesman in a shoe store on Saturdays and other rush days. He had no previous experiences as a shoe salesman or in any other regular business. He described his experience in this store thus:

> One day I was standing in the front part of the store, waiting for the next customer. A man came in and asked if we had any high, tan button shoes. I told him that we had no shoes of that style. He thanked me and walked out of the store. The floor-walker came up to me and asked me what the man wanted. I told him what the man asked for and what I replied. The floor-walker said angrily: "Damn it! We're not here to sell what they want. We're here to sell what we've got." He went on to instruct me that when a customer came into the store, the first thing to do was to get him to sit down and take off his shoe so that he couldn't get out of the store. "If we don't have what he wants," he said, "bring him something else and try to interest him in that style. If he is still uninterested, inform the floor-walker and he will send one of the regular salesmen, and if that doesn't work, a third salesman will be sent to him. Our policy is that no customer gets out of the store without a sale until at least three salesmen have worked on him. By that time he feels that he must be a crank and will generally buy something whether he wants it or not."
>
> I learned from other clerks that if a customer needed a 7-B shoe and we did not have that size in the style he desired, I should try on an 8-A or 7-C or some other size. The sizes were marked in code so that the customer did not know what the size was, and it might be necessary to lie to him about the size; also his foot might be injured by the misfit. But the rule was to sell him a pair of shoes, preferably a pair that fit but some other pair if necessary.
>
> I learned also that the clerks received an extra commission if they sold the out-of-style shoes left over from earlier seasons, which were called "spiffs." The regular salesmen made a practice of selling spiffs to anyone who appeared gullible and generally had to claim either that this was the latest style or that it had been the style earlier and was coming back this season, or that it was an old style but much better quality than present styles. The clerk had to size up the customer and determine which one of these lies would be most likely to result in a sale.
>
> Several years later I became acquainted with a man who worked for several years as a regular salesman in shoe stores in Seattle. When I described to him the methods I had learned in the shoe store where I worked, he said: "Every shoe store in Seattle except one does exactly the same things and I learned to be a shoe salesman in exactly the same manner you did."

Another young man who was holding his first position as a shoe salesman in a small city wrote an autobiographical statement in which he included the following instructions given him by the manager of the shoe store:

> My job is to move out shoes and I hire you to assist in this. I am perfectly glad to fit a person with a pair of shoes if we have his size, but I am willing to misfit him if it is necessary in order to sell him a pair of shoes. I expect you to do the same. If you do not like this, some one else can have your job. While you are working for me, I expect you to have no scruples about how you sell shoes.

A man who had been a school teacher and had never been officially involved in any delinquencies secured a position as agent of a book-publishing company and was assigned to public school work. He soon learned that the publishing company bribed the members of the textbook committee in order to secure adoptions of their books. With considerable shame he began to use this method of bribery because he felt it was necessary in order to make a good record. Partly because he disliked this procedure but principally because this work kept him away from home much of the time, he decided that he would become a lawyer. He moved to a large city, registered for night courses in a law school, and secured a daytime job as a claim agent for a casualty insurance company. About two years later he was convicted of embezzling the funds of the insurance company. A portion of his autobiography describes the process by which he got into this difficulty:

> Almost immediately after I got into this business I learned two things: first, the agents who got ahead with the company were the ones who made settlements at low figures and without taking cases into court; second, the settlements were generally made by collusion with the lawyers and doctors for the claimants. Most of the lawyers for the claimants were ambulance-chasers and were willing to make settlements because they got their fees without any work. The claim agent for the insurance company got a secret kick-back out of the settlement. When I learned this was the way to get ahead in the casualty insurance business, I went in for it in a big way. Accidentally I left some papers loose in my office, from which it was discovered that I was "knocking down" on the settlements. The insurance company accused me of taking money which belonged to them, but actually I was taking money which belonged to the claimants.

The following statement was made by a young man who had graduated from a recognized school of business, had become a certified public accountant, and had been employed for several years in a respected firm of public accountants in a large city.

> While I was a student in the school of business I learned the principles of accounting. After I had worked for a time for an accounting firm I found that I had failed to learn many important things about accounting. An accounting firm gets its work from business firms and, within limits, must make the reports which those business firms desire. The accounting firm for which I work is respected and there is none better in the city. On my first assignment I discovered some irregularities in the books of the firm and these would lead anyone to question the financial policies of that firm. When I showed my report to the manager of our accounting firm, he said that was not a part of my assignment and I should leave it out. Although I was confident that the business firm was dishonest, I had to conceal this information. Again and again I have been compelled to do the same thing in other assignments. I get so disgusted with things of this sort that I wish I could leave the profession. I guess I must stick to it, for it is the only occupation for which I have training.

The documents above were written by persons who came from "good homes" and "good neighborhoods" and who had no official records as juvenile delinquents. White collar criminals, like professional thieves, are seldom recruited from juvenile delinquents. As a part of the process of learning practical business, a young man with idealism and thoughtfulness for others is inducted into white collar crime. In many cases he is ordered by the manager to do things which he regards as unethical or illegal, while in other cases he learns from those who have the same rank as his own how they make a success. He learns specific techniques of violating the law, together with definitions of situations in which those techniques may be used. Also, he develops a general ideology. This ideology grows in part out of the specific practices and is in the nature of generalization from concrete experiences, but in part it is transmitted as a generalization by phrases such as "we are not in business for our health," "business is business," or "no business was ever built on the beatitudes." These generalizations, whether transmitted as such or abstracted from concrete experiences, assist the neophyte in business to accept the illegal practices and provide rationalizations for them.

The preceding documents all came from young men in subordinate positions and are in no sense a random sample of persons in such positions. Even if they came from a random sample of persons in such subordinate positions, they would not demonstrate the genesis of illegal practices by the managers of large industries. Unfortunately similar documents, even of a scattered nature, are not available for the managers of large industries. No first-hand research study from this point of view has ever been reported. Gustavus Meyer in his *History of American Fortunes* and Ferdinand Lundberg in his *America's Sixty Families* have demonstrated that many of the large American fortunes originated in illegal practices. However, these books pay little attention to the process by which illegal behavior develops in the person. Bits of information may be gleaned from biographies of men like Armour, du Pont, Eastman, Firestone, Ford, Gary, Guggenheim, Havemeyer, McCormick, Marshall Field, Mellon, Morgan, Rockefeller, Seiberling, Swift, Woolworth, and others. Many of the biographies are subscription books written on order of the businessmen for advertising purposes; criminal behavior is seldom admitted and never explained. Bouck White's *The Book of Daniel Drew* is a forthright description of an actual person but is classed in the *Dictionary of American Biography* as semi-fiction.

DIFFUSION OF ILLEGAL PRACTICES

The diffusion of illegal practices is the second type of evidence that white collar crime is due to differential association. Business firms have the objective of maximum profits. When one firm devises a method of increasing profits, other firms become aware of the method and adopt it, perhaps a little more quickly and a little more generally if the firms are competitors in the same market than if they are not competitors. The diffusion of illegal practices which increase profits is facilitated by the trend toward centralization of the control of industry by investment banks and by the conferences of business concerns in trade associations. The process of diffusion will be considered first in relation to competition, and subsequently with reference to other relations.

The diffusion of illegal practices among competitors is illustrated in the following incident in a food manufacturing concern. A chemist who had been employed to advise this firm as to the scientific basis for claims in advertisements made the following statement regarding his experiences.

> When I got members of the firm off in a corner and we were talking confidentially, they frankly deplored the misrepresentations in their advertisements. At the same time they said it was necessary to advertise in this manner in order to attract the attention of customers and sell their products. Since other firms are making extravagant claims regarding their products, we must make extravagant claims re-

garding our products. A mere statement of fact regarding our products would make no impression on customers in the face of the ads of other firms.

One of the important automobile companies began to advertise the interest rate on the unpaid balance in installment purchases as six percent, when in fact the rate was more than eleven percent. Within a few weeks the other automobile companies began to advertise their interest rates as six percent, although their actual rates, also, were more than eleven percent. Again, when one automobile company published an advertisement of the price and specification of a certain car, together with a picture of a more expensive model, thus misrepresenting its cars, the other companies in the industry generally published similar advertisements with similar misrepresentation. Within a few months after the tire dealers had solemnly adopted a code of ethics in advertising, including a pledge not to use misrepresentations, one tire manufacturer announced a special cut-rate price for tires on the Fourth of July, in which the savings were grossly misrepresented; several other tire manufacturers promptly made similar announcements of cut-rate sales with similar misrepresentations. Thus competition in advertising drives the participants to the extreme, and when one corporation violates the law in this respect the other corporations do the same. The illegal behavior of the other corporations, at least, grows out of differential association.

Practices in restraint of trade are similarly diffused. One tire manufacturer made a discriminatory price on tires to a mail-order house; as soon as the other tire manufacturers and large distributors of tires learned of this arrangement, they made similar agreements for discriminatory prices, which were declared to be in restraint of trade. Sometimes definite coercion is used in forcing competitors into illegal agreements in restraint of trade. This has occurred especially in the form of threats of suits of patent infringement.

Illegal practices are diffused, also, when competition is not directly involved. This will be illustrated by the diffusion of misrepresentation in regard to the quality of gas sold by public utility corporations. The heating value of gas is customarily measured in terms of British Thermal Units, or BTU's. A BTU is the amount of heat that will raise the temperature of one pound of water one degree under standardized conditions. Until 1921, the Public Service Company of Colorado, a subsidiary of Cities Service, furnished gas in Denver with 600 BTU's. In that year this company secretly reduced the heating value of the gas, without reducing the price, until it had only 400 BTU's. The company made a statement to the Colorado State Commission that the experiment demonstrated that families consumed no more gas with the reduction of BTU's, and asked for authorization to adopt such heating values as they found to be most economical and efficient. This request was granted without an inspection of the detailed evidence and without a consultation with other authorities. This practice of reduction of BTU's with the accompanying argument, then spread to other gas companies.

In June, 1924, the executive committee of the American Gas Association adopted a resolution that, since the Denver experiment showed no decrease in efficiency with the reduction of BTU's, the state utility commission should generally authorize the reduction of BTU's to as low as 300 without change in rates. In 1925, the Spokane Gas and Fuel Company requested authorization to reduce its gas to 450 BTU's, giving as supporting evidence the testimony of the Public Service Company of Colorado that the consumption of gas had not increased when BTU's were reduced, and with the further explanation that Alabama had adopted this standard and Illinois was considering it. The state commission of Washington, with no conflicting evidence available, granted the request. In May, 1926, the Iowa Committee on Public Utilities published a pamphlet for use in the public schools which contained the statement: "Government research has shown that the lower British Thermal Unit produces the same results in practical operation and can be more economically manufactured." In the meantime the Bureau of Standards of the federal government had been collecting evidence on this question. In 1925, it wrote a report to the effect that the efficiency of gas for heating purposes was directly proportional to the BTU's and that a decrease in BTU's was equivalent to an increase in price. This government report was discussed in 1924, before publication, with the members of the American Gas Association. The president of this Association wrote to the director of the Bureau of Standards: "Many members of the Gas Association would not want to send out a report that would indicate that the charge for gas should be inversely proportional to the calorific value of gas." A. Gordon King, a service engineer of the Gas Association, stated: "The more I study this (government) document, the less value or good to any one I see in it, and if it were possible I believe it should be suppressed."

The Bureau of Standards in 1926 asked permission to examine the data on which the Public Service Company of Colorado based their conclusions, but this request was refused. A paper on this subject was written by a gas engineer for the Bureau of Standards, which dealt specifically with the Denver situation. This paper was submitted to the Public Service Company of Colorado for criticisms. The officers of this corporation wrote to the officers of the National Electric Light Association, who wrote a personal letter to Paul S. Clapp, assistant to Secretary Herbert Hoover of the Department of Commerce, urging that the Secretary prohibit publication of the paper. Although consent to publish the paper was given to the author, both the *Gas Age Record* and the *American Gas Journal*, which had given space to the Denver claims, refused to publish this paper. It was not published anywhere until placed in evidence in 1935 by the Federal Trade Commission. This paper stated that the Public Service Company of Colorado had refused to make available the data on which they based claims that reduction of BTU's did not increase consumption of gas, that the evidence of the Bureau of Standards demonstrated the exact opposite of this, and that if the policy used in Denver were extended throughout the United States, consumers would pay $490,000,000 a year more for their gas. In 1927, the directors of the American Gas Association informed the Bureau of Standards that they did not approve of a re-investigation of this question. In July, 1928, the Association issued a news-letter to the effect that the Illinois Commerce Commission had conducted an investigation which sustained the Denver conclusion.

The Bureau of Standards appraised this Illinois study, which was made under conditions very favorable to the gas companies, as "a beautiful demonstration of an almost exact inverse proportion between the heating value and the volume of gas demanded by domestic consumers." The diffusion of these claims, which the

Bureau of Standards held to be misrepresentation, was stopped by the trend toward natural gas; in fact, with the new developments, the gas companies have tended to reverse the position which they had taken during the decade of the twenties. The misrepresentation stopped as soon as it ceased to have economic value to the gas companies.[1]

Other illustrations of the diffusion of criminal practices are found in the customer-ownership campaigns of utility corporations and in the sales-quota system of many manufacturing companies. These campaigns are not in themselves criminal, but they have included fraudulent methods in so many cases that their significance is practically comparable to that of the burglar's "jimmy." It is not necessary to describe the details of the diffusion of these practices.[2]

General attitudes or mental sets, as well as specific practices, are diffused. This is illustrated in the following statement by Daniel Drew:

> With this panic year of which I am now writing (1857) a new state of affairs came about in financial circles. The panic was known as the "Western Blizzard." It put old fogeyism out of date forevermore. The men who conducted business in the old-fashioned slowpoke method—the think-of-the-other-fellow method—were swept away by this panic, or at least were so crippled up that they didn't figure much in the world of affairs afterwards. A new generation of men came in—a more pushful set. I was one of them. We were men who went ahead. We did things. We didn't split hairs about trifles. Anyhow, men of this skin, with a conscience all the time full of prickles, are out of place in business dickerings. A prickly conscience would be like a white silk apron for a blacksmith. Sometimes you've got to get your hands dirty, but that doesn't mean that the money you make is also dirty. Black hens can lay white eggs. . . . It isn't how you get your money but what you do with it that counts.[3]

ISOLATION

Businessmen are not only in contact with definitions which are favorable to white collar crime but they are also isolated from and protected against definitions which are unfavorable to such crime. Most of them, to be sure, were reared in homes in which honesty was defined as a virtue, but these home teachings had little explicit relation to business methods. The persons who define business practices as undesirable and illegal are customarily called "communists" or "socialists" and their definitions carry little weight.

The public agencies of communication, which continually define ordinary violations of the criminal code in a very critical manner, do not make similar definitions of white collar crime. Several reasons for this difference may be mentioned. The important newspapers, the motion picture corporations, and the radio corporations are all large corporations, and the persons who own and manage them have the same standards as the persons who manage other corporations. These agencies derive their principal income from advertisements by other business corporations and would be likely to lose a considerable part of this income if they were critical of business practices in general or those of particular corporations. Finally, these public agencies of communication themselves participate in white collar crimes and especially in restraint of trade, misrepresentation in advertising, and unfair labor practices. Thus businessmen are shielded from harsh criticisms by the public agencies of communication and remain in relative isolation from the definitions which are unfavorable to their practices.

Businessmen are shielded also against harsh criticisms by persons in governmental positions. Congress provided special implementation of the Sherman Antitrust Law and of many subsequent laws so that the stigma of crime might not attach officially to businessmen who violated these laws. This special implementation is almost, if not wholly, an exclusive feature of the laws which apply to businessmen. Moreover, the administrators select the less critical procedures in dealing with businessmen. They generally select equity procedures for businessmen accused of restraint of trade and criminal procedures for trade unionists accused of the same crime.

The less critical attitude of government toward businessmen than toward persons of lower socio-economic status is the result of several relationships. (a) Persons in government are, by and large, culturally homogeneous with persons in business, both being in the upper strata of American society. (b) Many persons in government are members of families which have other members in business. (c) Many persons in business are intimate personal friends of persons in government. Almost every important person in government has many close personal friends in business, and almost every important person in business has many close personal friends in government. (d) Many persons in government were previously connected with business firms as executives, attorneys, directors, or in other capacities. In times of war, especially, many persons in government retain their business connections. (e) Many persons in government hope to secure employment in business firms when their government work is terminated. Government work is often a step toward a career in private business. Relations established while in business, as well as inside information acquired at that time, carry over after the person joins a business firm. (f) Business is very powerful in American society and can damage or promote the governmental programs in which the governmental personnel are interested. (g) The program of the government is closely related to the political parties, and for their success in campaigns these political parties depend on contributions of large sums from important businessmen. Thus, the initial cultural homogeneity, the close personal relationships, and the power relationships protect businessmen against critical definitions by government.

The United States Steel Corporation, organized in 1900 by J. P. Morgan after he had directed the combination of many of the constituent parts, was the largest merger that had occurred in American industry. Amos Pinchot described some of the connections between this corporation and government officials which may have assisted in protecting this corporation for many years against prosecution under the antitrust laws:

> Philander C. Knox, former counsel for the Carnegie Steel Company and close personal friend of U.S. Steel director Henry Clay Frick, was U.S. Attorney General when the corporation was formed. Steel was well represented in high places throughout the administration of Theodore Roosevelt and W. H. Taft. Elihu Root, former attorney for the Carnegie Steel Company, was Secretary of State under Roosevelt and was succeeded by Knox, while Knox was replaced as Attorney General by George F. Wickersham, formerly attorney for the U.S. Steel Corporation.

Truman Newberry, president of a subsidiary of U.S. Steel, was Secretary of the Navy, an important post in steel politics. Herbert Satterlee, son-in-law of J. P. Morgan, was Assistant Secretary of the Navy. Robert Bacon, a partner of J. P. Morgan and a director of U.S. Steel, was for a time Secretary of State.[4]

Although the Aluminum Company of America had the most complete monopoly of any corporation in the United States and for many years stamped out all competitors, the many complaints did not result in effective suits against this corporation for several decades. The principal power in this corporation was Andrew W. Mellon, who was a very important member of the Republican Party and a Secretary of the Treasury; it has been said that three presidents served under him. When the Democrats came into power in 1932, this corporation was not without influence in the federal government. Oscar Ewing, who had been counsel for the Aluminum Company for many years, had been treasurer of the Democratic Party and was at the time a vice-president of this party. It was understood prior to the death of President Franklin D. Roosevelt that Ewing was to be appointed Solicitor General of the United States. That plan did not materialize, perhaps because Harry S. Truman, as a member of a Senate Committee, had been very critical of the contracts secured by the Aluminum Company for the production of war materials. Other important persons were ready to assist this corporation to maintain its monopolistic position, despite the fact that it had been convicted of participating in cartels, which were a serious handicap to the efficiency of the United States in its preparations for the Second World War. The Reynolds Metal Company had developed in this emergency to assist in the production of aluminum, but great pressure was placed on the administration to restrict the sale of public power to the Aluminum Company of America. Secretary Harold Ickes testified that W. Averill Harriman, Robert R. Patterson, William S. Knudsen, and others appealed to him not to sell Bonneville power to the Reynolds Metal Company (which would leave the Aluminum Company of America as the recipient of that power), although the Bonneville Act prohibited sale of this power under conditions which would tend to create a monopoly.[5]

Harold Judson was appointed Assistant Solicitor General of the United States and in that capacity had the duty, among others, of representing the government in suits regarding the submerged oil lands of California. Judson had been an attorney for the oil companies of California and he appeared on the record as having contributed $380,500 in the California campaign of 1939. When an inquiry was made regarding this, he testified that he had not contributed any of that amount himself but all of it for oil companies in California. Although the law requires that the names of all persons making contributions either directly or indirectly be listed, Judson's name was the only one that appeared. Despite this evidence he retained his position.[6]

Another businessman who has had extensive connections with government is Victor Emanuel. He is or has been the controlling power in Standard Gas and Electric, American Aviation, Consolidated Vultee, Station WLW in Cincinnati, Republic Steel, and other large corporations. He has been affiliated, also, with a banking firm which has been reported to have had connections with I. G. Farben under the Nazi régime. After Pearl Harbor, General Amiline and Film, the principal American subsidiary of I. G. Farben, was indicted for a cartel in war materials. The German-owned patents of that corporation were seized by the Alien Property Custodian, as were other German-owned patents. The Alien Property Custodian at that time was Leo Crowley, who was also chairman of Standard Gas and Electric. In a conference of federal departments the recommendation was made that all German-owned patents be made freely available to American industry. This recommendation was unanimously approved by all participants in the conference except James E. Markham, who had become Alien Property Custodian and who was a director of Standard Gas and Electric, in which Emanuel was a powerful influence. Markham appealed to George Allen, an influential person in Washington, to oppose the recommendation of this interdepartmental committee, and Allen, too, was a director of several of Emanuel's corporations.

In some cases persons have been nominated for important positions in the government but have not been appointed when their business connections were made known. Charles Beecher Warren was nominated for the position of Attorney General of the United States in 1925, in which position he would control prosecutions under the antitrust law. It was revealed in Congressional hearings that Warren had been indicted (but not convicted) in 1910, along with the American Sugar Refining Company, which was convicted on several occasions of violations of the antitrust law, and that he had acted as an agent of that corporation from 1906 to 1925 in purchasing the stock of competing sugar corporations. His nomination was not confirmed. Also, Edwin Pauley was nominated in 1946 for the position of Under-Secretary of the Navy, which had jurisdiction over the oil reserves. Pauley had been engaged in the oil industry in California and had worked strenuously in opposition to the United States in the suits regarding submerged oil lands. He was treasurer of the Democratic Party. Secretary Ickes testified that Pauley had promised that $300,000 would be contributed to the campaign by California oil men if the government dropped the suit on submerged oil lands. Because of this publicity, Pauley's name was withdrawn.

Although some individuals may be sacrificed, those of greater power are protected. Richard Whitney, president of the New York Stock Exchange, was indicted on March 12, 1938, for stealing securities from trust funds of the Exchange, and was committed to prison on April 12, 1938. It is reported that subsequent investigations revealed that this crime was known three months before the indictment to other officers of the Exchange and to two partners of J. P. Morgan. At that earlier date Whitney made restitution to the trust funds by borrowing more than a million dollars from his brother, who was a partner of J. P. Morgan; and his brother, in turn, borrowed most of this amount from another partner, both knowing that his loan was for the purpose of restoring to the trust funds the securities which had been stolen. The New York statutes define the concealment of such knowledge as a felony. The prosecutors in the case knew that restitution had been made but made no inquiry as to the source of funds used in the restitution or as to other financiers who might have been accessory to this act. Moreover, the New York Stock Exchange, presumably with the hope of restoring public confidence, appointed Robert M. Hutchins, president of the University of Chicago, as a public representative on the Board of Governors of the Exchange. Within a short time Hutchins resigned from this Board with the public explanation that he did so because the Board of Governors refused to assist in the search for others who were implicated in the Whitney crime.[7]

SOCIAL DISORGANIZATION

Differential association is a hypothetical explanation of crime from the point of view of the process by which a person is initiated into crime. Social disorganization is a hypothetical explanation of crime from the point of view of the society. These two hypotheses are consistent with each other and one is the counterpart of the other. Both apply to ordinary crimes as well as to white collar crimes.

Social disorganization may be either of two types: *anomie*[8] or the lack of standards which direct the behavior of members of a society in general or in specific areas of behavior; or the organization within a society of groups which are in conflict with reference to specific practices. Briefly stated, social disorganization may appear in the form of lack of standards or conflict of standards.

Two conditions are favorable to disorganization of our society in the control of business behavior: first, the fact that the behavior is complex, technical, and not readily observable by inexperienced citizens; second, the fact that the society is changing rapidly in its business practices. In any period of rapid change, old standards tend to break down and a period of time is required for the development of new standards.

The *anomie* form of social disorganization is related to the change from the earlier system of free competition and free enterprise to the developing system of private collectivism and governmental regulation of business. The tradition has been that a government should not intervene in the regulation of business but that free competition and supply and demand should regulate economic processes. This tradition was generally held by the people of the United States in the earlier period. While the tradition has been largely abandoned in practice, it retains great force as an ideology, which has been designated "the folklore of capitalism." In practice businessmen are more devoted than any other part of current society to the policy of social planning. This is social planning in the interest of businessmen. Social planning for the more inclusive society is criticized by businessmen as "regimentation," "bureaucracy," "visionary," and "communistic." In this transition from one social system toward a different social system, *anomie* has existed in two forms. First, the businessmen passed through a period of uncertainty. They were dissatisfied with the system of free competition and free enterprise and had no substitute on which they could agree. This period cannot be sharply limited but is located within the three to six decades after the Civil War. Second, the general public has passed or is passing through the same uncertainty, starting at a later period than did the businessman and continuing after businessmen had reached a new consensus.

Conflict of standards is the second form of social disorganization. This is similar to differential association in that it involves a ratio between organization favorable to violation of law and organization unfavorable to violation of law. For this reason it may be called, with greater precision, differential social organization rather than social disorganization. Business has a rather tight organization for the violations of business regulations, while the political society is not similarly organized against violations of business regulations.

Evidence has been presented in previous chapters that crimes of business are organized crimes. This evidence refers not only to gentlemen's agreements, pools, trade associations, patent agreements, cartels, conferences, and other formal and informal understandings, but also to the tentacles which business throws out into the government and the public for the control of those portions of the society. The definition of specific acts as illegal is a prerequisite to white collar crime, and to that extent the political society is necessarily organized against white collar crime. The statutes, however, have little importance in the control of business behavior unless they are supported by an administration which is intent on stopping the illegal behavior. In turn, the political administration has little force in stopping this behavior unless it is supported by a public which is intent on the enforcement of the law. This calls for a clear-cut opposition between the public and the government, on the one side, and the businessmen who violate the law, on the other. This clear-cut opposition does not exist and the absence of this opposition is evidence of the lack of organization against white collar crime. What is, in theory, a war loses much of its conflict because of the fraternization between the two forces. White collar crimes continue because of this lack of organization on the part of the public.

The explanation of crime in general in terms of social disorganization has been at the focus of attention of many criminologists for at least a generation. This has not proved to be a very useful hypothesis up to the present time. A precise definition of social disorganization has been lacking, and the concept has often included ethical implications which have interfered with its utility as an analytical concept. Also, this hypothesis cannot be tested for validity. Finally, it does not explain the content of the criminal behavior or the reasons for the conflicts of standards; the hypothesis points to and describes the conflicts of standards but provides no satisfactory explanation of the genesis of the conflicts.

Notes

1. Federal Trade Commission, *Utility Corporations*, vol. 81A, pp. 237–244.

2. Federal Trade Commission, *Utility Corporations*, "customer-ownership" in index, vol. 84.

3. Bouck White, *The Book of Daniel Drew* (New York, 1910), pp. 144–145.

4. Amos Pinchot, "Walter Lippman," *Nation*, 137:9, July 5, 1933.

5. Associated Press, April 15, 1945.

6. *PM*, February 19, 1945, p. 3.

7. I. F. Stone, "Questions on the Whitney Case," *Nation*, 148: 55–58, January 14, 1939; "Dewey as Prosecutor," *New Republic*, 111:389–390, September 23, 1944.

8. This word was introduced into American sociological literature from the writings of the French sociologist Durkheim.

ANOMIE: THEORY AND FACT

Marshall B. Clinard

*Most influential theories generate a good deal of criticism. Criticism usually fo-
cuses on the clarity and consistency of the concepts and on how well the theory
fits the facts. In this excerpt, Clinard summarizes the criticisms of anomie theory
that six sociologists made during a special symposium on the subject. The major
criticisms are as follows: uniform values seem most unlikely in a complex society;
there is no evidence of higher rates of deviant behavior among the lower classes;
status discontent does not uniformly lead to deviant behavior; the so-called deviant's role in selecting a deviant style is much more complex than the theory
allows for; and social control, as either cause or deterrent of deviant behavior, is
completely overlooked by the theory.*

THE UNIFORMITY OF CULTURAL VALUES

Merton's theory of anomie tends to consider the social structure as consisting of
more uniform values than an empirical examination of the diverse nature of most
societies shows, according to Lemert. His main criticism of anomie is directed
at the difficulty of identifying a set of values that could be considered universal
in most societies today. There are not many societies, even pre-literate ones, in
which "values learned in childhood, taught as a pattern, and reinforced by structured controls, serve to predict the bulk of the everyday behavior of members
and to account for prevailing conformity to norms."[1] He adds also that to maintain that contemporary, urban, secular, and technologically based societies, such
as the United States, "have a common value hierarchy, either culturally transmitted or structurally induced, strains credulity."[2] In societies where there is
ethnic pluralism or newly migrant groups, or where a set of foreign values has
been imposed, as on a colonial population, criminal behavior, for example, can
be explained in the same way as conformity among members of the dominant
group, i.e., by reference to traditionally patterned values and norms where there
is *no* structural restriction of means.[3]

Rather than assuming "goals" to exist in American culture, as Merton does,
Lemert believes that the "ends sought" grow out of the nature of associations in
modern complex societies, the multi-value claims made on individuals, and the
influence of modern technology. In this way it is possible to explain conformity
as well as deviations without assuming "inherent" qualities or goals which apply
to all members of a modern society. Individual members of a modern complex

From Marshall B. Clinard, *Anomie and Deviant Behavior*, pp. 40–47, 49–52. Copyright © 1964
by The Free Press of Glencoe, a division of The Macmillan Company. Reprinted by permission.

society may, as a result of interaction with diverse groups, modify their cultural values or change the order of their satisfaction. Consequently, it is doubtful whether study of the "ideal pattern" or those values and norms presumably indoctrinated into individuals, will generally predict conformity in modern society.

EVIDENCE OF CLASS VARIATIONS IN THE DISTRIBUTION OF DEVIANT BEHAVIOR

In his discussion, Lemert claims that Merton over-emphasizes one aspect of social structure, class-limited access to means, in explaining deviant behavior. He questions whether we even have sufficient empiric evidence to support the contention that deviant behavior is disproportionately more common at lower class levels of society. A more discriminating concept or concepts than social class should, therefore, be utilized in explaining how social structure influences deviation. Moreover, there is insufficient evidence to support the view that deviation is the result of individual adaptations. . . .

PRESSURES TOWARD DEVIATION DEPENDENT ON POSITION IN THE SOCIAL STRUCTURE

Several authors are critical of Merton's position that limited access to the goals of society through legitimate means by the lower socioeconomic groups is a principal source of deviance. For example, while recognizing that social position may play an important role in determining what means become available to reach certain ends, Lemert feels that other factors are equally important, namely, group or collective adaptations, technology, psychic processes, and socio-biological handicaps. All of these factors Merton largely neglects in his emphasis on social class.

Lemert, moreover, maintains that "the discrete individual remains for Merton the unit of analysis; the group as an arena of interaction, influencing conformity and deviation, nowhere comes to the fore in his treatment."[4] Many forms of deviant behavior such as professional crime, prostitution, and opiate addiction, are collective acts in which group-maintained values, as well as private values, are involved. Much of white collar crime is of this order, as several studies have demonstrated. Likewise, much of what is termed conformity is a collective rather than an individual phenomenon or form of adaptation.

In their implementation of Merton's theory, Cohen, Cloward, and Ohlin made much of gang delinquency as a reflection of position or status discontent. In a test of this hypothesis, Short found this to be a chief component of those pressures toward deviant behavior, as measured by the magnitude of the mean discrepancy between the boys' occupational aspirations and occupational expectations; position discontent orders the boys in approximately the same manner as does their delinquency involvement, as measured by police records.[5] When position discontent was measured by a comparison of the occupational aspirations and expectations of the boys with the occupational achievements of their fathers, the Negro boys as a group had aspirations and expectations much higher than that of the white boys. On the other hand, there was an even higher degree of such position discontent among non-gang lower class boys, who had a lower rate of delinquency. A similar overall picture was presented for perceiving educational opportunities as closed, but again, there were internal contradictions.

These contradictory findings suggest to Short the difficulty of conducting research on anomie theory. "High educational and occupational aspirations . . . seem clearly not to pressure the boys toward deviance, despite limitations, perceived and objective, in opportunities for achievement of these aspirations."[6] He offers a possible hypothesis that "high aspirations are indicative of identification with conventional values and institutions. The stake in conformity . . . serves to protect the boys from delinquency involvement."[7]

Again, contrary to Cohen and Cloward and Ohlin, Short found that gang boys recognized the moral validity and legitimacy of middle class values. As opposed to Cohen, no rebellion against the social system nor evidence of reaction against middle class values was found. Short then advanced a significant point when he maintained that the conception of "social" which is basic to the anomie paradigm of opportunity structures and status deprivation must be "broadened to include situations which are more immediate to the boys, such as local community norms and opportunities, and normative and status considerations *within* the group."[8]

Short goes on to argue that while status considerations are important in explaining a gang boy's behavior, they do not have to be sought in middle class institutions and criteria of success. Status deprivation can also be important in a more immediate context, such as the boy's status as a male or as a member of a particular gang. As a tentative conclusion therefore, let us take the position that the "behavior of gang boys may be understood as an attempt by these boys to seek and create alternative status systems in the form of the gang, and that delinquency arises sometimes as a by-product and sometimes as a direct product of this attempt."[9] He enlarges the thesis that while gang boys encounter status deprivation within "respectable society," the status situations which are of immediate concern are those which relate to ongoing processes which involve their daily lives. Each boy then must adjust to a variety of statuses, a process which Short terms "status management."

This view is far removed from one which seeks to explain delinquency by the economic, educational, and other deprivations of the larger social structure, although Short says one may consider his explanation as an extension of the larger theory. He believes that the social structure operates to determine or to influence strongly economic and educational goals, aspirations, and opportunities. The theory of anomie, however, fails to take into account the ongoing group processes of interaction, from which delinquent behavior may develop. . . .

THE ROLE OF THE ACTOR

Lemert has a major objection to Merton's view of choice and action by individuals in our type of society. He feels that Merton simplifies something that is actually quite complex. The individual is not a free agent in his choice of values, but rather is restricted by the claims of various groups to which he belongs. The "pressures" on individuals come from these conflicting claims rather than from cultural emphasis on goals. Special interest groups in our society attempt to advance or protect their own sets of values. . . . As Lemert says, . . . the "emphasis placed on normative means is determined by their cost, that is, by the *particular* values that must be sacrificed in order to adopt means."[10] . . .

In his paper on delinquency, Short states that anomie is too mechanical a theory and that it disregards the actor. "What is lacking in most models of gang behavior is precisely this type of Meadian act, in which behavior is seen as a process of *continuous adjustment* of actors to one another, rather than as a sort of mechanical reaction to some one factor or combination of factors in the situation, whether they be characteristics of actors, or subcultures, or other features. It is this conception, too, which is lacking in anomie theory."[11] What the theory of anomie refers to as "pressures toward deviance" needs both theoretical and empirical specification. . . .

RETREATISM AS AN ADAPTATION OF MEANS AND GOALS

Three characteristic types of retreatism are generally considered by anomie theory to be drug addiction, alcoholism, and mental disorder. Lindesmith and Gagnon maintain that drug addicts are not retreatists but rather claim that difficulties in securing the drug make the addict of necessity an "active" rather than retreatist person. Snyder, while recognizing the research difficulties in studying the phenomenon of alcoholism, which has a prolonged history and by definition is "retreatist," feels that there is evidence to support the contention that the alcoholic was anomic even before his addiction began. . . .

Lindesmith and Gagnon point out that while some of the characteristics ascribed to retreatism apply to some drug addicts, none is accurate as a general description. Addicts are not persons who have abandoned both goals and means and who are characterized, in Merton's terms, by "defeatism, quietism, and resignation." In actuality, there are substantial numbers of addicts to whom such a description does not apply; there are addicts who are "responsible and productive members of society, who share the common frame of values, who have not abandoned the quest for success and are not immune to the frustrations involved in seeking it."[12] They go on to point out that Merton's description of the retreatist, while it does not adequately describe the actual addict, "does provide a reasonably accurate portrait of the current popular stereotype of the addict."

The "double failure" hypothesis of drug addiction advanced by Cloward and Ohlin, and in part implicit by Merton, namely, that the addict cannot achieve success goals by either legitimate or illegitimate means, comes in for pointed criticism by Lindesmith and Gagnon. They state: (1) It is not clear whether there is an actual objective performance failure or whether the individual tends to feel simply frustrated by a perceived block to success. (2) The hypothesis is not applicable to the doctor addict, among others. (3) The addicted person is not necessarily a failure in crime. (4) One cannot judge early adolescents, among whom such phenomena might occur, as double failures because of the age factor. . . . (5) While it may be conceded that there are many addicts who are failures in both the criminal and noncriminal world, it may be argued that addiction is probably more potent as a cause of failure than failure is a cause of addiction.[13]

For the addict in American society, the pursuit of drugs becomes a stimulus to action, not an escape from the requirements of society. One might describe the successful drug user as a "double success" rather than a double failure, the conventional rewards of accomplishment being an assured and adequate supply of drugs. In fact, one of the defects in the theory of anomie is the contention that the inner strain of anomie supposedly is reduced by the use of drugs, when actually, addiction ordinarily widens the "gap between aspirations and the means of achievement and to intensify, rather than resolve, inner anomie-generated conflict."[14]

The use of opiates by real addicts does not have the euphoric effect often described by those who assume that drugs are used for escape. As Lindesmith and Gagnon maintain, "The paradox anomie theory faces is that while opiates can be used for retreatist motives, they are used in this way primarily by those who are not addicted to them."[15] Addiction to opiates is not retreatism; rather, many persons are able to overcome retreatism through the use of drugs and to carry on their daily activities.

In an analytical paradigm they show that there is no invariant relationship between anomie, deviance, retreatism, and drug addiction. Not all drug addiction arises from anomie or is retreatist or deviant, and drug addiction may produce anomia. Addiction may, therefore, occur in any combination with the other three and also when all are absent. Likewise, anomie, deviance, and retreatism might also occur singly or in combination in the absence of addiction. Anomie as a theory does not, therefore, "specify the conditions under which the phenomenon being explained will occur and in the absence of which will not occur."[16]

Lindesmith and Gagnon disagree with the assumption that the use of drugs necessarily constitutes deviation, whether retreatist or otherwise, for like other forms of deviant behavior, the definition may shift according to time, place, the definer, and other considerations. They cite evidence that a substantial part of marijuana and opiate use today cannot be viewed as deviant behavior. Similarly, the nondeviant use of opiates can be illustrated by their wide use in Western society, in the past and today, either in therapy or to relieve pain. This may lead to addiction without the patient having voluntarily administered the drug. Their conclusion is: "Since the theory of anomie is proposed as a theory of deviance, and since some drug use is not deviant, the theory can hardly be relevant to the non-deviant portion. If the theory is applied to the non-deviant drug use, or if it is restricted to 'deviant drug use,' it meets substantial difficulties."[17]

Notes

1. Marshall B. Clinard, *Anomie and Deviant Behavior: A Discussion and Critique*, New York: The Free Press, 1964, p. 64.

2. *Ibid.*, 66.

3. *Ibid.*, 65.

4. *Ibid.*, 76.

5. *Ibid.*, 111–113.

6. *Ibid.*, 115.

7. *Ibid.*, 116.

8. *Ibid.*, 115.

9. *Ibid.*, 117.

10. *Ibid.*, 70.

11. *Ibid.*, 124.

12. *Ibid.*, 178.

13. *Ibid.*, 177.

14. *Ibid.*, 180.

15. *Ibid.*, 183.

16. *Ibid.*, 188.

17. *Ibid.*, 163.

AN EVALUATION OF THE THEORY OF DIFFERENTIAL ASSOCIATION

Donald R. Cressey

Sutherland's differential association theory is fifty years old. It is very influential and has inspired a good deal of research. Yet it is also misunderstood and widely criticized. In this excerpt, Cressey answers some critics and evaluates its current status as a theory of crime. He points out that Sutherland derived the theory of differential association from the principle of normative conflict and showed how it made sense of the data on crime rates. As a statement of how people become criminal, however, it is neither complete nor precise, and the lack of precision makes it difficult to test. At the same time, since accurate predictors of criminal behavior can be deduced from the theory of differential association, Cressey concludes, it goes further than any other current theory in explaining how people become criminals.

One popular form of criticism of differential association is not, strictly speaking, criticism at all. A number of scholars have speculated that some kinds of criminal behavior are exceptions to the theory. Thus, it has been said that the theory does not apply to rural offenders, to landlords who violate rent control regulations, to criminal violators of financial trust, "naïve check forgers," to white-collar criminals, to certain delinquents,[1] to perpetrators of "individual" and "personal" crimes, to irrational and impulsive criminals, to "adventitious" and/or "accidental" criminals, to "occasional," "incidental," and "situational" offenders, to murderers, nonprofessional shoplifters and noncareer types of criminals, to persons who commit crimes of passion and to persons whose crimes were perpetrated under emotional stress.[2] It is important to note that only the first six comments—those referring to rural offenders, landlords, trust violators, check forgers, some white-collar criminals, and some delinquents—are based on research. . . .

The fact that most of the comments are not based on research means that the criticisms are actually proposals for research. Should a person conduct research on a particular type of offender and find that the theory does not hold, then a revision of the theory is called for, provided the research actually tested the theory, or part of it. As indicated, this procedure has been used in six instances, and these instances need to be given careful attention. Hirschi, for example, has concluded on the basis of empirical research that *absence* of control, not the presence of behavior patterns favorable to delinquency, is what increases the likelihood that delinquent acts will be committed.[3] But in most cases, there is no evidence that the kind of behavior said to be exceptional is exceptional. For example, we do not know that "accidental" or "incidental" or "occasional" criminals have not gone through the process specified in the theory. Perhaps it is sometimes assumed that some types of criminal behavior are "obviously exceptional." However, one theoretical analysis indicated that a type of behavior that appears to be obviously exceptional—"compulsive criminality"—is not necessarily exceptional at all.[4]

A second principal kind of criticism attacks the theory because it does not adequately take into account the "personality traits," "personality factors," or "psychological variables" in criminal behavior. This is real criticism, for it suggests that the statement neglects an important determinant of criminality. Occasionally, the criticism is linked with the apparent assumption that some kinds of criminality are "obviously" exceptional. However, at least a dozen authors have proposed that the statement is defective because it omits or overlooks the general role of personality traits in determining criminality.

In an early period Sutherland stated that his theory probably would have to be revised to take account of personality traits.[5] Later he pointed out what he believed to be the fundamental weakness in his critics' argument: *Personality traits* and *personality* are words that merely specify a condition, like mental retardation, without showing the relationship between that condition and criminality. He posed three questions for advocates of personality traits as supplements to differential association: (1) What are the personality traits that should be regarded as significant? (2) Are there personal traits to be used as supplements to differential association, which are not already included in the concept of differential association? (3) Can differential association, which is essentially a *process* of learning, be combined with personal traits, which are essentially the *product* of learning?[6]

Sutherland did not attempt to answer these questions, but the context of his discussion indicates his belief that differential association does explain why some persons with a trait like "aggressiveness" commit crimes, while other persons possessing the same trait do not. It also reveals his conviction that terms like *personality traits, personality,* and *psychogenic trait components* are, when used with no further elaboration to explain why a person becomes a criminal, synonyms for *unknown conditions.*[7]

Closely allied with the "personality trait" criticism is the assertion that the theory does not adequately take into account the "response" patterns, "acceptance" patterns, and "receptivity" patterns of various individuals. The essential notion here is that differential association emphasizes the social process of transmission but minimizes the individual process of reception. Stated in another way, the idea is that the theory deals only with external variables and does not take into account the meaning to the recipient of the various patterns of behavior presented in situations which are objectively quite similar but nevertheless variable, according to the recipient's perception of them. One variety of this type of criticism takes the form of asserting that criminals and noncriminals are sometimes reared in the "same environment"—criminal behavior patterns are presented to two persons, but only one of them becomes a criminal.

Sutherland was acutely aware of the social psychological problem posed by such concepts as "differential response patterns." Significantly, his proposed solution to the problem was his statement of the theory of differential association.[8] One of the principal objectives of the theory is to account for differences in individual responses to opportunities for crime and in individual responses to criminal behavior patterns presented. To illustrate, one person who walks by an unguarded and open cash register, or who is informed of the presence of such a condition in a nearby store, may perceive the situation as a "crime-committing" one, while another person in the identical circumstances may perceive the situation as one in which the owner should be warned against carelessness. The difference in these two perceptions, the theory holds, is due to differences in the prior associations with the two types of definition of situation, so that the alternatives in behavior are accounted for in terms of differential association. The differential in "response pattern," or the difference in "receptivity" to the criminal behavior pattern presented, then, is accounted for by differential association itself.[9] Cressey has argued that one of the greatest defects in the theory is its implication that receptivity to any behavior pattern presented is determined by the patterns presented earlier, that receptivity to those early presentations was determined by even earlier presentations, and so on back to birth.[10] But this is an assertion that the theory is difficult to test, not an assertion that it does not take into account the differential response patterns of individuals.

If receptivity is viewed in a different way, however, the critics appear to be on firm ground.[11] The theory does not identify what constitutes a definition favorable to or unfavorable to the violation of law. The same objective definition might be favorable or unfavorable, depending on the relationship between the donor and the recipient. Consequently, the theory indicates that differential associations may vary in "intensity," which is not precisely defined but "has to do with such things as the prestige of the source of a criminal or anticriminal pattern and with emotional reactions related to the associations." This statement tells us that some associations are to be given added *weight*, but it does not tell us how, or whether, early associations affect the *meaning* of later associations. If earlier associations determine whether a person will later identify specific behavior patterns as favorable or unfavorable to law violation, then these earlier associations determine the very meaning of the later ones, and do not merely give added weight to them. In other words, whether a person is prestigeful or not prestigeful to another may be determined by experiences that have nothing to do with criminality and anticriminality. Nevertheless, these experiences affect the meaning (whether favorable or unfavorable) of patterns later presented to the person and, thus, they affect receptivity to the behavior patterns.[12] For example, in one experiment a rich-looking person and a poor-looking person were employed as models. The models crossed a street against a traffic light, and the experimenters noted how many pedestrians followed them in their lawbreaking. More people imitated the rich-looking model, possibly because to many persons, observing another person crossing the street against the light is not objectively favorable or unfavorable. If a poor person does it, it might be a behavior pattern unfavorable to law violation, but if a rich person does it, the pattern might have a quite different meaning.[13]

A fourth kind of criticism is more damaging than the first three, for it insists that the ratio of learned behavior patterns used to explain criminality cannot be determined with accuracy in specific cases. Short, for example, has pointed out the extreme difficulty of operationalizing terms such as "favorable to" and "unfavorable to"; nevertheless, he has devised various measures of differential association and has used the term in a series of significant studies.[14] Glaser has noted that the "phrase 'excess of definitions' itself lacks clear denotation in human experience." Glueck has asked, "Has anybody actually counted the number of definitions favorable to violation of law and definitions unfavorable to violation of law, and demonstrated that in the predelinquency experience of the vast majority of delinquents and criminals, the former exceeds the latter?" And Hirschi has concluded both that the theory is "virtually nonfalsifiable" and that predictions from it "tend to be trivial."[15] In a study of trust violators, Cressey found that embezzlers could not identify specific persons or agencies from whom they learned their behavior patterns favorable to trust violation. The general conclusion was, "It is doubtful that it can be shown empirically that the differential association theory applies or does not apply to crimes of financial trust violation or even to other kinds of criminal behavior."[16] Similarly, Stanfield has noted the extreme difficulty of measuring the variation and content of "frequency, duration, priority, and intensity."[17]

It should be noted that these damaging criticisms of the theory of differential association as a precise statement of the mechanism by which persons become criminals do not affect the value of the theory as a general principle which organizes and makes good sense of the data on crime rates. As we shall see below, a theory accounting for the distribution of crime, delinquency, or any other phenomenon can be valid even if a presumably coordinate theory specifying the process by which deviancy occurs in individual cases is *incorrect*, let alone untestable.

The fifth kind of criticism states in more general terms than the first four that the theory of differential association oversimplifies the process by which criminal behavior is learned. At the extreme are assertions that the theory is inadequate because it does not allow for a process in which criminality is said to be "chosen" by the individual actor. Some such assertions maintain that a social psychology and sociology of criminals and crime is impossible, and their authors ask for a return to something like the "free will" tenets of the classical school of criminology. Interestingly enough, such assertions have in recent years been announced by social psychologists and sociologists.[18] More realistic criticism ranges from simple assertions that the learning process is more complex than the theory states or implies, to the idea that the theory does not adequately take into account some specific type of learning process, such as differential identification or operant conditioning.

But it is one thing to criticize the theory for failure to specify the learning process accurately and another to specify which aspects of the learning process should be included and in what way.[19] Clinard, Glaser, and Matthews, among others, have introduced the process of identification.[20] Weinberg, Sykes and Matza, Cressey and Frazier, among others, have stressed other aspects of more general social psychological theory.[21] Adams has, on the basis of a laboratory experiment, noted the importance of such "nonsocial" variables as money, drugs, and sex in the reinforcement and maintenance of delinquent behavior.[22] Jensen consistently found that boys who associate with delinquents are more likely to be delinquent than boys who do not, but this occurs independently of the effect of these associations on their attitudes and beliefs.[23] Even these attempts are, like the differential association statement itself, more in the nature of general indications of the kind of framework or orientation one should use in formulating a theory of criminality than they are statements of theory. Burgess and Akers have given a most promising lead in this area by specifying that the conditions and mechanisms through which delinquent and criminal behavior are learned are those indicated in the theory of human learning variously referred to as reinforcement theory, operant behavior theory, and operant conditioning theory.[24]

The theory of differential association does not concentrate exclusively on individual criminality. It is also concerned with making sense of the gross facts about delinquency and crime.[25] Examination of Sutherland's writings clearly indicates that when he formulated the theory he was greatly, if not primarily, concerned with organizing and integrating the factual information about crime rates. In his account of how the theory of differential association developed, he made the following three relevant points:

> More significant for the development of the theory were certain questions which I raised in class discussions. One of these questions was, Negroes, young-adult males, and city dwellers all have relatively high crime rates: What do these three groups have in common that places them in this position? Another question was, even if feeble-minded persons have a high crime rate, why do they commit crimes? It is not feeble-mindedness as such, for some feeble-minded persons do not commit crimes. Later I raised another question which became even more important in my search for generalizations. Crime rates have a high correlation with poverty if considered by areas of a city but a low correlation if considered chronologically in relation to the business cycle; this obviously means that poverty as such is not an important cause of crime. How are the varying associations between crime and poverty explained?[26]
>
> It was my conception that a general theory should take account of all the factual information regarding crime causation. It does this either by organizing the multiple

factors in relation to each other or by abstracting them from certain common elements. It does not, or should not, neglect or eliminate any factors that are included in the multiple-factor theory.[27]

The hypothesis of differential association seemed to me to be consistent with the principal gross findings in criminology. It explained why the Mollaccan children became progressively delinquent with length of residence in the deteriorated area of Los Angeles, why the city crime rate is higher than the rural crime rate, why males are more delinquent than females, why the crime rate remains consistently higher in deteriorated areas of cities, why the juvenile delinquency rate in a foreign nativity group is high while the group lives in a deteriorated area and drops when the group moves out of the area, why second-generation Italians do not have the high murder rate their fathers had, why Japanese children in a deteriorated area of Seattle had a low delinquency rate even though in poverty, why crimes do not increase greatly in a period of depression. All of the general statistical facts seem to fit this hypothesis.[28]

The formal statement of the theory indicates, for example, that a high crime rate in urban areas can be considered the end product of criminalistic traditions in those areas. Similarly, the fact that the rate for all crimes is not higher in some urban areas than it is in some rural areas can be attributed to differences in conditions which affect the probabilities of exposure to criminal behavior patterns.[29] The important general point is that in a multigroup type of social organization, alternative and inconsistent standards of conduct are possessed by various groups, so that an individual who is a member of one group has a high probability of learning to use legal means for achieving success, or learning to deny the importance of success, while an individual in another group learns to accept the importance of success and to achieve it by illegal means. Stated in another way, there are alternative educational processes in operation, varying with groups, so that a person may be educated in either conventional or criminal means of achieving success. As indicated above, this situation may be called "differential social organization" or "differential group organization." "Differential group organization" should explain the crime rate while differential association should explain the criminal behavior of a person. The two explanations must be consistent with each other.

It should be noted that, in the three quotations above, Sutherland referred to the differential association statement as both a "theory" and a "hypothesis," and did not indicate any special concern for distinguishing between differential association as it applies to the epidemiology of crime and differential association as it applies to individual conduct. In order to avoid controversy about the essential characteristics of theories and hypotheses, it seems preferable to call differential association, as it is used in reference to crime rates, a principle. Many "theories" in sociology are in fact principles that order facts about rates—now called epidemiology—in some way. Durkheim, for example, invented what may be termed a "principle of group integration" to account for, organize logically, and integrate systematically the data on variations in suicide rates. He did not invent a theory of suicide, derive hypotheses from it, and then collect data to determine whether the hypotheses were correct or incorrect. He tried to make sense of known facts about rates, and the principle he suggested remains the most valuable idea available to understand the differences in the rates of suicide between Protestants and Jews, urban-dwellers and rural-dwellers, and so on.

The differential association statement, similarly, is a "principle of normative conflict" which proposes that high crime rates occur in societies and groups characterized by conditions that lead to the development of extensive criminalistic subcultures. The principle makes sense of variations in crime rates by observing that modern societies are organized for crime as well as against it, and then observing further that crime rates are unequally distributed because of differences in the degree to which various categories of persons participate in this normative conflict.[30] Sutherland invented the principle of normative conflict to account for the distribution of high and low crime rates; he then tried to specify the mechanism by which this principle works to produce individual cases of criminality. The mechanism proposed is differential association:

> The second concept, differential association, is a statement of [normative] conflict from the point of view of the person who commits the crime. The two kinds of culture impinge on him or he has association with the two kinds of cultures and this is differential association.[31]

THE VALUE OF DIFFERENTIAL ASSOCIATION

As an organizing principle, normative conflict makes understandable most of the variations in crime rates discovered by various researchers and observers, and it also focuses attention on crucial research areas.[32] The principle of normative conflict does not make good sense out of all the statistical variations, but it seems to make better sense out of more of them than do any of the alternative theories.

On the other hand, it also seems safe to conclude that differential association is not a precise statement of the process by which one becomes a criminal. The idea that criminality is a consequence of an excess of intimate associations with criminal behavior patterns is valuable because, for example, it negates assertions that deviation from norms is simply a product of being emotionally insecure or living in a broken home, and then indicates in a general way why only some emotionally insecure persons and only some persons from broken homes commit crimes. Also, it directs attention to the idea that an efficient explanation of individual conduct is consistent with explanations of epidemiology. Yet the statement of the differential association process is not precise enough to stimulate rigorous empirical test, and it therefore has not been proved or disproved. This defect is shared with broader social psychological theory. Although critics agree, as we have indicated, that the differential association statement oversimplifies the process by which normative conflict "gets into" persons and produces criminality, an acceptable substitute that is consistent with the principle of normative conflict has not appeared.

It is important to observe, however, that the "individual conduct" part of the theoretical statement does order data on individual criminality in a general way and, consequently, might be considered a principle itself. Thus, "differential association" may be viewed as a restatement of the principle of normative conflict, so that this one principle is used to account for the distribution of criminal and noncriminal behavior in both the life of the individual *and* in the statistics on collectivities. In this case, both individual behavior data and epidemiological rate data may be employed as indices of the variables in the principle, thus providing

two types of hypotheses for testing it.[33] Glaser has shown that differential association makes sense of both the predictive efficiency of some parole prediction
items and the lack of predictive efficiency of other items.[34] In effect, he tested
the principle by determining whether parole prediction procedures which could
have proven it false actually failed to prove it false. First, he shows that a majority
of the most accurate predictors in criminology prediction research are deducible
from differential association theory, while the least accurate predictors are not
deducible at all. Second, he shows that this degree of accuracy does not characterize alternative theories. Finally, he notes that two successful predictors of
parole violation—type of offense and noncriminal employment opportunities—
are not necessarily deducible from the theory, and he suggests a modification
that would take this fact into account.

Notes

1. Marshall B. Clinard, "The Process of Urbanization and Criminal Behavior," *American
Journal of Sociology*, 48: 202–13, 1942; idem, "Rural Criminal Offenders," *American Jour-
nal of Sociology*, 50: 38–45, 1944; idem, "Criminological Theories of Violations of Wartime
Regulations," *American Sociological Review*, 11: 258–70, 1946; Donald R. Cressey, "Ap-
plication and Verification of the Differential Association Theory," *Journal of Criminal Law,
Criminology, and Police Science*, 43: 43–52, 1952; Edwin M. Lemert, "Isolation and Clo-
sure Theory of Naïve Check Forgery," *Journal of Criminal Law, Criminology, and Police
Science*, 44: 293–307, 1953; Daniel Glaser, "Criminality Theories and Behavioral Images,"
American Journal of Sociology, 61: 441, 1956; and Travis Hirschi, *Causes of Delinquency*
(Berkeley: University of California Press, 1969), pp. 14–15, 229–30.

2. See [Gwynn] Nettler, *Explaining Crime* [New York: McGraw-Hill, 1974], p. 197; and
Steven Giannell, "Criminosynthesis," *International Journal of Social Psychiatry*, 16: 83–
95, 1970.

3. Hirschi, *Causes of Delinquency*, p. 229. See also Gary F. Jensen, "Parents, Peers, and
Delinquent Action: A Test of the Differential Association Perspective," *American Journal
of Sociology*, 78: 562–75, 1972; John R. Hepburn, "Testing Alternative Models of Delin-
quency Causation," *Journal of Criminal Law and Criminology*, 67: 450–60, 1977; and
Joseph H. Rankin, "Investigating the Interrelations Among Social Control Variables and
Conformity," *Journal of Criminal Law and Criminology*, 67: 470–80, 1977.

4. Donald R. Cressey, "The Differential Association Theory and Compulsive Crimes,"
Journal of Criminal Law, Criminology, and Police Science, 45: 49–64, 1954.

5. Sutherland, "Development of the Theory," pp. 25–27.

6. Edwin H. Sutherland, *White Collar Crime* (New York: Dryden Press, 1949), p. 272.
See also Harwin L. Voss, "Differential Association and Containment Theory—a Theoretical Convergence," *Social Forces*, 47: 381–91, 1969.

7. See the discussion in Chapter 7 [of *Criminology*, the source of this excerpt].

8. See Edwin H. Sutherland, "Susceptibility and Differential Association," in *Edwin H.
Sutherland on Analyzing Crime*, ed. Schuessler, pp. 42–43. See also Solomon Kobrin, "The
Conflict of Values in Delinquency Areas," *American Sociological Review*, 16: 653–61, 1951.

9. Cf. Elihu Katz, Martin L. Levin, and Herbert Hamilton, "Traditions of Research on the Diffusion of Innovation," *American Sociological Review*, 28: 237–52, 1963.

10. Cressey, "Application and Verification of the Differential Association Theory."

11. I am indebted to Albert K. Cohen for assistance with this paragraph and with other points.

12. See also Don C. Gibbons, *Society, Crime and Criminal Careers: An Introduction to Criminology* (Englewood Cliffs, NJ: Prentice-Hall, 1968), pp. 204–6.

13. M. M. Lefkowitz et al., "Status Factors in Pedestrian Violation of Traffic Signals," *Journal of Abnormal and Social Psychology*, 51: 704–6, 1955.

14. James F. Short, Jr., "Differential Association and Delinquency," *Social Problems*, 4: 233–39, 1957; and James F. Short, Jr. and Fred L. Strodtbeck, *Group Process and Gang Delinquency* (Chicago: University of Chicago Press, 1965).

15. Glaser, "Criminality Theories and Behavioral Images"; Glueck, "Theory and Fact in Criminology," p. 96; and Hirschi, *Causes of Delinquency*, pp. 14–15.

16. Cressey, "Application and Verification of the Differential Association Theory," p. 52.

17. Robert E. Stanfield, "The Interaction of Family Variables and Gang Variables in the Aetiology of Delinquency," *Social Problems*, 13: 411–17, 1966.

18. David Matza, *Becoming Deviant* (Englewood Cliffs, N.J.: Prentice-Hall, 1969), p. 107; Steven Box, *Deviance, Reality, and Society* (London: Holt, Rinehart and Winston, 1971), p. 21; Ian Taylor, Paul Walton, and Jock Young, *The New Criminology: For a Social Theory of Deviance* (London: Routledge and Kegan Paul, 1973), p. 128.

19. Despite the fact that Sutherland described a learning process, it should be noted that he also said, "The process of learning criminal and anticriminal behavior patterns involves all the mechanisms that are involved in any other learning."

20. Clinard, "The Process of Urbanization and Criminal Behavior"; idem, "Rural Criminal Offenders"; idem, "Criminological Theories of Violations of Wartime Regulations"; Glaser, "Criminality Theories and Behavioral Images"; idem, "Differential Association and Criminological Prediction," *Social Problems*, 8:6–14, 1960; idem, "The Differential Association Theory of Crime," in *Human Behavior and Social Process*, ed. Arnold Rose (Boston: Houghton Mifflin, 1962), pp. 425–43; Victor Matthews, "Differential Identification: An Empirical Note," *Social Problems*, 15: 376–83, 1968.

21. S. Kirson Weinberg, "Theories of Criminality and Problems of Prediction," *Journal of Criminal Law, Criminology, and Police Science*, 45: 412–29, 1954; idem, "Personality and Method in the Differential Association Theory," *Journal of Research in Crime and Delinquency*, 3: 165–72, 1966; Gresham Sykes and David Matza, "Techniques of Neutralization: A Theory of Delinquency," *American Sociological Review*, 22: 664–70, 1957; Cressey, "Application and Verification of the Differential Association Theory"; idem, "The Differential Association Theory and Compulsive Crimes"; idem, "Social Psychological Foundations for Using Criminals in the Rehabilitation of Criminals," *Journal of Research in Crime and Delinquency*, 2: 49–59, 1965; idem, "The Language of Set Theory and Differential Association," *Journal of Research in Crime and Delinquency*, 3: 22–26, 1966; Charles E. Frazier, *Theoretical Approaches to Deviance* (Columbus, OH: Bobbs-Merrill, 1976), pp. 113–114.

22. Reed Adams, "The Adequacy of Differential Association Theory," *Journal of Research in Crime and Delinquency*, 11: 1–8, 1974. See also Clarence Ray Jeffery, "Criminal Behavior and Learning Theory," *Journal of Criminal Law, Criminology, and Police Science*, 56: 294–300, 1965.

23. Jensen, "Parents, Peers and Delinquent Action."

24. Robert L. Burgess and Ronald L. Akers, "A Differential Association—Reinforcement Theory of Criminal Behavior," *Social Problems*, 14: 128–47, 1968. See also Ronald L. Akers, Robert L. Burgess, and Weldon T. Johnson, "Opiate Use, Addiction, and Relapse," *Social Problems*, 15: 459–69, 1968.

25. One of Sutherland's own students, colleagues, and editors has said, "Much that travels under the name of sociology of deviant behavior or of social disorganization is psychology—some of it very good psychology, but psychology. For example, Sutherland's theory of differential associations, which is widely regarded as preeminently sociological, is not the less psychological because it makes much of the cultural milieu. It is psychological because it addresses itself to the question: How do people become the kind of individuals who commit criminal acts? A sociological question would be: What is it about the structure of social systems that determines the kinds of criminal acts that occur in these systems and the way in which such acts are distributed within these systems?" (Albert K. Cohen, "The Study of Social Disorganization and Deviant Behavior," chap. 21 in *Sociology Today*, ed. Robert K. Merton, Leonard Broom, and Leonard S. Cottrell, Jr. [New York: Basic Books, 1959], p. 462).

26. Sutherland, "Development of the Theory," p. 15.

27. Ibid., p. 18.

28. Ibid., pp. 19–20.

29. Cf. Henry D. McKay, "Differential Association and Crime Prevention: Problems of Utilization," *Social Problems*, 8: 25–37, 1960.

30. See Raymond D. Gastil, "Homicide and a Regional Culture of Violence," *American Sociological Review*, 36: 412–27, 1971.

31. Sutherland, "Development of the Theory," pp. 20–21.

32. Cf. Llewellyn Gross, "Theory Construction in Sociology: A Methodological Inquiry," chap. 17 in *Symposium on Sociological Theory*, ed. Llewellyn Gross (Evanston, IL: Row, Peterson, 1959), pp. 548–55. See also Donald R. Cressey, "The State of Criminal Statistics," *National Probation and Parole Association Journal*, 3: 230–41, 1957; and DeFleur and Quinney, "Reformulation of Sutherland's Differential Association Theory."

33. I am indebted to Daniel Glaser for calling this point to my attention.

34. Glaser, "Differential Association and Criminological Prediction." See also idem, "A Reconsideration of Some Parole Prediction Factors," *American Sociological Review*, 19: 335–41, 1954; and idem, "The Efficiency of Alternative Approaches to Parole Prediction," *American Sociological Review*, 20: 283–87, June, 1955; and Daniel Glaser and Richard R. Hangren, "Predicting the Adjustment of Federal Probationers," *National Probation and Parole Association Journal*, 4: 258–67, 1958; and David M. Downes, *The Delinquent Solution: A Study in Subcultural Theory* (London: Routledge and Kegan Paul, 1966), pp. 97–98.

Questions for Discussion

1. Sutherland and Cressey discuss different levels of causal analysis. How do Merton's anomie and Sutherland's differential association theories differ in their levels?

2. How does Sutherland's theory of differential association integrate the multiple factors that may help to explain criminal behavior?

3. In "A Theory of White Collar Crime," how does Sutherland show that social disorganization and differential association are counterparts of one another?

4. Consider Clinard's critique of Merton's anomie theory. Do you see it as a plea for integration with differential association theory? How so, or why not?

5. Do you agree with any of the criticisms of Sutherland's theory? If yes, which one(s) and why?

Selected References

Adler, Freda, and William S. Laufer, eds. *The Legacy of Anomie Theory.* New Brunswick, NJ: Transaction, 1995.

The first compilation of essays documenting the revival of anomie theory as it bears on the social problems of crime.

Agnew, Robert. "A Longitudinal Test of Social Control Theory and Delinquency." *Journal of Research in Crime and Delinquency* 28 (May 1991): 126–56.

A study which shows, among the variables researched, the best predictions of delinquency to be prior delinquent involvement and deviant peer associations, results which support social learning theory.

Agnew, Robert. "Foundation for a General Strain Theory of Crime and Delinquency." *Criminology* 30 (February 1992): 47–87.

Robert Agnew has revitalized and extended Merton's theory. He amplifies the strain concept so that it might explain all forms of delinquent behavior.

Akers, Ronald L. *Deviant Behavior. A Social Learning Approach.* 3rd ed. Belmont, CA.: Wadsworth, 1985.

Seven of Sutherland's postulates of differential association use the word "learning." Akers rephrased them in the language of reinforcement psychology in his opening chapters and then employed them to analyze alcohol and drug use, mental illness, suicide, sexual deviance, and several varieties of criminal behavior.

Blake, Judith, and Kingsley Davis. "Norms, Values, and Sanctions." In *Handbook of Modern Sociology*, ed. Robert E. L. Faris. Chicago: Rand McNally, 1964, pp. 456–84.

Focuses on the sources of unintentional deviance, the sources of deviant motivation, and the factors preventing deviant motives from erupting into deviant behavior. The answers are provided from existing sociological literature.

Clinard, Marshall B., ed. *Anomie and Deviant Behavior: A Discussion and Critique.* New York: Free Press, 1964.

A useful dialogue regarding anomie theory. Clinard restates Merton's anomie theory and its implications. Six sociologists then give criticisms of the application of anomie theory to particular types of deviant acts. Finally, Merton responds to these critics. A useful appendix inventories eighty-eight empirical and theoretical studies of anomie—a testimony to the tremendous influence of this theory.

Clinard, Marshall B., and Robert F. Meier. *Sociology of Deviant Behavior.* 10th ed. Fort Worth, TX: Harcourt Brace, 1991.

Clinard and Meier point out that Sutherland's differential association theory can be applied not only to crime, but also to both the causes and the distribution of many different varieties of deviance among various groups in the population. Broadening his conception to a more general socialization theory, they apply it to numerous forms of deviant behavior, including physical disabilities.

Cloward, Richard A., and Lloyd E. Ohlin. *Delinquency and Opportunity: A Theory of Delinquent Gangs.* New York: The Free Press, 1960.

Cloward and Ohlin argue that access to both legitimate and illegitimate means can explain the formation of three types of delinquent gangs. The absence of access to legitimate means and the presence of access to illegitimate means increases the chances of *criminal* gang-formation. Absence of both legitimate and illegitimate means increases the chances of *fighting* gang-formation. And absence of access to legitimate means along with access to opportunities for drug use increases the chances of *drug* gang-formation.

Cohen, Albert K. *Delinquent Boys: The Culture of the Gang*. Glencoe, Ill.: Free Press, 1955.

A creative synthesis of the theories of anomie and differential association in which Cohen develops an influential theory of delinquent subcultures. A landmark in the tradition of deviant behavior analysis.

Cohen, Albert K. "Deviant Behavior." In *International Encyclopedia of Social Sciences*, ed. David L. Sills. New York: Macmillan and The Free Press, 1968, vol. 4, pp. 148–55

A scholarly essay on the rise and development of the deviant behavior perspective.

Cohen, Albert K., Alfred Lindesmith, and Karl Schuessler, eds. *The Sutherland Papers*. Bloomington: Indiana University Press, 1956.

Unsolicited self-criticism is rare. In this book, Sutherland examines his own theory of differential association, and his criticisms are almost as trenchant as the theory itself.

Durkheim, Emile. *Suicide: A Study in Sociology*. Trans. John A. Spaulding and George Simpson. Glencoe, IL: Free Press, 1951.

The classic statement regarding anomie. Durkheim shows that rates of suicide are higher under certain types of social conditions. One such condition is anomie, or normlessness.

Hirschi, Travis. *The Causes of Delinquency*. Berkeley: University of California Press, 1968.

Hirschi devises a systematic deviant behavior perspective on why teenagers become delinquent and then proceeds to test his hypothesis on some 4,000 California high-school students. His results offer ample support for his contention that the weakening of social bonds is the major cause of juvenile delinquency.

Kornhauser, Ruth Rosner. *Social Sources of Delinquency: An Appraisal of Analytic Models*. Chicago: University of Chicago Press, 1978.

After a systematic review of numerous studies of juvenile delinquency, Kornhauser finds that control theories (such as Hirschi's and others) explain delinquency much better than disorganization, anomie, or differential association.

Leonard, Eileen B. *Women, Crime and Society: A Critique of Criminology Theory*. New York: Longman, 1982.

According to Leonard, as more women aim to achieve financial success, thus challenging traditional restrictions and expectations, this can lead to anomie and, hence, to an increase in female crime.

Passas, Nikos, and Robert Agnew, eds. *The Future of Anomie Theory*. Boston: Northeastern University Press, 1997.

Anomie theory dominated the study of crime as a social problem during the 1950s and 1960s, declined during the 1970s and 1980s, and experienced a revival in the 1990s. Passas and Nikos collected eighteen essays that show that anomie theory can account for the social problems of crime and deviance—both of organizations and persons. These revisions and extensions of anomie theory clearly demonstrate that a disjunction between institutionalized means and any cultural goals (not only economic ones) generates pressures that culminate in severe social problems.

Rosenfeld, Richard, and Steven F. Messner, "Crime and the American Dream: An Institutional Analysis." In *The Legacy of Anomie Theory*, eds. Freda Adler and William S. Laufer. *Advances in Criminological Theory*. Volume 6. New Brunswick, NJ: Transaction, 1989, pp. 159–181.

Criminologists are at a loss to explain the extremely high rates of serious crimes in the United States when compared with all other developed nations. This failure, Rosenfeld and Messner argue, stems from criminologists' defining Merton's theory as a strain theory rather than as a structural explanation for deviant behavior. Merton's anomie theory, they say, seeks to explain *variation in rates of deviant behavior* rather than personal conduct (why A commits a crime whereas B doesn't). They point out that Merton noted that the overemphasis in the United States of defining success in economic terms sets the stage for deviant behavior when access to the legitimate means are scarce or absent. But the sufficient condition for excessive rates of crime, they argue, resides in the economy, which dominates the three other major social institutions: the family, education, and government.

Simon, William, and John H. Gagnon. "The Anomie of Affluence: Post-Mertonian Conception." *American Journal of Sociology* 82 (September 1976): 356–78.

The authors maintain that Merton's famous anomie theory presupposes an economy of scarcity. Since 1938, when Merton first presented his typology of responses to strains between culture and social structure, most of the societies in the Western world have become affluent. The situation of affluence produces different kinds of strains between means and goals, and the authors posit nine types of responses to the strains experienced in the affluent society, a number of which contribute to social problems.

Warr, Mark, and Mark Stafford. "The Influence of Delinquent Peers: What They Think or What They Do?" *Criminology* 29 (November 1991): 851–66.

In studying marijuana use, the authors find that in addition to attitude transmission (Sutherland's version of social learning) such mechanisms as "imitation" can be involved in the effect peers have on one's behavior.

6/LABELING

Perspectives differ in the questions they ask and the answers they yield. The sociology of deviant behavior, for example, initially asks *why people commit* crimes or other deviant acts. Sociologists in this tradition attempt to determine the necessary and sufficient conditions that produce deviant acts. The labeling perspective,[1] on the contrary, examines the social definition of deviance. Sociologists in this tradition want to know *how people define* situations, persons, processes, or events as problematic.

Inspired by Fuller, most sociologists agree that a social problem consists of a subjective definition and an objective condition. But, with few exceptions, sociologists have paid more attention to the objective condition than to the subjective definition. Students of labeling, however, reversed the emphasis by taking a closer look at the process of subjective definition, and this has led to an entirely different line of sociological questioning.

This chapter discusses the people who developed the labeling perspective, the questions they raised, and the events in sociology that contributed to the development of this perspective.

FOCUS AND CONCERNS OF THE LABELING PERSPECTIVE

Included in the labeling perspective is a set of assumptions about how people define situations. Perhaps the principal assumption is that people define all the recurrent situations in which they find themselves by means of interests and values. If so, then of course all definitions are related to people's positions in a given situation, the values they hold, and the interests they wish to further.

One line of attack of the labeling approach has been to look at the world from the vantage point of persons who have been socially defined by others as deviant, as well as from the vantage point of those who do the defining. Another has been to study the making of social rules (laws, organizational definitions, and so on) and the practices by which they are enforced. Both lines of attack have led to some very

---

1. A growing number of sociologists now prefer to call this approach the "interactionist perspective" rather than "labeling theory." The newer name was first used by Earl Rubington and Martin S. Weinberg, eds., *Deviance: The Interactionist Perspective* (New York: Macmillan, 1968) to connote that the "labeling" perspective fits into the broader tradition of "symbolic interactionism." Howard S. Becker, in the 1973 edition of *Outsiders: Studies in the Sociology of Deviance,* says that he now also prefers the term "interactionist."

important research findings. They have also, however, led some sociologists to accuse the labeling approach of having a vested interest in the underdog, almost to the point of accepting a "distorted" view of social reality.[2] We turn now to some of the conditions that gave rise to the labeling perspective.

THE DISCIPLINE AND ITS PROBLEMS

The labeling perspective arose relatively late in American sociology's fourth period (cultivating specialties: 1954–1970). During this period, the study of crime, deviance, and social control became specialties. Thus, sociologists working from both the deviant behavior and the labeling perspectives generally restricted themselves to the study of these social problems.

What transpired during this period to foster the labeling perspective? Three factors contributed: extension of concepts, conflict between schools, and interest in questions left unanswered by the deviant behavior perspective.

Extension of Concepts. The drive to refine and extend concepts characterizes the history of most sciences because of the efforts of scientists to explain a greater number of phenomena by means of a smaller number of concepts. During sociology's fourth period, theorists worked on refining concepts while researchers extended these concepts to new areas. This combination of labors contributed to the growing body of sociological knowledge. As a tradition called symbolic interactionism developed, researchers began to extend its concepts to the study of social problems, and the labeling perspective evolved out of this extension. (The role of the interactionist tradition in the development of the labeling perspective is dealt with more fully in the section on philosophical sources.)

Conflict Between Schools. Competition between Chicago sociology and Harvard sociology, noted in the preceding chapter, grew out of different conceptions of the sociological enterprise. Harvard emphasized structure, and many of its students developed, refined, and extended the concepts of structural-functionalism. Chicago, on the contrary, emphasized social process and developed, refined and extended the concepts of symbolic interactionism. Of course, notions of the differences between these schools of thought were exaggerated and frequently bordered on caricature. Nonetheless, opposition between the two schools almost required that one segment of sociologists study the processes involved in social problems, while the others look for their sources in social structure. Thus, the politics of sociology, as it were, led sociologists congenial to the Chicago school to join the labeling camp and followers of the Harvard school to oppose it.

Unanswered Questions. There are limitations in the deviant behavior perspective related to the specialized and complex nature of the society. In a multigroup society, conforming to the rules of one's own group sometimes requires violating another group's rules, whether legal, moral, or social. Similarly, not all violators are caught or punished, even though their offenses may be widely known. Finally, of those who are officially caught, not everyone is classified and treated in the same way.

2. See, for example, David Bordua, "Deviant Behavior and Social Control," *The Annals* 369 (January 1967): 149–63, and Alvin W. Gouldner, "The Sociologist as Partisan," *The American Sociologist* 3 (May 1968): 103–16.

These aspects of social problems seemed inexplicable from the deviant behavior perspective, leading some sociologists to begin to ask different sorts of questions: When are violations sanctioned, by whom, regarding whom, and with what social consequences? With these questions, the labeling perspective was born.

For those in the deviant behavior tradition, the labeling perspective stereotypes and oversimplifies the phenomenon of deviance. For those in the labeling tradition, it signifies a legitimate extension of interactionist concepts. Some differences between the interests of the two perspectives are summarized below.

Etiology.   Whereas the underlying causes of deviant behavior (for example, broken homes, social class, anomie, psychiatric disorder) are of great interest from the deviant behavior perspective, they are of little interest from the labeling perspective.

Initiating Factor.   The initiating factor, or the last act in the etiological chain, is of considerable interest to those who use the deviant behavior perspective, but of less interest to students of labeling.

Social Reactions.   Social reactions to alleged deviance are the central concern of labeling theory but not of the deviant behavior perspective.

The Official Record.   The deviant behavior perspective takes official records for granted, using them as indicators of deviant behavior. The labeling perspective finds official records interesting in and of themselves.[3] The acts that are recorded, how they are categorized, as well as where, when, and with what consequences, constitute a major focus of attention. The labeling perspective assumes that official records reflect primarily the processes of the organization compiling them. Thus, they are not assumed to present literal descriptions of the behaviors that they supposedly document.

In summary, the labeling perspective focuses on process rather than structure, on subjectivity rather than objectivity, and on reactions to deviance rather than the initiation of deviance.

PHILOSOPHICAL SOURCES OF THE LABELING PERSPECTIVE

The labeling approach is an outgrowth of the social philosophies of George Herbert Mead[4] and Alfred Schutz.[5] Although both men were philosophers, each exerted tremendous influence on sociologists. Mead's influence has been felt for a longer period of time by a wider circle of sociologists, while Schutz's influence has been more recent and limited. Together, Mead and Schutz constitute the major background sources of the labeling perspective.

Mead.   Mead taught philosophy at the University of Chicago. In his lectures, Mead presented a model of people and of social reality that, as adopted and developed

3. A good example is John I. Kitsuse and Aaron V. Cicourel, "A Note on the Uses of Official Statistics," *Social Problems* 11 (Fall 1963): 131–39.

4. George Herbert Mead, *Mind, Self, and Society from the Standpoint of a Social Behaviorist* (Chicago: University of Chicago Press, 1934).

5. Alfred Schutz, *Collected Papers I: The Problem of Social Reality,* ed. Maurice Natanson (The Hague: Martinus Nijhoff, 1962).

by members of the Chicago department of sociology, came to be known as symbolic interactionism.

Mead held that the sense of self arises in the course of social interaction. People learn to take the "attitude of the other" toward themselves. In so doing, they come to see themselves as social objects, and they subsequently behave according to that self-conception.

Mead also conceived of social interaction as emergent and dynamic rather than static in character. By reading gestures and symbols, he stressed, people continually adjust their behavior to what others seem about to do. The labeling perspective highlights the relevance of this concept for the study of deviance.

Schutz.   Schutz sought to explain social order by showing that people produce a set of typifications about the world.[6] These typifications include persons, places, things, and events; and insofar as people assume that other people are defining situations in much the same way, social order is produced. Schutz concerned himself with three important questions: What is the essence of any particular phenomenon in question? How do people make typifications? By what processes do typifications come to be considered as shared? The labeling perspective picks up on these interests and asks related questions: What is the essence of deviance as a *sociological* phenomenon? What are the processes by which people typify others as deviant? How do people come to share these typifications?

FOUNDERS OF THE LABELING PERSPECTIVE

The "grandfather" of labeling theory is Edwin Lemert. In 1951, Lemert published a book titled (or mistitled) *Social Pathology*.[7] In this book he set forth a systematic theory of deviant behavior based on the notion that deviance is defined by social reactions and that the frequency and character of deviation, together with the role of the deviant, are in large part shaped by the social reaction.

The labeling perspective was christened, however, in a book by Howard S. Becker, *Outsiders,* which appeared in 1963. The statement that helped to name the approach was:

> Social groups create deviance by making the rules whose infraction constitutes deviance, and by applying those rules to particular people and labeling them as outsiders. From this point of view, deviance is not a quality of the act the person commits, but rather a consequence of the application by others of rules and sanctions to an "offender." The deviant is one to whom that label has successfully been applied; deviant behavior is behavior that people so label.[8]

Though a change in thought on social problems was already under way, Becker's *Outsiders* crystallized it. Becker showed that becoming sociologically deviant is a dynamic interactive process, drawn out over time in a sequence orderly enough to be called a career. He also observed that not everyone who breaks the rules gets labeled deviant, that ultimately the definition and the enforcement of moral rules are

6. In his work, Schutz provides an important synthesis of the thought of Edmund Husserl, George Herbert Mead, and Max Weber.

7. Edwin M. Lemert, *Social Pathology: A Systematic Approach to the Theory of Sociopathic Behavior* (New York: McGraw-Hill, 1951).

8. Howard S. Becker, *Outsiders: Studies in the Sociology of Deviance* (New York: Free Press, 1963), p. 9.

political acts, and that the meaning of a deviant act can change over time for the people involved.

In the years since Becker's book appeared in 1963, a number of other sociologists have contributed to the labeling perspective. These sociologists have dealt primarily with the applications of rules to people who have apparently breached them, the conditions under which rules or labels are applied, and the consequences for the labeled person's self-image and future.[9]

CHARACTERISTICS OF THE LABELING PERSPECTIVE

Central to the labeling perspective is the notion that social problems and deviance exist in the eye of the beholder. The perspective seeks to study the process of and responses to social differentiation. The principal elements in the labeling perspective are as follows:

Definition. A social problem or social deviant is defined by social reactions to an alleged violation of rules or expectations. This perspective focuses on the conditions under which behaviors or situations come to be defined as problematic or deviant.

Causes. The cause of a social problem is ultimately *the attention it receives* from the public or from social control agents, for social reactions cannot occur until the alleged behavior or situation is recognized.

Conditions. When a person or situation is labeled problematic or deviant, the labeler is usually in a position to gain by affixing such a label. The labeler must have a negative label to apply and the power to make it stick. Very often, the labeling is done by someone whose job it is to apply labels (for example, social control agents, journalists), and assigning labels is often a mark of success in such jobs.[10] Occasionally, people may label themselves, and in doing so they may gain some advantages (for example, people have reported that they are homosexual in order to be discharged from the military).[11]

Consequences. The definition of a person or situation as socially problematic or deviant may lead to a reordering of human relations in a way that promotes further "deviance." For example, after a person has been labeled "deviant," most people expect him or her to continue violating norms of conventional behavior. This may limit the labeled person's life chances and lead him or her to elaborate the deviant role; for example, an ex-convict may be unable to obtain employment in a conventional job and may thus return to crime in order to make a living. This elaboration of deviant roles because of other people's reactions is called "secondary deviance."[12]

9. Despite their contributions, several of these writers disavow that they are proponents of labeling theory. For a useful discussion, see Erich Goode, "On Behalf of Labeling Theory," *Social Problems* 22 (June 1975): 570–83.

10. Examples are provided in Rubington and Weinberg, *Deviance*.

11. For example, see Colin J. Williams and Martin S. Weinberg, *Homosexuals and the Military: A Study of Less than Honorable Discharge* (New York: Harper & Row, 1971).

12. For an extended discussion of secondary deviance, see Edwin M. Lemert, *Human Deviance, Social Problems, and Social Control,* 2nd ed. (Englewood Cliffs, NJ: Prentice-Hall, 1972), pp. 62–92.

Solutions. The labeling perspective suggests two solutions: definitions can be changed, and the profit can be taken out of labeling. Changing definitions would mean becoming more tolerant, so that people stop labeling certain people and situations as problematic. Taking the profit out of labeling would mean a consequent decrease both in people's labeling of themselves and others as deviant, and in the problems that result from such labeling.

SUMMARY AND CONCLUSION

In the period after 1954, sociology was characterized as *the cultivation of specialties.* Early in this period, the deviant behavior perspective became prominent. Nonetheless certain problems remained unexplained by that perspective, and these unexplained problems generated the labeling perspective. The labeling point of view was rooted in symbolic interactionism, formulated by Mead and later elaborated by Schutz. As symbolic interactionism was extended to the study of the social processes surrounding deviance, the gap between structure and process views in sociology widened.

The labeling perspective examines certain taken-for-granted aspects of social problems. Sociologists working within this perspective focus on the people who define problems, the conditions under which a person or situation is labeled problematic, and the consequences of this labeling. Thus, social problems and deviance are defined by social reactions to a presumed violation of rules or expectations. The cause is presumed knowledge of the violation, and the conditions affecting the labeling process are power relations and the gains to be made by labeling. The major consequences of successful labeling are an elaboration of deviance (secondary deviance) and expectations of continued violations. Solutions suggested by the labeling perspective are to change definitions and to eliminate labeling profits.

OUTSIDERS

Howard S. Becker

Traditionally, sociologists studied deviance by examining the attributes of persons who violated rules, why they did so, what distinguished violators from nonviolators, and what could be done about it in a practical sense. Becker's excerpt exemplifies a more recent trend, in which deviance is studied in terms of the successful application of labels. With this reconceptualization, many sociologists have turned their attention from studying deviant behaviors to studying the social definition of deviance and the consequence of such definitions.

DEVIANCE AND THE RESPONSES OF OTHERS

[One sociological view] . . . defines deviance as the infraction of some agreed-upon rule. It then goes on to ask who breaks rules, and to search for the factors in their personalities and life situations that might account for the infractions. This assumes that those who have broken a rule constitute a homogeneous category, because they have committed the same deviant act.

Such an assumption seems to me to ignore the central fact about deviance: it is created by society. I do not mean this in the way it is ordinarily understood, in which the causes of deviance are located in the social situation of the deviant or in "social factors" which prompt his action. I mean, rather, the *social groups create deviance by making the rules whose infraction constitutes deviance,* and by applying those rules to particular people and labeling them as outsiders. From this point of view, deviance is *not* a quality of the act the person commits, but rather a consequence of the application by others of rules and sanctions to an "offender." The deviant is one to whom that label has successfully been applied; deviant behavior is behavior that people so label.[1]

Since deviance is, among other things, a consequence of the responses of others to a person's act, students of deviance cannot assume that they are dealing with a homogeneous category when they study people who have been labeled deviant. That is, they cannot assume that these people have actually committed a deviant act or broken some rule, because the process of labeling may not be infallible; some people may be labeled deviant who in fact have not broken a rule. Furthermore, they cannot assume that the category of those labeled deviant will contain all those who actually have broken a rule, for many offenders may escape apprehension and thus fail to be included in the population of "deviants"

From Howard S. Becker, *Outsiders: Studies in the Sociology of Deviance*, pp. 8–14, 31–33. Copyright © 1963 by The Free Press of Glencoe, a division of The Macmillan Company. Reprinted by permission.

they study. Insofar as the category lacks homogeneity and fails to include all the cases that belong in it, one cannot reasonably expect to find common factors of personality or life situation that will account for the supposed deviance.

What, then, do people who have been labeled deviant have in common? At the least, they share the label and the experience of being labeled as outsiders. I will begin my analysis with this basic similarity and view deviance as the product of a transaction that takes place between some social group and one who is viewed by that group as a rule-breaker. I will be less concerned with the personal and social characteristics of deviants than with the process by which they come to be thought of as outsiders and their reactions to that judgment.

Malinowski discovered the usefulness of this view for understanding the nature of deviance many years ago, in his study of the Trobriand Islands:

> One day an outbreak of wailing and a great commotion told me that a death had occurred somewhere in the neighborhood. I was informed that Kima'i, a young lad of my acquaintance, of sixteen or so, had fallen from a coconut palm and killed himself. . . . I found that another youth had been severely wounded by some mysterious coincidence. And at the funeral there was obviously a general feeling of hostility between the village where the boy died and that into which his body was carried for burial.
>
> Only much later was I able to discover the real meaning of these events. The boy had committed suicide. The truth was that he had broken the rules of exogamy, the partner in his crime being his maternal cousin, the daughter of his mother's sister. This had been known and generally disapproved of but nothing was done until the girl's discarded lover, who had wanted to marry her and who felt personally injured, took the initiative. This rival threatened first to use black magic against the guilty youth, but this had not much effect. Then one evening he insulted the culprit in public—accusing him in the hearing of the whole community of incest and hurling at him certain expressions intolerable to a native.
>
> For this there was only one remedy; only one means of escape remained to the unfortunate youth. Next morning he put on festive attire and ornamentation, climbed a coconut palm and addressed the community, speaking from among the palm leaves and bidding them farewell. He explained the reasons for his desperate deed and also launched forth a veiled accusation against the man who had driven him to his death, upon which it became the duty of his clansmen to avenge him. Then he wailed aloud, as is the custom, jumped from a palm some sixty feet high and was killed on the spot. There followed a fight within the village in which the rival was wounded; and the quarrel was repeated during the funeral. . . .
>
> If you were to inquire into the matter among the Trobrianders, you would find . . . that the natives show horror at the idea of violating the rules of exogamy and that they believe that sores, disease and even death might follow clan incest. This is the ideal of native law, and in moral matters it is easy and pleasant strictly to adhere to the ideal—when judging the conduct of others or expressing an opinion about conduct in general.
>
> When it comes to the application of morality and ideals to real life, however, things take on a different complexion. In the case described it was obvious that the facts would not tally with the ideal of conduct. Public opinion was neither outraged by the knowledge of the crime to any extent, nor did it react directly—it had to be mobilized by a public statement of the crime and by insults being hurled at the culprit by an interested party. Even then he had to carry out the punishment himself. . . . Probing further into the matter and collecting concrete information, I found that the breach of exogamy—as regards intercourse and not marriage—is by no means a rare occurrence, and public opinion is lenient, though decidedly hypocritical. If the affair is carried on *sub rosa* with a certain amount of decorum, and if

no one in particular stirs up trouble—"public opinion" will gossip, but not demand any harsh punishment. If, on the contrary, scandal breaks out—everyone turns against the guilty pair and by ostracism and insults one or the other may be driven to suicide.[2]

Whether an act is deviant . . . depends on how other people react to it. You can commit clan incest and suffer from no more than gossip as long as no one makes a public accusation; but you will be driven to your death if the accusation is made. The point is that the response of other people has to be regarded as problematic. Just because one has committed an infraction of a rule does not mean that others will respond as though this had happened. (Conversely, just because one has not violated a rule does not mean that he may not be treated, in some circumstances, as though he had.)

The degree to which other people will respond to a given act as deviant varies greatly. Several kinds of variation seem worth noting. First of all, there is variation over time. A person believed to have committed a given "deviant" act may at one time be responded to much more leniently than he would be at some other time. The occurrence of "drives" against various kinds of deviance illustrates this clearly. At various times, enforcement officials may decide to make an all-out attack on some particular kind of deviance, such as gambling, drug addiction, or homosexuality. It is obviously much more dangerous to engage in one of these activities when a drive is on than at any other time. (In a very interesting study of crime news in Colorado newspapers, Davis found that the amount of crime reported in Colorado newspapers showed very little association with actual changes in the amount of crime taking place in Colorado. And, further, the people's estimate of how much increase there had been in crime in Colorado was associated with the increase in the amount of crime news but not with any increase in the amount of crime.)[3]

The degree to which an act will be treated as deviant depends also on who commits the act and who feels he has been harmed by it. Rules tend to be applied more to some persons than others. Studies of juvenile delinquency make the point clearly. Boys from middle-class areas do not get as far in the legal process when they are apprehended as do boys from slum areas. The middle-class boy is less likely, when picked up by the police, to be taken to the station; less likely when taken to the station to be booked; and it is extremely unlikely that he will be convicted and sentenced.[4] This variation occurs even though the original infraction of the rule is the same in the two cases. Similarly, the law is differentially applied to Negroes and whites. It is well known that a Negro believed to have attacked a white woman is much more likely to be punished than a white man who commits the same offense; it is only slightly less well known that a Negro who murders another Negro is much less likely to be punished than a white man who commits murder.[5] This, of course, is one of the main points of Sutherland's analysis of white-collar crime: crimes committed by corporations are almost always prosecuted as civil cases, but the same crime committed by an individual is ordinarily treated as a criminal offense.[6]

Some rules are enforced only when they result in certain consequences. The unmarried mother furnishes a clear example. Vincent[7] points out that illicit sexual relations seldom result in severe punishment or social censure for the offenders.

If, however, a girl becomes pregnant as a result of such activities, the reaction of others is likely to be severe. (The illicit pregnancy is also an interesting example of the differential enforcement of rules on different categories of people. Vincent notes that unmarried fathers escape the severe censure visited on the mother.)

Why repeat these commonplace observations? Because, taken together, they support the proposition that deviance is not a simple quality, present in some kinds of behavior and absent in others. Rather, it is the product of a process which involves responses of other people to the behavior. The same behavior may be an infraction of the rules at one time and not at another; may be an infraction when committed by one person, but not when committed by another; some rules are broken with impunity, others are not. In short, whether a given act is deviant or not depends in part on the nature of the act (that is, whether or not it violates some rule) and in part on what other people do about it.

Some people may object that this is merely a terminological quibble, that one can, after all, define terms any way he wants to and that if some people want to speak of rule-breaking behavior as deviant without reference to the reactions of others they are free to do so. This, of course, is true. Yet it might be worthwhile to refer to such behavior as *rule-breaking behavior* and reserve the term *deviant* for those labeled as deviant by some segment of society. I do not insist that this usage be followed. But it should be clear that insofar as a scientist uses "deviant" to refer to any rule-breaking behavior and takes as his subject of study only those who have been *labeled* deviant, he will be hampered by the disparities between the two categories.

If we take as the object of our attention behavior which comes to be labeled as deviant, we must recognize that we cannot know whether a given act will be categorized as deviant until the response of others has occurred. Deviance is not a quality that lies in behavior itself, but in the interaction between the person who commits an act and those who respond to it. . . .

In any case, being . . . branded as deviant has important consequences for one's further social participation and self-image. The most important consequence is a drastic change in the individual's public identity. Committing the improper act and being publicly caught at it place him in a new status. He has been revealed as a different kind of person from the kind he was supposed to be. He is labeled a "fairy," "dope fiend," "nut" or "lunatic," and treated accordingly.

In analyzing the consequences of assuming a deviant identity let us make use of Hughes' distinction between master and auxiliary status traits.[8] Hughes notes that most statuses have one key trait which serves to distinguish those who belong from those who do not. Thus the doctor, whatever else he may be, is a person who has a certificate stating that he has fulfilled certain requirements and is licensed to practice medicine; this is the master trait. As Hughes points out, in our society a doctor is also informally expected to have a number of auxiliary traits: most people expect him to be upper middle class, white, male, and Protestant. When he is not there is a sense that he has in some way failed to fill the bill. Similarly, though skin color is the master status trait determining who is Negro and who is white, Negroes are informally expected to have certain status traits and not to have others; people are surprised and find it anomalous if a Negro turns out to be a doctor or a college professor. People often have the master status trait but lack some of the auxiliary, informally expected character-istics; for example, one may be a doctor but be female or Negro.

Hughes deals with this phenomenon in regard to statuses that are well thought of, desired and desirable (noting that one may have the formal qualifi-cations for entry into a status but be denied full entry because of lack of the proper auxiliary traits), but the same process occurs in the case of deviant stat-uses. Possession of one deviant trait may have a generalized symbolic value, so that people automatically assume that its bearer possesses other undesirable traits allegedly associated with it.

To be labeled a criminal one need only commit a single criminal offense, and this is all the term formally refers to. Yet the word carries a number of conno-tations specifying auxiliary traits characteristic of anyone bearing the label. A man who has been convicted of house-breaking and thereby labeled criminal is pre-sumed to be a person likely to break into other houses; the police, in rounding up known offenders for investigation after a crime has been committed, operate on this premise. Further, he is considered likely to commit other kinds of crimes as well, because he has shown himself to be a person without "respect for the law." Thus, apprehension for one deviant act exposes a person to the likelihood that he will be regarded as deviant or undesirable in other respects.

There is one other element in Hughes's analysis we can borrow with profit: the distinction between master and subordinate statuses.[9] Some statuses, in our society as in others, override all other statuses and have a certain priority. Race is one of these. Membership in the Negro race, as socially defined, will override most other status considerations in most other situations; the fact that one is a physician or middle-class or female will not protect one from being treated as a Negro first and any of these other things second. The status of deviant (depend-ing on the kind of deviance) is this kind of master status. One receives the status as a result of breaking a rule, and the identification proves to be more important than most others. One will be identified as a deviant first, before other identifi-cations are made. . . .

Notes

1. The most important earlier statements of this view can be found in Frank Tannenbaum, *Crime and the Community* (New York: McGraw-Hill Book Co., Inc., 1951), and E. M. Lemert, *Social Pathology* (New York: McGraw-Hill Book Co., Inc., 1951). A recent article stating a position very similar to mine is John Kitsuse, "Societal Reaction to Deviance: Problems of Theory and Method," *Social Problems*, 9 (Winter 1962), 247–256.

2. Bronislaw Malinowski, *Crime and Custom in Savage Society* (New York: Humanities Press, 1926), pp. 77–80. Reprinted by permission of Humanities Press and Routledge & Kegan Paul, Ltd.

3. F. James Davis, "Crime News in Colorado Newspapers," *American Journal of Sociol-ogy*, LVII (January 1952), 325–330.

4. See Albert K. Cohen and James F. Short, Jr., "Juvenile Delinquency," in Robert K.

Merton and Robert A. Nisbet, editors, *Contemporary Social Problems* (New York: Harcourt, Brace and World, Inc., 1961), p. 87.

5. See Harold Garfinkel, "Research Notes on Inter- and Intra-Racial Homicides," *Social Forces*, 27 (May 1949), 360–381.

6. Edwin H. Sutherland, "White Collar Criminality," *American Sociological Review*, V (February 1940), 1–12.

7. Clark Vincent, *Unmarried Mothers* (New York: The Free Press of Glencoe, 1961), pp. 3–5.

8. Everett C. Hughes, "Dilemmas and Contradictions of Status," *American Journal of Sociology*, L (March 1945), 353–359.

9. *Ibid.*

PRIMARY AND SECONDARY DEVIATION
Edwin M. Lemert

The causes of deviant acts, Lemert claims, must be distinguished from the causes of deviant roles. The latter phenomenon, which he calls "secondary deviation," arises out of social interaction between the deviant and his community. If the deviant behavior continues long enough and the community responds with escalating social penalties, then the sequence culminates in "a stigmatizing of the deviant . . . in the form of name calling, labeling, or stereotyping" and a resulting "deviant role." In the absence of severe social reaction, however, a deviant role is less likely since the person is not assigned a disvalued role which would require him to defend himself against real or imagined social punishment.

There has been an embarrassingly large number of theories, often without any relationship to a general theory, advanced to account for various specific [deviations] in human behavior. For certain types of [deviance], such as alcoholism, crime, or stuttering, there are almost as many theories as there are writers on these subjects. This has been occasioned in no small way by the preoccupation with the origins of [deviant] behavior and by the fallacy of confusing *original* causes with *effective* causes. All such theories have elements of truth, and the divergent viewpoints they contain can be reconciled with the general theory here if it is granted that original causes or antecedents of deviant behaviors are many and diversified. This holds especially for the psychological processes leading to similar [deviance], but it also holds for the situational concomitants of the initial aberrant conduct. A person may come to use excessive alcohol not only for a wide variety of subjective reasons but also because of diversified situational in-fluences, such as the death of a loved one, business failure, or participating in some sort of organized group activity calling for heavy drinking of liquor. What-ever the original reasons for violating the norms of the community, they are important only for certain research purposes, such as assessing the extent of the "social problem" at a given time or determining the requirements for a rational program of social control. From a narrower *sociological viewpoint* [Italics added] . . . deviations are not significant until they are organized subjectively and trans-formed into active roles and become the social criteria for assigning status. The deviant individuals must react symbolically to their own behavior aberrations and fix them in their sociopsychological patterns. The deviations remain primary de-viations or symptomatic and situational as long as they are rationalized or oth-erwise dealt with as functions of a socially acceptable role. Under such conditions normal and pathological behaviors remain strange and somewhat tensional bed-fellows in the same person. Undeniably a vast amount of such segmental and partially integrated [deviant] behavior exists in our society and has impressed many writers in the field of [deviance].

Just how far and for how long a person may go in dissociating his [deviant] tendencies so that they are merely troublesome adjuncts of normally conceived roles is not known. Perhaps it depends upon the number of alternative definitions of the same overt behavior that he can develop. . . . However, if the deviant acts are repetitive and have a high visibility, and if there is a severe societal reaction, which, through a process of identification is incorporated as part of the "me" of the individual, the probability is greatly increased that the integration of existing roles will be disrupted and that reorganization based upon a new role or roles will occur. (The "me" in this context is simply the subjective aspect of the societal reaction.) Reorganization may be the adoption of another normal role in which the tendencies previously defined as ["deviant"] are given a more acceptable social expression. The other general possibility is the assumption of a deviant role, if such exists; or, more rarely, the person may organize an aberrant sect or group in which he creates a special role of his own. *When a person begins to employ his deviant behavior or a role based upon it as a means of defense, attack, or adjustment to the overt and covert problems created by the consequent societal reaction to him, his deviation is secondary.* Objective evidences of this change will be found in the symbolic appurtenances of the new role, in clothes, speech, posture, and mannerisms, which in some cases heighten social visibility, and which in some cases serve as symbolic cues to professionalization.

ROLE CONCEPTIONS OF THE INDIVIDUAL MUST BE REINFORCED BY REACTIONS OF OTHERS

It is seldom that one deviant act will provoke a sufficiently strong societal reaction to bring about secondary deviation, unless in the process of introjection the in-dividual imputes or projects meanings into the social situation which are not present. In this case anticipatory fears are involved. For example, in a culture where a child is taught sharp distinctions between "good" women and "bad" women, a single act of questionable morality might conceivably have a profound meaning for the girl so indulging. However, in the absence of reactions by the person's family, neighbors, or the larger community, reinforcing the tentative "bad-girl" self-definition, it is questionable whether a transition to secondary deviation would take place. It is also doubtful whether a temporary exposure to a severe punitive reaction by the community will lead a person to identify himself with a [deviant] role, unless, as we have said, the experience is highly traumatic. Most frequently there is a progressive reciprocal relationship between the deviation of the individual and the societal reaction, with a compounding of the societal reaction out of the minute accretions in the deviant behavior, until a point is reached where ingrouping and outgrouping between society and the deviant is manifest.[1] At this point a stigmatizing of the deviant occurs in the form of name calling, labeling, or stereotyping.

The sequence of interaction leading to secondary deviation is roughly as follows: (1) primary deviation; (2) social penalties; (3) further primary deviation; (4) stronger penalties and rejections; (5) further deviation, perhaps with hostilities and resentment beginning to focus upon those doing the penalizing; (6) crisis reached in the tolerance quotient, expressed in formal action by the community stigmatizing of the deviant; (7) strengthening of the deviant conduct as a reaction to the stigmatizing and penalties; (8) ultimate acceptance of deviant social status and efforts at adjustment on the basis of the associated role.

As an illustration of this sequence the behavior of an errant schoolboy can be cited. For one reason or another, let us say excessive energy, the schoolboy engages in a classroom prank. He is penalized for it by the teacher. Later, due to clumsiness, he creates another disturbance and again he is reprimanded. Then, as sometimes happens, the boy is blamed for something he did not do. When the teacher uses the tag "bad boy" or "mischief maker" or other invidious terms, hostility and resentment are excited in the boy and he may feel that he is blocked in playing the role expected of him. Thereafter, there may be a strong temptation to assume his role in the class as defined by the teacher, particularly when he discovers that there are rewards as well as penalties deriving from such a role. There is, of course, no implication here that such boys go on to become delinquents or criminals, for the mischief-maker role may later become integrated with or retrospectively rationalized as part of a role more acceptable to school authorities.[2] If such a boy continues this unacceptable role and becomes delinquent, the process must be accounted for in the light of the general theory of this volume. There must be a spreading corroboration of a [deviant] self-conception and societal reinforcement at each step in the process.

The most significant personality changes are manifest when societal definitions and their subjective counterpart become generalized. When this happens, the range of major role choices becomes narrowed to one general class.[3] This was very obvious in the case of a young girl who was the daughter of a paroled convict and who was attending a small Middle Western college. She continually argued with herself and with the author, in whom she had confided, that in reality she belonged on the "other side of the railroad tracks" and that her life could be enormously simplified by acquiescing in this verdict and living accordingly. While in her case there was a tendency to dramatize her conflicts, nevertheless there was enough societal reinforcement of her self-conception by the treatment she received in her relationship with her father and on dates with college boys to lend it a painful reality. Once these boys took her home to the shoddy dwelling in a slum area where she lived with her father, who was often in a drunken condition, they abruptly stopped seeing her again or else became sexually presumptive. . . .

Notes

1. Mead, G., "The Psychology of Punitive Justice," *American Journal of Sociology*, 23, March, 1918, pp. 577–602.

2. Evidence for fixed or inevitable sequences from predelinquency to crime is absent. Sutherland, E. H., *Principles of Criminology*, 3rd ed. Philadelphia: Lippincott, 1939. p. 202.

3. Sutherland seems to say something of this sort in connection with the development of criminal behavior. *Ibid.*, p. 86.

THE DEVALUATION OF WOMEN

Edwin M. Schur

Power, wealth, respect, and knowledge are scarce values that people seek. Because women tend to be labeled with an inferior status simply on the basis of their gender, however, this reduces their chances of achieving these values in competition with men. Similarly, their ascribed gender status increases their chances of becoming a victim with regard to a variety of social problems. Schur argues that women are apt to become members of a stigmatized minority group who are overexposed to disrespect in interpersonal relations. They are also likely to become objects of discrimination in politics, corporations, and numerous occupations, skilled as well as unskilled.

Deviant statuses, Becker (1963) has emphasized, tend to exhibit a "master status" quality. They "override all other statuses and have a special priority." The imputation of an identity that is deviant "proves to be more important than most others. One will be identified as a deviator first, before other identifications are made" (Becker, 1963, p. 33; see also Hughes, 1945). Numerous studies have demonstrated that when individuals are "seen" in terms of a deviant status and identity (past or present)—be it "criminal," "homosexual," "madman," "prosti-

From Edwin M. Schur, *Labeling Women Deviant: Gender, Stigma, and Social Control*, pp. 24–28, 34–40. Copyright © 1984 by Random House. Reprinted by permission of The McGraw-Hill Company.

tute," "drug addict," "cripple," or "retardate"—other people's responses to them are heavily influenced by that identification. The tendency is for that to be all the other persons "see." Such imputed deviant identity becomes, in the eyes of others, the individual's essential character; Goffman terms it a "virtual" social identity as distinguished from the actual one (Goffman, 1963, p. 2; see also Garfinkel, 1956).

Reactions to perceived deviance thus emerge through a process of categorical "typing" (Rubington and Weinberg, 1981, pp. 5–7). The individual is responded to, first and foremost, in terms of his or her presumed membership in the devalued category. Furthermore, once this categorical label is applied, people tend to impute to the individual various "auxiliary traits" they believe (however erroneously) to be "characteristic of anyone bearing the label" (Becker, 1963, p. 33; also Hughes, 1945). It can easily be seen that this process is central to the general phenomenon of "prejudice," and that it is therefore manifest in the categorical devaluation of persons on the basis of race, ethnicity, or religion (see Allport, 1958).

Much the same thing is true of responses to women. Since it is indeed a basic mode of human differentiation, we would expect biological sex to carry some "master status" implications. Yet in fact this does not hold true equally for the two sexes. On the contrary, being a female, more than being a male (and in even more distorting ways), "conditions all social interactions; whether or not the individual is conscious of her femaleness, others are" (Laws, 1979, p. 2). Individual women are perceived and reacted to at least initially, and often primarily, in terms of their femaleness. Only secondarily, if at all, do their other identities and qualities determine responses to them. They are perpetually thought to be acting "just like a woman." They regularly have ascribed to them numerous "auxiliary traits" which reflect much refuted but nonetheless persisting "sex role stereotypes" (see Chafetz, 1974, p. 61; also Friedan, 1963; Epstein, 1971; Stoll, 1974; Rothman, 1978; Stockard and Johnson, 1980; Richardson, 1981).

One of the most widespread cultural indicators of the master status tendency is the "hyphenization" phenomenon. Although the practice has been widely criticized, it remains common to describe someone as a "woman-doctor," a "woman-executive," a "woman-novelist," a "woman-athlete," or as the apocryphal "woman-driver." Despite what one might infer from the fact that there are also a few instances in which comparable designations may be applied to men (e.g., "male-nurse," "male-secretary"), such usage clearly represents more than just a convenient means of noting numerically infrequent patterns. In either case, there is an imputation of "occupational deviance." . . . But in addition, since high status occupations and prized competencies tend to be stereotypically "male," the hyphenated designations of women imply a further "put-down." Because she is female, a woman is assumed not to have the same overall competence for the prized role that a man would have. Hence she should be described and assessed only relative to the occupation's other female occupants, rather than in terms of universalistic (i.e., sex-neutral) criteria. (Or, as we shall see shortly, she must be labeled an "exceptional" female.)

Two well-known empirical studies also illustrate the master status aspect of femaleness. A study by Philip Goldberg (1968) relates closely to the assumptions underlying hyphenization, and also shows how women themselves may devalue other women. Goldberg had female college students read excerpts of six journal articles drawn from the professional literature of six different fields—two of the fields being stereotypically "male," two stereotypically "female," and two deemed stereotypically neutral. In preparing the study materials, Goldberg had systematically varied the sex of the indicated authors. For example, one set of respondents reading a given article believed it to have been written by John T. McKay, while for another set of respondents the identical writing was attributed to Joan T. McKay. Asked to evaluate the articles and their authors, Goldberg's respondents consistently rated the articles attributed to men more highly than the identical articles attributed to women. Although the apparent bias against women was strongest in the evaluations of articles from traditionally male fields, the ratings favored presumed male authors in all the fields. Of fifty-four points at which comparisons were possible (each of the six articles was followed by nine questions), three were tied, seven favored the "female" authors, and forty-four favored the "male" authors.

In her study of "token" female sales personnel in a large industrial corporation, Rosabeth Kanter (1977a; 1977b) explicitly used the master status concept in describing and analyzing the responses to these women displayed by male members of the sales force. Kanter found much evidence that these women were perceived and reacted to more as females than as fellow workers. Because they were only "tokens" (i.e., constituted a small numerical minority) their femaleness "stood out." Their "technical abilities were likely to be eclipsed by their physical appearance," and both "male peers and customers would tend to forget information women provided about their experiences and credentials, while noting and remembering such secondary attributes as style of dress" (Kanter, 1977a, p. 973). They were viewed as objects of sexual attention, they were not fully trusted, and male workers made jokes at their expense. Often, in dealing with customers and managers, they "felt themselves to be treated in more wifelike and datelike ways than a man would be treated by another man, even though the situation was clearly professional" (ibid., p. 981).

Treated as "outsiders," these women could not easily enter into the existing (male) camaraderie of the work force. They felt pressured to play out male stereotypes of female roles (such as "the mother," "the seductress," and "the pet"), and if they did not succumb to these "role traps" they were seen as "tough" types who should be kept at a distance. Kanter's analysis emphasizes the matter of numerical frequency. She sees the skewed sex ratio as significantly influencing these modes of interaction. A good deal of experimental research on groups supports this claim—by showing, for example, that the size of a numerical minority within the group affects its members' ability to withstand majority-imposed pressures to conform. Yet it should be realized that Kanter's study can be given a broader reading as well. Almost all the male responses revealed in her research that reflect the "master status" aspect of femaleness are found in most female-male interaction in our society, regardless of numerical frequencies in the particular situations. There is, then, a sense in which women in general continue to occupy a "token" position within our system as a whole. To recognize this is not to deny that there are variations in types and degrees of stigmatization—depending on the particular perceived "offenses" of women and on other features of the specific situation (including the numerical frequency factor).

The beliefs and attitudes revealed in these studies are no doubt undergoing considerable change at the present time. This is perhaps especially true with respect to women's own beliefs regarding female competence. It is not even clear whether Goldberg's findings were fully representative of attitudes held at the time of his research (for discussion of related studies see Stoll, 1974; Fransella and Frost, 1977, Ch. 3; and Spence and Helmreich, 1978). Since then, the women's liberation movement has promoted an increased public awareness of the full range of female competencies. (For more recent data see Levenson, et al., 1975; also England, 1979.) On the other hand, even among women, the tendency to evaluate males more highly may not yet have disappeared. For example, if one were to conduct today a nationwide survey exploring women's preferences in the choice of a personal physician, it is not at all clear that a systematic bias toward males would not be revealed.

If women's beliefs and attitudes are still ambivalent, men's perceptions and behaviors are probably even more resistant to change. Responses in direct interaction situations (of the kinds found in Kanter's research) frequently become habitual in character, almost reflexlike, *regardless* of the beliefs and attitudes—about the abilities of women, and so on—that males might express if questioned. . . . Male reactions to women are heavily affected by the fact of their femaleness—even in situations where that condition ought to be quite irrelevant. . . .

To what extent, overall, are we justified in viewing femaleness as a devalued or "deviant" status, one that—as Laws put it—"carries a stigma in and of itself"? The strength of heterosexual attraction, professed male reverence for certain (limited) women's roles (e.g., motherhood), and the persisting dominance of conventional heterosexual marriage, together suggest how difficult it is to answer that question. As Sheila Rowbotham (1973, p. 34) notes, "The relationship of man to woman is like no other relationship of oppressor to oppressed. It is far more delicate, far more complex. After all, very often the two love one another. It is a rather gentle tyranny. We are subdued at the very moment of intimacy."

It seems clear that the devaluation of women is not total. On the other hand, there is massive evidence showing that it is indeed very substantial, and that its manifestations are extremely wide-spread. . . . For a review of the depth and extent of sex inequality in our society, the reader must consult other sources (see, for example, Laws, 1979; Stockard and Johnson, 1980; Oakley, 1981). We can, however, at least briefly note here four major grounds for accepting the notion that womanhood is, on balance, a devalued status. The first has just been referred to: namely, the well-documented existence of pronounced sex inequality within our social and economic system. An evaluative component is inextricably linked with placement in such a scheme of stratification. Highly valued persons are not systematically relegated (in the way women have been) to the lower echelons of the socioeconomic and occupational prestige ladders. Occupancy of such positions, in turn, tends to be a basis for evaluating people unfavorably.

A second reason to accept the claim that femaleness is devalued has to do with . . . widespread categorical perception and objectification tendencies. . . . It should be apparent that some measure of devaluation is always present in these modes of perceiving and responding to women. At times this element is only implicit, but at other times it becomes quite explicit, even blatant. Women are routinely—and to an extent that we cannot simply attribute to the general impersonality of modern life—treated in ways that suggest they are being little valued for their own selves.

A third and closely related point is the pervasive devaluation of women in "cultural symbolism" (Stockard and Johnson, 1980, Ch. 1; see also, Firestone, 1971; Gornick and Moran, eds., 1972; and Goffman, 1979). Common language usage often trivializes, slights, derogates, or unnecessarily sexualizes woman (see Lakoff, 1975; Adams and Ware, 1979; Richardson, 1981, Ch. 2; also Thorne and Henley, eds., 1975). The same can be said about images of women in the mass media and advertising—some specific aspects of which we will consider below. Widespread public exposure to softcore pornography, let alone the hardcore varieties, currently adds much sexually objectifying imagery of the most blatant sort to this constellation of cultural symbols. . . .

The fourth, and perhaps overriding, reason to view femaleness as devalued is reflected in the central concern of this text—namely, woman's relation to definitions of deviance. Both the multitude of specific "deviances" imputed to women under our gender system, and the failure to strongly condemn male offenses against women, illustrate the low value placed on femaleness. When the extensiveness of these phenomena is explored, the devaluation thesis is once again confirmed.

In the light of these four important types of evidence, the male claim that far from being devalued woman has been kept on "a pedestal" appears highly disingenuous. The treatment of women as "special" that this implies is itself a denial of their ordinary and full humanity. And the little "courtesies" (door opening, cigarette lighting, etc.) that often are cited in connection with the "pedestal" notion trivialize relations with women as well as seeming to deny their capacities for everyday living. Kate Millett's comment (1971, p. 37) on male chivalry is most cogent. She describes it as "a sporting kind of reparation to allow the subordinate female certain means of saving face. While a palliative to the injustice of woman's social position, chivalry is also a technique for disguising it."

A 1960 news account (*The New York Times*, August 10, 1960) nicely suggests the phenomenon of subordination *via* the "pedestal." The article reports a magistrate's criticism of a woman for wearing slacks to traffic court (thus illustrating in retrospect the changeability over time of one type of gender-related "deviance"). In lecturing the woman, the judge explained that he took the matter seriously because he held women on a high plane, and didn't want to see them brought down from "this pedestal." In subsequent reported comments to the woman's husband, the judge inadvertently revealed the true nature of the pedestal. Saying that he would not go out with his own wife if she were dressed that way, he told the husband to "clamp down a little," or else it would be "too late."

Perhaps the most positive thing that can be said about overall male responses to women is that they are ambivalent (see Goffman, 1977, on reflections of such ambivalence in routine interaction). Social psychologist Irwin Katz (1981) has suggested that ambivalence may be a fairly common feature of responses to stigmatized persons. Focusing on reactions to blacks and persons with physical handicaps, Katz reviews findings from his own and other experimental studies to support an "ambivalence" model. Because they hold a mixture of positive and negative attitudes toward and feelings about the stigmatized, other people experience special tension in contacts with them—tension that in turn must be reduced. Thus, research subjects in various experiments attempted to justify or compensate for harm they did to blacks or handicapped person (e.g., by administering a shock), more than when the harm was done to white or nonhandicapped persons. In other experiments, research subjects were found more likely, under certain conditions, to "help out" a black or physically handicapped person than they were to help a white or nonhandicapped person.

At first glance, the ambivalence thesis seems applicable to the "gentle tyranny" of men over women. However, the consequences of dominant male responses to women may be such as to prevent the "positive" side of the ambivalent feelings from having much real social force. Such consequences (at least in the past) have included the partial "segregation" of women in a separate women's "sphere," the discouragement of aspirations and restriction of opportunities, the consistent subjection to objectifying treatment in ordinary interaction, and so on. As we shall note shortly, systematic "inferiorization" of this sort easily becomes self-fulfilling and self-perpetuating. It can create conditions that minimize the need for males to confront evidence contradicting their stereo-types, or to experience discomfort when they negate women. The same conditions may reduce the efforts of females to demonstrate their full potential. Under all of these circumstances, the "tokens" of affection and respect men may bestow on women hardly seem sufficient to refute the claim of (and women's experiences of) a pervasive devaluation.

EXPERIENCING STIGMA

Women face stigmatization on a number of fronts. As we have seen, a certain degree of devaluation attaches merely by virtue of being a female. On top of this, women may be more directly stigmatized and punished for a multitude of specific "deviances". . . . These definitions of female deviance are, in fact, so extensive that virtually every woman becomes a perceived offender of some kind. When these facts are considered, together with the devaluation implicit in woman's general social and economic subordination, it becomes clear that the combined weight of the stigma women may encounter is considerable.

The more concrete stigma experiences of particular women, and the impacts these experiences have on them, are bound to vary a good deal. Labeling analysts (see Lofland, 1969; Schur, 1971; Schur, 1979) have emphasized that the individual's relevant resources (socioeconomic, psychological, group support, etc.) will affect his or her ability to resist stigmatization or to avoid some of its negative impact. To the extent femaleness carries a stigma, avoidance of the "labeling" itself—as may be possible when the stigmatized condition is not immediately evident to others (see Goffman, 1963)—is not an option for women. As Helen Hacker noted (1951) in her important early discussion of similarities in the situations of women and blacks, both suffer from "high social visibility."

Other things being equal, stigmatization usually implies a number of negative social and psychological consequences for the "marked" individual (E. E. Jones, et al., 1984; also Goffman, 1963). Typically, social reactions aim to "isolate, treat, correct, or punish" such individuals (Schur, 1971, p. 24), and overall, in one or another way, to "contain" them (Schur, 1980). Many of the specific definitions of female deviance considered below, as well as the sanctions used to uphold them, appear to serve functions of this sort. Practical consequences of an individual's being stigmatized and treated in these ways can include the reduction of his or her social acceptability, a blocking of important social and economic opportunities, a diminishing of overall life chances.

Studies of deviance and also of racial and ethnic minorities have paid special attention to the psychological consequences of stigmatization. The central concept in such analysis has been the self-fulfilling prophecy, the possibility that a false definition—if acted upon sufficiently—can, in effect, become true. Thus the individual who has consistently been treated as inferior—and who also has been denied the opportunities to develop and demonstrate the capacities that would disprove this—may even come to see himself or herself as inferior. This possibility obviously is closely tied to the "master status" and "nothing but" aspects of categorical perception. The individual may not be able to avoid "engulfment" (Schur, 1971; Schur, 1979) or "entrapment" (Kanter, 1977a) in the devalued role. Edwin Lemert (1951, p. 77) depicted as the extreme endpoint of a stigmatization process the devalued person's "ultimate acceptance of deviant social status and efforts at adjustment on the basis of the associated role."

Again, the likelihood of such an outcome will be affected by the specific individual's personal resources. Also important will be the nature and extent of the specific stigmatizing. As John Lofland points out, "Other things being equal, the greater the *consistency, duration* and *intensity* with which a definition is promoted by Others about an Actor, the greater the likelihood that an Actor will embrace that definition as truly applicable to himself" (Lofland, 1969, p. 122). Studies invariably conclude that as a general proposition, and notwithstanding some individual variability, systematic devaluation implies a strong likelihood of impaired self-esteem. It is extremely difficult to maintain favorable self-conceptions in the absence of validation (that is, reinforcement) by others. Furthermore, as Goffman has noted, stigmatized persons have themselves been socialized to accept the beliefs and values on which the stigma is grounded. Accordingly, "The standards he [or she!] has incorporated from the wider society equip him to be intimately alive to what others see as his failing, inevitably causing him, if only for moments, to agree that he does indeed fall short of what he really ought to be" (Goffman, 1963, p. 7).

Hence stigmatized persons often display what Allport called "traits due to victimization" (Allport, 1958, Ch. 9; see also, Hacker, 1951; Fanon, 1952, 1968; and Adam, 1978). These can include various patterns of withdrawal and defensiveness, passivity, in-group hostility and identification with the oppressors, as well as seriously impaired self-esteem. The last-named consequence has been emphasized in studies of the psychological problems of black persons, which at times have found the impairment to verge on self-hatred and to kindle severe psychological despair and rage (see Kardiner and Ovesey, 1951; Fanon, 1952, 1968; Grier and Cobbs, 1968; also Ladner, 1972).

Self-esteem has been a major focus also in studies of women's situation. Thus Hacker (1951, p. 61) stated that "women reveal their introjection of prevailing attitudes toward them," and Daly (1974, p. 48) has noted further that "As contradictory, divided beings, the oppressed do not fully grasp the paralyzing fact that the oppressor, having invaded the victims' psyches, now exists within themselves. They are caught in a web of self-defeating behavior." Gornick and Moran (eds., 1972, xx) similarly charge sexism with having produced in women "an image of the self that paralyzes the will and short-circuits the brain, that makes them deny the evidence of their senses and internalize self-doubt to a fearful degree."

References

Adam, Barry D. (1978) *The Survival of Domination*. New York: Elsevier.

Adams, Karen L. and Norma C. Ware (1979) "Sexism and the English Language," in Jo Freeman, ed., *Women: A Feminist Perspective*. 2nd ed., Palo Alto, Ca.: Mayfield Pub. Co.

Allport, Gordon W. (1958) *The Nature of Prejudice*. Garden City, NY: Doubleday Anchor Books.

Becker, Howard S. (1963) *Outsiders*. New York: Free Press.

Chafetz, Janet Saltzman (1974) *Masculine, Feminine, or Human?* Itasca, IL: F. E. Peacock.

Daly, Mary (1974) *Beyond God the Father*. Boston: Beacon Press.

England, Paula (1979) "Women and Occupational Prestige," *Signs*, 5 (Winter), 252–265.

Epstein, Cynthia Fuchs (1971) *Woman's Place*. Berkeley: University of California Press.

Fanon, Franz (1952, 1968) *Black Skin, White Masks*. New York: Grove Press.

Firestone, Shulamith (1971) *The Dialect of Sex*. New York: Bantam Books.

Fransella, Fay and Kay Frost (1977) *On Being a Woman*. London: Tavistock.

Friedan, Betty (1963) *The Feminine Mystique*. New York: W. W Norton.

Garfinkel, Harold (1956) "Conditions of Successful Degradation Ceremonies," *American Journal of Sociology*, 61 (March), 420–424.

Goffman, Erving (1963) *Stigma*. Englewood Cliffs, N.J.: Prentice-Hall.

Goffman, Erving (1977) "The Arrangement Between the Sexes," *Theory and Society*, 4 (Fall), 301–332.

Goffman, Erving (1979) *Gender Advertisements*. New York: Harper Colophon Books.

Goldberg, Philip (1968) "Are Women Prejudiced Against Women?" *Transaction*, 5 (April), 28–30.

Gornick, Vivian and Barbara K. Moran, eds. (1972) *Women in a Sexist Society*. New York: Signet Books.

Grier, William H. and Price M. Cobbs (1968) *Black Rage*. New York: Basic Books.

Hacker, Helen Mayer (1951) "Women as a Minority Group," *Social Forces*, 30 (Oct.), 60–69.

Hughes, Everett C. (1945) "Dilemmas and Contradictions of Status," *American Journal of Sociology*, 50 (March), 353–359.

Jones, Edward E., Amerigo Farina, Albert H. Hastorf, Hazel Markus, Dale T. Miller, and Robert A. Scott (1984) *Social Stigma: The Psychology of Marked Relationships*. New York: W. H. Freemen.

Kanter, Rosabeth Moss (1977a) "Some Effects of Proportions on Group Life: Skewed Sex Ratios and Responses to Token Women," *American Journal of Sociology*, 82 (March), 965–990.

Kanter, Rosabeth Moss (1977b) *Men and Women of the Corporation*. New York: Basic Books.

Kardiner, Abram and Lionel Ovesey (1951) *The Mark of Oppression*. New York: W. W. Norton.

Katz, Irwin (1981) *Stigma: A Social Psychological Analysis*. Hillsdale, NJ: Lawrence Erlbaum Assocs.

Ladner, Joyce A. (1972) *Tomorrow's Tomorrow: The Black Woman*. Garden City, NY: Doubleday Anchor Books.

Lakoff, Robin (1975) *Language and Woman's Place*. New York: Harper Colophon Books.

Laws, Judith Long (1979) *The Second X: Sex Role and Social Role*. New York: Elsevier.

Lemert, Edwin M. (1951) *Social Pathology*. New York: McGraw-Hill.

Levenson, H. B. Burford, B. Bonno, and L. Davis (1975) "Are Women Still Prejudiced Against Women?" *Journal of Psychology*, 89, 67–71.

Lofland, John (1969) *Deviance and Identity*. Englewood Cliffs, NJ: Prentice-Hall.

Millet, Kate (1971) *Sexual Politics*. New York: Avon Books.

Oakley, Ann (1981) *Subject Women*. New York: Pantheon Books.

Richardson, Laurel Walum (1981) *The Dynamics of Sex and Gender*. 2nd ed., Boston: Houghton Mifflin.

Rothman, Sheila M. (1978) *Woman's Proper Place*. New York: Basic Books.

Rowbotham, Sheila (1973) *Woman's Consciousness, Man's World*. Baltimore: Penguin Books.

Rubington, Earl and Martin S. Weinberg, eds. (1981) *Deviance: The Interactionist Perspective*. 4th ed., New York: Macmillan.

Schur, Edwin M. (1971) *Labeling Deviant Behavior*. New York: Harper and Row.

Schur, Edwin M. (1979) *Interpreting Deviance*. New York: Harper and Row.

Schur, Edwin M. (1980) *The Politics of Deviance*. Englewood Cliffs, NJ: Prentice-Hall.

Spence, Janet T. and Robert L. Helmreich (1978) *Masculinity and Femininity*. Austin: University of Texas Press.

Stockard, Jean and Miriam M. Johnson (1980) *Sex Roles*. Englewood Cliffs, NJ: Prentice-Hall.

Stoll, Clarice Stasz (1974) *Female and Male*. Dubuque, IA: Wm. C. Brown.

Thorne, Barrie and Nancy Henley, eds. (1975) *Language and Sex*. Rowley, MA: Newbury House.

THE SAINTS AND THE ROUGHNECKS
William J. Chambliss

Becker had argued in Outsiders *that one contingency of labeling was social class. This, he said, was particularly true in the case of juvenile delinquency, control agents showing more tolerance for middle-class delinquents, much less for working-class delinquents. Chambliss, in this oft-reprinted field study, documents how class background can make a big difference when it comes to being labeled a juvenile delinquent. The Saints and the Roughnecks engaged in roughly the same amount of deviant behavior. But because of class bias, visibility of delinquent acts, and behavior when in the presence of control agents, the Roughnecks were tagged as troublemakers, young men whose future lay in only more deviant behavior. By contrast, the community expected the Saints to be successes after high school. Where six of the eight Saints went on to higher degrees, five of the seven Roughnecks lived up to the community's expectation that none of them would come to a good end. As Chambliss notes: "The community responded to the Roughnecks as boys in trouble, and the boys agreed with that perception."*

Eight promising young men—children of good, stable, white upper-middle-class families, active in school affairs, good pre-college students—were some of the most delinquent boys at Hanibal High School. While community residents and parents knew that these boys occasionally sowed a few wild oats, they were totally unaware that sowing wild oats completely occupied the daily routine of these young men. The Saints were constantly occupied with truancy, drinking, wild driving, petty theft and vandalism. Yet not one was officially arrested for any misdeed during the two years I observed them.

This record was particularly surprising in light of my observations during the same two years of another gang of Hanibal High School students, six lower-class white boys known as the Roughnecks. The Roughnecks were constantly in trouble with police and community even though their rate of delinquency was about equal with that of the Saints. What was the cause of this disparity? The result? The following consideration of the activities, social class and community perceptions of both gangs may provide some answers.

THE SAINTS FROM MONDAY TO FRIDAY

The Saints' principal daily concern was with getting out of school as early as possible. The boys managed to get out of school with minimum danger that they

Reprinted by permission of Transaction, Inc., from *Society*, 11:1 (November/December 1973), pp. 24–31. Copyright © 1973 by Transaction, Inc.

would be accused of playing hookey through an elaborate procedure for obtaining "legitimate" release from class. The most common procedure was for one boy to obtain the release of another by fabricating a meeting of some committee, program or recognized club. Charles might raise his hand in his 9:00 chemistry class and ask to be excused—a euphemism for going to the bathroom. Charles would go to Ed's math class and inform the teacher that Ed was needed for a 9:30 rehearsal of the drama club play. The math teacher would recognize Ed and Charles as "good students" involved in numerous school activities and would permit Ed to leave at 9:30. Charles would return to his class, and Ed would go to Tom's English class to obtain his release. Tom would engineer Charles' escape. The strategy would continue until as many of the Saints as possible were freed. After a stealthy trip to the car (which had been parked in a strategic spot), the boys were off for a day of fun.

Over the two years I observed the Saints, this pattern was repeated nearly every day. There were variations on the theme, but in one form or another, the boys used this procedure for getting out of class and then off the school grounds. Rarely did all eight of the Saints manage to leave school at the same time. The average number avoiding school on the days I observed them was five.

Having escaped from the concrete corridors the boys usually went either to a pool hall on the other (lower-class) side of town or to a cafe in the suburbs. Both places were out of the way of people the boys were likely to know (family or school officials), and both provided a source of entertainment. The pool hall entertainment was the generally rough atmosphere, the occasional hustler, the sometimes drunk proprietor and, of course, the game of pool. The cafe's entertainment was provided by the owner. The boys would "accidentally" knock a glass on the floor or spill cola on the counter—not all the time, but enough to be sporting. They would also bend spoons, put salt in sugar bowls and generally tease whoever was working in the cafe. The owner had opened the cafe recently and was dependent on the boys' business which was, in fact, substantial since between the horsing around and the teasing they bought food and drinks.

THE SAINTS ON WEEKENDS

On weekends, the automobile was even more critical than during the week, for on weekends the Saints went to Big Town—a large city with a population of over a million, 25 miles from Hanibal. Every Friday and Saturday night most of the Saints would meet between 8:00 and 8:30 and would go into Big Town. Big Town activities included drinking heavily in taverns or nightclubs, driving drunkenly through the streets, and committing acts of vandalism and playing pranks.

By midnight on Fridays and Saturdays the Saints were usually thoroughly high, and one or two of them were often so drunk they had to be carried to the cars. Then the boys drove around town, calling obscenities to women and girls; occasionally trying (unsuccessfully so far as I could tell) to pick girls up; and driving recklessly through red lights and at high speeds with their lights out. Occasionally they played "chicken." One boy would climb out the back window of the car and across the roof to the driver's side of the car while the car was moving at high speed (between 40 and 50 miles an hour); then the driver would move over and the boy who had just crawled across the car roof would take the driver's seat.

Searching for "fair game" for a prank was the boys' principal activity after they left the tavern. The boys would drive alongside a foot patrolman and ask directions to some street. If the policeman leaned on the car in the course of answering the question, the driver would speed away, causing him to lose his balance. The Saints were careful to play this prank only in an area where they were not going to spend much time and where they could quickly disappear around a corner to avoid having their license plate number taken.

Construction sites and road repair areas were the special province of the Saints' mischief. A soon-to-be-repaired hole in the road inevitably invited the Saints to remove lanterns and wooden barricades and put them in the car, leaving the hole unprotected. The boys would find a safe vantage point and wait for an unsuspecting motorist to drive into the hole. Often, though not always, the boys would go up to the motorist and commiserate with him about the dreadful way the city protected its citizenry.

Leaving the scene of the open hole and the motorist, the boys would then go searching for an appropriate place to erect the stolen barricade. An "appropriate place" was often a spot on a highway near a curve in the road where the barricade would not be seen by an oncoming motorist. The boys would wait to watch an unsuspecting motorist attempt to stop and (usually) crash into the wooden barricade. With saintly bearing the boys might offer help and understanding.

A stolen lantern might well find its way onto the back of a police car or hang from a street lamp. Once a lantern served as a prop for a reenactment of the "midnight ride of Paul Revere" until the "play," which was taking place at 2:00 A.M. in the center of a main street of Big Town, was interrupted by a police car several blocks away. The boys ran, leaving the lanterns on the street, and managed to avoid being apprehended.

Abandoned houses, especially if they were located in out-of-the-way places, were fair game for destruction and spontaneous vandalism. The boys would break windows, remove furniture to the yard and tear it apart, urinate on the walls and scrawl obscenities inside.

Through all the pranks, drinking and reckless driving the boys managed miraculously to avoid being stopped by police. Only twice in two years was I aware that they had been stopped by a Big City policeman. Once was for speeding (which they did every time they drove whether they were drunk or sober), and the driver managed to convince the policeman that it was simply an error. The second time they were stopped they had just left a nightclub and were walking through an alley. Aaron stopped to urinate and the boys began making obscene remarks. A foot patrolman came into the alley, lectured the boys and sent them home. Before the boys got to the car one began talking in a loud voice again. The policeman, who had followed them down the alley, arrested this boy for disturbing the peace and took him to the police station where the other Saints gathered. After paying a $5.00 fine, and with the assurance that there would be no permanent record of the arrest, the boy was released.

The boys had a spirit of frivolity and fun about their escapades. They did not view what they were engaged in as "delinquency," though it surely was by any reasonable definition of that word. They simply viewed themselves as having a little fun and who, they would ask, was really hurt by it? The answer had to be no one, although this fact remains one of the most difficult things to explain about the gang's behavior. Unlikely though it seems, in two years of drinking, driving, carousing and vandalism no one was seriously injured as a result of the Saints' activities.

THE SAINTS IN SCHOOL

The Saints were highly successful in school. The average grade for the group was "B," with two of the boys having close to a straight "A" average. Almost all of the boys were popular and many of them held offices in the school. One of the boys was vice-president of the student body one year. Six of the boys played on athletic teams.

At the end of their senior year, the student body selected ten seniors for special recognition as the "school wheels"; four of the ten were Saints. Teachers and school officials saw no problem with any of these boys and anticipated that they would all "make something of themselves."

How the boys managed to maintain this impression is surprising in view of their actual behavior while in school. Their technique for covering truancy was so successful that teachers did not even realize that the boys were absent from school much of the time. Occasionally, of course, the system would backfire and then the boy was on his own. A boy who was caught would be most contrite, would plead guilty and ask for mercy. He inevitably got the mercy he sought.

Cheating on examinations was rampant, even to the point of orally communicating answers to exams as well as looking at one another's papers. Since none of the group studied, and since they were primarily dependent on one another for help, it is surprising that grades were so high. Teachers contributed to the deception in their admitted inclination to give these boys (and presumably others like them) the benefit of the doubt. When asked how the boys did in school, and when pressed on specific examinations, teachers might admit that they were disappointed in John's performance, but would quickly add that they "knew he was capable of doing better," so John was given a higher grade than he had actually earned. How often this happened is impossible to know. During the time that I observed the group, I never saw any of the boys take homework home. Teachers may have been "understanding" very regularly.

One exception to the gang's generally good performance was Jerry, who had a "C" average in his junior year, experienced disaster the next year and failed to graduate. Jerry had always been a little more nonchalant than the others about the liberties he took in school. Rather than wait for someone to come get him from class, he would offer his own excuse and leave. Although he probably did not miss any more classes than most of the others in the group, he did not take the requisite pains to cover his absences. Jerry was the only Saint whom I ever heard talk back to a teacher. Although teachers often called him a "cut up" or a "smart kid," they never referred to him as a troublemaker or as a kid headed for trouble. It seems likely, then, that Jerry's failure his senior year and his mediocre performance his junior year were consequences of his not playing the game the proper way (possibly because he was disturbed by his parents' divorce). His teachers regarded him as "immature" and not quite ready to get out of high school.

THE POLICE AND THE SAINTS

The local police saw the Saints as good boys who were among the leaders of the youth in the community. Rarely, the boys might be stopped in town for speeding or for running a stop sign. When this happened the boys were always polite, contrite and pled for mercy. As in school, they received the mercy they asked for. None ever received a ticket or was taken into the precinct by the local police.

The situation in Big City, where the boys engaged in most of their delinquency, was only slightly different. The police there did not know the boys at all, although occasionally the boys were stopped by a patrolman. Once they were caught taking a lantern from a construction site. Another time they were stopped for running a stop sign, and on several occasions they were stopped for speeding. Their behavior was as before: contrite, polite and penitent. The urban police, like the local police, accepted their demeanor as sincere. More important, the urban police were convinced that these were good boys just out for a lark.

THE ROUGHNECKS

Hanibal townspeople never perceived the Saints' high level of delinquency. The Saints were good boys who just went in for an occasional prank. After all, they were well dressed, well mannered and had nice cars. The Roughnecks were a different story. Although the two gangs of boys were the same age, and both groups engaged in an equal amount of wild-oat sowing, everyone agreed that the not-so-well-dressed, not-so-well-mannered, not-so-rich boys were heading for trouble. Townspeople would say, "You can see the gang members at the drugstore night after night, leaning against the storefront (sometimes drunk) or slouching around inside buying cokes, reading magazines, and probably stealing old Mr. Wall blind. When they are outside and girls walk by, even respectable girls, these boys make suggestive remarks. Sometimes their remarks are downright lewd."

From the community's viewpoint, the real indication that these kids were in for trouble was that they were constantly involved with the police. Some of them had been picked up for stealing, mostly small stuff, of course, "but still it's stealing small stuff that leads to big time crimes." "Too bad," people said. "Too bad that these boys couldn't behave like the other kids in town; stay out of trouble, be polite to adults, and look to their future."

The community's impression of the degree to which this group of six boys (ranging in age from 16 to 19) engaged in delinquency was somewhat distorted. In some ways the gang was more delinquent than the community thought; in other ways it was less.

The fighting activities of the group were fairly readily and accurately perceived by almost everyone. At least once a month, the boys would get into some sort of fight, although most fights were scraps between members of the group or involved only one member of the group and some peripheral hanger-on. Only three times in the period of observation did the group fight together: once against a gang from across town, once against two blacks and once against a group of boys from another school. For the first two fights the group went out "looking for trouble"—and they found it both times. The third fight followed a football game and began spontaneously with an argument on the football field between one of the Roughnecks and a member of the opposition's football team.

Jack had a particular propensity for fighting and was involved in most of the brawls. He was a prime mover of the escalation of arguments into fights.

More serious than fighting, had the community been aware of it, was theft. Although almost everyone was aware that the boys occasionally stole things, they did not realize the extent of the activity. Petty stealing was a frequent event for the Roughnecks. Sometimes they stole as a group and coordinated their efforts; other times they stole in pairs. Rarely did they steal alone.

The thefts ranged from very small things like paperback books, comics and ballpoint pens to expensive items like watches. The nature of the thefts varied from time to time. The gang would go through a period of systematically lifting items from automobiles or school lockers. Types of thievery varied with the whim of the gang. Some forms of thievery were more profitable than others, but all thefts were for profit, not just thrills.

Roughnecks siphoned gasoline from cars as often as they had access to an automobile, which was not very often. Unlike the Saints, who owned their own cars, the Roughnecks would have to borrow their parents' cars, an event which occurred only eight or nine times a year. The boys claimed to have stolen cars for joy rides from time to time.

Ron committed the most serious of the group's offenses. With an unidentified associate the boy attempted to burglarize a gasoline station. Although this station had been robbed twice previously in the same month, Ron denied any involvement in either of the other thefts. When Ron and his accomplice approached the station, the owner was hiding in the bushes beside the station. He fired both barrels of a double-barreled shotgun at the boys. Ron was severely injured; the other boy ran away and was never caught. Though he remained in critical condition for several months, Ron finally recovered and served six months of the following year in reform school. Upon release from reform school, Ron was put back a grade in school, and began running around with a different gang of boys. The Roughnecks considered the new gang less delinquent than themselves, and during the following year Ron had no more trouble with the police.

The Roughnecks, then, engaged mainly in three types of delinquency: theft, drinking and fighting. Although community members perceived that this gang of kids was delinquent, they mistakenly believed that their illegal activities were primarily drinking, fighting and being a nuisance to passersby. Drinking was limited among the gang members, although it did occur, and theft was much more prevalent than anyone realized.

Drinking would doubtless have been more prevalent had the boys had ready access to liquor. Since they rarely had automobiles at their disposal, they could not travel very far, and the bars in town would not serve them. Most of the boys had little money, and this, too, inhibited their purchase of alcohol. Their major source of liquor was a local drunk who would buy them a fifth if they would give him enough extra to buy himself a pint of whiskey or a bottle of wine.

The community's perception of drinking as prevalent stemmed from the fact that it was the most obvious delinquency the boys engaged in. When one of the boys had been drinking, even a casual observer seeing him on the corner would suspect that he was high.

There was a high level of mutual distrust and dislike between the Roughnecks and the police. The boys felt very strongly that the police were unfair and corrupt. Some evidence existed that the boys were correct in their perception.

The main source of the boys' dislike for the police undoubtedly stemmed from the fact that the police would sporadically harass the group. From the standpoint of the boys, these acts of occasional enforcement of the law were whimsical and uncalled for. It made no sense to them, for example, that the police would come to the corner occasionally and threaten them with arrest for loitering when the night before the boys had been out siphoning gasoline from cars and the police had been nowhere in sight. To the boys, the police were stupid on the one hand, for not being where they should have been and catching the boys in a serious offense, and unfair on the other hand, for trumping up "loitering" charges against them.

From the viewpoint of the police, the situation was quite different. They knew, with all the confidence necessary to be a policeman, that these boys were engaged in criminal activities. They knew this partly from occasionally catching them, mostly from circumstantial evidence ("the boys were around when those tires were slashed"), and partly because the police shared the view of the community in general that this was a bad bunch of boys. The best the police could hope to do was to be sensitive to the fact that these boys were engaged in illegal acts and arrest them whenever there was some evidence that they had been involved. Whether or not the boys had in fact committed a particular act in a particular way was not especially important. The police had a broader view: their job was to stamp out these kids' crimes; the tactics were not as important as the end result.

Over the period that the group was under observation, each member was arrested at least once. Several of the boys were arrested a number of times and spent at least one night in jail. While most were never taken to court, two of the boys were sentenced to six months' incarceration in boys' schools.

THE ROUGHNECKS IN SCHOOL

The Roughnecks' behavior in school was not particularly disruptive. During school hours they did not all hang around together, but tended instead to spend most of their time with one or two other members of the gang who were their special buddies. Although every member of the gang attempted to avoid school as much as possible, they were not particularly successful and most of them attended school with surprising regularity. They considered school a burden—something to be gotten through with a minimum of conflict. If they were "bugged" by a particular teacher, it could lead to trouble. One of the boys, Al, once threatened to beat up a teacher and, according to the other boys, the teacher hid under a desk to escape him.

Teachers saw the boys the way the general community did, as heading for trouble, as being uninterested in making something of themselves. Some were also seen as being incapable of meeting the academic standards of the school. Most of the teachers expressed concern for this group of boys and were willing to pass them despite poor performance, in the belief that failing them would only aggravate the problem.

The group of boys had a grade point average just slightly above "C." No one in the group failed either grade, and no one had better than a "C" average. They were very consistent in their achievement or, at least, the teachers were consistent in their perception of the boys' achievement.

Two of the boys were good football players. Herb was acknowledged to be the best player in the school and Jack was almost as good. Both boys were criticized for their failure to abide by training rules, for refusing to come to practice as often as they should, and for not playing their best during practice. What they lacked in sportsmanship they made up for in skill, apparently, and played every game no matter how poorly they had performed in practice or how many practice sessions they had missed.

TWO QUESTIONS

Why did the community, the school and the police react to the Saints as though they were good, upstanding, nondelinquent youths with bright futures but to the Roughnecks as though they were tough, young criminals who were headed for trouble? Why did the Roughnecks and the Saints in fact have quite different careers after high school—careers which, by and large, lived up to the expectations of the community?

The most obvious explanation for the differences in the community's and law enforcement agencies' reactions to the two gangs is that one group of boys was "more delinquent" than the other. Which group *was* more delinquent? The answer to this question will determine in part how we explain the differential responses to these groups by the members of the community and, particularly, by law enforcement and school officials.

In sheer number of illegal acts, the Saints were the more delinquent. They were truant from school for at least part of the day almost every day of the week. In addition, their drinking and vandalism occurred with surprising regularity. The Roughnecks, in contrast, engaged sporadically in delinquent episodes. While these episodes were frequent, they certainly did not occur on a daily or even a weekly basis.

The difference in frequency of offenses was probably caused by the Roughnecks' inability to obtain liquor and to manipulate legitimate excuses from school. Since the Roughnecks had less money than the Saints, and teachers carefully supervised their school activities, the Roughnecks' hearts may have been as black as the Saints', but their misdeeds were not nearly as frequent.

There are really no clear-cut criteria by which to measure qualitative differences in antisocial behavior. The most important dimension of the difference is generally referred to as the "seriousness" of the offenses.

If seriousness encompasses the relative economic costs of delinquent acts, then some assessment can be made. The Roughnecks probably stole an average of about $5.00 worth of goods a week. Some weeks the figure was considerably higher, but these times must be balanced against long periods when almost nothing was stolen.

The Saints were more continuously engaged in delinquency but their acts were not for the most part costly to property. Only their vandalism and occasional theft of gasoline would so qualify. Perhaps once or twice a month they would siphon a tankful of gas. The other costly items were street signs, construction lanterns and the like. All of these acts combined probably did not quite average $5.00 a week, partly because much of the stolen equipment was abandoned and presumably could be recovered. The difference in cost of stolen property between the two groups was trivial, but the Roughnecks probably had a slightly more expensive set of activities than did the Saints.

Another meaning of seriousness is the potential threat of physical harm to members of the community and to the boys themselves. The Roughnecks were more prone to physical violence; they not only welcomed an opportunity to fight; they went seeking it. In addition, they fought among themselves frequently. Although the fighting never included deadly weapons, it was still a menace, however minor, to the physical safety of those involved.

The Saints never fought. They avoided physical conflict both inside and outside the group. At the same time, though, the Saints frequently endangered their own and other people's lives. They did so almost every time they drove a car, especially if they had been drinking. Sober, their driving was risky; under the influence of alcohol it was horrendous. In addition, the Saints endangered the lives of others with their pranks. Street excavations left unmarked were a very serious hazard.

Evaluating the relative seriousness of the two gangs' activities is difficult. The community reacted as though the behavior of the Roughnecks was a problem, and they reacted as though the behavior of the Saints was not. But the members of the community were ignorant of the array of delinquent acts that characterized the Saints' behavior. Although concerned citizens were unaware of much of the Roughnecks' behavior as well, they were much better informed about the Roughnecks' involvement in delinquency than they were about the Saints'.

VISIBILITY

Differential treatment of the two gangs resulted in part because one gang was infinitely more visible than the other. This differential visibility was a direct function of the economic standing of the families. The Saints had access to automobiles and were able to remove themselves from the sight of the community. In as routine a decision as to where to go to have a milkshake after school, the Saints stayed away from the mainstream of community life. Lacking transportation, the Roughnecks could not make it to the edge of town. The center of town was the only practical place for them to meet since their homes were scattered throughout the town and any noncentral meeting place put an undue hardship on some members. Through necessity the Roughnecks congregated in a crowded area where everyone in the community passed frequently, including teachers and law enforcement officers. They could easily see the Roughnecks hanging around the drugstore.

The Roughnecks, of course, made themselves even more visible by making remarks to passersby and by occasionally getting into fights on the corner. Meanwhile, just as regularly, the Saints were either at the cafe on one edge of town or in the pool hall at the other edge of town. Without any particular realization that they were making themselves inconspicuous, the Saints were able to hide their time-wasting. Not only were they removed from the mainstream of traffic, but they were almost always inside a building.

On their escapades the Saints were also relatively invisible, since they left Hanibal and travelled to Big City. Here, too, they were mobile, roaming the city, rarely going to the same area twice.

DEMEANOR

To the notion of visibility must be added the difference in the responses of group members to outside intervention with their activities. If one of the Saints was confronted with an accusing policeman, even if he felt he was truly innocent of a wrongdoing, his demeanor was apologetic and penitent. A Roughneck's attitude was almost the polar opposite. When confronted with a threatening adult authority, even one who tried to be pleasant, the Roughneck's hostility and disdain were clearly observable. Sometimes he might attempt to put up a veneer of respect, but it was thin and was not accepted as sincere by the authority.

School was no different from the community at large. The Saints could manipulate the system by feigning compliance with the school norms. The availability of cars at school meant that once free from the immediate sight of the teacher, the boys could disappear rapidly. And this escape was well enough planned that no administrator or teacher was nearby when the boys left. A Roughneck who wished to escape for a few hours was in a bind. If it were possible to get free from class, downtown was still a mile away, and even if he arrived there, he was still very visible. Truancy for the Roughnecks meant almost certain detection, while the Saints enjoyed almost complete immunity from sanctions.

BIAS

Community members were not aware of the transgressions of the Saints. Even if the Saints had been less discreet, their favorite delinquencies would have been perceived as less serious than those of the Roughnecks.

In the eyes of the police and school officials, a boy who drinks in an alley and stands intoxicated on the street corner is committing a more serious offense than is a boy who drinks to inebriation in a nightclub or a tavern and drives around afterwards in a car. Similarly, a boy who steals a wallet from a store will be viewed as having committed a more serious offense than a boy who steals a lantern from a construction site.

Perceptual bias also operates with respect to the demeanor of the boys in the two groups when they are confronted by adults. It is not simply that adults dislike the posture affected by boys of the Roughneck ilk; more important is the conviction that the posture adopted by the Roughnecks is an indication of their devotion and commitment to deviance as a way of life. The posture becomes a cue, just as the type of the offense is a cue, to the degree to which the known transgressions are indicators of the youths' potential for other problems.

Visibility, demeanor and bias are surface variables which explain the day-to-day operations of the police. Why do these surface variables operate as they do? Why did the police choose to disregard the Saints' delinquencies while breathing down the backs of the Roughnecks?

The answer lies in the class structure of American society and the control of legal institutions by those at the top of the class structure. Obviously, no representative of the upper class drew up the operational chart for the police which led them to look in the ghettoes and on street corners—which led them to see the demeanor of lower-class youth as troublesome and that of upper-middle-class youth as tolerable. Rather, the procedures simply developed from experience— experience with irate and influential upper-middle-class parents insisting that their son's vandalism was simply a prank and his drunkenness only a momentary "sowing of wild oats"—experience with cooperative or indifferent, powerless, lower-class parents who acquiesced to the laws' definition of their son's behavior.

ADULT CAREERS OF THE SAINTS AND THE ROUGHNECKS

The community's confidence in the potential of the Saints and the Roughnecks apparently was justified. If anything, the community members underestimated the degree to which these youngsters would turn out "good" or "bad."

Seven of the eight members of the Saints went on to college immediately after high school. Five of the boys graduated from college in four years. The sixth one finished college after two years in the army, and the seventh spent four years in the air force before returning to college and receiving a B.A. degree. Of these seven college graduates, three went on for advanced degrees. One finished law school and is now active in state politics, one finished medical school and is practicing near Hanibal, and one boy is now working for a Ph.D. The other four college graduates entered submanagerial, managerial or executive training positions with larger firms.

The only Saint who did not complete college was Jerry. Jerry had failed to graduate from high school with the other Saints. During his second senior year, after the other Saints had gone on to college, Jerry began to hang around with what several teachers described as a "rough crowd"—the gang that was heir apparent to the Roughnecks. At the end of his second senior year, when he did graduate from high school, Jerry took a job as a used-car salesman, got married and quickly had a child. Although he made several abortive attempts to go to college by attending night school, when I last saw him (ten years after high school) Jerry was unemployed and had been living on unemployment for almost a year. His wife worked as a waitress.

Some of the Roughnecks have lived up to community expectations. A number of them were headed for trouble. A few were not.

Jack and Herb were the athletes among the Roughnecks and their athletic prowess paid off handsomely. Both boys received unsolicited athletic scholarships to college. After Herb received his scholarship (near the end of his senior year), he apparently did an about-face. His demeanor became very similar to that of the Saints. Although he remained a member in good standing of the Roughnecks, he stopped participating in most activities and did not hang out on the corner as often.

Jack did not change. If anything, he became more prone to fighting. He even made excuses for accepting the scholarship. He told the other gang members that the school had guaranteed him a "C" average if he would come to play football—an idea that seems far-fetched, even in this day of highly competitive recruiting.

During the summer after graduation from high school, Jack attempted suicide by jumping from a tall building. The jump would certainly have killed most people trying it, but Jack survived. He entered college in the fall and played four years of football. He and Herb graduated in four years, and both are teaching and coaching in high schools. They are married and have stable families. If anything, Jack appears to have a more prestigious position in the community than does Herb, though both are well respected and secure in their positions.

Two of the boys never finished high school. Tommy left at the end of his junior year and went to another state. That summer he was arrested and placed on probation on a manslaughter charge. Three years later he was arrested for murder; he pleaded guilty to second degree murder and is serving a 30-year sentence in the state penitentiary.

Al, the other boy who did not finish high school, also left the state in his senior year. He is serving a life sentence in a state penitentiary for first degree murder.

Wes is a small-time gambler. He finished high school and "bummed around." After several years he made contact with a bookmaker who employed him as a runner. Later he acquired his own area and has been working it ever since. His position among the bookmakers is almost identical to the position he had in the gang; he is always around but no one is really aware of him. He makes no trouble and he does not get into any. Steady, reliable, capable of keeping his mouth closed, he plays the game by the rules, even though the game is an illegal one.

That leaves only Ron. Some of his former friends reported that they had heard he was "driving a truck up north," but no one could provide any concrete information.

REINFORCEMENT

The community responded to the Roughnecks as boys in trouble, and the boys agreed with that perception. Their pattern of deviancy was reinforced, and breaking away from it became increasingly unlikely. Once the boys acquired an image of themselves as deviants, they selected new friends who affirmed that self-image. As that self-conception became more firmly entrenched, they also became willing to try new and more extreme deviances. With their growing alienation came freer expression of disrespect and hostility for representatives of the legitimate society. This disrespect increased the community's negativism, perpetuating the entire process of commitment to deviance. Lack of a commitment to deviance works the same way. In either case, the process will perpetuate itself unless some event (like a scholarship to college or a sudden failure) external to the established relationship intervenes. For two of the Roughnecks (Herb and Jack), receiving college athletic scholarships created new relations and culminated in a break with the established pattern of deviance. In the case of one of the Saints (Jerry), his parents' divorce and his failing to graduate from high school changed some of his other relations. Being held back in school for a year and losing his place among the Saints had sufficient impact on Jerry to alter his self-image and virtually to assure that he would not go on to college as his peers did. Although the experiments of life can rarely be reversed, it seems likely in view of the behavior of the other boys who did not enjoy this special treatment by the school that Jerry, too, would have "become something" had he graduated as anticipated. For Herb and Jack outside intervention worked to their advantage; for Jerry it was his undoing.

Selective perception and labelling—finding, processing and punishing some kinds of criminality and not others—means that visible, poor, nonmobile, outspoken, undiplomatic "tough" kids will be noticed, whether their actions are seriously delinquent or not. Other kids, who have established a reputation for being bright (even though underachieving), disciplined and involved in respectable activities, who are mobile and monied, will be invisible when they deviate from sanctioned activities. They'll sow their wild oats—perhaps even wider and thicker than their lower-class cohorts—but they won't be noticed. When it's time to leave adolescence most will follow the expected path, settling into the ways of the middle class, remembering fondly the delinquent but unnoticed fling of their youth. The Roughnecks and others like them may turn around, too. It is more likely that their noticeable deviance will have been so reinforced by police and community that their lives will be effectively channelled into careers consistent with their adolescent background.

A CRITIQUE OF LABELING

Gwynn Nettler

The labeling perspective is more interested in definitions of deviance than in deviant behaviors per se. Thus, it is less concerned with what so-called deviants actually do than with how others react. The advantage of the labeling perspective, Nettler says, is that it helps us see that in some cases people respond more to labels than to actual behaviors, and that by doing so they sometimes produce the very behaviors they condemn. In terms of explaining crime, however, Nettler does not think the labeling perspective is very useful. Specifically, it fails to predict or explain criminal behavior, it uses circular reasoning in treating the response to crime as the cause of crime, and it cannot tell us how to reduce criminal behavior.

The most popular new set of ideas employed by sociologists to explain crime is a bundle of assumptions known as the "labeling" hypothesis. This hypothesis depends heavily upon the belief that social relations are "constructed," that reality is defined and interpreted before it becomes meaningful. This is a way of saying that we act in terms of the *meanings* attributed to events rather than to objective events. Conditions, it is said, are *defined* before they are reacted to. How we respond to each other is a function of the way we have categorized each other and of the significance we have assigned to our interactions.

From this point of view, "crime" is a word, not an act. Crime is socially defined and criminals are socially "produced" in a process which allows majorities to apply labels to minorities and which, in many cases, permits majorities to enforce the consequences of this labeling. As a result, the "labeled" person—the stigmatized person—may be unable to act in any way different from the role ascribed to him.

THE TRANSCENDENCE OF ROLES OVER BEHAVIORS

Labeling theory emphasizes the processes of human interaction that result in the attribution and acceptance of *roles*. The emphasis upon role construction calls attention to the way behavior may be shaped by the expectations of those with whom one is interacting and to the way our perceptions of each other are reinforced by the early assignment of labels to samples of our acts. Once roles are defined, clusters of attributes are inferred. Such inference stimulates a selective

From Gwynn Nettler, *Explaining Crime*, pp. 202–12. Copyright © 1974 by McGraw-Hill, Inc. Reprinted by permission of the McGraw-Hill Book Company.

perception that permits a linking together of diverse acts under some meaningful label (Turner, 1972, p. 310).

The emphasis upon role formation means that less attention is paid to how people behave than to how they categorize each other on the basis of small segments of behavior. The tendency of the labeling theorist, then, is to deny or ignore differences in the ways in which people act and to stress the utility and the consequences of having the power to categorize. Throughout the literature, the prevailing sentiment is to deny differences and to cast doubt upon the validity and the justice of popular images of minorities.

TRANSLATING "CRIMINALITY" INTO "DEVIANCE"

Given this attitude toward difference, the labeling theorists find it more convenient to talk about "deviance" than about "criminality." This translation directs attention to the fact that majorities are reacting to minorities and that it is being different in the sense of being powerless because of small numbers that permits arrest, censure, and punishment to be attached to a difference.

Such a viewpoint is, obviously, sympathetic to minorities. The labeling school has, consequently, been termed an "underdog philosophy." Its spokesmen ask, "Whose side are we on?" (Becker, 1967).

The philosophy of the underdog turns the tables on conventional thought. Instead of assuming that it is the deviant's difference which needs explanation, it asks why the majority responds to *this* difference as it does. This shift of the question reverses the normal conception of causation; the labeling school suggests that the other person's peculiarity has not caused us to regard him as different so much as our labeling has caused his peculiarity. This reversal, among other characteristics of the labeling hypothesis, has made the theory interesting and has contributed to its popularity (Davis, 1971).

Proponents of the labeling hypothesis distinguish between "primary deviance," that is, some offensive act, and "secondary deviance" (Lemert, 1951), that is, the process by which the reaction of society to an initial difference may confirm the deviant in the stigmatized behavior. Being cast out means being an outcast and makes it comfortable for stigmatized persons to band together in defense of their egos and in justification of their "peculiar" interests.

The labeling theorist deemphasizes the difference in the deviant. He holds that "initially" everyone deviates somewhat from some standards some of the time. What confirms the difference is some official attachment of a label to the apprehended deviant. The labeling theorist is concerned, then, to study how much deviance is produced by the very correctional agencies that are supposed to reduce difference. How much delinquency do reform schools manufacture? How much crime do prisons create? How much psychosis is perpetuated by mental hospitals?

What is to be explained is not so much the deviant as the people who have the power to attach the scarlet letter and thus to confirm the deviation. The labeling theorist sees the judicial response to crime as "the dramatization of evil" (Tannenbaum, 1938).

IMPLICATIONS FOR METHODOLOGY

The research method advocated by the labeling theorist is intensive observation of labelers and their victims. Field work is preferred to the collection of statistics. The result of such study is a description of how the labeler comes to recognize and define the deviant and of how the deviant reacts to and interprets his own world. The test of the adequacy of such a description is understanding and insight rather than prediction and control.

As compared with statistical and experimental studies, the reportorial field work recommended by the labeling theorist is more fun for students. It is good sport to engage in "participant observation," particularly among people who are "different." To this element of pleasure, labeling theory has added the advocacy of the "rights" of minorities. Its appreciative methodology and its political stance have combined to make it a fashionable way of thinking about undesirable behaviors and "social problems." The fashion has spread from its application to crime and has been extended, with variations, to attempts to understand blindness (Scott, 1969), stuttering (Lemert, 1967), illness (Lorber, 1967), civil disturbances (Turner, 1969), "welfarism" (Beck, 1967), paranoia (Lemert, 1962), death and dying (Sudnow, 1966), mental retardation (Mercer, 1965), and neurosis and psychosis (Braginsky et al., 1969; Plog and Edgerton, 1969; Scheff, 1966). An evaluation of this popular mode of explanation must recognize both its advantages and its liabilities.

THE ADVANTAGES OF THE LABELING HYPOTHESIS

The value of the labeling hypothesis lies in its attention to the possibilities that (1) people may respond more to their definitions of others than to the behaviors of others and (2) stigmatizing definitions may produce the bad behaviors they condemn.

1. *The labeling hypothesis asks "society" whether it is reacting to the deviant's behavior or to its own definition of the deviance.* The idea that deviance is produced in some process of interaction that results in our pinning tags on each other calls attention to the possible inaccuracy of the names we apply. To say that "deviance" is created by labeling is to suggest that the labels may be inappropriate, and to raise the question whether we are responding more to what the other person did or more to the image of the other person that is called up by the name we have given him.

This is a valuable question, and it deserves a scientific answer. Thus far, the answer has been assumed by the labeling theorists rather than tested. This assumption partakes of a tradition in social psychology that has itself applied a label to the common-sense categories which most of us use to order our social worlds. The label applied by social psychologists to such popular concepts is "stereotype." Calling a popular image a "stereotype" assumes, without adequate evidence, that the ordinary citizen's notions about the "different" kinds of people around him are mostly wrong. However, the sociopsychological assumption itself seems more false than true. The few studies that have attempted to test the accuracy of popular images have shown that "stereotypes" are more accurate than inaccurate.

This has been found true of popular perceptions of occupations (Rice, 1928) and of ethnic groups (Mackie, 1971, 1973). No adequate research has yet been completed on the validity of popular images of various kinds of criminals, although one such study is under way (Solhaug, 1971). Until some research on this matter has been completed, we can appreciate the point made by the labeling theorists without subscribing to it.

2. *The labeling hypothesis alerts us to the possibility that official reactions to some disapproved behaviors may do more harm than good.* The chief value of the labeling hypothesis has been to call attention to the possibility that official reactions to some kinds of disapproved behaviors may confirm the actors in their deviant ways. It is suggested, for example, that some "sick behaviors" improve more rapidly when they are untreated and that some cures are worse than the diseases they treat.

The labeling theorist emphasizes how minor events in the stream of life may become major events through official reaction. The careers of some different kinds of people are made even more different by the fact that some portion of their lives must be spent in dodging the consequences of the official response to their deviance. The model here is that of the marijuana user,[1] whose life may be changed by the criminalization of his preference.

Labeling theory gains credence as it develops biographies showing that being "officially handled" increases the chances of future official attention. There is evidence that some part of this risk is incurred by the discrimination associated with a criminal label. *There is no way of knowing, however, how much of repeated offense is so caused.*

The labeling hypothesis could prove more useful if its ideas were associated with a taxonomy of offenders in such a way that we might know who could be best "saved" from future criminality by ignoring his present offense. This is not an easy question.[2] It is, however, part of what probation is about.

The labeling hypothesis is politically important because it challenges the *status quo.* This is congenial to revolutionaries, of course, whose ideology translates the label "convict" as "political prisoner." Less radically, the labeling hypothesis stimulates thinking about the costs of applying the criminal law to certain categories of disapproved behaviors. It suggests that there may be limits to the efficacy of the legal sanction (Packer, 1968) and urges assessment of the relative costs and benefits of the criminalization or decriminalization of immoral, peculiar, or unhealthful conduct.

THE LIABILITIES OF THE LABELING PERSPECTIVE

(1) Labeling theory has been criticized for ignoring the differences in behavior described by labels. The labeling schema draws attention from deeds to the public definitions of those deeds. Such diversion means that (2) labeling theory does not increase, and may well decrease, our ability to predict individual behavior. Its low predictive power is a result not only of its neglect of individual differences but also of the fact that (3) it contains a defective model of causation. This in turn means that (4) its relevance to social policy is lessened. Each of these points will be amplified.

1. Labeling theory does not explain the behaviors that lead to the application of labels. The labeling theorists argue as if popular and legal categories were devoid of content, as if they were never "well earned." The labeling explanation pays little or no attention to the fact that people do *not* behave similarly. It slights the possibility that a label may *correctly* identify consistent differences in conduct, and it pays little attention to the reasons why "society" continues to apply a label once it has been used.

Labeling theory denies, therefore, the causal importance and explanatory value of personality variables. In fact, labeling theorists regard as futile the search for personality differences that might distinguish categories of more or less criminal persons. The labeling hypothesis prefers a political interpretation to such a psychological one. It prefers to believe that deviants are minorities lacking power to challenge the rules by which a majority has labeled them. The theory denies, then, that a label may be properly applied to describe personality differences which may underlie real behavioral differences. This denial has unfortunate consequences for the prediction of individual behavior.

It has unfortunate consequences, too, for the development of public policy. The prescription that follows from the labeling hypothesis is to change the attitudes of majorities toward misbehaving minorities. In reply, majorities tell us that they are not yet convinced that a more compassionate attitude toward the robber or the burglar will change the offender's behavior and reduce the pain he gives.

2. When applied to the understanding of individual behavior, the labeling hypothesis has low predictive power. The low predictive power of labeling theory results from its denial of personality differences. The interactional bias of the labeling theorist encourages such optimistic but risky beliefs as these:

He will be honest if I trust him.

She will be reasonable if you are.

He will be pacific if we are.

Her psychosis is not "in her," but "in her situation." When the mirrors in which she sees herself are changed, she will change.

On the contrary, there *are* personality differences that are reliably associated with behavioral differences and that are remarkably persistent. These persistent ways of feeling and acting are not readily changeable with changes in the labels attached to them. Regardless of what we have been called, *most of us continue to be what we have been a long time becoming.*

The research literature on this subject is vast. It may be sampled in the works of Honzik (1966), Kelly (1963), Mischel (1969), Robins and O'Neal (1958), Roff (1961), Schaefer and Bayley (1960), Thomas et al. (1970), Witkin (1965), and Zax et al. (1968). The point is made in the autobiography of the playwright S. N. Behrman (1972) who, after years of failure and impoverished struggle, wrote a play that was a hit. Behrman comments, "With the production of a successful play, . . . you acquire overnight a new identity—a public label. But this label is pasted on you. It doesn't obliterate what you are and have always been—doesn't erase the stigmata of temperament" (p. 37).

The statement that there are persistent temperamental and cognitive differences underlying our behaviors can be qualified by adding that such personality variables have more of an impact upon behavior as circumstances are equalized. Nevertheless, most of us can tell the difference between behavior—our own and others'—that is only situationally reactive and behavior that is characteristic. All of us operate, implicitly or explicitly, with the idea of *character*—the idea that there *are* enduring personal predispositions relevant to moral behavior. This means that, unless there are tremendous changes in environments, people are likely to continue to behave as they have behaved. Against the optimistic recommendations of the interactionist, it seems more sensible to believe that:

The embezzler may need to be arrested, and stigmatized, before he "turns honest."

Being reasonable with a fanatic is futile.

A soft answer turns away the wrath of some men, but not of others, and there is no point in pleading for your life with a Charles Manson.

The cures of psychoses are exceptional. Most people who are "peculiar" are not disordered in all ways, all the time. Misbehavior may be episodic; but ordinarily, safety lies in the assumption of behavioral continuity.

3. *The model of causation implicit in the labeling hypothesis is questionable.* Every explanation of human behavior makes assumptions about its causes. The labeling theory locates the causes of adult behavior in an unusual place—in the people who respond to it. It shifts the "responsibility" for my action from me to you. It stresses how much of what I do is a result of what you have done to me, and for me. My "self," it is said, is reflected to me by the social mirrors available to me. My "self" is the presumed agent of my actions, but my "self" is itself largely constructed by the responses of "significant others" to my initial efforts.

This is a shorthand statement of the hypothesis of "socialization." In its general formulation, there is no quarrel with such a hypothesis. All theories that would explain human behavior, including popular theories, assume that our behavior has been shaped by the actions of others. The sociopsychological hypotheses of the "control" variety pay particular attention to the "how" of this socialization process.

It is not denied, then, that how people respond to us when we misbehave may affect our subsequent conduct. The lively questions are, however, at what periods of our development, and to what degree, others mold us. What is at issue is *how much* of the adult behavior to be explained varies with the response of others to it.

It is our ignorance that permits the continuing quarrel, for no one knows which kinds of behaviors, in which kinds of personalities, at which "stage" of life, are affected how much, by which kinds of response, from which others, in which situations. Some generalization about this is part of our popular wisdom, but much of that is truistic. We expect more than truisms from criminological theories.

The valuable contributions of the labeling hypothesis have tended to obscure its deficiencies. It is one thing to study the way in which a defining process affects our response to the behavior of others. It is another matter to study the causes of the events we are defining. Studying how we respond to deviant others may suggest to us a more economical (more rational) mode of reacting. This suggestion should not be confused, however, with information about the causes of the crimes that concern us.

Such confusion is created when spokesmen of the labeling theory tell us, for example, that "*social groups create deviance by making the rules whose infraction constitutes deviance,* and by applying those rules to particular people and labeling them as outsiders" (Becker, 1963, p. 9). Some readers will translate statements like this as saying that "social groups create crime by making the laws whose infraction constitutes crime." This translation is slippery: it slides between the truth that social groups create the *definition* of "crime" and the falsehood that the *injuries* condemned by these definitions would disappear (or would not have been "created") if the definition had not been formulated. To the layman, it sounds as though the labeling theorist believed that people would not wish to defend themselves against burglary or murder if they had not learned a rule defining these acts as crimes. It sounds, also, as though the labeling theorist believed that there would be less "burglary" if we did not use that term. The nonprofessional consumer of criminological explanations recognizes this for the semantic trick that it is—the trick of saying, "If a crime is a breach of a rule, you won't have the crime if you don't have the rule." The ordinary reaction to this sematic sleight of hand is to say, "A mugging by any other name hurts just as much."

Applied to "real life" the labeling hypothesis functions as another of the "power of positive thinking" philosophies: "If disease is an error of thought, positive thinking will cure it." "If crime resides in our definitions of deviance, redefining it will change it."

Our question has to do with the location of causation. When the causation implied by the labeling hypothesis is tested, it fails. The causes specified by this schema do not account for the production of the behaviors that disturb us. "Mental hospitals" do not cause "mental illness" (Gove, 1970), nor do the agencies of social control, or the labels they apply, account for crime (Ward, 1971).

The assumption of labeling theory is that those who become "criminal" are mostly those who, while behaving much like everyone else, just happened to get tagged, or that those labeled "criminals" were more liable to the tagging because they fit some public's prejudiced stereotype of the criminal. Contrary to these assumptions, however, studies of the operation of the system of justice show that it works like a sieve: as we have seen, the people who end up caught in the sieve tend to be the more serious and persistent lawbreakers (Black and Reiss, 1970; Bordua, 1967; Terry, 1967).

In summary, the labeling theorist does not think about causes and effects, about antecedents and consequents; he prefers to think about interactions. This preference does not eliminate the idea of causation; it only obscures it by shifting the locus of causes from actors to their judges. This shift has some moral and political value in the fight between outsiders and insiders. It justifies a challenge of the police and the courts, or any other mechanism of social control, that would condemn the conduct of minorities. When the labeling hypothesis is applied to the explanation of the serious crimes, however, its model of causation reduces its value for public policy.

4. On the level of social concerns, the labeling hypothesis does not answer the perennial questions about crime. We are reminded that explanatory theories are only as good as the questions they answer. The answers provided by the labeling theorists are not addressed to the questions about crime that are asked by most people. These questions are, again, "What causes crime?" "What accounts for increases or decreases in crime rates?" "How can crime be reduced?"

To these questions, the labeling theorists give no good reply. The policy recommendation of the labeling hypothesis comes down to "Avoid unnecessary labeling" (Schur, 1971, p. 171). This may be helpful in decriminalizing some activities. It is a recommendation that is already being followed in some areas, as in the euphemistic use of language that substitutes kind words for harsh ones—"sanitary engineer" for "garbage collector" and "special child" for "imbecile." Such transitions bespeak a change in attitude, yet the categories persist. Categorizing is an inevitable part of our response to the world. We should wish our categories to be clean, accurate, and useful, as social psychologists have urged. It is doubtful, however, whether attention to our vocabularies will tell citizens and public officials how better to reduce robbery and rape.

Notes

1. The labeling theorist's point can be made by substituting for marijuana the criminalization of any other chemical, like tobacco or alcohol, that many people habitually use.

2. The answer to this question is made difficult by the possible antagonism among the various goals of justice. The antagonism is the desire to rehabilitate some apprehended offenders, the need to deter others, and the need to express, through the symbolism of punishment, society's rejection of criminal conduct.

References

Beck, B. 1967. "Welfare as a moral category." *Social Problems* 14 (Winter): 258–277.

Becker, H. S. 1963. *Outsiders: Studies in the Sociology of Deviance.* Glencoe, Ill.: The Free Press.

————. 1967. "Whose side are we on?" *Social Problems* 14 (Winter): 239–247.

Behrman, S. N. 1972. "People in a diary, I." *The New Yorker* 48 (13 May): 36–94.

Black, D. J., and A. J. Reiss, Jr. 1970. "Police control of juveniles." *American Sociological Review* 35 (February): 63–77.

Bordua, D. J. 1967. "Recent trends: Deviant behavior and social control." *The Annals of the American Academy of Political and Social Science* 369 (January): 149–163.

Braginsky, B. M., et al. 1969. *Methods of Madness: The Mental Hospital as a Last Resort.* New York: Holt, Rinehart, and Winston, Inc.

Davis, M. S. 1971. "That's interesting!" *Philosophy of the Social Sciences* 1 (December): 309–344.

Gove, W. R. 1970. "Societal reaction as an explanation of mental illness: An evaluation." *American Sociological Review* 35 (October): 873–884.

Honzik, M. P. 1966. "Prediction of behavior from birth to maturity." In J. Rosenblith and W. Allinsmith (Eds.), *The Causes of Behavior.* Second Edition. Boston: Allyn and Bacon.

Kelly, E. L. 1963. "Consistency of the adult personality." *American Psychologist* 10 (November): 659–681.

Lemert, E. M. 1951. *Social Pathology.* New York: McGraw-Hill Book Company.

————. 1962. "Paranoia and the dynamics of exclusion." *Sociometry* 25 (March): 2–20.

————. 1967. *Human Deviance, Social Problems and Social Control.* Englewood Cliffs, N.J.: Prentice-Hall.

Lorber, J. 1967. "Deviance as performance: The case of illness." *Social Problems* 14 (Winter): 302–310.

Mackie, M. M. 1971. *The Accuracy of Folk Knowledge Concerning Alberta Indians, Hutterites and Ukrainians: An Available Data Stereotype Validation Technique.* Edmonton: The University of Alberta, Department of Sociology, Ph.D. dissertation.

————. 1973. "Arriving at 'truth' by definition: The case of stereotype inaccuracy." *Social Problems* 20 (Spring): 431–447.

Mercer, J. R. 1965. "Social system perspective and clinical perspective: Frames of reference for understanding career patterns of persons labelled as mentally retarded." *Social Problems* 13 (Summer): 18–34.

Mischel, W. 1969. "Continuity and change in personality." *American Psychologist* 24 (November): 1012–1018.

Packer, H. L. 1968. *The Limits of the Criminal Sanction.* Stanford: Stanford University Press.

Plog, S. C., and R. B. Edgerton (Eds.) 1969. *Changing Perspectives in Mental Illness.* New York: Holt, Rinehart, and Winston, Inc.

Rice, S. A. 1928. *Quantitative Methods in Politics.* New York: Alfred A. Knopf, Inc.

Robins, L. N., and P. O'Neal. 1958. "Mortality, mobility, and crime." *American Sociological Review* 23 (April): 162–171.

Roff, M. 1961. "Childhood social interaction and young adult bad conduct." *Journal of Abnormal and Social Psychology* 63 (September): 333–337.

Schaefer, E. S., and N. Bayley. 1960. "Consistency of maternal behavior from infancy to preadolescence." *Journal of Abnormal and Social Psychology* 61 (July): 1–6.

Scheff, T. J. 1966. *Being Mentally Ill.* Chicago: Aldine.

Schur, E. M. 1971. *Labeling Deviant Behavior: Its Sociological Implications.* New York: Harper and Row, Publishers.

Scott, R. A. 1969. *The Making of Blind Men.* New York: Russell Sage.

Solhaug, M. L. 1971. "Accuracy of 'bad men' stereotypes: A comparison of autostereotyping by lawbreakers with stereotyping by more lawful others." Edmonton: The University of Alberta, Department of Sociology. M.A. thesis prospectus.

Sudnow, D. 1966. *Passing On.* Englewood Cliffs, N.J.: Prentice-Hall.

Tannenbaum, F. 1938. *Crime and the Community.* Boston: Ginn and Company.

Terry, R. M. 1967. "Discrimination in the handling of juvenile offenders by social-control agencies." *Journal of Research in Crime and Delinquency* 4 (July): 218–230.

Thomas, A., et al. 1970. "The origin of personality." *Scientific American* 223 (August): 102–109.

Turner, R. H. 1969. "The public perception of protest." *American Sociological Review* 34 (December): 815–831.

————. 1972. "Deviance avowal as neutralization of commitment." *Social Problems* 19 (Winter): 308–321.

Ward, R. H. 1971. "The labeling theory: A critical analysis." *Criminology* 9 (August–November): 268–290.

Witkin, H. 1965. "Psychological differentiation and forms of pathology." *Journal of Abnormal Psychology* 70 (October): 317–336.

Zax, M., et al. 1968. "Follow-up study of children identified early as emotionally disturbed." *Journal of Consulting and Clinical Psychology* 32 (August): 369–374.

Questions for Discussion

1. What is the difference between master and subordinate statuses, on the one hand, and master and auxiliary status traits, on the other? How do these apply to "deviants"?

2. Provide examples of primary and secondary deviance. How can the institutionalization of the "mentally challenged" produce secondary deviance?

3. What arguments does Schur present to back up his position that women have a "deviant" staus? To what extent and why do you agree or disagree with Schur's point of view?

4. Do you think Nettler misinterprets the labeling perspective? Why or why not? How applicable are Nettler's points to Chambliss's article?

Selected References

Becker, Howard S. *Outsiders: Studies in the Sociology of Deviance.* New York: Free Press, 1963.
    A succinct statement of the labeling perspective, together with some empirical studies of jazz musicians, marijuana use, and social controls on marijuana.

Glassner, Barry. "Labeling Theory." In *The Sociology of Deviance,* ed. M. Michael Rosenberg, Robert A. Stebbins, and Allan Turowetz. New York: St. Martin's Press, 1982, pp. 71–89.
    Since the emergence of the labeling perspective some twenty-five years ago, there has been widespread popular acceptance and considerable critical commentary. Though Becker and Lemert have urged that "labeling" be examined beyond its original applications, according to Glassner it has not been. He counsels that three aspects of labeling be studied: categorical, contextual, and potential labeling.

Gove, Walter R., ed. *The Labelling of Deviance.* New York: Sage, 1975.
    A collection of papers in which experts refute the alleged ability of the labeling perspective to account for alcoholism, drug addiction, mental retardation, and mental illness.

Harris, Anthony R., and Gary D. Hill. "The Social Psychology of Deviance: Toward a Reconciliation with Social Structure." *Annual Review of Sociology* 8. Palo Alto, CA: Annual Reviews, 1982, pp. 161–86.

Summarizes some of the literature which faults labeling explanations of deviance and social problems.

Lemert, Edwin M. *Social Pathology: A Systematic Approach to the Theory of Sociopathic Behavior.* New York: McGraw-Hill, 1951.

An early, influential, and systematic theory that centers its attention on the social reactions to rule-breaking behavior. Clearly a book that was ahead of its time.

Link, Bruce G., Francis T. Cullen, Elmer Struening, Patrick E. Shrout, and Bruce P. Dohrenwend. "A Modified Labeling Theory Approach to Mental Disorders." *American Sociological Review* 54 (June 1989): 400–423.

An empirical study which supports Scheff's labeling theory of mental illness. Mental patients, after their release from the hospital, anticipated rejection and adopted a role to defend against stigma (secondary deviance).

Mercer, Jane R. "Social System Perspective and Clinical Perspective: Frames of Reference for Understanding Career Patterns of People Labeled as Mentally Retarded." *Social Problems* 13 (Summer, 1965): 18–34.

High-status families label their children as retarded at an earlier age than low-status families. High-status families are more apt to accept official labels and are more likely to leave the child in an institution, whereas the low-status family "frequently rejects the official definition of the child as retarded and withdraws him from the institution at the first opportunity." Mercer's classic study supports the general labeling proposition that though peoples' behaviors may be similar, the response to those behaviors may vary with the definition that significant others and officials place upon them.

Plummer, Ken. "Misunderstanding Labelling Perspectives." In *Deviant Interpretations,* ed. David Downes and Paul Rock. New York: Barnes & Noble, 1979, pp. 85–121.

Plummer says that "the critics drastically overstate their case if they believe that they can announce the 'death' of labeling theory." He refutes charges that labeling theory has limited application and that when tested is usually found to be empirically wrong.

Rubington, Earl, and Martin S. Weinberg, eds. *Deviance: The Interactionist Perspective.* 1st ed. New York: Macmillan, 1968.

Broadened the labeling perspective and coined the term "interactionist perspective." The editors have amassed some fifty-five articles and organized them according to their relevance for the labeling perspective. This book is now in its eighth edition (2002).

Scheff, Thomas J. *Being Mentally Ill: A Sociological Theory.* 3rd ed. Aldine de Gruyter, 1999.

The revised edition of this systematic explanation of mental illness by means of the labeling perspective includes the theory as first expounded in 1966, a discussion of the considerable debate it engendered among sociologists, and research since its first publication that lends support to the theory.

Schur, Edwin M. *Labeling Deviant Behavior: Its Sociological Implications.* New York: Harper & Row, 1971.

Codifies a number of propositions on the development and application of deviant labels and on their personal, organizational, and social consequences.

Schur, Edwin M. *Labeling Women Deviant: Gender, Stigma, and Social Control.* New York: Random House, 1984.

Schur reviews a number of studies of gender and applies the labeling perspective to the social situations of women. Inequality between the genders establishes the conditions under which women come to be defined as deviant if they either fail to act as women are "expected to" or act "like men." He demonstrates how the basic concepts of the labeling perspective help to account for how men and women come to define certain women as deviant and the effects of those definitions on their self-concepts and life chances.

Scull, Andrew T. "Deviance and Social Control." In *Handbook of Sociology,* ed. Neil Smelser. Newbury Park, CA: Sage, 1988, pp. 667–93.

In this review article, Scull argues that the labeling perspective cannot account for the simultaneous presence of deviant behavior and the absence of its presumed effective cause, social control.

7/CRITICAL PERSPECTIVE

All societies and their cultures experience change. As part of the culture, perspectives on social problems also change. As we have seen, a sense of crisis in a society affects thinkers who try to develop a comprehensive understanding of the society and its problems. And, in a similar fashion, a sense of crisis within the discipline of sociology fosters the development of new perspectives on social problems. Thus, the emergence of a new perspective generally signifies that current perspectives do not explain social problems in a whole or consistent manner. Such a situation led to the development of the critical perspective.

THE MAIN IDEA OF THE CRITICAL PERSPECTIVE

Patterns of values, statuses, and norms come to center around important societal concerns. For example, maintenance of order becomes the task of the political institution; replenishment of the population, the task of the family; "learning," the task of the educational institution; and producing and distributing goods and services, the task of the economic institution. All social institutions are interrelated and exercise influence on one another, but of them all, many believe that the economic institution exerts the greatest influence on people, their prospects, and their patterns of interaction with one another. And similarly, though people have numerous social statuses, their position in the economic institution is viewed as the most important.

From the point of view of Marxian thought, there are essentially two positions available in the economic institution—one in which people own or control economic enterprises, and one in which they labor primarily for the benefit of the former. Each of these classes develops life patterns that stem from its position in the economic enterprise. People come to learn class interests and values through association with others similarly situated in the economic institution. Classes become the key social units because, through the dynamics of relations between these classes, one can predict the kinds of social problems that will come into being. Central to the array of problems is class dominance and conflict. When members of one of these classes act on behalf of their own class interests, they enter into conflict with the other class, whose interests are diametrically opposed.

For example, the class that owns and controls economic enterprises exercises considerable control over the government. In consequence, it exerts greater influence on the laws the government makes. This class gets civil laws passed that are in accord with its economic interests. In addition, it helps to mold the criminal law. It directs attention to those people most likely to break certain laws that buttress capitalism and brings pressure on agencies of social control to see that these people are caught, tried, and punished for any infractions of the law. The ruling class also deflects attention from any rule-breakers within its ranks and shields them from exposure to enforcement. Thus, the class that owns and controls economic enterprises extends its influence into a number of other aspects of life. So it is that the critical perspective seeks to account for a host of social problems.

THE SOCIAL SOURCES OF THE CRITICAL PERSPECTIVE

Crises call into question the ability of older viewpoints to offer either understanding or remedial action. These are the kinds of social and cultural circumstances that gave rise to the critical perspective. The persistent crises of interrelated social problems generated doubts in the minds of some thinkers that any of the prevailing perspectives could offer a meaningful account for what seemed to be the problems of society. Facing the double crisis that confronts social policy and social thought, some thinkers created the critical perspective by uniting various perspectives with an earlier tradition of social thought. Theorists in Germany drew on idealist philosophy[1]; those in England, on radical politics; and those in the United States, on a combination of philosophy and political activism. The result has been several strands of thought on social problems that share a number of characteristics, though they go by different names. Under "critical perspective," we have grouped a number of viewpoints labeled by the theorists themselves or others as "critical theory," "critical criminology," "new criminology," "radical criminology," "radical sociology," and "neo-Marxism." While having a number of viewpoints in common, these approaches exhibit some differences. Thus, within the "critical perspective," there are thinkers who emphasize philosophy, those who emphasize political activism and the need for social change, and those who focus on the perspective's explanatory potential.

What crises gave rise to these variants of the critical perspective? What were their sources in traditional social thought? And who were the thinkers who developed these versions of the critical perspective?

The critical perspective stems from the Marxist tradition. During his lifetime, Karl Marx (1818–1883) produced a host of works that do not easily lend themselves to classification. He wrote philosophy, social and political history, and a three-volume magnum opus on economics titled *Das Kapital* (*Capital* in English). He was both a theorist and a political activist for most of his life, devoting most of his energies to unseating the capitalists and bringing the working class to political power in Western Europe. His work had broad influence in the Western world during his lifetime. Since his death, his influence widened and deepened to the point that it became the basis of revolutionary political thought in Asia and the Third World. In addition, Marxist thought continues to influence the work of scholars in philosophy, economics, politics, and sociology.

As Marx and Engels argued in *The Communist Manifesto*, the history of all societies has been the history of class exploitation and struggle. First there was tribal society, then slavery, then feudalism, and then capitalism. The seeds of the new society are contained in the death of the old social forms. Just as the rising middle

---

1. A philosophy that considers the active contribution of the human mind in the formation of our knowledge of the world. Thus it provides a philosophical justification for taking the role of "culture" seriously.

class overthrew feudalism, thereby ushering in capitalism, so in time will the proletariat (the working class) unite and overthrow the bourgeoise (the capitalists) and usher in socialism, which, in time, will give way to a classless society.

The capitalist economic system is based on market competition and the pursuit of self-interest. Thus, each enterprise seeks to produce the most at the least cost for the highest possible profit. As a result, the working class experiences such miseries as poverty, unemployment, shorter life expectancy, poor physical and mental health, alcoholism, and high rates of crime against persons, property, and public order. The only solution to these miseries is for the workers to unite and take control of the capitalist republic.

In Germany, early members of what became known as the Frankfurt School—for example, Theodore Adorno, Max Horkheimer, and Herbert Marcuse—extended and developed Marx's ideas in a number of directions. With the rise of Nazism, they fled Germany. Fascism in Europe, along with the failure of the Soviet Union to develop into a democratic socialist state, led members of the Frankfurt School to doubt that the working class could ever achieve the role that Marx had both planned and predicted for it. Just as psychoanalysis seeks to liberate its patients from the unconscious conflicts that entrap them, so the Frankfurt School sought to liberate and emancipate people by bringing cultural factors to the forefront of Marxian analysis. Thus the Frankfurt sociologists showed how the basic assumptions of capitalism pervade all aspects of people's lives. Their major thrust (which they developed in the United States) was and is to develop a comprehensive and detailed critique of the culture of advanced capitalism.

In Britain, the 1960s were a period of declining influence on the international scene, of the emergence of a high rate of unemployment, and of growth in the immigration of Pakistanis and blacks. A number of British sociologists saw a pattern of social problems that seemed to have become both interwoven and intractable; depressed industries, high inflation, poverty, racism, increasing rates of crime, delinquency, drug use, and the like.

A group of these sociologists met to assess the extent to which the available perspectives on social problems made sense and offered some practical solutions to these pressing social problems. Their deliberations produced these conclusions: current perspectives on social problems of whatever school seemed unable to account for the pattern of social problems; the Marxist tradition seemed to offer the most fruitful way of both looking at and solving the problems; and a detailed focus on the social problem of crime would provide the best example of this holistic perspective on social problems.

The upshot of their labors was an important book, published in 1972. *The New Criminology,* written by Ian Taylor, Michael Walton, and Jock Young, set itself two important tasks. The first was to review and analyze the existing array of sociological theories of crime. The second was the development of a new theory of crime that would present satisfactory explanations of the major aspects of crime as a social problem: the promulgation of criminal laws, their violation, and their enforcement. Taylor, Walton, and Young outlined, analyzed, and criticized a number of sociological theories, including the deviant behavior perspective and the labeling perspective. Then, in their last chapter, they outlined the questions on crime that an adequate theory must answer. While their last chapter does not present a new theory, the line of questions they ask and the answers they presume the perspective will find make it quite clear that they have developed a systematic Marxist argument on crime as a social problem. A subsequent collection of readings that they edited, *Critical Criminology,* contains some additional arguments. The implications of their point of view for description, analysis, explanation, and action come forth quite explicitly in their second book. As Britain enters the more advanced stages of capitalist society, crime rates will only increase. The only remedy, the authors say, is to change Great Britain into a socialist society. The authors claim that the reduction of social inequalities will correspondingly reduce crime rates drastically. Like their mentor, Karl Marx, the new criminologists believe that the proof of any way of looking at the world rests on the ability of that perspective to help change that world.

In the United States, the 1960s also became an extremely turbulent decade, one characterized by the assassination of political and civil-rights leaders, the beginning of protests against the Vietnam War, the civil-rights movement, riots, the white back-lash and flight to the suburbs, and the rebirth of the feminist movement. The turbu-lence of the 1960s carried over into the 1970s, which saw the Watergate scandals, the winding down of the Vietnam War, economic recession, and the oil crisis. In the early 1970s, an American version of the critical perspective began to emerge. And, much as in Britain, a strand of this thought centered around the analysis of crime as a social problem.

The American version of the critical perspective grounded itself in the holistic orientation of Marx—that events in the history of any given society take place in specific social, economic, and political circumstances, and that these events gen-erally are interrelated. Class conflict came to be seen as the cause of the many problems that appeared in different institutional contexts. Theorists who extended and developed a neo-Marxist view of social problems in the United States also ar-gued that both the deviant behavior perspective and the labeling perspective had only limited explanatory potential compared with the broader and more systemic view that saw social problems as the inevitable outcome of the conflict between the owning-controlling class and the working class.

Two important writers who advanced and developed the American critical per-spective evolved in their thought from a position of value conflict to the more sys-tematic Marxist conception of class conflict. Both Richard Quinney and William J. Chambliss had already, by the late 1960s, contributed important works advancing a value conflict interpretation of social problems. By the early 1970s, each shifted and developed this perspective into its present critical form. For instance, Quinney's book *The Social Reality of Crime* located among a variety of different interest groups the power to define certain acts as criminal. In his later works, *Class, State, and Crime* and *Critique of Legal Order,* Quinney postulated that all crimes are a consequence of the capitalist society.

In 1964, Chambliss published a paper entitled "A Sociological Analysis of the Law of Vagrancy." In this paper, he showed how different interest groups, over time, came forward to define the crime of vagrancy as a way of pursuing or protecting their own interests. In essence, this work exemplified a value conflict approach to the social problem of vagrancy. In 1975, Chambliss published "The Political Economy of Crime," in which he demonstrated a basic assumption of the critical perspective about corruption.

A number of other sociologists have contributed to the critical perspective. They have added to the programmatic statement of the perspective, applied it to specific issues, or used it to point out the deficiencies of the other perspectives on social problems.

The most general criticism of the critical perspective has been that it is a political ideology, or a theory that, unlike most standard theories, does not specify the con-ditions under which it could be disproved. Regardless, the critical perspective con-tinues to remain an important perspective on social problems because of its close links to the Marxist tradition and because it offers a broad historical view on how social problems come into being and how they can be reduced, if not eliminated, by concerted political action.

CHARACTERISTICS OF THE CRITICAL PERSPECTIVE

Holism, a key assumption of the critical perspective, requires that analysts examine the whole social system, rather than any of its specific parts. Social problems are interrelated with a number of events, changes, and pressures operating on all social institutions. The main elements of the critical perspective are as follows:

Definition. A social problem is a situation that develops out of the exploitation of the working class.

Causes. In the broadest sense, the form of social organization that capitalist society produces causes a wide range of specific social problems. With regard to the social problem of crime, it is the system of class domination that creates and sustains it. For example, capitalists sustain poverty and make and enforce rules in their own interests.

Conditions. Important conditions of social problems are the extent and severity of class domination and conflict, working-class consciousness, and fluctuations in the business cycle. When domination and conflict are less visible or of lesser strength, if large segments of the working class are unaware of their common interests, and if there is an upturn in the business cycle, awareness of social problems will lag considerably behind their actual occurrence.

Consequences. Though capitalist societies go through cyclic periods, social problems are proportional to advances in the stages of the development of capitalism. Thus, writers using critical perspective predict, for example, that crime rates will rise with advances in the development of capitalism.

Solutions. Only political activism can resolve the consequences of the capitalist system. Either through reform or revolution, the working-class movement must struggle to achieve a classless society, thereby eliminating the host of social problems that are endemic in a social system based on social inequality.

SUMMARY AND CONCLUSION

Crises, turbulence, and upheaval seem to be common occurrences in modern, urban, industrial societies. These periods of crisis demand responses by members of society. These crises similarly reverberate within the discipline of sociology and affect prevailing perspectives on social problems. Thus, sociologists in Germany, Great Britain, and the United States found that crises that their particular societies were experiencing called into question the adequacy of the dominant social problems perspectives of the day.

In all three of these countries, a body of thought on social problems made its appearance under a variety of names. It developed into a profound critique of capitalist society and culture that sees social problems as endemic to capitalistic society. Thus, the essential causes of social problems reside in class dominance and conflict:

the "haves" hold on to what they have and maintain what they have at the continued expense of the "have-nots." Class conflict results from the system of class domination that perpetuates social inequality. Ultimately, the rich get richer and the poor get poorer. The only solution to the assortment of social problems that are common to advanced capitalist societies is for the working class to win the class struggle and usher in true socialism, which will lead to a classless society.

CRIME AND THE DEVELOPMENT OF CAPITALISM

Richard Quinney

"Crime," says Quinney, "is inevitable under capitalist conditions." Capitalists own and control the production of work, law, and culture. The working class, by contrast, has nothing to sell save its own labor. This economic, political, and cultural inequality provides both the dynamics and the consequences of the capitalist system. The consequences only increase the need of the capitalist class to dominate and of the working class to adapt. The responses of both classes to the situation produce a variety of crimes. The capitalist class commits crimes of domination, government, and control that produce such social injuries as corruption, sexism, racism, and economic exploitation. The working class commits crimes of accommodation and resistance. The only solution to the expanding and increasing rate of crime, Quinney says, comes about when the working class shifts from individual crimes of accommodation to crimes of collective resistance. Such a consciousness forged in a manifest struggle between the classes will ultimately change the system from capitalist to socialist, thereby reducing, if not eliminating, the many kinds of crimes the capitalist system engenders.

The state . . . arose to protect and promote the interests of the dominant class, the class that owns and controls the means of production. The state exists as a device for controlling the exploited class, the class that labors, for the benefit of the ruling class. Modern civilization, as epitomized in capitalist societies, is founded on the exploitation of one class by another. Moreover, the capitalist state is oppressive not only because it supports the interests of the dominant class but also because it is responsible for the design of the whole system within which the capitalist ruling class dominates and the working class is dominated.[1] The capitalist system of production and exploitation is secured and reproduced by the capitalist state.

The coercive force of the state, embodied in law and legal repression, is the traditional means of maintaining the social and economic order. Contrary to conventional wisdom, law, instead of representing the community custom, is an instrument of the state that serves the interests of the developing capitalist class.[2] Law emerged with the rise of capitalism. As human labor became a commodity, human relations in general began to be the object of the commodity form. Human beings became subject to juridic regulation; the capitalist mode of production called forth its equivalent mode of regulation and control, the legal system.[3] And criminal law developed as the most appropriate form of control for capitalist society. Criminal law and legal repression continue to serve the interests of the capitalist class and the perpetuation of the capitalist system.

Through the legal system, then, the state forcefully protects its interests and those of the capitalist class. Crime control becomes the coercive means of checking threats to the existing social and economic order, threats that result from a system of oppression and exploitation.

Yet the coercive force of the state is but one means of maintaining the social and economic order. A more subtle reproductive mechanism of capitalist society is the perpetuation of the capitalist concept of reality, a nonviolent but equally repressive means of domination. As Alan Wolfe has shown, in the manipulation of consciousness the existing order is legitimated and secured:

> The most important reproductive mechanism which does not involve the use of state violence is consciousness-manipulation. The liberal state has an enormous amount of violence at its disposal, but it is often reluctant to use it. Violence may breed counter-violence, leading to instability. It may be far better to manipulate consciousness to such an extent that most people would never think of engaging in the kinds of action which could be repressed. The most perfectly repressive (though not violently so) capitalist system, in other words, would not be a police state, but the complete opposite, one in which there were no police because there was nothing to police, everyone having accepted the legitimacy of that society and all its daily consequences.[4]

Those who rule in capitalist society—with the assistance of the state—not only accumulate capital at the expense of those who work but impose their ideology as well. Oppression and exploitation are legitimized by the expropriation of consciousness; since labor is expropriated, consciousness must also be expropriated.[5] In fact, *legitimacy* of the capitalist order is maintained by controlling the consciousness of the population. A capitalist hegemony is established.

Thus, through its various reproductive mechanisms capitalism is able to maximize the possibility of control over citizens of the state. Ranging from control of production and distribution to manipulation of the mind, capitalism operates according to its own form of dictatorship. André Gorz writes:

> The dictatorship of capital is exercised not only on the production and distribution of wealth, but with equal force on the manner of producing, on the model of consumption, and on the manner of consuming, the manner of working, thinking, living. As much as over the workers, the factories, and the state, this dictatorship rules over the society's vision of the future, its ideology, its priorities and goals, over the way in which people experience and learn about themselves, their potentials, their relations with other people and with the rest of the world. This dictatorship is economic, political, cultural and psychological at the same time: it is total.[6]

Although the capitalist state creates and manages the institutions of control (employing physical force *and* manipulation of consciousness), the basic contradictions of the capitalist order are such that this control is not absolute and, in the long run, is subject to defeat. Because of the contradictions of capitalism, the capitalist state is more weak than strong.[7] Eventually the capitalist state loses its legitimacy and no longer is able to perpetuate the ideology that capital accumulation for capitalists (at the expense of workers) is good for the nation or for human interests. The ability of the capitalist economic order to exist according to its own interests is eventually weakened.[8] The problem becomes especially acute in periods of economic crisis, periods that are unavoidable under capitalism.

In the course of reproducing the capitalist system, crimes are committed. One of the contradictions of capitalism is that some of its laws must be violated in order to secure the existing system.[9] The contradictions of capitalism produce their own sources of crime. Not only are these contradictions heightened during times of crisis, making for an increase in crimes of domination, but the nature of these crimes changes with the further development of capitalism.

The crimes of domination most characteristic of capitalist domination are those crimes that occur in the course of securing the existing economic order. These *crimes of economic domination* include the crimes committed by corporations, ranging from price fixing to pollution of the environment in order to protect and further capital accumulation. Also included are the economic crimes of individual businessmen and professionals.

Then there are the *crimes of government* committed by the elected and appointed officials of the capitalist state. The Watergate crimes, carried out to perpetuate a particular governmental administration, are the most publicized instances of these crimes. There are also those offenses committed by the government against persons and groups who would seemingly threaten national security. Included here are the crimes of warfare and the political assassination of foreign and domestic leaders.

Crimes of domination also occur in the course of state control. These are the *crimes of control.* They include the felonies and misdemeanors that law-enforcement agents, especially the police, carry out in the name of the law, usually against persons accused of other violations. Violence and brutality have become a recognized part of police work. In addition to these crimes of control, there are crimes of a more subtle nature in which agents of the law violate the civil liberties of citizens, as in the various forms of surveillance, the use of provocateurs, and the illegal denial of due process.

Finally, many *social injuries* committed by the capitalist class and the capitalist state are not usually defined as criminal in the legal codes of the state.[10] These systematic actions, involving the denial of basic human rights (resulting in sexism, racism, and economic exploitation), are an integral part of capitalism and are important to its survival.

Domination and repression are basic to class struggle in the development of capitalism. The capitalist class and the state protect and promote the capitalist order by controlling those who do not own the means of production. The labor supply and the conditions for labor must be secured. Crime control and crimes of domination are necessary features and natural products of a capitalist political economy.

ACCOMMODATION AND RESISTANCE

The contradictions of developing capitalism heighten the level of class struggle and thereby increase (1) the need to dominate by the capitalist class and (2) the need to accommodate and resist by the classes exploited by capitalism, particularly the working class. Most of the behavior in response to domination, including actions of the oppressed defined as criminal by the capitalist class, is a product of the capitalist system of production. . . .

[T]he class that does not own or control the means of production must adapt to the conditions of capitalism. Accommodation and resistance to the conditions of capitalism are basic to the class struggle. The argument here is that action by people who do not own and control the means of production, those who are exploited and oppressed, is largely an accommodation or resistance to the conditions produced by capitalist production. Thus, criminality among the oppressed classes is action (conscious or otherwise) in relation to the capitalist order of exploitation and oppression. Crime, with its many historical variations, is an integral part of class struggle in the development of capitalism. . . .

Many crimes of accommodation are of this . . . nature. Nevertheless, these actions occur within the context of capitalist oppression, stemming from the existing system of production. Much criminal behavior is of a parasitical nature, including burglary, robbery, drug dealing, and hustling of various sorts.[11] These are *predatory crimes*. The behavior, although pursued out of the need to survive, is a reproduction of the capitalist system. The crimes are nevertheless antagonistic to the capitalist order. Most police activity is directed against these crimes.

In addition to predatory crimes are *personal crimes*, which are usually directed against members of the same class. These are the conventional criminal acts of murder, assault, and rape. They are pursued by those who are already brutalized by the conditions of capitalism. These actions occur in immediate situations that are themselves the result of more basic accommodations to capitalism.

Aside from these lumpen crimes, actions are carried out, largely by the working class, that are in resistance to the capitalist system. These actions, sometimes directed against the work situation, are direct reflections of the alienation of labor—a struggle, conscious or unconscious, against the exploitation of the life and activity of the worker. For example, workers may engage in concrete political actions against their employers:

> On the assembly lines of the American automobile industry, this revolt extends as far as clandestine acts of sabotage against a product (the automobile body) which appears to the worker as the detestable materialization of the social uselessness and individual absurdity of his toil. Along the same lines is the less extreme and more complex example of miners fighting with admirable perseverance against the closing of the mines where they are exploited under inferior human and economic conditions—but who, individually, have no difficulty in recognizing that even if the coal they produced were not so bad and so expensive, their job, under the prevailing conditions, would still be abominable.[12]

Moreover, large numbers of workers under advanced capitalism become expendable. For the capitalist the problem becomes that of the kind and size of labor force necessary to maximize production and realize surplus value. The physical well-being and spiritual needs of the worker are not the concern; rather, capitalism requires an "industrial reserve army" that can be called into action when necessary and relieved when no longer needed—but that is always available. Marx observed in *Capital*:

> But if a surplus laboring population is a necessary product of accumulation or of the development of wealth on a capitalist basis, this surplus population becomes, conversely, the lever of capitalist accumulation, nay, a condition of existence of the capitalist mode of production. It forms a disposable industrial reserve army that belongs to capital quite as absolutely as if the latter had bred it at its own cost. Independently of the limits of the actual increase of population, it creates, for the changing needs of the self-expansion of capital, a mass of human material always ready for exploitation.[13]

Under these conditions, "the labor force consists of two parts, the employed and the unemployed, with a gray area in between, containing the part-time or sporadically employed. Furthermore, all these categories of workers and potential workers continuously expand or contract with technological change, the ups and downs of the business cycle, and the vagaries of the market, all inherent characteristics of capitalist production."[14] Many workers are further exploited by being relegated to the degradations and uncertainties of a reserve army of labor.

For the unemployed, as well as for those who are always uncertain about their employment, this life condition has its personal and social consequences. Basic human needs are thwarted when the life-giving activity of work is lost or curtailed. This form of alienation gives rise to a multiplicity of psychosocial maladjustments and psychic disorders.[15] In addition, unemployment means the loss of personal and family income. Choices, opportunities, and even life maintenance are jeopardized. For many people, the appropriate reaction consists not only of mental disturbance but also of outright acts of personal and social destruction.

Although the statistical evidence can never show conclusively the relation between unemployment and crime, largely because such statistics are politically constructed in the beginning to obscure the failings of a capitalist economy, there is sufficient observation to recognize the obvious fact that unemployment produces criminality. Crimes of economic gain increase whenever the jobless seek ways to maintain themselves and their families. Crimes of violence rise when the problems of life are further exacerbated by the loss of life-supporting activity. Anger and frustration at a world that punishes rather than supports produce their own forms of destruction. Permanent unemployment—and the acceptance of that condition—can result in a form of life where criminality is an appropriate and consistent response.

Hence, crime under capitalism has become a response to the conditions of life.[16] Nearly all crimes among the working class in capitalist society are actually a means of *survival*, an attempt to exist in a society where survival is not assured by other, collective means. Crime is inevitable under capitalist conditions. . . .

Class struggle involves a continuous war between two dialectically opposed interests: on one hand, capital accumulation for the benefit of a nonworking minority class that owns and controls the means of production and, on the other hand, control and ownership of production by those who actually labor. Since the capitalist state regulates this struggle, the institutions and laws of the social order are intended to assure the victory of the capitalist class over the working class. Yet the working class constantly struggles against the capitalist class, as shown in the long history of labor battles against the conditions of capitalist production.[17] The resistance continues as long as there is need for class struggle, that is, as long as capitalism exists.

With the instruments of force and coercion on the side of the capitalist class, much of the activity in the working-class struggle is defined as criminal. Indeed, according to the legal codes, whether in simply acting to relieve the injustices of capitalism or in taking action against the existence of class oppression, actions against the interests of the state are crimes. With an emerging consciousness that the state represses those who attempt to tip the scales in favor of the working class, working-class people engage in actions against the state and the capitalist class. This is crime that is politically conscious.

Crimes of accommodation and resistance thus range from unconscious re-actions to exploitation, to conscious acts of survival within the capitalist system, to politically conscious acts of rebellion. These criminal actions, moreover, not only cover the range of meaning but actually evolve or progress from *unconscious reaction* to *political rebellion*. Finally, the crimes may eventually reach the ulti-mate stage of conscious political action—*revolt*. In revolt, criminal actions are not only against the system but are also an attempt to overthrow it.

The movement toward a society can occur only with political consciousness on the part of those oppressed by capitalist society. The alternative to capitalism cannot be willed into being but requires the conscious activity of those who seek new conditions of existence. Political consciousness develops in an awareness of the alienation suffered under capitalism. The contradiction of capitalism—the disparity between actuality and human possibility—makes large portions of the population ready to act in ways that will bring about a new existence. When people become conscious of the extent to which they are dehumanized under the capitalist mode of production, when people realize the source and nature of their alienation, they become active in a movement to build a new society. . . .

The only lasting solution to the crisis of capitalism is socialism. Under late, advanced capitalism, socialism will be achieved in the struggle of all people who are oppressed by the capitalist mode of production, namely, the workers and all elements of the surplus population. An alliance of the oppressed must take place.[18] Given the objective conditions of a crisis in advanced capitalism and the conditions for an alliance of the oppressed, a mass socialist movement can be formed. . . .

Notes

1. David A. Gold, Clarence Y. H. Lo, and Erik Olin Wright, "Recent Developments in Marxist Theories of the State," *Monthly Review* 27 (November 1975): 36–51.

2. Stanley Diamond, "The Rule of Law Versus the Order of Custom," *Social Research* 38 (Spring 1971): 42–72; and Michael Tigar, with the assistance of Madeleine Levy, *Law and the Rise of Capitalism* (New York: Monthly Review Press, 1977).

3. E. B. Pashukanis, "The General Theory of Law and Marxism," in *Soviet Legal Philos-*

ophy, trans. and ed. Hugh W. Babb (Cambridge, Mass.: Harvard University Press, 1951), pp. 111–225; and Isaac D. Balbus, "Commodity Form and Legal Form: An Essay on the 'Relative Autonomy' of the Law," *Law and Society Review* 11 (Winter 1977): 571–88. Discussions of Pashukanis are found in C. J. Arthur, "Towards a Materialist Theory of Law," *Critique* 7 (Winter 1976–77): 31–46; and Steve Redhead, "The Discrete Charm of Bourgeois Law: A Note on Pashukanis," *Critique* 9 (Spring–Summer 1978): 113–20.

4. Alan Wolfe, "Political Repression and the Liberal State," *Monthly Review* 23 (December 1971): 20.

5. Alan Wolfe, "New Directions in the Marxist Theory of Politics," *Politics and Society* 4 (Winter 1974): 155–57.

6. André Gorz, *Strategy for Labor: A Radical Proposal,* tr. Martin A. Nicolaus and Victoria Oritz (Boston: Beacon, 1967), pp. 131–32.

7. Wolfe, "New Directions in the Marxist Theory of Politics," p. 155.

8. See Stanley Aronowitz, "Law, Breakdown of Order, and Revolution," in *Law Against the People: Essays to Demystify Law, Order and the Courts,* ed. Robert Lefcourt (New York: Random House, 1971), pp. 150–82; and John H. Schaar, "Legitimacy in the Modern State," in *Power and Community: Dissenting Essays in Political Science,* ed. Philip Green and Sanford Levinson (New York: Random House, 1970), pp. 276–327.

9. See Richard Quinney, *Criminology* (2nd ed.; Boston: Little, Brown, 1979), pp. 163–261.

10. Tony Platt, "Prospects for a Radical Criminology in the United States," *Crime and Social Justice* 1 (Spring–Summer 1974): 2–10; and Herman and Julia Schwendinger, "Defenders of Order or Guardians of Human Rights?" *Issues in Criminology* 5 (Summer 1970): 123–57.

11. Judah Hill, *Class Analysis: United States in the 1970's* (Emeryville, Calif.: Class Analysis, 1975), pp. 86–87.

12. Gorz, *Strategy for Labor,* pp. 57–58.

13. Karl Marx, *Capital,* vol. 1 (New York: International Publishers, 1967), p. 632.

14. Editors, "The Economic Crisis in Historical Perspective," *Monthly Review* 26 (June 1975): 2.

15. K. William Kapp, "Socio-Economic Effects of Law and High Employment," *Annals of the American Academy of Political and Social Science* 418 (March 1975): 60–71.

16. David M. Gordon, "Capitalism, Class, and Crime in America," *Crime and Delinquency* 19 (April 1973): 163–86.

17. Sidney Lens, *The Labor Wars: From the Molly Maguires to the Sitdowns* (New York: Doubleday, 1973); Jeremy Brecher, *Strike!* (Greenwich, Conn.: Fawcett, 1972); Samuel Yellin, *American Labor Struggles* (New York: Russell, 1936); and Richard O. Boyer and Herbert M. Morais, *Labor's Untold Story* (New York: Cameron Associates, 1955).

18. James O'Connor, *The Fiscal Crisis of the State* (New York: St. Martin's, 1973), pp. 221–56.

TOWARD A POLITICAL ECONOMY OF CRIME

William J. Chambliss

In this reading Chambliss shows that members of the dominant class break the criminal law but get punished for doing so much less frequently than do their criminal counterparts in the lower class. Chambliss describes such a situation in Ibados, Nigeria, and Seattle, Washington. He concludes that this study generally supports "the Marxian assertion that criminal acts which serve the interests of the ruling class will go unsanctioned while those that do not will be punished."

It is obviously fruitless to join the debate over whether or not contemporary theories of criminal etiology are adequate to the task. The advocates of "family background," "differential association," "cultural deprivation," "opportunity theory," and a host of other "theories" have debated the relative merits of their explanations *ad infinitum*. . . . I should like, however, to present a summary of data from a study of crime and criminal law which compares selected aspects of these phenomena in Nigeria and the United States. In so doing I hope to shed some light on the Marxian paradigm without pretending to resolve all the issues.

My data come from research in Seattle, Washington, and Ibadan, Nigeria. The research methods employed were mainly those of a participant observer. In Seattle the research spanned almost ten years (1962–1972), and in Ibadan the research took place during 1967–1968. In both cities the data were gathered through extensive interviewing of informants from all sides of criminal law—criminals, professional thieves, racketeers, prostitutes, government officials, police officers, businessmen and members of various social class levels in the community. Needless to say, the sampling was what sociologists have come to call (with more than a slight bit of irony) "convenience samples." Any other sampling procedure is simply impossible in the almost impenetrable world of crime and law enforcement into which we embarked.

Nigeria and America both inherited British common law at the time of their independence. Independence came somewhat later for Nigeria than for America, but the legal systems inherited are very similar. As a result, both countries share much the same foundation in statutes and common law principles. While differences exist, they are not, for our purposes, of great significance.

In both Nigeria and the United States, it is a crime punishable by imprisonment and a fine for any public official to accept a bribe, to solicit a bribe or

Excerpted from William J. Chambliss, "Toward a Political Economy of Crime," *Theory and Society*, 2, Summer 1975, pp. 157–170. Reprinted by permission of Kluwen Academic Publishers. Copyright © 1975 by Martinus Nijhoff Publishers.

to give special favors to a citizen for monetary considerations. It is also against the law in both countries to run gambling establishments, to engage in or solicit for prostitutes, to sell liquor that has not been inspected and stamped by a duly appointed agency of the government, to run a taxi service without a license, etc. And, of course, both nations share the more obvious restrictions on murder, theft, robbery, rape and the standard array of criminal offenses. In both countries there is striking similarity in the types of laws that do *not* and those that do get enforced.[1]

CRIME AND LAW ENFORCEMENT IN NIGERIA

In both Nigeria and the United States, many laws can be, and are, systematically violated with impunity by those who control the political and economic resources of the society. Particularly relevant are those laws that restrict such things as bribery, racketeering (especially gambling), prostitution, drug distribution and selling, usury and the whole range of criminal offenses committed by businessmen in the course of their businesses (white collar crimes).

In Nigeria the acceptance of bribes by government officials is blatantly public and virtually universal. When the vice president of a large research organization that was just getting established in Nigeria visited the head of Nigerian Customs, he was told by the Customs Director that "at the outset it is important that we both understand that the customs office is corrupt from the top to the bottom." Incoming American professors were usually asked by members of the faculty at the University if they would be willing to exchange their American dollars on the black market at a better exchange rate than banks would offer. In at least one instance the Nigerian professor making this request was doing so for the military governor of the state within which the university was located. Should the incoming American fail to meet a colleague who would wish to make an illegal transfer of funds, he would in all likelihood be approached by any number of other citizens in high places. For example, the vice president of the leading bank near the university would often approach American professors and ask if they would like to exchange their money through him personally, and thereby receive a better exchange rate than was possible if they dealt directly through the bank.

At the time of my study, tithes of this sort were paid at every level. Businessmen desiring to establish businesses found their way blocked interminably by bureaucratic red tape until the proper amount of "dash" had been given to someone with the power to effect the result desired. Citizens riding buses were asked for cigarettes and small change by army soldiers who manned check points. The soldiers, in turn, had to pay a daily or weekly tithe to superior officers in order to be kept at this preferential assignment. At the border one could bring French wine, cigarettes and many other prohibited commodities into Nigeria, so long as prior arrangements had been made with the customs officers either in Lagos (the capital of the country) or at the check point itself. The prior arrangements included payment of a bribe.

As a result of bribes and payoffs, there flourished a large and highly profitable trade in a wide variety of vices. Prostitution was open and rampant in all of the large cities of Nigeria—it was especially well developed in those cities where commerce and industry brought large numbers of foreigners. Gambling establishments, located mainly in large European-style hotels, and managed incidentally by Italian visitors, catered to the moneyed set with a variety of games of chance competitive with Monte Carlo or Las Vegas. There was a large, illicit liquor trade (mostly a home-brewed gin-like drink), as well as a smaller but nevertheless profitable trade in drugs that received political and legal protection through payoffs to high-level officials.

In at least Ibadan and Lagos, gangs of professional thieves operated with impunity. These gangs of thieves were well organized and included the use of beggars and young children as cover for theft activities. The links to the police were sufficient to guarantee that suspects would be treated leniently—usually allowed to go with no charges being brought. In one instance an entire community within the city of Ibadan was threatened by thieves with total destruction. The events leading up to this are revealing. The community, which I shall call Lando, had been victimized by a gang of thieves who broke into homes and stole valuable goods. The elders of Lando hired four men to guard the community. When thieves came one evening the hired guards caught and killed three of them. The next day the Oba of the community was called on by two men from another part of the city. These men expressed grave concern that some of their compatriots had been killed in Lando. The Oba informed them that if any other thieves came to Lando they would be dealt with similarly. The thieves' representatives advised the Oba that if such a thing happened the thieves would burn the community to the ground. When the Oba said he would call the police, it was pointed out to him that the chief of police was the brother-in-law of one of the thieves. Ultimately an agreement was reached whereby the thieves agreed to stop stealing in Lando in return for the Oba's promise that the thieves could sell their stolen property in Lando on market day.

Ibadan is a very cosmopolitan city which lies in the Yoruba section of western Nigeria. Although dominated by the Yoruba, there are nonetheless a large number of Hausa, Ibo and other ethnic groups in the city. The Hausa who are strongly Muslim (while the Yoruba are roughly 50% Christian) occupy a ghetto within Ibadan which is almost exclusively Hausa. Despite the fact that the Hausa are an immigrant group where one might expect the crime rate to be high, there are very few Hausa arrested for crime. (See Table 1.) This is particularly impressive since there is general belief that the Hausa are responsible for some of the more efficient and effective groups of professional thieves in the area. The explanation for this apparently lies in the fact that the Hausa have a strong leadership which intervenes with payoffs and cash to government and police officials whenever a member of their community is in any difficulty. Payment of bribes to the police is usually possible whenever an arrest is likely. An incoming American who illegally photographed an airport was allowed to (without even

Table 1. Arrest Rate for 1,000 Population, Ibadan, Nigeria 1967

Immigrant areas	Indigenous area	Hausa area
1.41	.61	.54

destroying his film), upon payment of $15.00 to the arresting officer. Six dollars was sufficient for the wife of an American professor to avoid arrest for reckless driving. A young son of a wealthy merchant was arrested on numerous occasions for being drunk, driving without a license, stealing and getting into fights. On every occasion the police returned him to the custody of his parents without charges being filed when the father paid the arresting officer (or the policeman on the desk) thirty to forty-five dollars.

Such practices are not atypical, but were instead the usual procedure. It was said, and research bears this out, that one with money could pay to be excused from any type or amount of crime.

Who, then, did get arrested? In general, those who lacked either the money or the political influence to "fix" a criminal charge. The most common youth arrest was for "street trading"—that is, selling items on the street. The second most frequent offense was "being away from home" or "sleeping out without protection." Among adults, "suspiciousness," public indecency, intoxication and having no visible means of support were the most common offenses. Although robbery, theft and burglary were common offenses (in a sample of 300 residents of Ibadan, 12.7% reported having been the victim of burglary), arrests for these offenses were much less frequent.

Anyone who has lived or traveled in foreign countries will not be surprised by these findings. What is usually not recognized, however, is that these same kinds of things characterize crime and criminal law enforcement in the United States (and possibly every other nation) as well.

CRIME AND LAW ENFORCEMENT IN SEATTLE

Seattle, like Ibadan, is a city of 1,000,000 people with its own police, government, and set of laws inherited from Great Britain. In Seattle, as in Ibadan, any type of vice can be found. It is only necessary to travel away from the middle- and upper-class suburbs that ring the city, and venture into the never-never land of skidrow derelicts, the Black ghetto or a few other pockets of rundown hotels, cafes and cabarets that are sprinkled along freeways and by the docks. Here there is prostitution, gambling, usury, drugs, pornography, bootleg liquor, book-making and pinball machines.

The most profitable of these are gambling and usury. Gambling ranges from bookmaking (at practically every street corner in the center of the city), to open poker games, bingo parlors, off-track betting, casinos, roulette and dice games (concentrated in a few locations and also floating out into the suburban country clubs and fraternal organizations), and innumerable two and five dollar stud-poker games scattered liberally throughout the city.

The most conspicuous card games take place from about ten in the morning (it varies slightly from one "fun house" to the next) until midnight. But there are a number of other twenty-four hour games that run constantly. In the more public games the limit ranges from one to five dollars for each bet; in the more select games that run twenty-four hours a day there is a "pot limit" or "no limit" rule. These games are reported to have betting as high as twenty and thirty thousand dollars. I have seen a bet made and called for a thousand dollars in one of these games. During this game, which was the highest stakes game I witnessed in the six years of the study, the police lieutenant in charge of the vice squad was called in to supervise the game—not, need I add, to break up the game or make any arrests, only to insure against violence.

Prostitution covers the usual range of ethnic groups, age, shape and size of female. It is also found in houses with madams as in New Orleans, on the street through pimps, or in suburban apartment buildings and hotels. Prices range from five dollars for a short time with a street walker to two hundred dollars for a night with a lady who has her own apartment (which she usually shares with her boyfriend, who is discreetly gone during business operations).

High interest loans are easy to arrange through stores that advertise "your signature is worth $5,000." It is really worth considerably more; it may, in fact, be worth your life. The interest rates vary from twenty per cent for three months to as high as one hundred per cent for varying periods. Repayment is demanded not through the courts, but through the help of "The Gaspipe Gant" who call on recalcitrant debtors and use physical force to bring about payment. The "interest only" repayment is the most popular alternative practiced by borrowers, and is preferred by the loan sharks as well. The longer repayment can be prolonged, the more advantageous it is to the loan agents.

Pinball machines are readily available throughout the city, and most of them pay off in cash. The gambling, prostitution, drug distribution, pornography, and usury (high interest loans) which flourish in the lower class center of the city do so with the compliance, encouragement and cooperation of the major political and law enforcement officials in the city. There is, in fact, a symbiotic relationship between the law enforcement-political organizations of the city and a group of *local* (as distinct from national) men who control the distribution of vices.

The payoffs and briberies in Seattle are complex. The simpler and more straightforward are those made by each gambling establishment. A restaurant or cabaret with card room attached had to pay around $200 each month to the police and $200 to the "syndicate." In reality these were two branches of the same group of men, but the payoffs were made separately. Anyone who refused these payments was harassed by fire inspectors, health inspectors, licensing difficulties and even physical violence from enforcers who worked for the crime cabal in the city. Similarly, places with pinball machines, pornography, bookmaking or prostitution had to pay regularly to the "Bagman" who collected a fee for the police.

Payoffs to policemen were also required of tow truck operators, cabaret owners and other businesses where police cooperation was necessary. Tow truck drivers carried with them a matchbox with $3.00 in it and, when asked for a light by the policeman who had called them to the scene of an accident, they gave him the matchbox with the $3.00 inside. Cabaret owners paid according to how large their business was. The police could extract payoffs because the laws were so worded as to make it virtually impossible to own a profitable cabaret without violating the law. For example, it was illegal to have an entertainer closer than 25 feet to the nearest customer. A cabaret, to comply with this ordinance, would have had to have a night club the size of a large ballroom, at which point the atmosphere would have been so sterile as to drive customers away, not to mention that such large spaces are exceedingly expensive in the downtown section of the city. Thus, the police could, if they chose to, close down a cabaret on a moment's notice. Payoffs were a necessary investment to assure that the police would not so choose.

The trade in licenses was notoriously corrupt. It was generally agreed by my informants that to get a tow truck license one had to pay a bribe of $10,000; a card room license was $25,000; taxicab licenses were unavailable, as were licenses for distributing pinball machines or juke boxes. These licenses had all been issued to members of the syndicate that controlled the rackets, and no outsiders were permitted in.

There were innumerable instances of payoffs to politicians and government officials for real estate deals, businesses and stock transactions. In each case the participants were a combination of local businessmen, racketeers, local politicians and government officials.

Interestingly, there is also a minority ghetto within Seattle where one might expect to find a high crime rate. In Seattle this is the Japanese-American section of the city.

It is widely believed that the Japanese-Americans have a very low propensity to crime. This is usually attributed to the family-centered orientation of the Japanese-American community. There is some evidence, however, that this perspective is largely a self-fulfilling prophecy.[2] Table 2 shows a comparison between the self-reported delinquency and arrest rates of Japanese-American youth for a selected year. The data suffer, of course, from problems inherent in such comparisons, but nonetheless, the point cannot be gainsaid that the actual crime rate among Japanese-American youth is considerably higher than the conventional view would suggest.

Table 2. Comparison of Arrests (for 1963) and Self-Reported Delinquency Involvement by Racial Groups[a]

Racial group	Per cent arrested	Per cent self-reporting high delinquency involvement[b]
White	11	53
Negro	36	52
Japanese	2	36

[a]Based on data from Richard H. Nagasawa, *Delinquency and Non-Delinquency: A Study of Status Problems and Perceived Opportunity*, unpublished M.A. thesis, University of Washington, 1965, p. 35.

[b]A self-reported delinquency scale was developed and the respondents were divided, so that 50 per cent of the sample was categorized as having high, and 50 per cent as having low delinquent involvement.

Thus we see that in both the Hausa area of Ibadan and the Japanese-American section of Seattle there is reason to suspect a reasonably high crime rate, but official statistics show an exceptionally low one. When discussing Hausa crime earlier, I attributed this fact to the payoffs made by Hausa leaders to the police and other government officials.

Somewhat the same sort of system prevails in Seattle as well, especially with regard to the rackets. Whereas prostitutes, pornography shops, gambling establishments, cabaret operators and tow truck operators must pay off individually to the police and the syndicate, the Japanese-American community did so *as a community*. The tithe was collected by a local businessman, and was paid to the police and the syndicate in a group sum. Individual prostitutes and vice racketeers might at times have to do special favors for a policeman or political figure, but by and large the payoffs were made collectively rather than individually.

This collective payoff was in large measure attributable to a common characteristic present in both the Hausa and the Japanese-American communities, namely, the heterogeneous social class nature of the community. Typically, wealthy or middle-class members of the lower-class white slum or the Black ghetto moved out of these areas as rapidly as their incomes permitted. So too with Yoruba, Ibo or other ethnic groups in Ibadan. But many, though certainly not all, upper- and middle-class Hausa in Ibadan, and Japanese-Americans in Seattle retained their residence in their respective communities. As a result, the enforcement of any law became more problematic for law enforcement agencies. Arrests made of any youth or adult always carried with it the possibility that the suspect would have a politically influential parent or friend. There was also the possibility that a payoff of some sort (including political patronage) would override the policeman's efforts. Since there was also the necessity to hide from the middle- and upper-class the extent to which the police closed their eyes to the rackets, it was then convenient to avoid having many police in the Hausa and Japanese-American community. The myth of these areas as "no crime" sections of the city was thus very convenient. By contrast, since only those members of the middle- and upper-class who were seeking vice would come to the skidrow area, or the Black ghetto, then the presence of the police was not problematic, and in fact helped to assure the "respectable" citizen that he could partake of his prurient interests without fear of being the victim of robbery or violence.

As in Nigeria, all of this corruption, bribery and blatant violation of the law was taking place, while arrests were being made and people sent to jail or prison for other offenses. In Seattle over 70% of all arrests during the time of the study were for public drunkenness.[3] It was literally the case that the police were arresting drunks on one side of a building while on the other side a vast array of other offenses were being committed with police support and management.

What then are we to conclude from these data about the etiology of criminal behavior? For a start, the data show that criminal behavior by *any reasonable* definition is *not* concentrated in the lower classes. Thus, to the extent that a theory of the causes of criminal behavior depends on the assumption that there is a higher rate of criminality in the lower classes, to that extent, the theory is suspect. These data on Seattle and Ibadan link members of the ruling class, legal and political officials and racketeers in joint ventures which involve them actively and passively in criminal activities as part of their way of life.

This conclusion, ironically, is identical with Edwin Sutherland's only he came to this view from his study of corporation ("white-collar") crime. However, he then went on to propose an explanation for criminality which was essentially socio-psychological: Sutherland asked why some *individuals* became involved in criminal behavior while others did not. My contention is that this question is meaningless. Everyone commits crime. And many, many people whether they are poor, rich or middling are involved in a way of life that is criminal; and furthermore, no one, not even the professional thief or racketeer or corrupt politician commits *crime all the time*. To be sure, it may be politically useful to say that people become criminal through association with "criminal behavior patterns," and thereby remove the tendency to look at criminals as pathological. But such a view has little scientific value, since it asks the wrong questions. It asks for a psychological cause of what is by its very nature a socio-political event. Criminality is simply *not* something that people have or don't have; crime is not something some people do and others don't. Crime is a matter of who can pin the label on whom, and underlying this socio-political process is the structure of social relations determined by the political economy. It is to Sutherland's credit that he recognized this when, in 1924, he noted that:

> An understanding of the nature of Criminal law is necessary in order to secure an understanding of the nature of crime. A complete explanation of the origin and enforcement of laws would be, also, an explanation of the violation of laws.[4]

But Sutherland failed, unfortunately, to pursue the implications of his remarks. He chose instead to confront the prevailing functionalist perspective on crime with a less class-biased but nonetheless inevitably psychological explanation.

The argument that criminal acts, that is, acts which are a violation of criminal law, are more often committed by members of the lower classes is not tenable. Criminal acts are widely distributed throughout the social classes in capitalist societies. The rich, the ruling, the poor, the powerless and the working classes *all* engage in criminal activities on a regular basis. It is in the enforcement of the law that the lower classes are subject to the effects of ruling class domination over the legal system, and which results in the appearance of a concentration of criminal acts among the lower classes in the official records. In actual practice, however, class differences in rates of criminal activity are probably negligible. What difference there is would be a difference in the type of criminal act, not in the prevalence of criminality.

The argument that the control of the state by the ruling class would lead to a lower propensity for crime among the ruling classes fails to recognize two fundamental facts. First is the fact that many acts committed by lower classes and which it is in the interests of the ruling class to control (e.g., crimes of violence, bribery of public officials, and crimes of personal choice, such as drug use, alcoholism, driving while intoxicated, homosexuality, etc.) are just as likely— or at least very likely—to be as widespread among the upper classes as the lower classes. Thus, it is crucial that the ruling class be able to control the discretion of the law enforcement agencies in ways that provide them with immunity. For example, having a legal system encumbered with procedural rules which only the wealthy can afford to implement and which, if implemented, nearly guarantees immunity from prosecution, not to mention more direct control through bribes, coercion and the use of political influence.

The Marxian paradigm must also account for the fact that the law will also reflect conflict between members of the ruling class (or between members of the ruling class and the upper class "power elites" who manage the bureaucracies). So, for example, laws restricting the formation of trusts, misrepresentation in advertising, the necessity for obtaining licenses to engage in business practices are all laws which generally serve to reduce competition among the ruling classes and to concentrate capital in a few hands. However, the laws also apply universally, and therefore apply to the ruling class as well. Thus, when they break these laws they are committing criminal acts. Again, the enforcement practices obviate the effectiveness of the laws, and guarantee that the ruling class will rarely feel the sting of the laws, but their violation remains a fact with which we must reckon.

It can also be concluded from this comparative study of Ibadan and Seattle that law enforcement systems are *not* organized to *reduce crime* or to enforce the public morality. They are organized rather to *manage* crime by cooperating with the most criminal groups and enforcing laws against those whose crimes are minimal. In this way, by cooperating with criminal groups, law enforcement essentially produces more crime than would otherwise be the case. Crime is also produced by law enforcement practices through selecting and encouraging the perpetuation of criminal careers by promising profit and security to those criminals who engage in organized criminal activities from which the political, legal and business communities profit.

Thus, the data from this study generally support the Marxian assertion that criminal acts which serve the interests of the ruling class will go unsanctioned while those that do not will be punished. The data also support the hypothesis that criminal activity is a direct reflection of class position. Thus, the criminality of the lawyers, prosecuting attorneys, politicians, judges and policemen is uniquely suited to their own class position in the society. It grows out of the opportunities and strains that inhere in those positions just as surely as the drinking of the skidrow derelict, the violence of the ghetto resident, the drug use of the middle-class adolescent and the white-collar crimes of corporation executives reflect different socializing experiences. That each type of criminality stems from social-psychological conditioning is to say nothing unique about crime and criminality, but only to posit what would have to be a general theory of human psychology—something which places the task beyond the scope of criminology and which has also been notoriously unsuccessful.

The postulates in the paradigm that deal with expected differences between capitalist and socialist societies have not been tested by the data presented, because our data come from two capitalist societies. Crime statistics which might permit a comparison are so unreliable as to be useless to the task. A comparison between East and West Germany would be most enlightening in this regard, as would a comparison between Yugoslavia and Italy, Cuba and Trinidad, or China and India. I have the impression that such a series of comparisons would strongly support the Marxist hypothesis of crime rates being highest in capitalist societies.

SUMMARY AND CONCLUSION

As Gouldner and Friedrichs have recently pointed out, social science generally, and sociology in particular is in the throes of a "paradigm revolution."[5] Predictably, criminology is both a reflection of and a force behind this revolution.

The emerging paradigm in criminology is one which emphasizes social conflict—particularly conflicts of social-class interests and values. The paradigm which is being replaced is one where the primary emphasis was on consensus, and within which "deviance" or "crime" was viewed as an aberration shared by some minority. This group had failed to be properly socialized or adequately integrated into society or, more generally, had suffered from "social disorganization."

The shift in paradigm means more than simply a shift from explaining the same facts with new causal models. It means that we stretch our conceptual framework and look to different facets of social experience. Specifically, instead of resorting inevitably to the "normative system," to "culture" or to socio-psychological experiences of individuals, we look instead to the social relations created by the political and economic structure. Rather than treating "society" as a full-blown reality (reifying it into an entity with its own life), we seek to understand the present as a reflection of the economic and political history that has created the social relations which dominate the moment we have selected to study.

The shift means that crime becomes a rational response of some social classes to the realities of their lives. The state becomes an instrument of the ruling class, enforcing laws here but not there, according to the realities of political power and economic conditions.

There is much to be gained from this re-focusing of criminological and sociological inquiry. However, if the paradigmatic revolution is to be more than a mere fad, we must be able to show that the new paradigm is in fact superior to its predecessor. In this paper I have tried to develop the theoretical implications of a Marxian model of crime and criminal law, and to assess the merits of this paradigm by looking at some empirical data. The general conclusion is that the Marxian paradigm provides a long neglected but fruitful approach to the study of crime and criminal law.

Notes

1. Throughout the paper we rely on data from Ibadan and Seattle as a basis for discussing the patterns in both countries. This lead may disturb some, and if so, then the study may be considered as directly referring only to the two cities—with only a possible application more generally. From a variety of research studies and my own impressions, I am convinced that what is true of Ibadan and Seattle is not only true of Nigeria and the United States, but whether or not this is the case should not affect the overall conclusions of this inquiry.

2. Richard H. Nagasawa, *Delinquency and Non-Delinquency: A Study of Status Problems and Perceived Opportunity*, Unpublished M.A. thesis, Seattle: University of Washington, 1965. See also William J. Chambliss and Richard H. Nagasawa, "On the Validity of Official Statistics," *Journal of Research in Crime and Delinquency*, January, 1969, pp. 71–77.

3. James P. Spradley, *You Owe Yourself a Drunk*, Boston: Little Brown and Co., 1970, p. 128.

4. Edwin H. Sutherland, *Criminology*, Philadelphia: J. P. Lippincott, 1924, p. 11.

5. Alvin W. Gouldner, *The Coming Crisis in Western Sociology*, New York: Basic Books,

1970; Robert W. Friedrichs, *A Sociology of Sociology*, New York: The Free Press, 1970. For a more general discussion of paradigm revolution in science, see Thomas S. Kuhn, *The Structure of Scientific Revolutions* (2nd edition), Chicago: University of Chicago Press, 1970.

REPRESSION AND CRIMINAL JUSTICE IN CAPITALIST AMERICA

Raymond J. Michalowski and Edward W. Bohlander

In this excerpt, the authors offer a critical perspective explanation of why most people believe that "crime" is a social problem. Formal agencies of social control apply legal sanctions against those who commit common crimes against property. Constantly learning about these sanctions, most people come to share the view that these actions are criminal, against mainstream cultural values, and social problems. It could not be otherwise, the authors argue. The capitalist class controls the definition of crime. And capitalist class interests dictate that harms caused by the disadvantaged, more often than those inflicted by the advantaged, be seen as crimes.

In the U.S. the legal order serves the interests of the capitalist ruling class by (1) facilitating the pursuit of capitalist goals, (2) legitimizing the repression of the economically and politically disadvantaged classes which must exist to maintain a capitalist distribution of wealth and who threaten capitalist interests through criminal activity, and (3) creating and maintaining a definition of "crime" which guarantees the continued enjoyment of the first two benefits by the ruling class. Table 1 presents the effects of the capitalist legal order upon both the power-advantaged and the power-disadvantaged, and the overall contribution of these effects to the definition of crime. The following discussion examines each of these effects in greater detail.

SUBSTANTIVE LAW

Since the development of rational theories of jurisprudence, the justification for substantive criminal laws has been centered around the need to protect the conforming members of society from the "harmful" behaviors of deviants. Designing a social order within which the maximum number of individuals could enjoy freedom from the harmful acts of others has always been the ostensible reason

From Raymond J. Michalowski and Edward W. Bohlander, 1976, *Sociological Inquiry* 46: 95–106. By permission.

Table 1. Effects of the Capitalist Legal Order

Component	Effects upon the power-advantaged classes	Effects upon the power-disadvantaged classes	Effects upon perception of the crime problem
Substantive criminal law	a. Ensures a monopoly of force b. Excludes a majority of readily accessible harmful behavior (corporate crimes)	a. Includes all readily accessible harmful behaviors (common-law crimes)	a. Crime is seen primarily as common-law offenses
Formal sanctions	c. Qualitatively and quantitatively minimal for crimes most readily accessible	b. Qualitatively and quantitatively severe for crimes most readily accessible	b. Common-law offenses appear to be far more serious than corporate crimes
Procedural law	d. Have the best chance of avoiding prosecution e. Have the best chance of avoiding conviction	c. Have the worst chance of avoiding prosecution d. Have the worst chance of avoiding conviction	c. The majority of people prosecuted and convicted are members of the power-disadvantaged classes who have committed common-law crimes, giving the impression that the power-disadvantaged classes are the "dangerous" classes
Interpretive institutions	f. Devote little attention to crimes most readily accessible	e. Devote nearly all attention to crimes most readily accessible	
Discretionary actions	g. Further reduce likelihood of prosecution h. Further reduce likelihood of conviction	f. Further increase likelihood of prosecution g. Further increase likelihood of conviction	

for the creation of criminal codes. However, the specific definition of "harm" has always reflected the perceptions and interests of the ruling classes. In fact, Diamond (1971) argues convincingly that it is the emergence of a ruling class with self-interests distinct from those of the society as ruled by custom which has occasioned the creation of legal states.

Substantive criminal law in the U.S. is characterized by a strong emphasis upon common-law crimes involving the perpetration of some harm upon one individual by another acting out of relatively immediate self-interest. Harms committed by individuals serving corporate interests and perpetrated upon either large segments of the society, or upon the society as a whole, are for all practical purposes omitted from our substantive criminal law.

The effects of this upon the power-advantaged group are two-fold. First, the high priority given common-law crimes insures that harms involving individual victims will be seen as attacks upon the state rather than the occasion for personal retribution. By identifying these conflicts as attacks upon the legal order, the state can appropriate to itself the sole right of capturing and punishing offenders (Schafer, 1968). This right defined by class fiat thereby insures the ruling classes "that monopoly of force which characterizes the mature state" (Diamond, 1971).

Secondly, by de-emphasizing or not including harms resulting from the search for corporate profit, the substantive criminal law gives owners and managers a relatively free reign in the pursuit of capitalist goals. This distinction exists even where the harms caused in the search for corporate profit are more socially injurious than common-law offenses.

The law, for example, did not prohibit the Ford Motor Company from placing automobile gas tanks in such a position that there is a high risk of explosion in a rear-end collision. While such poor design costs approximately 5,000 lives per year, Ford reasoned that design changes were not warranted since their cost would exceed the "cost" of the lives lost. While individual murders causing one, or even several deaths are never overlooked by the criminal law, disregard for human life exhibited by major corporations is not legally defined as criminal behavior in capitalist America.

While the substantive criminal law de-emphasizes corporate crimes, it insures that nearly all of the socially harmful behaviors readily *accessible* to members of the power-disadvantaged classes are defined as "criminal" acts. Attempts to gain material advantage in some manner not authorized by the capitalist opportunity structure (property crimes), or acts which threaten the state monopoly of force (personal crimes), are given the greatest emphasis. This emphasis upon the harmful behavior most accessible to the disadvantaged gives the impression that the disadvantaged class is also the "dangerous" class, and diverts the conventional definition of crime away from the harmful behaviors of the ruling class.

FORMAL SANCTIONS

The statutorily prescribed sanctions for common-law crimes are generally far more severe than those attached to corporate crimes. This difference is both qualitative and quantitative.

The most common form of sanction prescribed for common-law crimes is incarceration, while for business-related offenses the most common form of penalty is a monetary fine. In the State of Ohio, for example, all of the acts listed under "offenses against property" are punishable by incarceration, while only forty percent of the offenses listed under the "pure food and drug law" can result in a deprivation of liberty. Furthermore, while nearly all of the property crimes are determined to be felony offenses punishable by prison sentences, ranging from one year to life, there is not a single violation of the pure food and drug law classified as a felony, and the maximum period of incarceration for any of these violations is 100 days. Generalized harms resulting from corporate crime when formally addressed by state are in the main handled through administrative or civil processes which seldom if ever result in individual loss of liberty and more often than not the penal sanction imposed is merely nominal.

Since common-law crimes are more readily accessible to members of the disadvantaged classes and corporate crimes more readily accessible to members of the ruling class, and since incarceration is a qualitatively more severe form of sanction than a nominal fine, it can be concluded that the sanctions applied to members of the power-disadvantaged group are quantitatively *and* qualitatively more severe than those applied to corporate criminals.

The penalties attached to crimes play a significant role in informing citizens of the seriousness of an offense. Since the penalties attached to corporate crimes are quantitatively less severe than those attached to common-law crimes, the sanction component of the criminal justice process emphasizes the "dangerous" nature of common-law offenses while presenting the harms perpetrated against large numbers of citizens by individuals serving corporate interests as minor offenses.

PROCEDURAL LAW

The procedural law component of the criminal justice process guarantees that the bulk of those individuals prosecuted and convicted will be members of the power-disadvantaged group. It serves the interests of the power-advantaged group by insuring that they have the least likelihood of being prosecuted, and, if prosecuted, the dominant class enjoys the maximum advantage in defending against the charges.

Procedural rules permit the arrest of common-law felons on the basis of probable cause, while violations of many laws governing corporate behavior require a complex sequence of complaint, show-cause orders, injunctions and violations of injunctions before criminal prosecutions result. Consider for a moment why is it *not* the case that burglars are given the opportunity to show cause why they should not be enjoined from burglarizing homes. Our procedural laws maximize the number of common-law offenders—who by the nature of the substantive law are generally members of the disadvantaged class—and minimize the number of corporate offenders who will ever face criminal proceedings following from the harms they cause.

Even in those unusual circumstances where criminal charges are indeed faced by the power-advantaged, procedural law creations such as money bail and the demand for legal counsel greatly improve the position of those from the power-advantaged group. The substantial body of literature on the effects of both pre-trial release through bail opportunity and public versus privately retained counsel on one's success in avoiding conviction serves as evidence of the procedural law in service of the power-advantaged.

INTERPRETIVE INSTITUTIONS

The interpretive institutions of the criminal justice process are the sub-systems of police, courts and corrections. The police sub-system is comprised of those agencies who must identify violations of law and bring the offenders before the court for prosecution. The organization of our policing efforts are directed toward controlling the common-law crimes of the power-disadvantaged. Few agencies exist to police the activities of corporate criminals, and where they do exist they are often drastically understaffed and underfunded. For example, it was recently reported that the Internal Revenue Service seldom conducts detailed audits of corporate tax returns since it generally lacks staff with sufficient expertise to understand the complexity of such returns (*Charlotte Observer*, April 14, 1974). Furthermore, many of the agencies designed to police corporate activities are staffed by representatives from the very agencies being policed. These represen-tatives serve more a liaison capacity benefitting the corporate community than as unbiased agents of societal control. Yet, it is exceedingly unlikely that we would allow even "reformed" housebreakers to police other housebreakers.

Every city police defines its basic responsibility as the control of common-law crimes. Violations against consumers of the commonwealth, such as air and water pollution, are generally handled, if at all, by small regulatory agencies with little power and only minimal funding relative to the task at hand.

The courts and their related processes are clearly disadvantageous to those who are not members of the power-advantaged classes. The effects of the near-total breakdown of balance in our adversary system of prosecution are felt most heavily by those who cannot afford high-powered and equally high-priced legal counsel. The failure of those in political power to provide for a court system of sufficient size to handle even those criminal cases defined as serious, coupled with the overloading of court calendars with insignificant offenses of the poor, such as public intoxication and drug possession, gives criminal courts the squalid, overcrowded appearance which clearly identifies those prosecuted there as "undesirables."

The correctional sub-system exists almost entirely for the management and control of common criminals of the disadvantaged class. Historically, offenders who have committed corporate crimes or political power crimes have seldom undergone the pains of imprisonment. On those few occasions when they have, as in the case of the criminals in the Nixon Administration, they have been sentenced to short terms in minimum security institutions.

These facts—that the police devote most of their attention to, that the courts generally convict, and that the prisons only punish common-law offenders—give further credence to the conventional impression that the "true" harms in society are common-law offenses and that the only harm-producers are members of the identifiable disadvantaged classes.

DISCRETIONARY ACTIONS

It is this component of the criminal justice process which most clearly demonstrates the repressive role of capitalist criminal justice. At every stage in the criminal justice process discretionary actions are taken which generally either benefit members of the power-advantaged group or which solidify and fix harmful effects on the politically and economically disadvantaged. The most prominent uses of this discretion are found in the decision to take into custody, the setting of bail, and the application of sentence. While these are the most well-established modes of repressive discretion, the potential for repression exists each time an actor in an interpretive institution decides upon a course of action.

The closer an individual is perceived as being to the locus of power—middle or upper status—the less likely he is of being arrested following an actual law violation; the less likely he will be denied release through excessive bail; and the less likely he will be subjected to incarceration as a penal sanction, as would be the risk of a member of the "dangerous" disadvantaged class.

The current efforts to adjust bail inequities reflect the entrenched nature of such discretionary biases. An individual's acceptability for release on recognizance is generally based upon his perceived social proximity to the powerful classes. An individual's geographic and job stability, the nature of his occupation and whether or not he owns property in the area are basic considerations in evaluating candidates for pre-trial release. On the basis of such "community stability" criteria, it is clear that the closer an individual's life-style conforms to one which is perceived as serving capitalist interests, the more likely he will be released on his own recognizance.

In the imposition and execution of sentence, similar discretionary favors are given members of the ruling class. That a presidential advisor could receive a sentence of six months for his part in the burglary of Daniel Ellsberg's psychiatrist's office, while disadvantaged "common offenders" spend years in prison for essentially the same offense is the archetype of discretionary repression.

REPRESSION AND CONSENSUS IN CAPITALIST AMERICA

While the interests of those with the power to make and enforce law receive immediate support from the criminal justice process, by far the greatest gain is through the power-advantaged class' control of the definition of crime.

Individuals learn the social meaning of actions through the responses those actions elicit from others. This learning can be either personal or imitative. At the personal level, we learn the meaning of our own behaviors through the consequences we experience as a result of those behaviors. At the level of imitative learning, the meaning of actions is acquired by observing the consequences experienced by others as a result of their actions (Bandura and Walters, 1963, p. 47).

The meaning of crime, like all other behaviors, is acquired through social learning, and for most individuals the social meaning of crime is acquired through imitative learning. The official responses—both dramatized and real—experienced by others for harmful acts prohibited by law provide a definition of crime.

The understanding of what constitutes crime, the relative seriousness of various criminal acts and the established perception of who is "criminal" are based upon observations of the types of harmful acts prosecuted as criminal, the relative severity of the sanctions applied to these acts, and the types of individuals associated with these acts. Thus, those who control law making, establish penal sanctions, and administer justice also control the definition of crime.

While the substantive criminal law proscribes nearly all of those harmful acts accessible to the disadvantaged, it fails to include a large proportion in the harmful acts accessible only to members of the ruling class in search of corporate profits. This initial codification and dichotomous classification of harmful acts into criminal, and, by omissions non-criminal, sets the stage for a perception of crime which rests almost exclusively upon the common-law crimes of the power-disadvantaged.

Where harms committed in the service of capitalist goals are included in either the criminal law or in administrative regulatory codes, the penalties attached for violation are substantially less than those applied to common-law crimes. Persons socialized into a society where they observe that an individual can be deprived of his liberty for several years for breaking into a house, but will only pay a small fine for selling adulterated foods will *tend to assume that breaking into the house is the more serious of the two behaviors.*

The substantive laws and formal sanctions determine, for the most part, what behaviors we define as criminal and the relative seriousness we attach to these behaviors. The procedural laws, interpretive institutions and discretionary actions operate to guarantee that the bulk of individuals made accessible for social-observation and, to use Garfinkel's term, "public degradation" as convicted criminals, are members of the power-disadvantaged classes.

The procedural law makes an independent contribution to the definition of "criminal" by establishing a structure incomprehensible and problematic to negotiate successfully by those who are not economically and politically advantaged. The very procedures ostensibly designed to insure a balance in the adversary process between the individual and the state actually operate to give the disadvantaged an exceedingly poor chance of avoiding conviction.

The interpretive institutions, and the discretionary decisions made within them, are a result of the definition of crime created by the substantive and procedural laws and formal sanctions, while at the same time serving as contributors to the definition of the "crime problem." The laws and penalties concerning crime dictate that these agencies focus upon the apprehension and conviction of common-law offenders. Since common-law offenders have been conventionally defined as the most dangerous criminals, they become the least likely to benefit from police, courtroom, or "correctional" discretion. These factors further reinforce the perception that the true source of the crime problem is rooted in the relatively poor and powerless who commit common-law offenses, since citizen-observers see only that dimension of the crime problem wherein the poor and the powerless are convicted and punished for individual crimes against persons or property.

Members of the ruling class control the making of substantive and procedural laws, the statutory and discretionary determination of sentences, the character of interpretive institutions and both the detrimental and beneficial results of discretionary actions. Through all of this the powerful class shapes a definition of crime which supports their capitalist interests by insuring that the bulk of offenses from which individuals will acquire the meaning of crime bear no resemblance to the harmful acts of corporate profiteers, and that the majority of offenders—by the example of whom we learn to identify who is the criminal—bear no resemblance to members of the capitalist ruling class.

Given the nature of the law making and enforcing processes the fact that sub-groups in society would agree upon the relative seriousness of crimes is of little surprise. Each of these groups must derive its understanding of crime from the same basic pool of social responses to harmful acts. All members of society, regardless of sub-group membership, observe that the common-law crimes committed by the poor and the powerless are the most frequently prosecuted and most severely punished. Given this common universe of experience, it is unlikely that members of various subgroups would arrive at different evaluations of the seriousness of various crimes.

The existence of consensus, however, does not mean that the law serves the interests of all. The criminal justice process exists to insure the perpetuation of the established social order, and a primary method is through control of the definition of crime. Sub-groups tend to agree upon what is serious, not because this definition serves their own or society's interests but because it is difficult to understand a social creation such as crime outside of the social context in which it is presented.

Criminal justice in America serves the interests of the capitalist ruling class primarily through its creation of a consciousness which helps all believe that their interests are being served by a capitalist definition of "crime." Such consciousness manipulation preserves the "legitimacy" of the state and, unlike violent repression, does not run the risk of generating counter-violence.

References

Bandura, A. and Walters, R. 1963. *Social Learning and Personality Development*. N.Y.: Rinehart and Winston.

Diamond, S. 1971. "The Rule of Law Versus the Order of Customs," *Social Research* 38: 42–47.

Schafer, S. 1968. *The Victim and His Criminal*. N.Y.: Random House.

THE UNIVERSALIZATION OF SOCIAL PROBLEMS

David Wagner

Since the 1960s, more and more claims-makers have argued in the media that all people in the society, regardless of age, class, gender, or race, are equally at risk of becoming victims of social problems—that is, that they can "happen to anyone." Wagner points out, however, that the findings from numerous social researchers show that generally social problems are most heavily concentrated in the lower classes. He argues that the idea of the universalization of social problems (that they cross all lines) derives directly from the interests and values of capitalism. It is in the interest of a capitalist society to endorse solutions to social problems that treat individual persons, thereby creating a market for treatment industries while discouraging solutions that call for a radical change in the social structure.

It has become common parlance for media, social service, health, and social science experts to discuss social problems as universal issues affecting everyone. A rhetoric of social problems has become almost obligatory, which describes numerous issues as "cutting across" class, race, age, gender, and so on. Such statements are widely found in the literature regarding a host of different problems (italics added):

Child abuse can happen in any kind of home, at any time, at any level of society (Gilmour, 1988: 1).

This book tells how people from the very ordinary to the very famous are affected by *alcoholism*—many more than you can imagine (Wholey, 1986: 1).

In cities and suburbs all across the nation, a generation of American children (is) increasingly at risk to the nightmare of *cocaine addiction* (*Newsweek*, 1986, cited in Orcutt and Turner, 1993: 192).

Teen pregnancy is a serious problem. Indeed it is epidemic among all races and classes of American youth today. It could happen to your daughter, your niece, your grandchild, your friend's child (Edelman, 1991: 150).

Money in the bank or an executive car is no guarantee against [*domestic*] *violence*, abusers can be found in any walk of life (*US News and World Report*, cited in Loseke, 1989: 195).

Overeating is a problem for most Americans . . . We must fight the prevalence

From David Wagner, "The Universalization of Social Problems: Some Radical Explanations," *Critical Sociology* 23, pp. 3–23. Copyright © 1997. Reprinted by permission.

of *obesity* which crosses all lines of American society (*1988 Surgeon General's Report*, cited in Levenstein, 1993: 242).

If some social problem claims assert that issues "cross lines," others describe a problem as an "equal opportunity" risk. For example, the popular poster, the "Typical Alcoholic American," pictures a range of affluent people (along with a few more ordinary people) and a variety of ethnic, age, and gender groups (cited in Peele, 1989: 69). AIDS prevention groups and activists have also strained to present the disease as an "equal opportunity killer," despite the concentration of new HIV/AIDS cases for many years among low income inner city residents (Laumann et al., 1994: chapter 11). Others characterize "typical" perpetrators of crime or substance users as being of high social class or status. For example, O. J. Simpson has been described as the "typical" wife batterer (Tucker, 1994); Joel Steinberg (the affluent New York lawyer who brutally killed his young daughter) was said to be a typical child abuser (Hentoff, 1988); while some describe the average drug user as affluent (see, for example, Inciardi, 1986: 79; Miller, 1991; Nixon, 1991).

This article suggests that while much of the new social problem rhetoric is well meaning—a vehicle to raise funds for worthy causes and an attempt to remedy social prejudices against groups of people often discriminated against—there are also latent social and political functions are at work. First, since it would seem self-evident that such problems potentially *can* happen to anyone, it is of interest that public service announcements, public health and political leaders, and social service professionals feel a need to repeat these slogans again and again. One might even suggest that they "protest too much," that perhaps political leaders and professionals recognize the public knows that these problems are *not* evenly distributed throughout the population. Second, at least in regard to the topics explored in this paper (teen pregnancy, crime, domestic violence, long term substance use, poor diet, and obesity), empirical evidence often suggests that these problems cluster in the lower social classes.

I will suggest, then, that in addition to the more manifest purposes of the universalist rhetoric, that there may be other purposes to this popular discourse. . . . In the last two decades, as social problems have come to be constructed as problems of "middle Americans" (if not the affluent), self-interested for-profit industries have emerged to satisfy these needs. The non-profit sector has developed a similar imperialistic stance in which growth is predicated on problem expansion, an increased clientele or a combination of both. Second, the new more liberal, post-1960s approach to social problems, while minimizing older moralistic and discriminatory treatment of issues, also appears to paradoxically disguise the power arrangements of capitalist society. It obscures, in particular, the role of social class in social problems. This obfuscation may be critical to middle class audiences because it serves a double purpose: it frees the middle class to become self-absorbed with its own problems, while supporting the social distance the middle class places between itself and those it regards as "deviant," "grungy" or "underclass." Since overt reliance on classism or racism is now frowned upon, a new discourse must be carried out in which behavioral codes replace the earlier designations for "deviance."[1]

In raising criticisms of this "new universalism," it is more important to be clear that I am *not* referring to efforts to secure universal social benefits, e.g., universal health coverage, pensions, income guarantees, etc. Interestingly, this type of "universalism" has proceeded in a completely opposite way to what I am referring to. In nations with many universal social benefits, struggles for social justice usually led by working class parties and labor unions have made claims for redistribution based on *class equality and justice, not* on the fact that upper or middle income people may be vulnerable to social problems. The new American discourse on social problems, for the most part, has not been one that stresses social or economic justice or income redistribution, but rather emphasizes either social control, on the one hand, or treatment and social services, on the other.

I will briefly review the demographics of several social problems and note some difficulties in making empirical statements about them. I will then suggest some explanations of why social class often seems to structure personal behavior which is identified as "deviant" or undesirable. I will then return to drawing some tentative conclusions regarding the rhetoric of universality.

PROBLEMS WITH DISCUSSING SOCIAL PROBLEM PREVALENCE

There are reasons to be cautious in generalizing about the demographics of stigmatized behaviors. Some of the easy repetition of the universalist rhetoric flows from this reluctance. First, problems which are highly personal, stigmatized or illegal—drug use or child abuse, for example—present unique challenges to social scientists in collecting good data because of the justifiable fear of subjects. Second, as sociologists, criminologists, and other social problem experts have pointed out since the 1960s, behavioral problems which are stigmatized lend themselves to discrimination against the poor, racial minorities, and other disenfranchised people. "Deviant behavior," from child abuse to theft to mental illness, has always been policed more in the lower classes than in other classes. The social control agencies police poorer areas more, and at least some personal problems are harder to hide in the absence of the privacy of middle class homes.[2]

Third, we know that the structure of society often forces people to take divergent paths because of class, race, and/or gender. A pregnant young girl in an inner city may find abortion unavailable, not to mention unaffordable (in many states it is not reimbursable by Medicaid), while an affluent peer would probably have easier access to abortion. Middle class people with drinking and drug problems are more easily accepted into treatment facilities and other programs, and have health insurance to pay for it. Still, another complexity is definitional. Does the poor person and rich person, African-American and Caucasian, young and old, always mean the same thing when they say they have a problem, such as drinking too much? Stanton Peele, an addiction critic, notes that middle class people have been so bombarded by public service announcements and "warnings . . . of the danger that alcoholism can appear in average people's live without their recognizing it" that often what the middle class calls addiction is "the new Betty Ford kind, which is marked by a general dull malaise, a sense that one is drinking too much" or "like Kitty Dukakis, [that they are] relying on prescribed drugs to make life bearable" (Peele, 1989: 2, 123). To some extent, depending on the problem being discussed, the association of once stigmatized behavior with the poor may be reversed as more and more affluent or middle class people, through recovery groups and other movements, come to see themselves as victims of particular diseases or syndromes. The problem for the social scientist is whether the oft repeated personal problems of the middle class should always be fully accepted at face value.

Finally, given America's allergy to acknowledging the existence of social classes, there is little research which actually explores social class as a coherent variable, as opposed to inadequate surrogates such as educational level, parental education or occupational status. Hence, though I will argue for a class perspective, my arguments can only be tentative and suggestive as I am extrapolating from incomplete data often consisting of imperfect indicators of social class.[3]

Despite all these concerns, it makes little sense to completely abandon all empirical evidence about the prevalence of social problems. First, some major social problems are hard to keep hidden or disguised. Murder or serious injury and disfigurement can rarely be kept from police, health officials, and social agencies. In the year of the Steinberg case in New York, for example, as the news devoted page after page to this one affluent family, 103 other children died from parental abuse and neglect in New York City (two a week), nearly all in lower class and ghetto neighborhoods (Hentoff, 1988). Although charges of neglect are certainly correlated with differentials in social service scrutiny of poor families, it is hard to believe that affluent people are killing their children or their wives, husbands, fathers or mothers and somehow bribing police or media not to report it. Similarly, many conditions are subject to reporting requirements. To argue there is significant long term deception or misdirection by reporters on issues such as child abuse is a serious charge, and cannot simply be asserted. That is, if massive middle class child abuse is occurring without detection, this data need presentation and support, and evidence of expert "cover up" revealed.

Second, a considerable body of data collection is now based on self-reporting. Although hardly perfect, this type of data provides relatively reliable results in that it avoids the above mentioned pitfalls of official records. NIDA, for example, performs surveys on substance use, and, with a few exceptions, its data supports strong differentials in drug, alcohol, and cigarette use among youth, particularly heavy and long term usage, by education and self-assessment of low prospects for further education, both of which are our only surrogates here for social class (see, NIDA, 1993, for example). In fact, on issues such as racial differentials in serious drug use, there is evidence that compared with reports from emergency rooms and drug testing, NIDA probably underrates class and racial distinctions (see Tonry, 1995, Chapter 3). Self-reports not only generally confirm the class divisions (as well as gender and age divisions) discussed below, but may even suggest underreporting by disenfranchised groups rather than the middle class hiding its deviancy.[4]

So despite the need for caution, use of data such as self-reports in addition to official reports, ethnographic, longitudinal, and participant observation data, in addition to quantitative data, and cross-national as well as American data, suggest that behavior that is the subject of universalist claims can be examined and suggested to be fairly stable and predictable demographic features.

THE DEMOGRAPHICS OF SELECTED BEHAVIORS

When certain behaviors are examined, we often find they actually *do* cluster among those in the lower classes, as well as often by gender (for example, there is little dispute that men commit most serious crime, domestic violence, and are most engaged in substance use), age (aggression and substance use is associated with relative youth), and sometimes by race and ethnicity. Of course, I would not argue that *every* social problem clusters in this fashion—for example, eating disorders have the opposite demographics, being found predominantly among more affluent women—but, for a variety of reasons (see below), the most stigmatized behaviors usually occur within the most disenfranchised groups. For example, on the six issues below,[5] while the dynamics of each issue differs, their prevalence can be summarized as follows:

Teen Pregnancy.   The U.S., along with most other Western nations, shows a dramatic class difference in rates of teen pregnancy, as well as a strong independent racial difference for African-Americans.[6] Some of this sharp difference seems to be cultural, relating to stronger support, for example, in the African-American community for the rearing of children despite the biological mother's young age.[7]

Substance Use.   It is often forgotten that the stigmatization of alcohol use, cigarette smoking, and various illicit drugs *followed* the adaptation of those habits among the "dangerous classes" in the 19th century. That is, the Temperance Movement's campaign against alcohol was inextricably tied to the use of "demon rum" among the immigrant poor and working class (see Gusfield, 1963, for example), the anti-"cigaret" movement of the late 19th century targeted the young tough "cigarette fiend" of the lower class (Dillow, 1981; Klein, 1993), and the panic about opium, cocaine, and marijuana were associated with racial fears of the Chinese, African-Americans, and Mexicans respectively (Musto, 1973; Morgan, 1981; Reinarman and Levine, 1989). By comparison with the turn of the century, of course, the use of all alcohol or tobacco became democratized in the 20th century, as the "demon rum" and the "soot weed" did spread to the respectable classes.

Nevertheless, long term and heavy use of alcohol, most illicit drugs, and tobacco continue to be correlated throughout Western societies with those who are less educated, poor and working class, males (though with cigarette smoking, women have recently approached the level of men), younger people (with the partial exception of cigarette smoking), and, in some cases, ethnic cultures. In the latter case, ethnic cultures highly stratify usage, such as differences in alcoholism between Irish-Americans, Jews, and Asians in America.[8]

Obesity and Fitness. Like substance use, healthy diet and exercise has had symbolic class and status meanings in America since the 19th century when "healthism" was very much a part of the constellation of middle class Protestant revivalist and temperance movements. Historians of diet and food note, however, that the prosperity of mid-20th century, as well as cultural assimilation, tended to democratize eating habits by the post World War II period (Levenstein, 1993: 87, see also Stacey, 1994). Since then, as the economic positions of the social classes have polarized in the U.S. and health concerns have grown in the middle class, both eating and exercise habits have considerably diverged. U.S. Center for Disease Control (CDC) figures (1994) show strong educational differences (our only surrogate for social class) on both obesity and healthy diet and exercise, with poorer persons more likely to eat fatty diets and engage in less healthy habits.[9]

Felony Crime. Western data on felony crimes, against property (burglary, larceny) and person (homicide, robbery, assault, rape) are highly class stratified, and, given the location of most racial minorities in the class structure, their crime rates are also higher than among Whites. Vast differentials exist for crime by gender (with males committing about 90 percent of felonies) and by age (generally under 25) as well.[10]

Child Abuse. Putting aside child neglect, which as noted is almost entirely policed among the poor, charges of child abuse are still made in dramatically disproportionate numbers against poor people, again usually younger people (under 30).[11]

Wife and Partner Abuse. Like felony crime, wife and partner abuse is overwhelmingly found among relatively young men from poor or working class backgrounds with unemployment, underemployment, and poverty particularly leading to dramatic differential rates.[12]

THE SOCIAL STRUCTURE OF BEHAVIOR

The reasons for the structuring of these often stigmatized behaviors among those in the lower classes, and often (in the cases of substance use, crime, and aggression) among young males, is a topic far too broad to be adequately discussed here. I hasten to add that I support neither a "blame the victim" view of the poor or working class as being immoral or irresponsible nor do I support an essentialist gender view which sees men as "naturally" aggressive or malevolent. Rather I would stress, briefly, the following.[13]

As noted, stigmatization of many behaviors *often follow* the association of behavior with the lower class, so, for example, the use of alcohol and drugs, the construction of sexual issues including teen sex and pregnancy, proper diet, and exercise, *cannot be separated out easily* from their historic associations with social class. When the upper class heavily used morphine, cigars, and cigarettes and ate steaks, these behaviors were not stigmatized or disapproved of. "Age of consent" laws and changes in the late 19th century middle class view of sexuality, particularly for women, heavily structured how lower class and racial minority women were viewed and has strongly affected a whole range of issues such as teen pregnancy, sexual abuse, and runaway youth (Snitow, 1983; Hobson, 1990).

Limitations in opportunity and the economic structure always lead to stronger involvement of the poor and disenfranchised in illegal markets (drugs, prostitution, other crime). These markers often produce secondary characteristics (because of their policing) of inducing aggression, carrying weapons, and the inability to turn to police or other formal social control agencies for aid (e.g., leading to violence or the threat of violence as self-protection in low income areas).

The poor environment characterized by lack of adequate prenatal care, nutrition, housing, health care, education, and recreation no doubt combine with unemployment and underemployment to contribute to the social stress creating high rates of substance use, criminal activities, and family violence among the poor. The stress of life in poverty affects all the issues discussed including the relative availability of healthy foods and concern with exercise and diet.

Cultural arguments are important to understanding different norms and socialization patterns around food, sexuality, and use of substances among different classes and races. Issues of sexuality, food, and substance use are particularly mediated by ethnic subculture and tradition, and many pockets of difference remain with dominant white Protestant ideals around these issues. Youth culture and cultural norms even in White low income communities also must be understood as mediating forces.

Undoubtedly, there are important roles for biological and developmental theories (the role of age in aggression, for example), and cultural and anthropological theories about gender socialization as well as social structural theories. These must be put together to explain how young men, in particular, engage in certain types of cultural resistance that are often aggressive in nature. In turn, as Cloward and Piven note (1979), women in Western society tend to "deviate" by "internalized" aggression such as perceived psychological problems or eating disorders or have been labeled historically as sexually "deviant" rather than deviant by acts of aggression. The more successful theories that account for differential rates of aggression and sexuality in the lives of the poor must look at both patterned gendered and social class responses to stress and disappointment, and at the failure of social control when lower classes do not need to conform to dominant social norms which middle and upper class people must conform to maintain their jobs and status.

MANIFEST AND LATENT REASONS FOR UNIVERSALISM

Given the existing data about behavior by social class, why is it that journalists, prominent experts, and social service agencies since the 1960s have emphasized that every problem "crosses all lines" or that middle class people are "typical" perpetrators and so on? I suggest that there are two manifest reasons for universalism: securing funding for various causes and trying to reverse the past discrimination by class, race, and sex. Yet I also propose that universalism may have latent functions, representing a middle class world view that is self-interested and that is ultimately less concerned about addressing the root causes of many of these problems. This discussion can also be viewed as paralleling the contradictions of modern liberal ideology, where issues of inequality are transformed into service issues and the previously militant social movements change into reform movements devoid of interest in social structural change.

The Profit in Social Problems. . . . Fundraisers for AIDS do not want the disease associated only with gays, IV drugs users or the inner cities. They want to gain money and support from "straight" affluent givers who are afraid of the disease spreading. Charities for the poor play on the middle class' fear of downward mobility to tug at the heart strings by implying that middle class people often fall into homelessness, and advocates for battered women or rape victims stress universal vulnerability, not that poor minority women are those most often raped, murdered, and mugged. As Loseke (1989: 202) notes about domestic violence, the structure of funding and appeals to a middle class audience dictate the way a problem is framed. Noting that domestic violence is often not dramatic, and noting that poor women are the most likely victims, she asks: "After all, we only need ask ourselves: What is the likelihood that images of poor women being "pushed" or "shoved" would generate mass sympathy?" Organizations rely on appeals that stress the "deservedness" of the victim and generate feelings of commonality between the audience, constructed as white middle class people of middle age, and those presumed to be the sufferers or victims of problems.

The idea that universalism is *only* well meaning would be naive, however. Universalism also assists in a growing market of middle class professionals and businesses that have been booming since the 1960s. Although the market in personal problems was started long ago, the development of "third party" insurance reimbursement in the 1960s, with the consequent availability of coverage for middle class consumers of therapy and substance abuse treatment, marked a turning point in the history of social service. Not only have personal problems become profitable to doctors, private hospitals, health suppliers, social workers, psychologists, psychiatrists, and nurses, but the very burgeoning of this middle class industry creates its own market. Reinarman and colleagues, in exploring why middle class drug use is so advertised, while its prevalence among the poor is less newsworthy, note:

> [After] lobbyists pushed through insurance coverage for treatment . . . there are now billboard advertisements for Cokenders (for which clients or their insurance companies pay $2000–3000 for a weekend retreat) and full page ads in national magazines and regular TV spots for chemical dependency hospitals (where costs range from $10,000 to 28,000 for inpatient therapy). The growth of the treatment industry is not simply a response to existing "demand." Chemical dependency units have become a profitable way for hospitals to utilize excess plant capacity (Reinarman, Waldorf, and Murphy, 1987: 23).

The marketing of personal problems goes well beyond drugs or alcohol or psychotherapy, however. Since the 1960s the diet industry has been one of the most profitable industries in America, followed by a host of other businesses from gyms to fitness centers to running equipment and aerobics, as well as books and videos on diet and exercise. Cigarette smoking cessation has now become an industry ranging from nicotine patches to hypnotism to groups run by medical and mental health professionals. Crime prevention is even more lucrative than the industries mentioned; from security systems to private correctional companies, there is a considerable lobby for crime, often profiting from exaggerating the true extent of crime, particularly among middle and upper income Americans. While it is true that there are lucrative markets in intemperate behaviors (tobacco, liquor companies, the pornography industries, etc.), the industries focused on health and temperance are *"upscale"* and hence need to stress the *middle class* nature of social problems, while industries such as tobacco and pornography have become decidedly *"downscale."*

It is not only far more profitable to seek out the middle class drinker or pill user, overeater or sexual addict, cigarette smoker, or therapy patient with insurance coverage than to serve the poor, but most counselors, physicians, and other health and mental health personnel prefer the middle or upper class client. The consumer of counseling who is middle class shares the language of the social worker or psychologist, is more often not in "denial" about his or her problem, and is more likely to be compliant with treatment goals. The abandonment of the poor by social workers and other mental health disciplines is the subject of several interesting works including Specht and Courtney (1994) and Funiciello (1993). Servicing "ourselves" (particularly paying middle class consumers) has become one of the few growth industries of late 20th century America.

Further, beginning in the 1970s with the widespread "contracting out" of government services to private non-profit agencies, the "charity" business has become increasingly privatized. Estimates in the mid-1980s put the non-profit sector at more than seven million employees and a $300 billion budget (Odendahl, 1990: 14). Many people fail to realize that "non-profit" status only means that hospitals, colleges, social agencies, etc. are prohibited from legally distributing a profit, not from accruing large surpluses. Surpluses can be used to increase profitable investment (sometimes in spin-off companies or in for-profit corporations in which board members of non-profits have interests), to enrich executives, to provide infrastructure growth, or to provide more travel, dining expense, and other frills to board members or executives.

The economics of the non-profits do not differ sharply from the imperatives of capitalists for-profit economics. Since most agencies are paid on a "fee-for-service" or per capita basis by government, insurers or private parties, the major vehicle for expansion is either increased clientele (e.g., the creation of large "at risk" populations needing service, often involving the organizations in "outreach" to obtain new clients) or an increase in social problem designation of the same general group of clients to achieve more funding (the category of "dually diagnosed" provides a good example; by re-labeling some of the mentally ill and substance users into a new category, greater funding per capital is achieved from government and insurers). Clients become commodities whose value is enhanced by either increased diagnosis or problem area. Generally, like businesses, even small non-profit must grow or die. Hence, they spend an increasing percentage of their money and time on public relations, the non-profit equivalent of advertising to stay viable.

The economics of the non-profits does much to explain the new universalism. Non-profits not only need to increase their funding, but also they must compete with one another for charitable and government funds. Moreover, a growing workforce has become dependent on social problems and has ideologically come to subscribe to therapy, counseling or other treatment as a way of life. Just as consumer goods are sold by persuasion that individuals and their families are incomplete without a certain product, the public, particularly the insured and educated public, is sent into a panic because personal deficiencies exist in themselves, their family or neighborhood—and must be remedied.

I do not mean to suggest that the overwhelming numbers of workers in the non-profit sector are not well meaning and altruistic or that treatment or counseling does not play an important role in helping some people. Nevertheless, as the private health-education-social welfare bureaucracy grows, it develops a particular ideological view of the world that sees personal problems multiplying everywhere and sees "services" (not income redistribution or radical social change) as the solution to all problems. Problems such as substance use or "at risk" behavior of youth convert people into manageable categories where "services" are "provided," rather than conceiving of people as active social actors.

Liberalism, the Middle Class and the Embrace of Universalism.   Throughout American history prior to the civil rights and other movements of the 1960s, the discourse about "misbehavior," particularly drugs, sex, and violence, would be characterized by today's standards as racist and classist. To take just one example, in the early years of the 20th century, fear of drugs (leading to passage of the Harrison Act) was linked to Black sexuality and violence. Cocaine was said to make Blacks so strong that they could "withstand bullets which would kill [the] normal person" (Musto: 1973: 244–5). The American Pharmaceutical Association pronounced in 1903 that "the Negroes, the lower and immoral classes, are naturally more readily influenced, and therefore . . . give little thought to the seriousness of the habit forming [drug]" (cited in Morgan, 1981: 92). . . . Drugs, crime, and "animal" sexuality were associated with "lower" racial and class groups.

It is quite appropriate then, in the face of American history, for post-1960s journalists, professionals, and experts to attempt to eliminate this discriminatory treatment of people by race, class and sex. Yet American professionals, while often influenced by (or perhaps afraid of) demands from the civil rights, women's, gay and lesbian movements, have had no similar exposure to class movements in America. While the effort to present "bad" behavior has strained not to antagonize organized groups who will vocally demand relief if upset, they face no such lobby to acknowledge class or even mention income or poverty. So what probably began as a well meaning "political correctness" on the part of media, social service personnel, and other liberal professionals can turn into something of an opposite: a denial of class that serves to *encode* class prejudice and thus privilege other explanations for social problems.

The lack of discussion of class is not merely an omission. The politics of lobbying and advocacy for reform, on the one hand, and the ideology of "identity movements" from the mid-1970s onward (particularly the women's and gay and lesbian movements) has dictated a universalist approach. To convince media, Congress, and other decision makers to aid stigmatized groups is difficult work, to say the least. Nathanson (1991: 48) argues that as long as Congress framed family planning and other reproductive issues as problems of poor and minority women, these efforts were doomed to failure. When liberal advocates turned issues of teen pregnancy, birth control, and abortion from the "the image . . . of a poor, black inner city resident [to] in her place . . . the girl next door, a rhetorical shift of major proportions," they had considerably more success. Similarly, as the women's movement moved from its origins in the New Left to a reform movement seeking to unite all women regardless of social class (and often of different political views), it targeted male violence (from domestic violence to rape to child sexual abuse) as a compelling cross-class, cross-race phenomenon to develop social movement solidarity. Issues that might be seen as more related to the intersection of social class and gender, such as women's low pay, women on welfare or "wages for housework," have by comparison faded from view in the conservative last two decades.[14] The gay and lesbian movement also tended to minimize class and race in its need for movement coherence. By the 1980s, the campaigns against AIDS accepted the mantra that "AIDS crosses all lines" as a defense against the homophobia that accompanied the epidemic.[15] The new social movement of recovery groups and 12 step programs has further reinforced the politics of universalism, insisting that alcoholism, drug addiction, sexual addiction, and gambling compulsions (to name only a few issues) "cross all lines."

All of these movements deny class not only to avoid division and not only because their goals are more limited than the radical changes sought by the activists of the 1960s, but also because, as Ehrenreich (1989) has noted, the middle class sees itself as a "universal class." When middle class leaders (even those on the political Left), say a certain problem "can happen to anyone" or "everyone," the subtext can be deconstructed as "this could happen to *us*, i.e., middle class people." As Ehrenreich (1989: 1) notes, "in our culture, the professional, and largely white, middle class is taken as the social norm—a bland and neutral mainstream—from which every other group or class is ultimately a kind of deviation." In fact, even when economic issues are mentioned by advocates and political leaders (homelessness is a good example), they are treated as universal issues that have little to do with class relationships.

While the universalist dicta does at times lead to short term successful strategies to achieve funding, legislation, and media sympathy, there are a number of paradoxes in this approach to social problems. In addition to the spread of misinformation, social policy can be misdirected away from the most serious resource issues. For example, David Kirp (1994: 91), in a critique of the AIDS activism, suggests "the insistence that everybody is at risk, though useful for funding, has undermined efforts to concentrate energies where the need is greatest." Put more strongly, it is unclear how the emphasis on educating middle class suburban school kids helps the large number of HIV-positive people in our nation's ghettos with their health care needs, much less the devastation of their communities. Moreover, once the middle class (the "we") decide in actuality the problem does not seriously involve us, the sympathetic "politics of compassion" media and charity coverage disappears. Such is already the case with homelessness, which a number of years ago was a "crisis," but now is either met with media silence or with active hostility among middle class opinion shapers (see Egan, 1993; Smolowe, 1993; Spencer, 1994; Uzelac, 1990). Since the solutions proposed by universalism (one thinks of "hands across America") rarely involve redistribution, the social "problem" festers, and enthusiastic middle class volunteers and givers move on to other issues since they see no quick gain or solution in sight.

A broader problem with equating the middle and upper class experience of social problems with that of the poor, or of Whites with non-whites or the middle aged with youth, is that it frequently allows the dominant group to become absorbed in its own problems, while the less dominant groups suffer the containment and repression for what is presumed a universalistic problem. Foucault saw the construction of "allegedly universal moral categories" of "deviance" beginning in the 18th and 19th centuries as a power strategy of the emerging bourgeois state. If we follow his argument, construction of categories such as "mental illness," "criminality," "sexual deviance," etc., divide humans (particularly those in weakest social positions) into categories where containment, surveillance and punishment is justified. Whereas if we simply referred to those people only as "working class," "the poor," or "the masses," such justification for containment and surveillance would be missing. In describing the origin of pathologization. Foucault discusses the logic of power that denies class.

> He steals because he is poor certainly, but we all know that *all* poor people don't steal. So for this individual to steal, there has to be *something wrong with him* and this is his character, his psyche, his upbringing, his unconscious, his desires (Foucault 1980: 44).

Foucault's logic here is critical to understanding liberal universalism. Since social workers, criminologists, health workers, and other labelers now must recognize that not all poor people (or racial minorities) are sick or immoral, they refrain from stigmatizing statements and draw little attention to class. Yet by *denying or disguising* the class (and often racial and age basis) of social problems, we also allow for easier social control and discrimination against the poor and young while upholding the limited medical model of deviance. Whites move out of African-American neighborhoods *not* because they are racist or classist, we believe, but because there is too much drug use there or too much crime. Large percentages of the poor go to jail and prison, but it is *not* because they are poor, we believe, but because they use drugs or engage in deviant acts. The middle class radical decides not to attend a political meeting with some poorer people *not* because he or she is prejudiced (of course) but he or she can't stand the cigarette smoke or the greasy foods being served (Ehrenreich, 1989: 226–227). Curfews are declared against youth for "their own good" to protect them from drugs, crime, and sexual abuse, but most kids on the streets of our cities at night are not affluent.

This is not to argue that middle and upper class people don't suffer serious personal problems or that all poor people suffer the social problems we are discussing. As a general rule, however, the "crossing all lines" rhetoric places a veil of neutrality on state policy which is usually most repressive to the poor, racial minorities, and youth. The middle class public asserts that it simply wants to "help" the drug user, teen parent, street kid, etc., without regard to poverty, class or race. But as it denies social class and other power relations, universalism "brackets" much of the underlying reality of life. It allows the same middle class liberals who use "politically correct" language about social problems to *simultaneously* support repressive action against the poor and social "deviants." To discuss and admit economic power would threaten the middle class, both in its occupational role as professional labeler of the "deviant," and in other roles as beneficiaries of a degree of economic power. Moreover, to admit that campaigns against, say, drug use or tobacco will be a campaign against poor people complicates the middle class self-image as a heroic class.[16]

Anatole France once said that in the fairness of the law, both rich and poor may sleep under the bridge, and hence all is equal in bourgeois society. In a sense, universalism maintains a similar neutralistic ideology. The universalist dicta that addiction ruins lives and "crosses all lines" contains some truth, but it also obscures other truths, such as the fact that the drug war has led to more than a million arrests and thousands of deaths in the African-American community, and wholesale policing and surveillance of the ghettos. In other words, both the particular problems under discussion (from drugs to cigarette smoking to teen pregnancy), and the current wars against them (the mass repression of drug users, the bans on smoking, the repressive welfare rules against teen mothers being proposed) are *primarily* problems that most affect poorer people despite the fact that, yes, there are middle class drug users and cigarette smokers and middle class teen parents. The ideology of universalism, in denying that policies directed against certain forms of behavior are class bound, upholds the legitimacy of government policy and dominant social norms.

Notes

1. I am particularly indebted to Ehrenreich (1989) for her discussion of middle class status cues, and the boundary markers which developed in the 1970s and 1980s to reerect social class lines.

2. I observed some of this phenomenon in my study of street people (Wagner, 1993) in which drug and alcohol use, cigarette smoking and consumption of "junk food," was more policed and commented on by the public because of the subjects' visibility. But—and this point is key—their observability should not obscure that the homeless and formerly homeless I met did appear to drink more heavily, take more drugs, use more tobacco, eat more unhealthy food, and engage in more crime than the middle class denizens of the Northeastern city I studied. The deviation of the poor from middle class norms must be treated in its own right, not only as an artifact of biased policing or reporting.

3. Because of the way demographic data is presented in the United States, it is difficult to fully enunciate and flesh out a class analysis that corresponds with the way data is reported. For example, my own view of social class would most resemble a neo-Marxist one, but the role of the very rich or ruling class is less clear here nor can the overall prevalence of working class "deviance" or "misbehavior" be easily described or defined. The clearest class in the labeling and processing of "deviants" are those professionals in the liberal, human and social sciences whom Barbara and John Ehrenreich referred to as part of "the professional managerial class" (see Walker, 1979), while those most labeled as behavioral "deviants" are those occupying the lower fifth in income in the United States,

who can be referred to as the "poor" or the "marginal working class" or the "reserve army of labor." For a historical analysis of how behavioral classification itself shapes the class structure (and hence becomes a self-fulfilling prophecy), see my discussion based on Gramsci and Foucault (on Puritanism and Fordism and moralization and class respectively) in Wagner (1997:51–56).

4. Some research has found that lower income people may reveal less deviance. For example, in the case of crime, self-reports reveal that poorer people commit more criminal acts, but also when subjects are asked about their own actions, poorer people under-report their actions compared to middle class people (Kleck, reported in Argyle, 1994: 250). Similarly, while there is a tendency of police to stop and arrest Black men (see Chambliss, 1994), and perhaps poorer white men in the drug war, this itself does not mean that middle class people use more drugs and are just undetected. For example, Mensch and Kandel (1988) report that racial minorities may underreport their drug use in surveys. This would make good sense, given the increased penalties that Blacks and poor people generally suffer upon arrest or detection. In other words, the well known bias in the modern state to police the poor does not in itself prove that widespread middle class behavior of the same sort is being engaged in. On some issues, such as marijuana use, sexuality, and minor crime, it is even likely that the more "sophisticated" ideology of the middle class would tend to lead youth to overstate their maturity or daring, while lower class and working class youngsters may underrate these acts because they fear detection more.

5. The issues chosen are not arbitrary but reflect my own interest in behavioral issues that are provoking state sanctioned actions or social movement activity aimed at deviant groups; see Wagner (1997).

6. A good discussion of how "teen pregnancy" was universalized into "everybody's problem" in the 1970s is contained in Nathanson (1991). See also Alan Guttmacher Institute estimates in Rosolf (1994) as well as Edelman (1991), Dash (1990), Farber (1990), and Males (1993).

7. See in particular the work of Arline Geronomius and colleagues on the functionality of teen pregnancy in the low income community, summarized in Cockburn (1994a, 1994b).

8. The issue of substance use is extremely complex to summarize for a number of reasons. First, there are so many substances that generalizing is difficult. Second, there is the issue of experimental use of substances which occurs in every class and ethnic group which needs distinguishing from long term use. Finally, many social scientists and other liberal minded people actually add to the stigmatization of substances by mixing any use of drugs with problem usage, e.g., the latter usage which can be documented as destroying health, stimulating violence, and so forth. As Peele (1989) well argues, in particular, when problem usage of illicit drugs and alcohol is separated from casual, experimental or moderate usage, the differentials in class and status are exponential.

For alcohol use, see Cahalan (1970), Cahalan and Room (1974), Crum, Helzer and Anthony (1993: 830–836), NIDA (1993: Tables 1, 6, 9), Peele (1989), and Valliant (1983). All indicate that long term use of alcohol is heavily gender and class stratified. For a good discussion of gender and alcohol, see Thompson (1989). On "ethnic subcultures" in drinking, see Greeley, McCready, and Theisen (1980) as well as Peele (1989) and Vaillant (1983).

On illicit drugs, self-reported data collected by NIDA and other agencies finds large differences even in marijuana use (NIDA, 1993. Table 9), with daily use among those not headed to college at nearly twice those headed to college. See also Table 1 which compares college students with young adults for higher rates of use among non-college young adults.

Although there are no major racial differences in those "ever using a drug," the rate of consistent drug usage is 50 percent higher among Blacks than whites (over a 30 day period), and the death rate is twice as high among Blacks from drug induced causes than Whites (cited in Chideya, 1995: 212, 214). See also discussion in Tonry (1995: Chapter 3) which notes NIDA leaves out the part of the population most likely to be troubled by drug use. As with alcohol use, drug use self-reports also show dramatic gender differences. For example, in high school, males are far more likely to use marijuana, hallucinogens, cocaine, and almost all other drugs than females (NIDA, 1993).

Rates of cigarette smoking even at the height of tobacco popularity always showed strong differential rates between professionals (teachers, doctors, lawyers), and farmers and small businessman, as opposed to poor, working class, and perhaps, some of the wealthy. In any event, since the 1970s, cigarette smoking has become dramatically class stratified with rates among blue collar and poor people more than double middle class people (see Hall, 1985: Mascie-Taylor, 1990: 124; Argyle, 1994: 11, 268: Wilkinson, 1986; Pierce et al., 1989).

9. In addition to Levenstein, Stacey and CDC, see Argyle (1994: Mascie-Taylor (1990: 130–31), and Wilkinson (1986: 15).

10. For cross-national data on crime, see Argyle (1994: 161–63, 249, 276), Braithwaite (1979), and Chiricos (1987). For some reviews of American data on crime and social class, see Kemper (1990: 71–77), Kurz (1991: 159), and Messerschmidt (1986, 1993).

11. Good reviews on this issue are in Kruttschnitt, McLeod, and Dornfeld (1994), Gelles and Straus (1988), Pelton (1981), and McNeil (1994).

12. A good summary of data on income, occupation, and domestic violence is Messerschmidt (1993: 148–50). Class and age data are supported as well by a recent CDC study (*New York Times*, 1994) and by historical data (Gordon, 1988: 174.)

13. I have included in the body of the text the explanations that seem to me in my reading of the social history and sociology of personal behavior to make the most sense. However, it is beyond the scope of this article to prove a particular theory of why social class (or age or gender) structures behavior. I agree with Argyle (1994) that we know more about how social class structures most behavior than why.

Others would raise issues I have not examined here. For example, some would assert that "downward drift" is playing a role; e.g., in the case of, say, substance abuse, the drinker or drug user is naturally falling in class or perhaps even a high school student drug user is perceiving himself to be likely to fall in class. Another perspective would simply assert only educational variables are key: e.g., education independent of social class may produce more middle class norms as increased awareness of, say, the harms of substance use, fatty foods or aggression are made known.

14. Of course, there have always been elements in these movements, socialist feminists and radical gay and lesbian authors, for example, who have criticized mainstream leaderships and strategies. But these criticisms have received little public attention and have had little influence on what the media at least perceives and presents as these movements' key issues.

15. For critical discussion of the American approach to AIDS, see Altman (1986) and Patton (1990). The controversy over the presentation of HIV and AIDS as a "universal" e.g., middle class heterosexual issue is discussed in Sears (1991: 46), Haney (1994), and Kirp (1994). Generally there is little disagreement that the risk of AIDS was universalized as a strategy by activists to alert the public that "anyone could get AIDS"; more controversial is the assessment of this strategy. On the one hand, to some activists who believe the encoding of homophobia, racism, and other discrimination was the key result of the

"risk group" logic, presumably efforts to reduce the "binary" logic of sexual risk and deviance would be politically "progressive" (see, for example, Cole and Denny, 1994). Yet there are arguments (see Haney [1994] and Laumann et al. [1994]) that such strategies have backfired with the public by overstating risk, and there are also countervailing activist arguments (for example, see Sears [1991]) that universalism denies the identities and specific needs of the populations struggling against AIDS.

16. My point here is not to support use of drugs or tobacco. Rather, I am suggesting the pretext of altruism among the many social problem claimsmakers and middle class opinion shapers would be weakened both by an actual examination of the class nature of the villains they attack, and by a de-construction of the categories they helped construct.

References

Argyle, Michael. 1994. *The Psychology of Social Class*. London: Routledge.

Altman, Dennis. 1986. *AIDS in the Mind of America*. Garden City, NY: Doubleday.

Braithwaite, John. 1979. *Inequality, Crime, and Public Policy*. London: Routledge.

Cahalan, Don. 1970. *Problem Drinkers*. San Francisco: Jossey-Bass Inc.

Cahalan, Don and Robin Room. 1974. *Problem Drinking among American Men*. New Brunswick, NJ: Rutgers Center for Alcohol Studies.

Chambliss, William. 1994. "Policing, the Ghetto Underclass: The Politics of Law and Law Enforcement." *Social Problems* 41: 177–194.

Chideya, Farai. 1995. *Don't Believe the Hype: Fighting Cultural Misinformation about African Americans*. New York: Plume Books.

Chiricos, Theodore, 1982. "Rates of Crime and Unemployment: An Analysis of Aggregate Research Evidence." *Social Problems* 34: 187–212.

Cloward, Richard and Frances Fox Piven. 1979. "Hidden Protest: The Channeling of Female Innovation and Resistance." *Signs* 4: 651–59.

Cockburn, Alexander. 1994a. "Beat the Devil." *The Nation* (February 28): 259.

——— 1994b. "Beat the Devil." *The Nation* (April 25): 549.

Cole, Cheryl and Harry Denny. 1994. "Visualizing Deviance in Post-Reagan America: Magic Johnson, AIDS, and the Promiscuous World of Professional Sport." *Critical Sociology* 20(3): 123–148.

Crum, Rosa, John Helzer, and James Anthony, 1993. "Level of Education and Alcohol Abuse and Dependence in Adulthood: A Further Inquiry." *American Journal of Public Health* 83: 830–836.

Dash, Leon. 1990. "When Children Want Children." *Society* 27: 17–20.

Dillow, Gordon. 1981. "The Hundred Year War against the Cigarette." *American Heritage* (February/March): 7.

Edelman, Marian Wright. 1991. "Reducing Teen Pregnancy Would Decrease Childhood Poverty." Pp. 149–156 in C. Wekesser, ed., *America's Children: Opposing Viewpoints*. San Diego: Greenhaven Press.

Egan, Timothy. 1993. "In 3 Progressive Cities, It's Law vs. Street People." *New York Times* (December 12): B1.

Ehrenreich, Barbara. 1989. *Fear of Falling. The Inner Life of the Middle Class*. New York: Pantheon.

Farber, Naomi. 1990. "The Significance of Race and Class in Marital Decisions among Unmarried Adolescent Mothers." *Social Problems* 37: 51–63.

Foucault, Michel. 1980. *Power/Knowledge: Selected Interviews and Other Writings 1972–77.* New York: Pantheon.

Funiciello, Theresa. 1993. *The Tyranny of Kindness: Dismantling the Welfare System to End Poverty in America.* New York: Atlantic Monthly.

Gelles, Richard and Murray Straus. 1988. *Intimate Violence: The Definitive Study of the Causes and Consequences of Abuse in the American Family.* New York: Simon and Schuster.

Gilmour, Alan. 1988. *Innocent Victims: The Question of Child Abuse.* London: Michael Joseph.

Gordon, Linda. 1988. *Heroes of Their Own Lives.* New York: Viking Press.

Greeley, Andrew, William C. McCready, and G. Theisen. 1980. *Ethnic Drinking Subcultures.* New York: Praeger.

Gusfield, Joseph. 1963. *Symbolic Crusade: Status Politics and the American Temperance Movement.* Urbana, IL: University of Illinois Press.

Hall, Trish. 1985. "Smoking of Cigarettes Seems to be Becoming a Lower-class Habit." *Wall Street Journal* (June 25): 1, 17.

Haney, Daniel (Associated Press). 1994. "Backlash Emerging over Risk of AIDS." *Maine Sunday Telegram* (April 17): 1C, 6C.

Hentoff. Nat. 1988. "Is it a Crime to do Nothing?" *Village Voice* (November 22).

Hobson, Barbara. 1990. *Uneasy Virtue.* Chicago: University of Chicago Press.

Inciardi, James. 1986. *The War on Drugs: Heroin, Cocaine, Crime and Public Policy.* Palo Alto, CA: Mayfield Publishing.

Kemper, Theodore. 1990. *Social Structure and Testosterone.* New Brunswick: Rutgers University Press.

Kirp, David. 1994. "Love Among the Ruins." *The Nation* (July 18): 89–93.

Klein, Richard. 1993. *Cigarettes are Sublime.* Durham: Duke University Press.

Kruttschnitt, Candace, Jane McLeod, and Maude Dornfeld. 1994. "The Economic Environment of Child Abuse." *Social Problems* 41: 299–314.

Kurz, Demie. 1991. "Corporal Punishment and Adult Use of Violence: A Critique of 'Discipline and Deviance.'" *Social Problems* 38: 155–61.

Laumann, Edward, John Gagnon, Robert Michael, and Stuart Michaels 1994. *The Social Organization of Sexuality: Sexual Practices in the United States,* Chicago: University of Chicago Press.

Levenstein, Harvey. 1993. *The Paradox of Plenty: A Social History of Eating in Modern America.* New York, Oxford University Press.

Loseke, Donileen. 1989. "Violence is 'Violence' . . . or Is It? The Social Construction of 'Wife Abuse' and Public Policy." Pp. 189–206 in J. Best, ed., *Images of Issues: Typifying Contemporary Social Problems.* 1st ed. New York: Aldine de Gruyter.

Males, Mike. 1993. "School Age Pregnancy: Why Hasn't Prevention Worked?" *Journal of School Health* 63: 10.

Mascie-Taylor, C. G. Nicholas. 1990. *Biosocial Aspects of Social Class.* Oxford: Oxford University Press.

McNeil, Brian. 1994. "Poverty Causes Child Abuse." Pp. 91–95 in Katie Koster and Karin Swisher, eds., *Child Abuse: Opposing Viewpoints*. San Diego: Greenhaven Press.

Mensch, Barbara and Kandel, Denise. 1988. "Underreporting of Substance Use in a National Longitudinal Youth Cohort." *Public Opinion Quarterly* 52: 100–124.

Messerschmidt, James. 1986. *Capitalism, Patriarchy, and Crime*. Totowa, NJ: Roman and Littlefield.

———. 1993. *Masculinities and Crime*. Totowa, NJ: Roman and Littlefield.

Miller, Mark. 1991. "Fatal Addiction." *Mademoiselle* (November).

Morgan, Howard Wayne. 1981. *Drugs in America: A Social History 1800–1980*. Syracuse: Syracuse University Press.

Musto, David. 1973. *The American Disease: The Origins of Narcotic Control*. New Haven: Yale University Press.

Nathanson, Constance. 1991. *Dangerous Passage: The Social Control of Sexuality in Women's Adolescence*. Philadelphia: Temple University Press.

National Institute on Drug Abuse. 1993. *Drug Use, Drinking and Smoking: National Survey Results from High School, College and Young Adult Populations*. NIDA: Rockville, MD.

New York Times. 1994. "Study Suggests 6 Percent of Pregnant Women are Battered" (March 4).

Nixon, Richard. 1991. "In the Arena." Excerpted in "Zero Tolerance for Drugs can Reduce Chemical Dependency." Pp. 230–33 in C. Cozic and Karin Swisher, eds., *Chemical Dependency: Opposing Viewpoints*. San Diego: Greenhaven Press.

Odendahl, Teresa. 1990. *Charity Begins at Home: Generosity and Self-interest among the Philanthropic Elite*. New York: Basic Books.

Orcutt, James and J. Blake Turner. 1993. "Shocking Numbers and Graphic Accounts: Quantified Images of Drug Problems in the Print Media." *Social Problems* 40: 190–206.

Patton, Cindy. 1990. *Inventing AIDS*. New York: Routledge.

Peele, Stanton. 1989. *The Diseasing of America: Addiction Treatment Out of Control*. Lexington, MA: D.C. Heath.

Pelton, Leroy. 1981. "Child Abuse and Neglect: The Myth of Classlessness." Pp. 23–38 in L. Pelton, ed., *The Social Context of Child Abuse and Neglect*. New York: Human Sciences Press.

Pierce, John, Michael Fiore, Thomas Novotny, Evridiki Hatziandreu, and Ronald Davis. 1989. "Trends in Cigarette Smoking in the United States." *Journal of the American Medical Association* 261: 56–60.

Reinarman, Craig and Harry Levine. 1989. "Crack Attack: Politics and Media in America's Latest Drug Scare." Pp. 115–137 in J. Best, ed., *Images of Issues: Typifying Contemporary Social Problems*. 1st ed. New York: Aldine de Gruyter.

Reinarman, Craig, Dan Waldorf, and Sheila Murphy. 1987. "Cocaine and the Workplace: Empirical Findings and Notes on Scapegoating and Social Control in the Construction of a Public Problem." *Research in Law, Deviance, and Social Control* 9: 37–62.

Rosoff, Jeannie. 1994. "For Most Teens, Chastity Isn't a Choice." *Wall Street Journal* (July 13): 12.

Sears, Alan. 1991. "AIDS and the Health of Nations: The Contradictions of Public Health." *Critical Sociology* 18: 2:31–50.

Smolowe, Jill. 1993. "Giving the Cold Shoulder." *Time* (December 6): 28–31.

Snitow, Ann, Christine Stansell, and Sharon Thompson, eds. 1983. *The Powers of Desire: The Politics of Sexuality*. New York: Monthly Review Press.

Specht, Harry and Courtney, Mark, 1994. *Unfaithful Angels*. New York: The Free Press.

Spencer, J. William. 1994. "From Burns to the New Homeless: Media Constructions of Homeless: Media Constructions of Homeless Persons in the 1980s." Paper presented at meeting of North Central Sociological Society, April 15.

Stacey, Michelle. 1994. *Consumed: Why Americans Love, Hate, and Fear Food*. New York: Simon and Schuster.

Thompson, Kevin. 1989. "Gender and Adolescent Drinking Problems: The Effects of Occupational Structure." *Social Problems* 36: 30–47.

Tonry, Michael. 1995. *Malign Neglect: Race, Crime, and Punishment in America*. New York: Oxford University Press.

Tucker, Cynthia. 1994. "You Can't Spot Abuser by his Table Manners." Syndicated column (June 25).

U.S. Center for Disease Control. 1994. "Prevalence of Selected Risk Factors for Chronic Disease by Education Level in Racial/Ethnic Groups—United States 1991–92." *Morbidity and Mortality Weekly Report* 43: 894–98.

Uzelac, E. 1990. "Compassion for the Poor Burns Out across the Nation." *Baltimore Sun* (December 1): 1.

Vaillant, George. 1983. *The Natural History of Alcoholism*. Cambridge, MA: Harvard University Press.

Wagner, David. 1993. *Checkerboard Square: Culture and Resistance in a Homeless Community*. Boulder, CO: Westview Press.

———. 1997. *The New Temperance: The American Obsession with Sin and Vice*. Boulder, Co: Westview/Harper Collins.

Walker, Pat, ed. 1979. *Between Labor and Capital*. Montreal: Black Rose Books.

Wholey, Dennis. 1986. *The Courage to Change*. Boston: Houghton-Mifflin.

Wilkinson, Richard. 1986. *Class and Health*. London: Tavistock.

EVALUATING THE CRITICAL PERSPECTIVE

Marshall B. Clinard and Robert F. Meier

The critical perspective regards deviance as conflict, generally as a rational adjustment to the contradictions of the capitalist social and economic system. The strengths of the perspective, as Clinard and Meier point out, rest on its focusing attention on how political, economic, and social structures shape legal definitions of crime and deviance. They claim that its explanatory scheme has much more

Excerpt, pp. 90–93, from *Sociology of Deviant Behavior*, Sixth Edition, by Marshall B. Clinard and Robert F. Meier, copyright © 1985 by Holt, Rinehart and Winston, Inc., reprinted by permission of the publisher.

to say about how groups make rules and enforce them than about how individuals come to violate them. Similarly, the inverse relationship between power and punishment ("those who commit conventional crimes (generally lower-class citizens) are much more likely to be arrested, convicted, and sentenced to longer prison terms than those who commit white-collar and corporate crimes") adds validity to the critical perspective. Its weaknesses, they say, inhere in the fact that there are many more sources of conflict than political or economic ones, that laws benefit all classes (not just the ruling or powerful class) and do not cause criminal or deviant behavior by themselves, that few empirical studies support the claims of the critical perspective, and that the perspective makes more sense as an ideology than as a theory.

The conflict model has made an important contribution to the study of deviance. It has focused attention on the role of political, economic, and social structure in the definition of deviance, particularly through laws of the political state. Conflict theorists point out basic problems and contradictions of contemporary capitalism. They note that much crime is a reflection of societal values and not merely a violation of those values.[1] The basic issue is how values are translated into crimes and other rules, and it is on this point that conflict theory focuses. Several problems are inherent in the conflict view.

EXPLANATION OF RULES OR BEHAVIOR?

Conflict theory does little to inform us about the process by which a person comes to commit crimes or to develop deviance. It does raise pertinent questions about the origin of laws and norms, but it is essentially an explanation for the formation and enforcement of certain rules and laws.[2] To conflict theorists, the basic structure of a society, both economic and social, shapes the behavior of individuals and not socialization processes or peer-group and subcultural patterns.[3] When the conflict approach does deal with the individual, it assumes that deviance is a rational and purposive activity. Because the socialization process is ignored, deviance is assumed to be a rational process in which behavior is selected from available norms, values, and roles.[4]

OTHER SOURCES OF CONFLICT

The Marxist view is overly restricted to the relation of social class and economic power interests to norms regulating deviance and crime. Such norms are outgrowths of much broader conflicts of interest groups that include not only social class and economic interests, but other power conflicts based, for example, on religion, sex, age, occupation, race and ethnicity, and those attempting to regulate morality or to protect the environment.[5]

WHO BENEFITS?

Not all laws are necessarily devised by and operated for the advantage of one particular group. The conflict approach may be more applicable to those acts that generate disagreement about their deviant nature, such as political crime, prostitution, the use of certain drugs, and homosexuality, than to acts that reveal no such disagreement. In fact, it would appear that there is general consensus about both the illegal nature of the behavior and the seriousness of the act in the case of most acts presently defined in the United States as conventional or ordinary crime.[6] Laws against homicide, robbery, burglary, and assault benefit all members of society, regardless of economic position. Any statement that the elite alone benefit from such laws neglects the fact that most victims of these offenses are poor, lower-class urban residents and not members of any elite, however broadly defined. Although certainly the elite have more property to lose from theft or robbery, persons who actually lose the most are those who are the least able to afford it. If, on the other hand, one regards the operations of the criminal justice system, one sees considerable validity in the conflict perspective in the sense that those who commit conventional crimes (generally lower-class citizens) are much more likely to be arrested, convicted, and sentenced to longer prison terms than those who commit white-collar and corporate crimes.[7]

THE POWERFUL MAKE THE RULES EVERYWHERE

The assumption that powerful groups dictate the content of the criminal law, as well as other rule-making processes, and their enforcement for the protection of their own interests is too broad. All types of groups are involved in lawmaking, each with specific interests and concerns.[8] Powerful groups do have substantial input into the legal structure, but this is the case in any social system, whether capitalist, socialist, or communist. By penalizing those who violate it, the criminal law always defends the existing order and those holding power in it. It means little to say that the rules are made by those who have something to gain from those rules. This leaves unanswered important questions related to the characteristics of the "powerful," the process whereby some norms are made into law and others are not, the selective enforcement of those laws, and differences in lawmaking and enforcement processes in different economic and political systems.

LAW DOES NOT "CAUSE" BEHAVIOR

Although the conflict perspective points to the criminal law, supported by certain interest groups, as the ultimate cause of criminal behavior, it does not follow logically that the law is responsible for the behavior. In referring to the labeling perspective, which generates similar confusion with its emphasis on rule-making and deviance by interest groups, Edward Sagarin observes that "without schools, there would be no truancy; without marriage, there would be no divorce; without art, there would be no art forgeries; without death, there would be neither body-snatching nor necrophilia. Those are not causes; they are necessary conditions."[9] There would be no crime if there were no laws to prohibit some behavior, but the existence of a law is not sufficient to account for the behavior.

EMPIRICAL EVIDENCE

The empirical evidence supporting the conflict perspective tends to be broad and selective. General statements are made, but substantiating empirical evidence in terms of objective scientific evidence is often lacking, or existing contradictory evidence is omitted. Paul Friday has noted: "Conclusions of research on the social control agencies are used as theoretical support in addition to journalistic and 'muckraking' techniques drawing major conclusions from isolated case studies. The opinion of most conflict-oriented criminologists is that traditional 'scientific' methodology cannot be effectively used to uncover social structural inconsistencies."[10]

Few well-designed and operationalized research studies have been made of the conflict perspective; most, in fact, have been designed to support the ideology of this viewpoint by sometimes overlooking negative evidence. Here are three examples. First, most evidence has been taken from an analysis of capitalist U.S. society as a whole, with little recognition of variations by state or differences between the United States and many Western European countries. Second, while it is true that conventional criminal laws are directed primarily at the behavior of the lower class, this does not mean that social control agents such as the police are always repressive (they also stop family quarrels)[11] or that large corporations are not sanctioned for violations.[12] The penalties imposed by the government on businesses are not in any way proportionate to those imposed on lower-class criminals, but it must be recognized that even the enormous corporate power in this country is subject to the control of the state. Third, variations in sentencing of conventional offenders frequently seem to rest on factors other than class bias and the political power of elite groups.[13]

THEORY AS IDEOLOGY

The ultimate acceptance of the conflict view, particularly the Marxist view, depends only partially on the availability of a body of empirical evidence supporting the claim of the perspective. Perhaps more than any other approach to deviance, this theory has an ideological base that will either hasten or retard its acceptance, depending upon the observer's political and social viewpoint. Other sociological perspectives are not completely free of ideology, but the conflict theorists' emphasis on combining theory with practice in a socialist framework makes more obvious and explicit the political connotations of its explanatory scheme. The movement toward socialism is the end product of a fully developed conflict theory. As Richard Quinney summarized: "The underclass, the class that must remain oppressed for the triumph of the dominant economic class, will continue to be the object of crime control as long as the dominant class seeks to perpetuate itself; that is, as long as capitalism exists."[14] If the elimination of deviation and crime through the dissolution of capitalism and the transition to socialism is perceived to be too costly, however, the appeal of the conflict view diminishes considerably. It is not sufficient merely to analyze the conditions under which deviance develops; one must also be willing to change those conditions in a political sense. We are thus talking about someone who is not only committed to science as a means to discover the "real" world but someone who is also a political being committed to a political ideology, an ideology that, it is believed, can eradicate deviance. Thus appeal to scientific evidence leaves untouched the ideological component of conflict theory.[15]

Notes

1. Paul C. Friday, "Changing Theory and Research in Criminology," *International Journal of Criminology and Penology*, 5 (1977), pp. 159–170.

2. Ronald L. Akers, *Deviant Behavior: A Social Learning Perspective*, 2nd edition (Belmont, Calif.: Wadsworth, 1977), p. 29.

3. Alex Thio, "Class Bias in the Sociology of Deviance," *The American Sociologist*, 8 (1973), pp. 1–12.

4. See Alvin W. Gouldner, *The Two Marxisms: Contradictions and Anomalies in the Development of Theory* (New York: Seabury Press, 1980). On pp. 58–60 Gouldner distinguishes two forms of Marxist thought, one that emphasizes the rational aspects of human conduct, the other stressing the view that behavior follows lawlike patterns.

5. See John Horton, "The Rise of the Right: A Global View," *Crime and Social Justice* 15 (1981), pp. 7–17. In his first book on conflict and crime, Quinney adopted a much broader approach than social class, particularly in his discussion of the conflict of religious interests, Richard Quinney, *The Social Reality of Crime* (Boston: Little, Brown, 1970), pp. 37–39, 60–72.

6. See V. Lee Hamilton and Steve Rytina, "Social Consensus on Norms of Justice. Should the Punishment Fit the Crime?" *American Journal of Sociology*, 85 (1980), pp. 1117–1144, and Peter H. Rossi, Emily Waite, Christine E. Bose, and Richard E. Berk, "The Seriousness of Crime: Normative Structure and Individual Differences," *American Sociological Review*, 39 (1974), pp. 224–237.

7. Jeffrey H. Reiman, *The Rich Get Richer and the Poor Get Prison: Ideology, Class, and Criminal Justice*, 2nd edition (New York: Wiley, 1984).

8. For a study examining the role of such groups see Richard A. Berk, Harold Brackman, and Selma Lesser, *A Measure of Justice: An Empirical Study of Changes in the California Penal Code, 1955–1971* (New York: Academic Press, 1977).

9. Edward Sagarin, *Deviance and Deviants* (New York: Holt, Rinehart and Winston, 1975), pp. 143–144.

10. Friday, p. 165.

11. See Otwin Marenin, "Parking Tickets and Class Repression: The Concept of Policing in Critical Theories of Criminal Law," *Contemporary Crises*, 6 (1982), pp. 241–266.

12. See Marshall B. Clinard and Peter C. Yeager, *Corporate Crime* (New York: Free Press, 1980).

13. This issue is debated, from each side, in Theodore G. Chiricos and Gordon P. Waldo, "Socioeconomic Status and Criminal Sentencing: An Empirical Assessment of a Conflict Proposition," *American Sociological Review*, 40 (1975), pp. 753–772, and Ivan Jankovic, "Social Class and Criminal Sentencing," *Crime and Social Justice*, 10 (1978), pp. 6–16.

14. Richard Quinney, *Critique of Legal Order* (Boston: Little, Brown, 1974), p. 16.

15. See, generally, Gouldner.

Questions for Discussion

1. Why is crime "inevitable under capitalist conditions"? For which social class(es)? What is the nature of these crimes? Is crime needed to solve the social problems produced by capitalism? What does Quinney think? What do you think?

2. Chambliss titles his article "Toward a Political Economy of Crime." What does this mean? Do you agree with Chambliss? Why or why not? How does his point of view enter into the article by Michalowski and Bohlander?

3. How does Wagner's article on "The Universalization of Social Problems" fit into the Critical Perspective?

4. Clinard and Meier outline the strengths and weaknesses of the critical perspective. Discuss these. What is your judgment: Do the strengths outweigh the weaknesses or the weaknesses, the strengths? Support your position.

Selected References

Anderson, Charles H. *Toward a New Sociology.* Rev. ed. Homewood, IL.: Dorsey Press, 1974.

An introductory sociology text based almost exclusively on the critical perspective. Anderson shows how many of the social problems in the United States derive from the social, cultural, and economic structure of contemporary corporate capitalism. He follows Marx in attributing most of these problems to alienation and sees the role of the sociologist as that of examining the causes and conditions of oppression and injustice, disseminating that information, and working for a more just and equitable society.

Antonio, Robert J. "The Origin, Development, and Contemporary Status of Critical Theory." *Sociological Quarterly* 24 (Summer 1983): 325–51.

The rise of Stalinism in the Soviet Union and of fascism in Germany, and the failure of the proletariat to revolt in all modern urban-industrial-capitalist orders contributed to the emergence of the Frankfurt School. Most of the scholars who composed the Frankfurt School fled Germany for the United States, where they continued their extensive writings in a broad area that came to be known as "critical theory." Antonio traces the development and spread of this broad Marxist perspective in sociology. He closes with a brief note on a research project that combined data collection, explicit values on the part of the researchers, and the use of research for political purposes.

Balkan, Sheila, Ronald J. Berger, and Janet Schmidt. *Crime and Deviance in America: A Critical Approach.* Belmont, CA: Wadsworth, 1980.

The authors examine crime and deviance from the critical perspective. They compare and contrast the crimes of the powerful with those of the powerless; they examine women as criminals and as victims; they analyze the political economy of mental illness; and they conclude by "blaming the system" rather than "blaming the victim." They say that if all social problems are rooted in capitalist society, then the solution to these problems will come about only through a transition from capitalism to democratic socialism.

Bernard, Thomas. "The Distinction Between Conflict and Radical Criminology." *Journal of Criminal Law and Criminology* 72 (Spring 1981): 362–79.

As additional perspectives on social problems come into being, there is the task of sorting them out and noting exactly where they fit in relation to the new as well as the earlier perspectives. In this piece, Bernard notes the similarities and the differences between two important viewpoints: conflict and radical criminology.

Chambliss, William J. *Power, Politics, and Crime.* Boulder, CO: Westview Press, 1999.

Despite the fact that crime rates have dropped markedly in the past twenty-five years, most Americans perceive themselves as being at high risk of victimization by violent criminals. This discrepancy between perception and reality has come about through what Chambliss calls the "politics of fear." He says a coalition of interest groups composed of conservative politicians, the media, and the law enforcement establishment ("the crime control industry") created crime as a social problem. "The issue of crime was raised for political purposes and was perpetuated by groups with a vested interest in elevating crime to the level of a national crisis." His short, concise, and pithy book is a very good example of the critical perspective.

Davis, Nanette J., and Clarice Stasz. *Social Control of Deviance: A Critical Perspective.* New York: McGraw-Hill, 1990.

The authors state that from the point of view of the critical perspective, political process is the central issue in deviance and control. This includes the importance of power in the creation of, organization of, and change in methods of control.

Eitzen, D. Stanley, and Maxine Baca Zinn. *Social Problems.* 7th ed. Boston: Allyn and Bacon, 1997.

Eitzen and Zinn organize their textbook around what they call a "system blame" view-point. The capitalist system results in the concentration of cultural, economic, and political power in the hands of a corporate "power elite." Most of the social problems that the text covers derive from the social conditions of inequality. This text overcomes Fuller's criticisms about the lack of theory in social problems textbooks and is an excellent example of a systematic treatise based on the critical perspective.

Feagin, Joe R., and Clairece Bocher Feagin. *Social Problems: A Critical Power-Conflict Perspective.* Englewood Cliffs, NJ: Prentice-Hall, 1995.

Another example of a text that overcomes Fuller's criticism about the lack of theory in social problems textbooks. This is a good example of the critical perspective. The text demonstrates the proposition that the greater the political and economic power, the greater the chances of influencing the definition of social problems.

Greenberg, David F. "Delinquency and the Age Structure of Society." *Contemporary Crises* 1 (April 1977): 189–223.

Contradictions in the political economy of capitalism produce rising rates of juvenile delinquency in advanced capitalist societies. Overproduction, exclusion of youth from the labor market (compulsory schooling, declining need for their labor) and teenagers' need for money combine to generate the social problem of juvenile delinquency.

Harring, Sidney L. *Policing a Class Society: The Experience of American Cities, 1865–1915.* New Brunswick, N.J.: Rutgers University Press, 1983.

Through a number of case studies, principally of the Buffalo, Chicago, and Milwaukee police, Harring shows how members of the business class gained direct or indirect control of the police in these cities and used the police to repress the working class in one of two ways: by breaking strikes and preventing the formation of labor unions, or by selectively enforcing laws prohibiting public drunkenness, vagrancy, gambling, and prostitution.

Inciardi, James A., ed. *Radical Criminology: The Coming Crises.* Beverly Hills, CA: Sage, 1980.

A collection of nineteen essays that outline radical criminology and offer arguments both for and against the development and acceptance of this perspective.

Jamrozik, Adam, and Luisa Nocella. *The Sociology of Social Problems: Theoretical Perspectives and Methods of Intervention.* New York: Cambridge University Press, 1998.

The authors argue that in contemporary post-industrial societies, social problems emerge, develop, and change through three stages which they describe as the "residualist conversion process." The political structure turns problems brought to its attention over to administration, which, in turn, transfers the problem to the helping professions. The result is the conversion of public problems into personal problems and the continued maintenance of the status quo.

Kellner, Douglas. *Critical Theory, Marxism, and Modernity.* Baltimore: Johns Hopkins University, 1989.
A review and examination of the various intellectual sources of the critical perspective. Closes with suggestions for forming alliances with various contemporary social movements.

Liazos, Alexander. *People First: An Introduction to Social Problems.* Boston: Allyn and Bacon, 1982.
Liazos's thesis is that capitalism causes many problems in the United States, intensifies others, and makes it difficult to solve most. The social issues he deals with include social stratification, democracy, work, the professions, imperialism and hunger, communities, women, racism, the environment, crime, health, and education. He argues that socialism will solve many social problems.

Lilly, Robert J., Francis T. Cullen, and Richard A. Ball. *Criminological Theory: Contexts and Consequences.* London: Sage, 1990.
Devotes one chapter to an assessment of the contributions of critical criminology.

Melossi, Dario. "Overcoming the Crisis in Critical Criminology: Toward a Grounded Labeling Theory." *Criminology* 23 (May 1985): 193–208.
Melossi suggests that a synthesis of labeling theory with critical criminology will very likely improve the predictive power of the critical perspective.

Messerschmitt, James W. *Capitalism, Patriarchy, and Crime.* Totowa, NJ: Rowman and Littlefield, 1986.
Messerschmitt attributes high rates of crime among young blacks to the way the capitalist system works. Constantly denied status, only aggressive criminality can restore their masculinity and self-respect. Similarly, subordination of women, one example being their decreased access to employment, reward, and promotion in the economic system, only increases their chances to engage in prostitution.

Skolnick, Jerome H., and Elliott Currie. *Crisis in American Institutions.* 9th ed. New York: Harper Collins, 1994.
A popular text-reader on social problems. A modified critical perspective collection.

Spitzer, Steven. "Toward a Marxian Theory of Deviance." *Social Problems* 22 (June 1975): 638–51.
Spitzer derives a set of propositions from Marxist theory that offer an explanation for increases in petty crimes and welfare problems in urban areas. The core of his argument rests on how the workings of the capitalist economy generate surplus labor, or what Marx called "the industrial reserve army."

Sykes, Gresham. "The Rise of Critical Criminology." *Journal of Criminal Law and Criminology* 65 (Spring 1974): 206–13.
A sympathetic appraisal of the conditions giving rise to the formulation of critical criminology and a prediction that the point of view is here to stay.

Taylor, Ian, Paul Walton, and Jock Young, eds. *Critical Criminology.* London: Routledge and Kegan Paul, 1975.
A collection of papers by three of the founders of critical criminology and a number of their followers.

Wagner, David. *The New Temperance: The American Obsession with Sin and Vice.* Boulder, CO: Westview Press, 1997.
In the 1980s a rash of problems clustered in a pattern that Wagner calls the "New Temperance." In reaction to the 1960s permissiveness, tolerance of deviant behavior among the lower classes aroused middle-class anxieties over lower-class excesses, as in crime, substance abuse, and sexuality. Concern about maintaining social distance from the lower classes led to a shift from tolerance to repression, from trying to change society

to changing or restraining individuals (the war on drugs, mandatory sentences, drug testing, from treatment programs to incarceration). This social movement reinforced conventional middle-class norms, made largely possible through dominance in the ownership and control of the means of production and of communication. In this book, Wagner makes a systematic application of the critical perspective to a range of social problems.

8 / SOCIAL CONSTRUCTIONISM

The turbulence of the 1960s and the early 1970s started to subside soon after the Vietnam War ended. Academics and their students returned to "business as usual." In terms of the dual mandate, the emphasis on the solution of social problems (which turmoil favors) became less salient and the development of sociology (which social tranquillity favors) became more of a focus. The social constructionist perspective became part of this change. It advanced a radical *subjectivist* perspective on the sociology of social problems.

THE LABELING PERSPECTIVE: THE CRITIQUE FROM OUTSIDE

Excluding the introductory course in sociology, the largest course in most sociology departments continues to be the course on social problems. As noted earlier in the book, since most of the students who take "Social Problems" are not majors in sociology, most colleges define it as a "service" course, and this important fact of academic life has played a role in the theory-research versus description-solution dilemma. To nonmajors, descriptions and solutions are more interesting than theories and research questions. Thus, textbook writers continue writing social problems texts in which detailed descriptions of social problems and their alleged objective conditions outweigh theoretical and research questions on how these situations came to be seen as social problems. As the reading of any one of the leading texts today will show, the best of them convey an enormous amount of information about a variety of social problems, teach sociology on the side, and still manage to remain silent on the development of sociological theory.

What set the groundwork for the theoretical breakthrough provided by social constructionism in the mid-seventies? Paradoxically, it all came about because of the success and the failure of the labeling perspective. First, we consider the "success," then, the "failure."

The "Success" of the Labeling Approach. All theories that have a lasting influence (e.g., Darwinism, Marxism, and Freudianism) ultimately get reduced to oversimplifications. In time, people need only repeat a key term to give the impression of both knowing and understanding the theory. That all of this happened with what came to be called "labeling theory" seems quite clear. A theory that said a good deal more about the sociology of deviance spread rapidly because of the apparent simplicity and neatness of its key concept, "labeling." This helped to produce its success.

The "Failure" of the Labeling Approach.   In Howard Becker's version of the labeling perspective, Edwin Sutherland's threefold classification of criminology still held sway: criminology is the study of the making, breaking, and enforcing of rules. Becker, in his book *Outsiders,*[1] says deviants are people who are labeled as such. There are three elements in this process: the making of labels, the application of labels, and the reaction to being labeled.

The sociological community ignored the making of labels and concentrated on who applied the labels to whom and how the people so labeled lived with these labels. Critiques, conceptual and empirical, centered on labeling's silence on etiology and on its central proposition that enforcement of rules increased deviant behavior, launched people on deviant careers, and engendered deviant subcultures.

Two different philosophies of social science governed the intellectual responses to the labeling perspective. The "objectivist" tradition, focusing on causal explanation, showed that labeling failed as a theory of deviant behavior on two counts: either no testable "hypotheses" could be deduced from its postulates or its "hypotheses" were refuted by the "facts." The "subjectivist" tradition, focusing more on how people came to understand their own and others' actions, concentrated on how people designated as social deviants coped with the problems of deviant roles and whether participation in deviant subcultures helped to solve those problems for them.[2] If objectivists relied heavily on official statistics and questionnaire data, subjectivists were more apt to gather their data through fieldwork.

While objectivists and subjectivists both examined, albeit with different research methods, the conditions under which deviant persons are made, they paid considerably less attention to its complementary question, namely, What are the conditions under which *alleged situations are made out to be deviant?* Furthermore, although the labeling perspective could just as easily be applied to social problems as to deviance, somehow both critical and sympathetic responses to the labeling perspective concentrated on the question of *labeling deviance* as opposed to *labeling social problems.*

In arguing for a subjectivist orientation, Becker pointed out that the emergence and enforcement of a rule had its own natural history. He cited Sutherland's groundbreaking 1950 study which set forth the conditions under which sexual psychopath laws were passed. He then went on to apply a similar argument to how the Marijuana Tax Act came into being and what followed its passage.

Subsequent students of social problems applied this point of view to examining other laws. The great bulk of research, following the publication of *Outsiders,* as already noted, however, was on labeling deviants, not social problems, and the consequences of the labeling.

The debate between two sociologists, Walter Gove and Thomas Scheff, throughout the next decade, symbolized for many what might be called "the rise and fall of the labeling perspective." Scheff argued in his book *Being Mentally Ill,* which first appeared in 1966, that the single most important causal factor in mental illness was labeling.[3] Gove, in a series of publications, argued that disturbed behavior rather

1. Howard S. Becker, *Outsiders: Studies in the Sociology of Deviance* (New York: Free Press, 1963).
2. See Earl Rubington and Martin S. Weinberg, eds., *Deviance: The Interactionist Perspective,* 8th ed. (New York: Allyn and Bacon, 2002).
3. Thomas Scheff, *Being Mentally Ill: A Sociological Theory* (Chicago: Aldine de Gruyter, 1966).

than social responses to such behavior was the main cause of mental illness. Gove later convened a conference in 1975, the proceedings of which were later published as *The Labeling of Deviance*.[4] This book rejected the labeling perspective with subsequent chapters refuting its application to mental retardation, drug addiction, mental illness, and alcoholism. Ronald Akers summed up the situation when he wrote as follows:

> The labeling perspective captured the imagination of researchers, theorists, and practitioners in the 1960s. It continued as a major but much less dominant theory in the 1970s. By the late 1970s, however, it was clear that labeling theory was in decline. It was criticized from several quarters for not being supported by research and was attacked by radicals for ideological impurity. It remains as a recognized and important approach, always included in textbook discussions of theories of deviance. . . . But labeling theory does not generate the interest and research it once did.[5]

But observers of debates between these two schools of thought often remarked that here was a good example of people talking past one another. A clarification and a focus on the third subject of Becker's book—the study of the conditions under which situations are made out to be problems—became the province of the social constructionist perspective.

THE RISE OF SOCIAL CONSTRUCTIONISM

Two papers, coauthored by John Kitsuse and Malcolm Spector, mark the birth of the *social constructionist perspective* in the area of social problems.[6] Kitsuse and Spector argued that sociologists had written about social problems for fifty years, but had yet to come forward with a real theory of social problems. A true sociology of social problems, they said, had yet to exist.

In effect, Kitsuse and Spector went on to show that none of the perspectives that we treat in the present book can answer the question, What truly makes a situation out to be a social problem in the first place? For instance, textbooks, particularly after Fuller and Myers's articles appeared, stated that a social problem consisted of a subjective as well as an objective condition. Yet none of them could answer the question as to why some situations got designated as a social problem while others did not. The authors simply took it for granted that everyone would concede that what they chose to include as social problems in their textbooks *were* social problems. This basis of inclusion, which either made the general public or the authors to be "judges" of social problems, only begged the question, How did this situation come to be defined as a social problem whereas another one did not?

Spector and Kitsuse noted that in the introduction to another of Becker's books, *Social Problems*,[7] Becker agreed with Fuller and Myers that social problems consisted of both an *objective condition* as well as a *subjective definition*. It is here that Kitsuse and Spector made their strongest and most critical point. Becker had said that social problems are what people think they are, but then he went on to presume

---

4. Walter Gove, *The Labeling of Deviance: Evaluating a Perspective* (New York: Halsted Press, 1975).

5. Ronald L. Akers, *Deviant Behavior: A Social Learning Approach,* 3d ed. (Belmont, CA: Wadsworth, 1985), p. 32.

6. John I. Kitsuse and Malcolm Spector, "Toward a Sociology of Social Problems: Social Conditions, Value Judgments, and Social Problems," *Social Problems* 20 (Spring 1973): 407–19; Malcolm Spector and John I. Kitsuse, "Social Problems: A Reformulation," *Social Problems* 21 (Fall 1973): 145–59.

7. Howard S. Becker, *Social Problems: A Modern Approach* (New York: John Wiley, 1966).

that *there was such a situation as that which they were complaining about.* This is where Spector and Kitsuse parted company with all previous perspectives on social problems. Their argument really centers on the process by which people come to think of something as a "social problem" without any reference to an "objective condition." Unlike all the other perspectives, Spector and Kitsuse asked a different set of questions. What did some people say was a social problem? How did they go about making that situation into a "social problem"? What did other people do in response to this conceptualization? What were the consequences of the definition of that situation as a social problem? In a word, what Spector and Kitsuse had done was to subjectify more fully the labeling perspective.

CONSTRUCTIONISM'S GROWTH, DEVELOPMENT, AND CHANGE

Spector wrote an important piece, "Legitimizing Homosexuality,"[8] which graphically demonstrates Becker's point that ultimately definitions of deviance are political (only groups with power can effectively label behavior as deviant and only pressure groups can muster enough power to redefine such behavior as acceptable). In addition, Spector served as editor of the journal *Social Problems* (1981–1984) and during that time published a number of important pieces in the new tradition of constructionism. Kitsuse and Spector's two 1973 articles in *Social Problems* set down the essentials of their sociology of social problems. They expanded these articles into chapters in their 1977 book, *Constructing Social Problems,* which has since come to be the locus classicus of the perspective.[9]

Conrad and Schneider's *Deviance and Medicalization,* first published in 1980, linked labeling with constructionism and indicated that a new perspective was forming.[10] Joseph Schneider later joined with Kitsuse to edit a book entitled *Studies in the Sociology of Social Problems,* a collection of readings on social constructionism.[11] And to mark the emergence of this latest perspective on social problems, Schneider wrote an important chapter reviewing work in this new and developing approach in the *Annual Review of Sociology* in 1985.[12] In turn, Schneider went on to serve as editor of *Social Problems* (1987–1990). Like Spector, he encouraged work in constructionism and the journal published a number of theoretical, critical, and research papers on constructionism during his tenure.

Joel Best later became editor of *Social Problems.* During his tenure (1996–1999), he also encouraged authors to submit papers that employed the constructionist perspective. Best, who had already published a seminal paper on the problem of "missing children" in 1987,[13] edited a collection of papers on social construction of social problems in 1989.[14] In 1995 he published a second edition with thirteen new

8. Malcolm Spector, "Legitimizing Homosexuality," *Society* 14 (May 1977): 52–56.

9. Malcolm Spector and John I. Kitsuse, *Constructing Social Problems* (Menlo Park, CA: Cummings, 1977).

10. Peter Conrad and Joseph W. Schneider, *Deviance and Medicalization: From Badness to Sickness* (St. Louis: Mosby, 1980).

11. John Kitsuse and Joseph Schneider, *Studies in the Sociology of Social Problems* (Norwood, NJ: Ablex, 1984).

12. Joseph W. Schneider, "Social Problems Theory: The Constructionist View," *Annual Review of Sociology* 11 (Palo Alto, CA: Annual Reviews, 1985): 209–29.

13. Joel Best, "Rhetoric in Claims-Making: Constructing the Missing Children Problem," *Social Problems* 43 (April 1987): 101–121.

14. Joel Best, *Images of Issues: Typifying Contemporary Social Problems* (New York: Aldine de Gruyter, 1989).

papers.[15] And in 1995, he became the editor of a series of some twenty books titled *Social Problems and Social Issues*. Best not only wrote papers and books employing the constructionist perspective, and edited and stimulated the work of many other sociologists in social constructionism, but also became a friendly and sympathetic critic of the perspective with his conception of "contextual constructionism." This increased production of both theoretical and empirical studies, stimulated by these three editors of *Social Problems*, promoted this perspective on social problems.

In that short time, Kitsuse and Spector had accomplished a number of things: they had synthesized the value-conflict and labeling perspectives; they had turned the field on its head by arguing that subjective definitions, not objective conditions, were the "source" of social problems and the proper object of study of those sociologists who sought to develop a sociological theory of social problems; they had pointed out the usefulness of "a natural history of social problems"; and they had stimulated a flood of studies that took quite seriously their radical definitional approach to the study of social problems.

CHARACTERISTICS OF THE CONSTRUCTIONIST PERSPECTIVE

To some degree, from a widened labeling perspective, Spector and Kitsuse argue that social problems are what people think they are. Objective conditions that may or may not exist and may in some ways give rise to the conception that a social problem exists are of no interest to them. Adopting a radically subjectivist position, they focus all attention on the problem-defining process, in who goes about defining a situation as a problem, what kind of a definition they formulate, how they present their arguments to others, how others respond to their complaints, and what the upshot of the interaction is between those who complain and those who respond.

Definition. Social problems are conditions that have become culturally defined as troublesome, widespread, changeable, and in need of change.

Cause. The problem-defining activities people engage in as they seek a redress of grievances.

Conditions. The process involving interaction between complainants, as initiators, and old or new agencies, as responders to their demands for redress.

Consequences. There are different stages in the natural history of social problems when examined from the point of view of social constructionism. But since these stages are contingent on such matters as clarity of definition, management and strategy of gaining and maintaining attention, the relative power of complainants, and the agencies from which they seek redress, only empirical research can offer tentative answers to the question of consequences.

Solutions. The constructionist perspective is silent on the question of solutions, deeming this a matter to be settled by research on the life course of the defining process.

15. Joel Best, *Images of Issues: Typifying Contemporary Social Problems*. 2nd ed. (New York: Aldine de Gruyter, 1995).

SUMMARY AND CONCLUSION

The 1960s saw the rise of the labeling perspective, a view that held that deviance is what people say it is. This point of view quickly caught on, and stimulated research, writing, and criticism. By the mid-1970s, however, numerous objectivist researchers questioned what they saw as the perspective's major proposition: that labeling either sustains or increases deviant behavior.

The mid-seventies saw the emergence of a radicalization of the labeling perspective, social constructionism, as an approach to the study of social problems. Radically subjective, constructionists argued that the true subject of the sociology of social problems lay in finding out how people arrived at a definition of a social problem, how they fashioned their complaints, claims, and demands into a process of defining activities, and who responded to these activities. As the 1980s came to a close, though, constructionism had already developed its own schools: those who would center all of their research efforts on the subjective definition of the problem (strict constructionists) and those who would include data on the objective conditions that provide the social context for such definitions (contextual constructionists). Perhaps most significant of all, social constructionism fostered more research in showing how problems became problems and less on telling how to solve them.

THE DEFINITION OF SOCIAL PROBLEMS
John I. Kitsuse and Malcolm Spector

In this excerpt, Kitsuse and Spector part company with the value-conflict perspective. Fuller and Myers, for example, said that social problems consisted of an objective condition and a subjective definition. By contrast, Spector and Kitsuse argue that the latter, the process by which a situation gets defined as a social problem, is what the sociology of social problems should focus on. Peoples' beliefs about situations, what they complain about, the form their protest takes, and so forth, should constitute the sociological study of social problems rather than a study of the objective facts. People can protest because of a material interest (they are affected by the situation in some way) or because of a moral interest (though personally unaffected by the situation, they consider it morally wrong and feel "that something should be done about it"). There is also a natural history to social problems: if some interest groups are able to convince others that a problem exists, others fail.

Definition, the work of interest groups, and whether or not people come to define the situation the way interest groups do, make up, for Spector and Kitsuse, the social problems process.

THE "VALUE-CONFLICT" POSITION

Fuller and Myers (1941b) stress both the objective conditions and the subjective awareness of social problems. They view the objective conditions as not *sufficient* (but rather as only *necessary*) for the existence of a social problem. This leads them to be concerned equally with explaining the causes of the objective conditions and the process by which they become defined as social problems.[1]

Here their formulation becomes confused. They use values, value-judgments and value-conflicts in several ways, leading them, in our judgment, to stray from the course they initiate in their definition of the field. Waller (1936) and Fuller and Myers use the concept of values in three senses. First, value-judgments lead people to denounce conditions as undesirable and repugnant to them and to define such conditions as social problems. This is the import of their statement that "value-judgments lead people to define conditions." Thus values are the key element in explaining the subjective elements of social problems.

. . . [I]n his attempt to *explain the objective condition* as well as its definition as a problem, Fuller (1938:419) invokes values again:

From John I. Kitsuse and Malcolm Spector, *Social Problems* 20:4 (Spring 1973), pp. 407–419. Reprinted by permission of The Society for the Study of Social Problems and the authors.

Value-judgments themselves are in most instances a formal cause of the *condition* which is regarded as undesirable.

In their typologies of social problems, Fuller and Myers (1941a) classify problems as to whether *the causes of the conditions include* physical events, value-judgments, or moral ambiguity.

In a third usage, value-judgments "not only help to create the condition but prevent its solution" (1941a:29) as well:

> A value-scheme which prohibits frank discussion of sex problems in the home and school is a causal item in the existence of the condition, venereal disease. The same taboos which contribute to the causation of the condition frustrate public programs which are designed to eradicate it. Similarly, value-judgments which deny social acceptance to the mother of a child born out of wedlock, not only contribute causally to such conditions as abortions, infant mortality, and abandoned children, all of which are socially disapproved, but such value-judgments also obstruct efforts to solve the illegitimacy problem by impeding free discussion of it (1941a:26).

Here Fuller and Myers point out with irony that the very people (social workers, liberal statesmen, and assorted other "do-gooders" among whom they included sociologists) who invoke their humanitarian mores to define conditions as social problems, themselves subscribe to and support policies *based on those same mores,* that insure the persistence of the social condition without alleviation, amelioration, or eradication.

Without questioning the validity of these last two formulations, we believe that the Fuller and Myers attempt to explain both *the objective and subjective* aspects of social problems deflects the thrust of their original statement. While they move away from the functionalist position that conditions in themselves are sufficient for the existence of social problems, they do not move to the position that *objective conditions* (italics added) are *not necessary.* To the extent that they attempt to explain the existence of the objective conditions themselves, their position comes close to the very social disorganization formulation of which they are so critical (see especially Fuller, 1939). This is particularly clear in their statement that values both cause the condition and inhibit its solution, and in Waller's position that conflicts *in and between the mores themselves* produce social problems, with the implication that different values or mores, acting independently, may interfere with each other or work at cross purposes. To the extent that values, rather than individuals or groups of people, are seen as the active agents in the society, the formulation becomes elliptical, reified, and abstracted.

Thus, their attempt to explain both the existence of the objective conditions and the process by which some condition, real or imaginary, becomes defined as a problem introduces an ambiguity into their position on just what the role of values is in the production of social problems. The result is that values seem to be the active forces everywhere: in producing the condition, in leading people to define the condition as a problem, and finally, in inhibiting a solution. We interpret this ambiguity as a hedge against the charge of subjectivism, solipsism and worse. The logic of their formulation, however, does not require a statement of position on the question of whether or not an objective condition "in fact" exists. Becker (1966:6) in his re-statement of the value-conflict view acknowledges that group definitions of social problems *usually do* have reference to some empirically verifiable social conditions. Groups do not typically get upset over "nothing." Our position is that one need not assume nor explain the existence of this *objective* (italics added) condition; indeed, to do so would deflect attention from investigation of the definitional process. The definition *may* be accompanied by empirically verifiable claims about the scale, intensity, distribution, and effects of the imputed social conditions; but it *may not* and theoretically it *need not.* . . .

SOCIAL PROBLEMS AS PROCESS

Our analysis . . . leads us to propose that the explanation of the "subjective element" of social problems—the process by which members of groups or societies define a putative condition as a problem—is the distinctive subject matter of the sociology of social problems. Thus, we define social problems as *the activities of groups making assertions of grievances and claims with respect to some putative conditions.* The *emergence* of a social problem, then, is contingent on the organization of group activities with reference to defining some putative condition as a problem, and asserting the need for eradicating, ameliorating, or otherwise changing the condition. The central problem for a theory of social problems, so defined, is to account for the *emergence and maintenance of claim-making and responding activities.* Such a theory should comprehend the activities of any group making claims on others for ameliorative action, material remuneration, alleviation of social, political, legal, economic disadvantage or other consideration.

The existence of social problems depends on the continued existence of groups or agencies that define some condition as a problem and attempt to do something about it. To ask what are the effective causes of social problems, or what keeps social problems activities going, is to ask what keeps these various groups going.

Fuller and Myers, in answer to this question, saw the causes of social problems in value-judgments and value-conflicts that lead members of a society to call attention to conditions that they find offensive. Values may lead some groups to become indignant about some condition and call for its change. This is the force behind humanitarian reformers, crusaders, and do-gooders.

However, not all social problems activities spring from this sort of "disinterested" principled activity. Humanitarian crusaders by definition set out to improve the lot of more disadvantaged others. They are not, themselves, victims of the conditions they set out to ameliorate. When those who complain are themselves the victims of the conditions, we will call them an "interest group." Interest may be defined as real and material advantages or stakes in the outcome of a given line of activity. Interest groups are those who have something to gain or lose, not just as everyone else would be affected but over and above the way everyone in a society would be affected by a given change in law or policy.

Groups defining conditions as social problems then, may be kept going by interests or values, or any mixture or combination of them. Some of the interesting varieties might include the following:

1. Value groups may find that as they raise a condition as a social problem, they gain as allies other groups who have a vested interest in their position. Similarly, they may be opposed by groups who have a vested interest in the *status quo*.
2. Interest groups may find that the dialogue of public debate must take place in terms of values or ideals. Thus, in order to present its claims effectively, or argue its position, it must acquire a set of values that legitimate their claim.
3. A given protest group may find a convenient overlap between their interests and their values. That is, the things they want to ask for are just those things that are easily justified and legitimated.
4. Alternatively, a group may find itself cross-pressured when their interest requires them to sacrifice or ignore some strongly felt value, or their values require them to work against their own best interests—the liberal position on school busing may be an example of this.
5. To the extent that a disinterested value-oriented group is successful in their activity, they may develop various interests to protect organizations, careers, reputations, etc. They may face a crisis of the "routinization of disinterest" when they become vulnerable to the charge of being interested and self-serving rather than humanitarian.

In the preceding . . . we have attempted to define a subject matter for the study of social problems in a clear and unambiguous manner amenable to empirical investigation. It remains now to justify the addition of this new conceptual category "social problems" by contrasting it to previously used or related and overlapping categories. We have suggested that previous treatments of social problems failed to distinguish their own subject matter from such related fields as social pathology, social disorganization, value-conflicts, and deviant behavior. As we have indicated, our approach has little (or nothing) in common with social pathology or disorganization formulations of social problems. We begin our analysis with the activities of individuals and groups in a society, not with a formulation about what any society must do or have for its survival, nor with any idea about whether protest activities are good (functional) or bad (dysfunctional) for its maintenance. Nor does our approach share the concerns of the study of deviant behavior conceived as the analysis of the etiology of certain acts or behaviors that violate norms or result in official responses to these acts. Such a conception forms a fundamentally different subject matter from our sociology of social problems. We are interested in the activities of making claims, and the response to these claims *as claims*. Deviant acts are not usually taken to be claims nor does the response to them typify them as claims. However, when claims and grievances are responded to *as deviance,* then these processes would be subject matter for investigation within our formulation (cf. Horowitz and Liebowitz: 1968).

The approach we take does, however, contain an affinity with some developments in the so-called labelling perspective on deviance. It shares an interest in the process by which a phenomenon (an act or a condition) comes to be defined in a specific way. It shares also an insistence that acts or conditions may be intelligibly studied only with difficulty or not at all if such definitional processes are ignored. Further, some studies within the labelling formulation provide examples of the initial processes that we take to be the bases of the phenomena we wish to identify as social problems. Becker's (1963) discussion of moral entrepreneurship and of the development of the marijuana tax act exemplify this theoretical articulation (see also Cook: 1969 and Dickson: 1968).

In addition to these several social problems categories, our formulation invites comparison to the study of social movements and to the study of interest groups. Indeed, our definition of social problems could be interpreted to include the whole of "political sociology." This, however, is not our intention. Specifically, the rise of political parties or revolutionary groups whose aim is to take control of social institutions falls at the margins of our definition, although they comprise the core of the study of social movements and political sociology. For the most part, groups that create social problems do so by making demands on existing institutions, not by trying to form institutions themselves. They share a concern to "get someone to do something" about the putative conditions. Such groups, of course, may transform themselves into genuine political parties if they fail to gain satisfaction from the existing regime. In doing so, however, their specific "social problems" are likely to be lost or transformed by intra- and inter-organizational political processes and concerns. By proposing these analytic distinctions, we wish to provide for the investigation of organized protests and social movements that do not conform to the models of political parties or revolutionary movements and thus tend to be ignored by political sociologists.

Finally, our formulation bears a similarity to the so-called "group approach" to politics exemplified in the classic formulations of Bentley (1908) and Truman (1951). It will, however, be instructive to contrast Truman's definition of interest group with our distinction between interest groups and "dis-interested" or value-oriented groups. Truman (1951:33–4) defines interest groups as

> any group, that, on the basis of one or more shared attitudes, makes certain claims upon other groups in the society for the establishment, maintenance or enhancement of forms of behavior that are implied by the shared attitudes. These shared attitudes (deal with) what is needed or wanted in a given situation, observable as demands or claims upon other groups in the society. The shared attitudes, moreover, constitute the interests.

Truman's definition is much broader than our own conception and would include both interested and dis-interested groups. In our formulation, an interest may be defined as any social arrangement upon which some individuals or groups claim to depend, rely, use, or need in the conduct of their daily activities. The scope of this definition is intentionally broad; it is meant to suggest that almost any aspect or object in social life may become the focal point for social problems activity. *Not all groups that enter the social problems arena, however, do so to defend some interest* (italics added). Similarly, not all activities of interest groups lead to the emergence of social problems.

As Truman (1951:38) points out, many interest groups are highly altruistic, supporting causes in which they have no vested interest. Although the vocabulary of motives in contemporary society leaves little room for altruism and self-sacrifice as explanations of conduct, we recognize that individuals and groups may be moved by moral indignation and outrage to demand that "something be done." Thus, our approach modifies Truman's conception of interest groups to recognize differences between those affected by the condition and those participating in the social problems enterprise for other reasons.

CONCLUSION

. . . [Prior] approaches [to social problems] harbor crucial ambiguities as to the distinctive nature of the phenomenon of social problems and the kind of theory one would have to develop to account for it.

We have presented a definition of social problems drawn from our analysis of the functionalist and value-conflict approaches [which also consider "objective" conditions as relevant to sociology]. It proposes that the explanation of the "subjective elements" of social problems—the process by which some groups successfully define a condition as a problem within their society—is the distinctive task of the sociology of social problems.

We believe the theoretical approach to this subject matter contains three elements. One is a theory of interests, for many of the groups that participate in the process of definition do so in order to pursue or protect their own social, political, economic, and other interests. A second element is a theory of moral indignation, for some groups attempt to define a condition as a social problem because it offends their sense of values; it seems wrong to them that the condition exists at all. The third element is a theory of natural history, because we conceive social problems not as static conditions or instantaneous events, but rather as a sequence of activities that may move through different stages.[2] These different stages may be characterized by different casts of characters, different kinds of activities, different dilemmas, and call for different kinds of analysis. Furthermore, the development of social problems through these stages may be marked by critical contingencies that impede or facilitate it.

Notes

1. It should be noted that Merton pays lip service also to the dual nature of social problems: "Social problems are not subjective states of mind; they are also objective states of affairs" (1971:788). However, his discussion of manifest and latent problems indicates quite clearly that the objective state of affairs takes precedence over subjective states of mind in the definition of social problems.

2. Blumer (1971) has recently proposed a five-stage career model of social problems that begins to address this question.

References

Becker, Howard S. 1963. *Outsiders: Studies in the Sociology of Deviance.* New York: Free Press.

————. 1966. *Social Problems: A Modern Approach.* New York: John Wiley.

Bentley, Arthur F. 1908. *The Process of Government: A Study of Social Pressures.* Bloomington, Indiana: The Principia Press.

Blumer, Herbert. 1971. "Social problems as collective behavior." *Social Problems* 18 (Winter): 298–306.

Cook, Shirley. 1969. "Canadian narcotics legislation, 1908–1923: A conflict model interpretation." *The Canadian Review of Sociology and Anthropology,* 6 (February): 36–47.

Dickson, Donald T. 1968. "Bureaucracy and morality: An organizational perspective on a moral crusade." *Social Problems* 16 (Fall): 143–157.

Fuller, Richard C. 1938. "The problem of teaching social problems." *American Journal of Sociology* 44: 415–435.

————. 1939. "Social problems," pp. 3–59 in Robert E. Park (ed.), *An Outline of the Principles of Sociology.* New York: Barnes and Noble.

————, and Richard R. Myers. 1941a. "Some aspects of a theory of social problems." *American Sociological Review* 6 (February): 24–32.

————. 1941b. "The natural history of a social problem." *American Sociological Review* 6 (June): 320–328.

Horowitz, Irving Louis, and Martin Liebowitz. 1968. "Social deviance and political marginality: Toward a redefinition of the relation between sociology and politics." *Social Problems* 15 (Winter): 280–296.

Merton, Robert K., and Robert A. Nisbet. 1971. *Contemporary Social Problems.* Revised. New York: Harcourt, Brace and World.

Truman, David B. 1951. *The Governmental Process.* New York: Alfred Knopf.

Waller, Willard. 1936. "Social problems and the mores." *American Sociological Review* 1 (December): 922–934.

HOW TO SUCCESSFULLY CONSTRUCT A SOCIAL PROBLEM

Donileen R. Loseke

Contemporary society generates numerous conditions that one could claim are social problems. But of the many candidates competing for social problem status, why is it that only a few achieve that status? While systematic research has yet to establish the difference between successful and unsuccessful claims, Loseke, after studying the relevant literature, has suggested her own recipe for how to effectively construct a social problem. Her key ingredients focus on the form and content of claims that increase the probability of their acceptance as in fact being a social problem. She deals with such elements as how complex the claims should be, what they should stress, how expansive they should be, and what kind of stories they should contain. If the claims generate sufficient fear and moral indignation, the audience will be more likely to clamor for "something being done about it."

What are some strategies claims-makers use to increase the chances that audiences will believe their claims? What are some techniques to convince audiences that a condition is prevalent and troublesome enough to violate morality, that it contains victims who deserve sympathy?[1]

CONSTRUCTING A POPULAR FRAME

Remember that each social problem must be constructed as a particular kind of a problem with a particular kind of a cause. There are two strategies for constructing such a frame that are associated with success because they key into larger cultural biases.

The first is the strategy of constructing *difference within sameness*. Constructing *difference* is important because there's a premium on novelty in the social problems game: The new and the different command audience attention because Americans tend to become bored with specific social problems.[2] The term here is *saturation*: Audiences become saturated with claims; when claims become boring, audiences stop listening. But while constructing something new—difference—is important, it also seems that this difference is best when it's *not* totally new. Many Americans tend to get confused when we hear about something *entirely* new; we seem to like novelty but we don't like the security of our worldview threatened by things that aren't understandable. For example, there's not a lot of public debate about the incredibly complex issues being raised by medical technology—human cloning, test-tube babies, and so on. One of the reasons for a lack of attention is that we simply don't know how to think about these things. What kinds of categories do we use to understand them when we haven't heard anything like it before? Entirely new claims can be unsuccessful if audiences don't have categories to understand them. Successful claims-making therefore changes the old in novel ways.[3] In two ways, claims can construct difference within sameness.

The first strategy is *piggybacking*. Piggybacking is when a new problem is constructed as a different instance of an already existing problem. A major example would be the modern-day social change groups working for equality. Historically, the civil rights movement to gain equal rights for African-Americans was the first equality movement after World War II in the United States. This social change group was doubly disadvantaged in gaining support for its claims. First and most clearly, racial inequality had been a part of the American social landscape from the beginning of this country. It was simply "the way things are"; it was unchallenged. The second disadvantage was related: When these claims started to receive public notice in the late 1950s, Americans in general didn't think much about a morality of equality. Sure, "equality" was a word in the constitution of the United States, yet Americans in general didn't tend to think about it; it wasn't an important morality in everyday life. My point here is that claims made by people fighting for racial equality brought a more general morality of equality into social life. This made it easier for claims to use this morality of equality to fight for other types of people such as women, students, gays, and disabled. In social constructionist terms, these claims have been piggybacked onto claims about equal rights for African-Americans. This strategy creates new types of problems with new types of victims and villains that are variations on older, already accepted types of problems and people.

A second strategy of constructing difference within sameness is called *domain expansion*. In domain expansion, the contents of a previously accepted social problem category expand. The category contents include more than in earlier constructions. The condition of "slavery," for example, began as a very narrow category used for a condition where people were *physically* prohibited from leaving the condition. But recent claims have greatly expanded this category. The domain of slavery expands as claims construct "immigrant labor" as "slavery," when they construct women prostitutes as "slaves" to their pimps, when they construct the new law requiring welfare recipients to work at low-wage jobs as "slave labor." Another clear example of domain expansion is the category of "child abuse." In the 1960s this started as a category for extreme physical abuse; now "child abuse" is used for instances of not so extreme violence as well as instances constructed as emotional, educational, or physical neglect. The domain of "child abuse" has expanded.[4] With each such expansion of conditions come new types of people constructed as victims and villains.

The strategies of piggybacking and domain expansion are two ways to create novelty while taking advantage of earlier successful claims-making. But this doesn't mean that categories are infinitely expandable. Audiences judge claims, mostly through our commonsense understandings of the world, and some expansions don't make good sense to many audience members. For example, there have been recent attempts to include "alcoholism" in the list of "disabilities" covered in the Americans with Disabilities Act. This expansion is meeting resistance. So too, feminists trying to expand the problem of "slavery" to include "housewives" haven't been very successful in convincing large numbers of Americans. Or, a six-year old boy was recently suspended from school for kissing a six-year old girl on the cheek. Although his behavior was categorized as "sexual harassment," many Americans (at least those writing editorials) took this as a joke rather than as a serious claim.

Constructing a problem frame of difference within sameness can be an effective claims-making strategy because it makes use of what already is generally accepted while it adds novelty, which encourages audiences' interest. A second strategy for constructing the frame relates specifically to *cause*. With the important exceptions of claims made by and for academic audiences, claims constructing *individual* causes are associated with success. Now granted, many of these claims simultaneously construct people as the problem and release these people from blame. But it remains that American audiences in general are more interested in hearing about individuals than we are in hearing about social causes of conditions. Consider the social problem of "rape." What kind of a problem is it? What causes it? We could look at the individual characteristics of men who rape

(rape as caused by something about these men as individuals) or we could rather look at social causes existing outside individual people (patriarchy, sexism). Even when claims-makers want to construct social causes, they will find many audience members are more interested in hearing about the characteristics of men who rape than about how the social world is set up in ways that allow (or even encourage) this behavior. Or, we often hear more about immigrants to the United States who don't quickly learn English (an individual failure) than we hear about how learning English might be difficult given characteristics of the structure of our social order (poorly paid work, which means immigrants don't have time to learn another language because they're working long hours; the inconvenient location of classes and the unavailability of public transportation; residential segregation, which means new immigrants often live around only others who speak their language).

Within such a frame constructing a new problem as being similar to—but different from—older problems, and within a frame constructing people rather than social structure as cause, there are other claims-making strategies for constructing the characteristics of the conditions and people in them.

CONSTRUCTING A VERY COMMON CONDITION

Remember that claims-makers must convince audiences that a condition is widespread. The social problems game uses a law of *large numbers*: The larger the number of victims created by a condition, the more likely audiences are willing to evaluate a condition as a social problem. This characteristic of the social problems game encourages claims-makers to cast wide nets in constructing victims. So for example, who is a victim of the condition of "drug abuse"? Some claims construct drug abusers as victims—they are ill people whose drug addiction is ruining their health and possibilities; they might be constructed as victims of poverty or racism. But this often isn't enough for audiences who tend to construct "drug abusers" as villains. So claims-makers can construct "people living with or close to the drug abusers" as victims. These people—mothers, sisters and brothers, neighbors, teacher—aren't responsible for the "drug abuse" so they are victims. But this still might not be convincing and to gain support we might have to construct more victims. This is easy. We might, for example, construct "drug abuse" as the cause of teenage pregnancy and school failure, and then we could construct these as leading to "welfare dependency." From there it is only a short step to constructing "American taxpayers" as victims. Or, we might go further and claim that "drug abuse" leads to crime and then we could construct the entire "American public" as the victims. The general rule: The greater the number of victims, the better.[5]

Of course, this strategy of emphasizing the great frequency of the condition also has its limits. A claim such as "one in six women are victims of rape" might be effective in convincing an audience that the condition is frequent, but a claim such as "all heterosexual intercourse is rape" might be convincing to a much smaller audience. I think about "nutrition" claims in this way. During the past few years, American audiences have been told to not eat fat; we have been warned about cholesterol and Chinese food, about most food sold in restaurants, as well as about the horrid nature of movie theater popcorn. Recent claims-makers seem to have stopped this tendency of constantly adding new foods to the list of the things we shouldn't eat—the list was becoming so long that, in commonsense reasoning, *all* food (except, perhaps, tofu and rice cakes) was constructed as a problem. Or, as a bumper sticker read: "Food causes cancer." If so, then it follows we might as well eat that double bacon cheeseburger. Audiences have their commonsense limits; claims that go beyond these limits will be ineffective.

Yet within these limits, this strategy of emphasizing the size of the condition and the number of victims is important because it encourages audience members to evaluate the condition as common enough to be called a social problem. This strategy of emphasizing size also is important because it can help convince audiences that the social problem is *close to home.* While humanitarian moralities construct the importance of helping people just because it's the moral thing to do, a characteristic of American audiences is that we tend to worry most about those things directly affecting us or our loved ones. When the numbers of people affected are huge then audience members are encouraged to believe that they or their loved ones can be harmed. This is especially so when conditions are constructed as "equal opportunity problems." These are claims such as that *any* woman is a likely victim of wife abuse, that *any* of us might find ourselves homeless through odd quirks of fate, that AIDS doesn't discriminate in choosing its victims. If audience members accept these claims constructing only "fate" or "bad luck" as causing the condition, there's a very personal reason to support claims: If anyone can be victimized then you and I can be victimized. We'd better listen to claims-makers; we'd better help them change the condition that could affect us. Claims encouraging audiences to be fearful are effective.[6]

Let's go one step further: It's also a strategy for claims about the commonness of the condition to emphasize *middle-class* victims. Because this is an economically and socially powerful audience, it makes sense to emphasize how conditions harm this type of person. Claims constructing victims of crime as middle-class or constructing drug abusers as teens in a suburban school, for example, tend to be more successful claims about the conditions of crime or drug abuse then are claims constructing poor or minority victims or villains. Constructing victims and villains as "any one," and emphasizing how middle-class people are victimized are effective claims-making strategies.

Finally, constructing middle-class victims—and villains—is also a kind of novelty that sparks audience interest. Americans are drawn to the unexpected, and therefore unexpected victims and villains are more interesting than are those we've come to expect. In this way, O. J. Simpson was a very good villain. Who would have expected someone that rich and powerful to be a "wife abuser" (and, depending on your view, a "wife killer")? So, too, JonBenet Ramsey, a murdered child commonly constructed as a "six-year-old beauty queen," has held public fascination for almost two years. She was a beautiful child, her parents are wealthy. Her story makes an effective claim because she was an unexpected victim. Likewise, stories of suburban teens who become mass murderers are very effective claims about social problem conditions. Remarks such as "We never thought it could happen here" or "This kind of thing isn't supposed to happen here" emphasize how the condition affects—or can affect—anyone. All audience members, especially those in the socially and economically powerful middle-class, are constructed as having a stake in the outcome of the social problems game.

CONSTRUCTING HORRIFYING CONSEQUENCES

Successful claims construct frequently occurring conditions; they also leave no doubt that the condition is morally *troublesome*. Social problems aren't mere "problems": they're often constructed in very strong language—they are a "crisis," an "epidemic," a "disaster." Claims construct horrifying consequences for social problems. Claims about the social problem of "poverty," for example, focus on people having much more than a "rough economic time." Claims tend to focus on examples of the most *extreme* poverty with the most *devastating* consequences imaginable. Likewise, claims about "drunk driving" emphasize the most extreme consequence—when such drivers kill others. This is an effective strategy in the social problems game: To convince audience members that a condition is morally troublesome, emphasize the extreme of the condition, which leads to the most extreme consequences.

Of course, we all know, given the complexity of social life, that objective consequences of specific social problem conditions will range from the "inconvenient" to the "pretty bad" to the "horrifying." Audience members know this. But there's a strategy that gets around this problem: Claims-makers tend to begin their claims (speeches, books, and so on) with one or two horror stories as examples and then they go on to talk about the condition in general. So claims about the condition of "missing children" often begin with a horrible example of a particular child who was abducted and brutally murdered by a stranger. Then, claims continue by constructing the "tens of thousands of children who are missing each year." Claims-makers haven't explicitly *said* that "tens of thousands of children" are the same as the example they started with (a child murdered by a stranger), but this strategy encourages audiences to construct an image that the "missing children" problem is that of children abducted and killed by strangers.[7]

Because successful claims construct really horrifying conditions, it follows that victims must suffer horribly. You'll notice that audiences don't hear much about teen mothers who manage to finish their education and go on to become good mothers and happy people. We hear about those who become trapped in poverty, those whose lives are essentially ruined. We don't hear about the "crack babies" who grow up healthy; we hear about those with continuing and devastating problems. We don't hear about "unemployment workers" who use their unemployment as an opportunity to go to school and enter new and more interesting work. The general rule: The more victims suffer, the more effective the claim.

PERSONALIZING THE CONDITION AND THE PEOPLE

Another important claims-making strategy is to *personalize* the problem. While American audiences in general want to know how *many* people are affected by a social problem condition, this isn't enough: We want to know the *details* of how conditions affect people and such details can be found only in personal stories. Big numbers offer audiences a *logical* reason why a condition should be taken seriously; personalizing stories is the route to encourage audiences' *feelings.* Stories are the way to encourage audiences to feel sympathy toward victims, to feel moral outrage toward villains.

Personal stories can be about regular people who might seem similar to audience members and therefore encourage audience members to support the social problem because "this might be me." The semifictional characters of Francine and Miki Hughes in *The Burning Bed* are claims about a condition called wife abuse and about the categories of persons called the battered woman and the abusive man. *Adam's Story*, a movie about a child abducted and brutally killed by a stranger, constructs the "missing children" problem and the "missing child" as a special category of victim. Rodney King was just a regular guy until a home video captured images that were used to construct a graphic and detailed image of the condition of "police brutality."

This strategy of personalizing social problem conditions also works well when it uses stories of well-known celebrities. These people often aren't similar to audience members, but audience members in the United States can have strong identifications with celebrities. Celebrity stories also serve to emphasize how *anyone* can be victimized by a social problem condition. For example, Rock Hudson, Magic Johnson, and Greg Louganis have been effective examples to make claims about the social problem of AIDS; the death of basketball star Len Bias in 1986 of a cocaine overdose led to a flurry of claims and the beginning of the current war against drugs. I'd bet that for the next several years claims about the problem of "drunk driving" will feature Princess Diana as the victim. Read celebrity's stories such as those in the *National Inquirer* and People Magazine as claims about the horrid personal consequences of social problems conditions.

Regardless of whether the story is that of a well-known celebrity or of "regular people" constructed as no different from audience members, it remains that American audiences like personal stories. General audiences to social problems claims tend to not judge claims solely on the logical basis of the scientific evidence; we judge them on the basis of how we *feel*, and how we feel can best be encouraged by the little details of personal anguish in individual stories. I think about this when I teach my class in Family Violence. In addition to lots of scientific research, I assign *The Bluest Eye* (a novel by Toni Morisson), and we watch *The Burning Bed* (the fictionalized true story of Francine and Miki Hughes). These are what students praise in their student evaluations; these images are the ones they tend to remember. Individual stories of people can be worth countless logic-based claims.

CONSTRUCTING SIMPLICITY

Throughout, I've been encouraging you to keep in mind that our real-life experiences are complex and confusing. But an effective claims-making strategy is to forget about this real-life complexity and to construct social problem conditions and the people in them as easy to understand. While there can be many competitions among claims, any given set of claims often tends toward constructing simple (if not downright simplistic) images of conditions and people. One way in which this can be done is to construct images of the conditions as containing *only* horrifying consequences. So, for example, if I'm trying to convince you that there's a problem of bad schools in this country, it wouldn't be effective for me to dwell upon the kinds of things that schools do well. Or, if I'm making claims about the condition of teenage parenting, it wouldn't make sense for me to talk about the possible ways in which young mothers might be better than older mothers in establishing friendships with their children. The same holds for constructing images of victims. If I want to convince you that "wife abuse" is a problem, it wouldn't be good for me to dwell upon the ways in which relationships can contain both "abuse" and "caring"; if I wanted to convince you that "child sexual abusers" should be locked up, it wouldn't be effective for me to dwell upon the ways in which such people might have positive personal qualities. Now, don't take me wrong: I'm *not* claiming that social problem conditions aren't as bad as we're led to believe; I'm *not* claiming that victims don't suffer. Certainly not. What I *am* claiming is that effective claims are those constructing only the characteristics of the condition that lead to images of the condition as a social problem; they contain only the characteristics of victims that construct them as victims; they contain only the characteristics of villains that construct them as villains.

Simplicity also is constructed by emphasizing victim purity. Remember that many audiences won't evaluate a person as a victim unless they also believe the person isn't responsible for his or her harm. It makes sense, then, that a claimsmaking strategy is to *emphasize* that victims are in no way responsible for the harm they experience. Think about the social problem of AIDS and the common question, How did people contact this disease? This is a veiled question about responsibility: Are people who have AIDS responsible? In the 1980s when AIDS first appeared in the United States, it didn't reach the status of a national social problem. Claims were made but socially and economically powerful audiences weren't particularly interested. Why? I'd suggest it was because in the beginning years, constructions of the victims of AIDS were of "homosexuals" and "drug users." Within dominant (middle-class, heterosexual) understandings, these persons "did something" (engaged in homosexual activities or took illegal drugs) that caused them to contract this disease. From middle-class, heterosexual folk reasoning, if follows that it wasn't the public's responsibility to do anything. AIDS became a national social problem only when constructions of AIDS victims started to use personal stories of hemophiliacs and babies born to AIDS-infected mothers.[8] Such categories of people are clearly not responsible for their plights. So we have a tilt in successful claims toward constructing not only "nonresponsibility" but also toward constructing what often seems to be victims' absolute *purity*.

STRATEGIES IN CONSTRUCTING VILLAINS

While constructing morality and purity almost always is an effective strategy in constructing victims, the situation is more complex when we turn to strategies for constructing villains. We live in an odd world where audiences often do want to hear about individual villains, but where these same audiences often hesitate to condemn or blame individuals. There are three possible strategies to construct villains. The likely effectiveness of each strategy depends on the situation and audience.

First, and probably the most common, villains can be constructed, yet blame deflected from them. We see this strategy when claims construct a murderer as a person "under considerable stress," when criminals are constructed as "former mental patients," as people who "never really had a chance in life," and so on. In such claims, we do have a villain, yet blame for the harm is deflected onto someone (such as a terrible mother) or something (such as poverty, racism, illness) else. In this case, claims construct an individual cause of the problem but audience members aren't asked to experience the very unpleasant emotion of hatred. Indeed, we can feel the more positive emotion of sympathy for the villain. This strategy is effective when it is emotionally appealing to audiences: It allows us to "hate the sin but love the sinner."

Second, just as it's often effective to construct victims as "anyone," claims can refuse to construct villains as a particular type of person. So how do we know that a person is a "child abuser"? We don't: Anyone can be this type of person, warns a handout on a bulletin board at the local laundromat. How do we predict that a child will become a "drug abuser"? We don't: parents are warned, any child can do this. This strategy has much to recommend it. I remember when I used to give public lectures about "wife abuse." Originally, I offered images of the "typical wife abuser." But audience members often disagreed: At times, an audience member would know an individual man who *was* a "wife abuser" but who *didn't* fit my image; at times, an audience member would know a man who *wasn't* a "wife abuser" but who *did* fit my image. Easier, I learned, to say "any man can be a wife abuser." This strategy can be effective because it *doesn't* typify. Because it doesn't typify, it doesn't run the risk of encouraging audiences to think about the complexity of real people, which might lead to counterclaims challenging the typification.

Third, a true villain deserving condemnation can be constructed. In these instances, the strategy is first to construct *unthinkable* harm done to victims. The harm must be so extreme that it encourages audience members to feel considerable anger. Then, the villain also must be so extremely constructed: There can be nothing good about this person; the construction must contain nothing but what reasonably can be defined as pure evil. What this extreme construction does is silence competing claims that might deflect blame; it constructs a villain as a dangerous outsider, as not one of us, as somehow less than human.[9] The news gives us a continuing assortment of such individual dangerous outsiders as Timothy McVeigh, the "Oklahoma City Bomber." Yet, given the tendency in our country to deflect blame from people doing harm to someone or something else, we have few *categories* of necessarily evil outsiders.

Before we continue to the final claims-making strategy of constructing types of conditions and people for mass media presentations, let's stop for a minute and put all this together to see what we would have if all of these strategies were combined. What kind of a condition, victim, and villain would we have if claims used all these strategies? If all strategies were combined we would have an image of a new problem, but not so new that it would ask audiences to develop whole new ways of seeing the world. It would be a condition confirming our cultural beliefs in individualism (problems are caused by people), and the social rules for sympathy (victims aren't responsible, victims are pure). It would be an image of an incredibly common condition with incredibly horrible consequences affecting middle-class Americans. It would be an image of a condition that was easy to understand because the typification wouldn't contain any real-life complexity. This package of claims about conditions and people would be successful because it would reflect typical American common sense and because it also would appeal emotionally: Audiences would be encouraged to feel positive human compassion for victims while they would be encouraged to blame only those villains who are clearly and most certainly pure evil.

In real-life claims-making, of course, claims simply tilt in these directions, but if we take this as an abstract model of a "perfect" claim, we are ready for the last claims-making strategy: Constructing claims for mass media presentations.

CONSTRUCTING TYPES OF PROBLEMS AND PEOPLE FOR MASS MEDIA PRESENTATION

Remember that in the previous chapter I talked about the importance of packaging claims for television. While network television is only one of many forms of mass media, it is extremely critical for two simple reasons: It has the power to reach inside almost all American homes, so it offers the largest possible audience for social problems claims; and what Americans know about our world increasingly comes from televised images. It follows that an effective claims-making strategy is to construct types of conditions and people in ways that make them attractive for television viewers. [T]hese viewers prefer programs that reflect larger cultural worries and it [is] risky to construct too much morality because there are many kinds of moral understandings in audiences measured in the millions of people.

The same holds here and I'll add only two additional strategies. The first is to claim at the right time. Sometimes, claims are made at the wrong time. For example, we might hold a very large and successful protest march today, but not receive any media coverage if, by chance, there's a hurricane elsewhere in the country or if another event becomes the focus of media attention. At other times, a fairly predictable cultural calendar can be used to advantage. For example, television viewers in December seem to be drawn toward human interest stories, so it follows that a good strategy would be to make claims about social problems harming people (especially children) during this time; winter months are better than summer months for making claims about the problems of "homelessness," and so on.

Claiming at the right time also means to make claims when there is a story already being covered by the media. A strategy for getting media coverage is to make claims when the world offers a *real-life example* of the condition at hand. When Princess Diana of Wales died in an automobile crash, her death quickly led to increased—and effective—claims-making about the two conditions of "drunk driving" and "celebrity stalking." In the same way, media personnel sought out "wife abuse" claims-makers after the murder of Nicole Brown Simpson and the charge of murder against her celebrity ex-husband. Or, claims about environmental ruin increased in both number and effectiveness when the Exxon Valdez dumped thousands of gallons of oil in Alaska. When the social world offers examples as perfect as these (extreme conditions, devastating consequences), it's only logical that claims-makers seize upon them and use them for their advantage.[10]

Claiming at the right time is an effective strategy for obtaining audience interest in general, media attention in particular. A second strategy for the media is to remember that most media, most of the time, is about *entertainment*. Television broadcasts, including the nightly news and the various news shows such as "20/20" or "60 Minutes," must be entertaining or viewers will turn them off and do something else.[11] So, ask yourself, what will encourage you to watch the news on television rather than, say, read or take your dog for a walk? The answer can take us right back to the strategies for constructing types of conditions and people.

Notes

1. I'll be drawing from much previous work by Joel Best (1990), who developed the concepts of domain expansion and piggybacking. I'll also draw from Stephen Hilgartner and Charles Bosk (1988), who examined the "principles of selection" in public arenas for attention to social problems.

2. There are reasons other than boredom for why audiences lose interest in social problems. Anthony Downs (1972), for example, outlines an "issue-attention cycle." According to him, social problems have several phases: (1) the preproblem stage, when the condition exists but hasn't yet captured public attention; (2) the stage of discovery and enthusiasm that the problem can be resolved; (3) the stage of realizing that solutions will not be as easy as originally believed; (4) decline of public interest as discouragement about resolution and boredom set in; and (5) the postproblem stage, when audiences are no longer interested and the problem receives little attention.

3. David Rochefort and Roger Cobb (1993) discuss this importance of constructing novelty—but not too much within the public policy arena. New issues are interesting, but totally new issues lack familiar solutions and there is no consensus within the political system for how to resolve them. This encourages claims and counterclaims and the political process becomes bogged down. Stephen Hilgartner and Charles Bosk (1988) advance a series of theoretical propositions for which social problem claims will receive public attention. Among these "principles of selection" are those that saturation with redundant claims dedramatizes problems and that new symbols or events must continually renew the drama or the problem will decline.

4. The category "child sexual abuse" also is very interesting. Consider an article by Frank Bruni (1997) in the *New York Times* that considers child sexual abuse "in an age of heightened sexual precociousness among children." The article begins: "Mention child

sexual abuse and the kind of image that creeps to mind is a depraved adult taking muscular advantage of an 8-year old's rag-doll frailty, strangling an incipient cry of protest with threats or promises." Against the image, the article questions readers about how we are to classify the thirty-five-year-old female teacher who had a sexual affair with, and bore the baby of, her thirteen-year-old male student. While the teacher went to jail, the student insisted that "we loved each other."

5. See Joel Best (1989) for an empirical example of the importance of, and problems with, statistics used to construct the "missing children" problem. See also Philip Jenkins (1994) for his examination of the data and claims for the "serial murder" problem.

6. See Connie Roser and Margaret Thompson (1995) for an empirical study demonstrating that fearful messages tend to transform low-involvement audiences into active publics wanting to do something about fearful conditions. See also David Altheide's (1997) argument that the news media promote a public-discourse of fear.

7. For empirical examples of how extreme stories become exemplars of social problems categories, see Joel Best (1990) for "missing children," John Johnson (1995) for "child abuse," and Donileen Loseke (1992) for "wife abuse."

8. Edward Albert (1989) argues that early constructions of the victims of AIDS (1982–1983) focused on how victims' lifestyles deviated from (middle-class) American values. Albert claims the homosexual men, Haitian immigrants, and intravenous drug users who were first identified as victims of AIDS can be understood as an "inventory of the powerless" (p. 43), the types of people having no claim to public resources. As another example, public opinion polls show that while about 80 percent of the general public expresses "a lot" or "some" sympathy for "people with AIDS," that figure drops to 39 percent when the disease was said to have been acquired from homosexual activity; it drops to 30 percent when said to be acquired from sharing needles while using illegal drugs (Rogers, Singer, and Imperio 1993).

9. Philip Jenkins (1994) argues that "serial murderers" have been constructed as such dangerous outsiders. Gina Petonito (1992) examines how "Japanese Americans" were constructed as such dangerous outsiders during World War II and how this construction justified internment camps. Brian Hufker and Gray Cavendar (1990) explored the changing constructions of "Mariel immigrants."

10. Ellen Paul (1994) claims that the social problem condition of "sexual harassment" was successful because Anita Hill, the "Tailhook Affair," and Senator Robert Packwood's "indiscretions" supplied a constant source of real-life happenings that could be easily constructed as graphic instances of the condition of "sexual harassment."

11. Richard Campbell claims that "60 Minutes" perfected the style of packaging news and entertainment. He quotes Don Hewitt, producer of "60 Minutes": "If we package reality as well as Hollywood packages fiction, I'll bet we could double the rating" (1991: 3).

References

Albert, Edward (1989). "AIDS and the Press: The Creation and Transformation of a Social Problem." Pp. 39–54 in *Images of Issues: Typifying Contemporary Social Problems*, edited by Joel Best. Hawthorne, NY: Aldine de Gruyter.

Altheide, David L. (1997). "The News Media, the Problem Frame and the Production of Fear." *Sociological Quarterly* 38: 645–66.

Best, Joel (1989). "Dark Figures and Child Victims: Statistical Claims About Missing Children." Pp. 21–35 in *Images of Issues: Typifying Contemporary Social Problems*, edited by Joel Best. Hawthorne, NY: Aldine de Gruyter.

———. (1990). *Threatened Children: Rhetoric and Concern about Child-Victims*. Chicago: University of Chicago Press.

Bruni, Frank (1997). "In an Age of Consent, Defining Abuse by Adults." *New York Times*, November 9, Section 3, p. 3.

Campbell, Richard (1991). *60 Minutes and the News: A Mythology for Middle America*. Urbana: University of Illinois Press.

Downs, Anthony (1972). "Up and Down with Ecology—The 'Issue Attention' Cycle." *Public Interest* 28: 38–50.

Hilgartner, Stephen, and Charles Bosk (1988). "The Rise and Fall of Social Problems: A Public Arenas Model." *American Journal of Sociology* 94: 53–78.

Hufker, Brian, and Gray Cavendar (1990). "From Freedom Flotilla to America's Burden: The Social Construction of the Mariel Immigrants." *Sociological Quarterly* 31: 321–35.

Jenkins, Philip (1994). *Using Murder: The Social Construction of Serial Homicide*. Hawthorne, NY: Aldine de Gruyter.

Johnson, John M. (1986). "The Changing Concept of Child Abuse and Its Impact on the Integrity of Family Life." Pp. 257–75 in *The American Family and the State*, edited by Joseph R. Peden and Fred R. Glahe. San Francisco: Pacific Research Institute for Public Policy.

Loseke, Donileen R. (1992). *The Battered Women and Shelters: The Social Construction of Wife Abuse*. New York: State University of New York Press.

Paul, Ellen Frankel (1994). "Sexual Harassment: A Defining Moment and Its Repercussions." Pp. 67–97 in *The Politics of Problem Definition: Shaping the Policy Agenda*, edited by David A. Rochefort and Roger W. Cobb. Lawrence: University of Kansas Press.

Petonito, Gina (1992). "Constructing 'Americans': Becoming 'American,' 'Loyalty,' and Japanese Internment during World War II." Pp. 93–108 in *Perspectives on Social Problems*, Vol. 4, edited by James A. Holstein and Gale Miller. Greenwich, CT: JAI.

Rochefort, David A., and Roger W. Cobb (1993). "Problem Definition, Agenda Access, and Policy Choice." *Policy Studies Journal* 21: 56–71.

Rogers, Theresa F., Eleanor Singer, and Jennifer Imperio (1993). "Poll Trends: AIDS-An Update." *Public Opinion Quarterly* 57: 92–114.

Roser, Connie, and Margaret Thompson (1995). "Fear Appeals and the Formation of Active Publics." *Journal of Communication* 45: 103–21.

VICTIMIZATION AND THE VICTIM INDUSTRY

Joel Best

*In 1941, Fuller said that "every social problem thus consists of an objective con-
dition and a subjective definition." He went on to say that ". . . social problems
are what people think they are [our emphasis]" (American Sociology Review, 6
[June 1941]: 320–28). In 1973, in first making the case for a constructionist
approach to the study of social problems, Spector and Kitsuse defined social
problems as a social process in which groups make claims about a "putative"
condition (Social Problems, 20 [Spring 1973]: 145–59). According to them, the
sole focus for sociological study should be the claims-making process. Joel Best,
in his 1989 critique, labeled Spector and Kitsuse's point of view as "strict constructionism" because of its lack of concern with objective conditions. Best labeled
his position and that of many other constructionists as "contextual constructionism," arguing that any theory of social problems needs to take into account the
interplay between subjective definitions and objective conditions. His piece on the
"victim industry" exemplifies his claim that objective conditions foster claims. He
shows how the civil rights movement set the stage for the victimization movement,
and how a heterogeneous array of groups, organizations, and persons, came to
discover, proselytize, and exploit the victim construction.*

Victimization has become fashionable, the focus of talk shows, political speeches,
and concerned commentaries as diverse as Alan Dershowitz's *The Abuse Excuse*
(1994), Robert Hughes's *Culture of Complaint* (1993), Wendy Kaminer's *I'm
Dysfunctional, You're Dysfunctional* (1992), and Charles Sykes's *A Nation of
Victims* (1992). Though these critics approach the topic from different directions,
they agree that claims of victimization are spreading, and they worry that this
threatens basic assumptions about personal responsibility that are fundamental
to the social order. Yet focusing on the moral consequences of claims about
victims causes most critics to overlook the social arrangements that foster those
claims.

The announcement of new forms of victimization has become commonplace
during the last twenty-five years. Journalists, activists, academics, and talk show
hosts have called attention to the neglected or unnoticed victims of marital rape,
acquaintance rape, date rape, elder abuse, sibling abuse, peer abuse, emotional
abuse, telephone abuse, clergy abuse, Satanic ritual abuse, sexual abuse, sexual
harassment, sexual addiction, love addiction, food addiction, eating disorders,

Reprinted by permission of Transaction Publishers. "Victimization and the Victim Industry" by
Joel Best, *Society* 34:4, pp. 9–17. Copyright © 1997 by Transaction, Inc.

post-traumatic stress disorder, multiple-personality disorder, chronic fatigue syndrome, false memory syndrome, credit-card dependency, codependency, dysfunctional families, hate crimes, battering, stalking, drunk driving, and UFO abductions. Some of these claims gained wide acceptance, whereas others met with considerable skepticism. But debating the merits of particular claims ignores underlying patterns in the way contemporary Americans interpret victimization. During the 1960s, Americans became sensitized to victims and victimization; by the 1970s, there was a widespread ideology of victimization. As this ideology gained acceptance in key institutions, it created a victim industry—a set of social arrangements that now supports the identification of large numbers of victims.

DISCOVERING VICTIMS IN THE 1960s

Whether human actions and experiences are best understood as products of individuals' choices or as shaped by social arrangements is a central issue in social theory. Focusing on victims discounts individuals' ability to control their own lives and emphasizes the power of social forces because victims cannot control what happens to them. Contemporary discussions of victimization have their roots in the 1960s and early 1970s, when several developments drew attention to—and reshaped attitudes toward—the social arrangements that produced victims and victimization. During this period, a broad array of activists, conservatives, liberals, therapists, lawyers, and victimologists spoke out about victims and their problems.

The civil rights movement's successes during the early 1960s inspired other social movements demanding equal rights for women, homosexuals, the disabled, the elderly, children, and others. Later movements borrowed tactics, rhetoric, and sometimes personnel from their predecessors. Typically, movement activists identified large segments of the population as victims of prejudice and discrimination (or, in more politicized language, by oppression and exploitation), described the processes of their victimization, and advocated reforms to correct the inequities.

The rhetoric of equal rights also inspired slogans about victims' rights. Many political conservatives deplored the Supreme Court decisions under Chief Justice Earl Warren extending the rights of criminal suspects and restricting police powers; the courts, they argued, protected the rights of criminals but ignored the rights of the criminals' victims. Republican political candidates began advocating victims' rights, and this rhetoric eventually spawned a victims' rights movement that demanded such reforms as victim compensation, victim impact statements, and victim allocution at sentencing and parole hearings.

The Left also adopted victim imagery. In 1971, William Ryan, a psychologist and civil rights activist, published a well-received book, *Blaming the Victim*, which focused on the problems of what would later be called the black underclass. Ryan argued that the underclass were victims of racial and class oppression and that criticizing street crime or welfare dependency amounted to blaming powerless people for their own victimization. The expression "blaming the victim" quickly took on a life of its own; Ryan's original focus on the underclass was lost, and the phrase became a rhetorical trump card, playable in almost any political contest. The notion was not new—earlier generations of psychiatrists and social workers had argued that delinquents were "victims of society"—but Ryan's rephrasing caught on. Part of its appeal may have been its ambiguity; it let one identify victims without necessarily specifying who was doing the victimizing.

Furthermore, since 1960 the ranks of mental health professionals has grown more rapidly than has the general population. Public and private medical insurance plans spread and their coverage for mental health services (for example, substance-abuse programs and personal counseling) expanded. These benefits fostered a growing number of therapeutic professionals—clinical psychologists, licensed clinical social workers, family counselors, and so on—whose eligibility to receive compensation from insurers was established in new state and federal legislation. These professionals medicalized family dynamics and other aspects of their patients' lives, often helping them interpret their experiences as forms of victimization. These therapists could apply a growing number of diagnoses; the American Psychiatric Association's *Diagnostic and Statistical Manual* (the official catalog of diagnostic categories) has grown with each revision.

Parallel developments occurred within the law, as reforms made it easier to litigate cases of alleged harms and risks. Following the U.S. Surgeon General's 1964 report on tobacco use, warnings proliferated about risks associated with a wide range of products, foods, and activities. Emerging health and consumer movements focused on those victimized by dangerous technologies, unsafe products, and inadequate regulation. Increasingly, government agencies sought to regulate risks, while hazard victims turned to the civil courts, demanding compensation for their suffering. These regulations and court cases attracted news coverage, contributing to the awareness of risk and victimization.

Increasingly, critical social scientists defined their task as exposing powerful institutions and defending society's most vulnerable members. Within criminology, a growing interest in victimization led to the emergence of victimology as a subspecialty, with its own professional societies, textbooks, and journals. Academics melded activists' calls for equal rights and victims' rights, warnings against blaming victims, therapeutic interpretations of family dynamics, and legal theories of liability into a general study of victims.

The net effect of these developments was to sensitize Americans to the plight of victims and the processes of victimization. Victim advocates argued that victims had long been neglected, even ignored. But by the mid-1970s, victims had become familiar figures on the social landscape.

THE IDEOLOGY OF VICTIMIZATION

This familiarity coalesced in an ideology of victimization, a set of widely accepted propositions about the nature of victimization. These propositions tend to be invoked piecemeal, that is, in individual campaigns by advocates drawing attention to particular kinds of victims rather than in a general theory of victimization. However, this ideology's seven central tenets underpin most contemporary claims about victims. Each proposition seems unexceptional by itself, but in combination they form a powerful ideology that makes it easy to identify large numbers of victims.

1. *Victimization is widespread.* Attempts to draw attention to social prob-

lems often emphasize the large numbers of people affected, and claims about victims routinely argue that victimization is widespread, sometimes almost ubiquitous. Thus, for example, we are told that 96 percent of families are dysfunctional or that 96 percent of the population is codependent. Even forms of victimization that might seem rare are alleged to be surprisingly common: A national survey suggested that 1 in 50 adults shows signs of having been abducted by UFOs.

Claims that victimization is common often depend upon broad definitions. Horror stories—especially severe and clear-cut examples—serve to focus attention on a category of victims, but the problem is defined in much broader terms. The problem's domain often expands once the initial claims gain widespread acceptance. Thus, for example, the contemporary campaign against child abuse first addressed the "battered-child syndrome" (typified by severe beatings of very young children); the acceptance of child abuse as a social problem then laid a foundation for expanding its domain to include neglect, sexual abuse, emotional abuse, and so on. Similarly, post-traumatic stress disorder (PTSD) originated as a diagnosis for combat-related psychiatric problems of Vietnam veterans; but the notion of "traumatic stress" proved remarkably flexible, and the PTSD label is now applied to victims whose experiences range from battering and incest to receiving contaminated fast food. Broad definitions, of course, help justify large estimates for the extent of victimization. If the domain of sexual violence includes flashing and "touching assaults by relatively young boys," then the proportion of females who have been victims of sexual violence will be far greater than if some narrower definition is applied.

2. *Victimization is consequential.* Even a single, brief incident can have consequences that extend throughout the victim's life. One analysis of sexual abuse, for instance, warns that one childhood experience of being flashed or fondled "can have profound and long-term consequences." Victimization's consequences are fundamentally psychological: The victim experiences anxiety, doubt, fear, or other psychological reactions. While victims may have impaired social relationships, the root cause of these problems is not social forces but lasting psychological damage. This characterization invites the medicalization of victimization, since therapists presumably have the appropriate knowledge and skills for treating psychological problems. The theme of lasting consequences is central to the claims of intergenerational victimization—cycles of abuse in which abused children become abusive parents—that have inspired movements of adult children (and grandchildren) of alcoholics, abusive parents, and divorced couples. These reverberating effects further support claims that victimization is widespread. If apparently minor incidents can be consequential, then victimization should be defined broadly.

3. *Relationships between victims and their victimizers are relatively straightforward and unambiguous.* Most claims about victims describe victimization as exploitative encounters between a victimizer who takes advantage and a victim who suffers. Usually, the perpetrator is portrayed as more powerful than the victim, more aware of the exploitative nature of their relationship, and more responsible for the victimization. In this view, victimization is morally unambiguous: The victimizer is exploitative, the victim innocent.

In practice, people identified as victimizers may dispute that characterization, and even people labeled victims may be unsure whether an offense "really" occurred (as suggested by the title of an influential book on date rape, *I Never Called It Rape*). Victim advocates define these denials and uncertainty as part of the pattern of victimization. Where those involved may see ambiguity, advocates perceive clear-cut, unambiguous exploitation. They make few distinctions among forms of victimization, emphasizing the similarities between, say, forcible rape and date rape rather than exploring any differences.

4. *Victimization often goes unrecognized.* If victimization is common, consequential, and clear-cut, it should be a visible, prominent part of social life. But victim advocates argue that victimization often goes unrecognized and unacknowledged, not only by the larger society but even by the victims themselves.

Society may simply be unaware of victimization. New ways of thinking about some form of victimization or new evidence or a new willingness of victims to speak up can make a neglected social problem visible. In this view, identifying new types of victims reflects social progress, as a more enlightened society gives victimization the attention it deserves. According to more critical advocates, language, culture, and institutional arrangements obscure victims' suffering. For example, feminists argue that the patriarchy discounts the significance of women's victimization and activists denounce police failures to treat hate crimes seriously.

Victimization also may be deliberately concealed. Some claims describe victimization concealed by numerous or powerful actors, such as a million-member Satanic blood-cult conducting undetected human sacrifices or highly advanced aliens in UFOs experimenting on abducted victims. But secrecy does not require great conspiracies. Offenders may convince individual victims, for example, sexually abused children, to keep the experience secret; if such secrets are widespread, then their sum may be collective invisibility.

Beyond society's failure to acknowledge victims, victims themselves may not recognize victimization for what it is. They may define victimization too narrowly, or they may be ashamed, afraid, or otherwise unwilling to reveal their victimization to others. Some therapists argue that many victims cannot remember their experiences, that a common response to the trauma of victimization is to repress memories of the experience (see Richard Ofshe and Ethan Watters, "Making Monsters," *Society*, March 1993). These victims cannot recall or acknowledge being victimized; they are "in denial." Here again, victimization is portrayed as a psychological problem requiring medical treatment.

5. *Individuals must be taught to recognize others' and their own victimization.* Because victimization often goes unrecognized by both victims and the larger society, people must be educated. Potential victims may need preventive education, such as "stranger, danger" and "good touch, bad touch" programs designed to warn preschoolers about abduction and sexual abuse or campus campaigns to make college students aware of—and help them avoid—date rape. Other educational efforts seek to inform the larger society about particular forms of victimization. Newsmagazine feature stories, talk shows, made-for-TV movies, and other press and entertainment genres regularly present information about victims; these treatments routinely adopt the views promoted by victim advocates.

In addition to educational programs aimed at potential victims or the general public, advocates seek to teach victims to recognize, acknowledge, and address their victimization. Therapy and support groups offer ways to deal with one's victimization—once the individual acknowledges that victimization has occurred. But what of those victims said to be in denial, unaware that some prior, now-forgotten victimization continues to trouble them? Though these individuals cannot recall their victimization, they are often aware that something is amiss.

Those unaware of their own victimization must be helped to recognize and identify the root of their problems. Victim advocates offer checklists of symptoms to help diagnose prior victimization. Thus, for example, adult children of alcoholics may "have difficulty following a project through from beginning to end," "feel they are different from other people," and "are either super responsible or super irresponsible"; codependents may "feel angry, victimized, unappreciated, and used," "blame themselves for everything," "come from troubled, repressed, or dysfunctional families," or "deny their family was troubled, repressed, or dysfunctional"; while child victims of ritual abuse may be preoccupied with urine, feces, and flatulation, be clingy, resist authority, destroy toys, or have nightmares. These inventories of symptoms may be lengthy; Melody Beattie's best-selling book *Codependent No More* lists more than 230 characteristics of codependents. Sometimes advocates' lists specify contradictory symptoms. For instance, a review of various guidelines for identifying sexually abused children notes: "Some believe . . . that a reluctance to disclose is characteristic of a true allegation, while others look for spontaneity in the child's disclosure as an index of veracity."

Of course, many—probably most—people display several symptoms on these lists yet deny having been victimized. To victim advocates, a denial of prior victimization may be just another symptom. Regarding her recently recovered memories of childhood sexual abuse, comedienne Roseanne declared: "When someone asks you, 'Were you sexually abused as a child,' there's only two answers. One of them is, 'Yes,' and one of them is, 'I don't know.' You can't say no." Similarly, a failure to display symptoms need not be significant; the review of guidelines for identifying sexual abuse warns: "The absence of positive indicators does not mean the child hasn't been sexually abused." Within such diagnostic frameworks, claims of victimization are easily made but difficult to dismiss. Coupled with the claim that victimization is widespread, these frameworks justify a suspicion that virtually anyone might be victim.

Such checklists of symptoms merely raise the possibility that someone is a victim; confirming this possibility requires additional investigation. Sometimes, the therapist's task is defined as helping the victim "recover the memories" of victimization. Critics note that transcripts of therapists' conversations with patients sometimes reveal leading questions and other tactics that encourage patients to acknowledge their victimization. Or therapists may adopt special techniques to elicit memories of victimization, including hypnosis, play with dolls or puppets, massage, and fantasizing. These methods are often successful. As *The Courage to Heal*, a popular guidebook for survivors of child sexual abuse, notes: "Assume your feelings are valid. So far, no one we've talked to thought she might have been abused, and then later discovered that she hadn't been. The progression always goes the other way, from suspicion to confirmation. If you think you were abused and your life shows the symptoms, then you were." The belief that victimization is widespread but largely hidden justifies extraordinary measures to identify individuals who have been victimized and to encourage them to acknowledge and address their victimization.

6. *Claims of victimization must be respected.* Once individuals learn, via education or therapeutic intervention, to recognize their victimization, their claims to be victims must not be challenged. Victim advocates insist that it takes great courage to step forward and acknowledge one's victimization, that such individuals take a precarious stand against the institutional forces that promote and conceal widespread victimization. Injunctions against challenging claims of victimization often warn against "blaming the victim"; victims have already suffered, and calling their claims into question can only constitute further victimization.

Advocates often argue that skepticism is unwarranted, asserting that some victims' claims should be seen as true by definition (for example, early activists sometimes insisted that children never lie about being sexually abused) or at least that there is no reason for individuals to make false claims about being victimized. Or advocates may suggest that similarities in the stories of many victims (for example, accounts of Satanic ritual abuse or UFO abduction) constitute strong evidence for the stories' truth. Memories of victimization that have been recovered through hypnosis or other therapeutic techniques receive validation from therapists who insist that these techniques elicit reliable information, that challenges are unwarranted and unfair, and that society should support the claims of vulnerable, innocent victims.

7. *The term "victim" has undesirable connotations.* Some advocates reject the very term "victim" on the grounds that it carries negative connotations of being damaged, passive, and powerless. They prefer more positive, "empowering" terms, such as "survivor," "adult child," "recovering," or even "persons" (for example, "persons with AIDS"). This renaming affirms that victimization occurred, while possibly serving to reduce individuals' reluctance to define themselves or others as victims. In addition, to the degree that these category names derive from therapeutic discourse, they offer further medical or scientific legitimacy to claims of victim status.

These seven ideological propositions appear routinely in contemporary discussions of victimization. Combined, they form an extremely powerful ideology, one that encourages identifying and labeling victims: It defines victimization as common, serious, morally unambiguous, yet largely unrecognized; it justifies methods to identify individuals (and help those individuals recognize themselves) as victims; it delegitimizes doubts about victims' claims; and it provides new, nonstigmatizing labels for those who have suffered.

Again, there is no overarching "victims movement"; rather, advocates address particular forms of victimization. Typically, these campaigns begin modestly, with the initial claims addressing clear-cut, outrageous instances of exploitation. Then, after these initial claims gain acceptance, the problem's domain expands to incorporate other cases. Thus, for example, early claims about sexual harassment focused on instances in which female workers' jobs were overtly threatened unless they complied with their male supervisors' sexual demands. Once sexual harassment gained recognition as a social problem, advocates began expanding its domain to include a broader range of behaviors and conditions, including "conduct that creates an intimidating, hostile, or offensive environment." Such domain expansion is self-reinforcing: Expanded definitions support claims of larger problems; larger problems justify increased attention; and increased attention in turn encourages further expanding the problem's domain.

INSTITUTIONAL RESPONSES TO VICTIMIZATION

Ideologies exist within institutional contexts, receiving more or less ratification and support from different institutions. Campaigns drawing attention to new forms of victimization seek recognition in several institutional arenas. Typically, advocates' initial appeals are sensitizing: They seek to draw an institution's attention to victims whose plights have been neglected. Once an institution acknowledges these victims, advocates call for accommodations to integrate victims' needs within the existing institutional structure. When such accommodation is deemed insufficient, advocates may call for institutional changes—significant alterations to meet the victims' needs.

Typically, the responses to sensitization—accommodation and change—have seemed modest; advocates sought particular reforms to protect particular victims from particular abuses. Thus, a state might pass a law to extend the period within which victims of sexual abuse can file charges or sue for damages, so that adults who recover memories of abuse can bring cases against their abusers, or a university might require all faculty to attend workshops on sexual harassment. Though each reform is limited, taken together they represent considerable institutional support for the ideology of victimization. This support extends across several major institutions, including law, the medical and therapeutic professions, academia, the mass media, and the recovery movement.

Law. Because much of the law concerns protecting individuals against exploitation, it becomes an important institutional arena for claims about victimization. The contemporary ideology of victimization has influenced the law's various facets, including legislation, the criminal justice and court systems, and legal scholarship.

Advocates often call for new laws prohibiting the exploitation of victims or requiring reporting of victimization. For example, following actress Rebecca Schaeffer's well-publicized murder by a fan, claims that stalking was widespread led to California's passing of an antistalking law in 1990. Within two years, forty-seven other states and the District of Columbia had similar laws, and Congress has ordered the National Institute of Justice to devise a model antistalking code and was considering proposals to make stalking a federal crime. Similarly, several states have added a "victims' bill of rights" to their constitutions; state and federal law enforcement agencies have been ordered to collect data on hate crimes; and state laws requiring reporting of various forms of child abuse continue to expand.

In addition to calling for new laws, victim advocates criticize the legal system's failure to protect individuals from victimization, as well as its further failure to treat victims appropriately once they complain to legal authorities. Thus, the criminal justice system's insensitive treatment of victims of rape and child sexual abuse (for example, not responding to all complaints, investigating some allegations with skepticism, and subjecting complainants to humiliating courtroom interrogations) represent a "second rape" or a "second form of child abuse." In this view, the law discourages victims, blames them for their suffering, forces them to humiliate themselves, and then fails to deliver justice. Such claims have inspired reforms to make the legal system more accessible to and protective of victims, ranging from relatively minor accommodations (such as letting child victims testify while seated in child-size chairs) to more substantial institutional changes (such as prohibiting or limiting the cross-examination of child victims giving testimony). The criminal justice system's relatively elaborate arrangements for preserving the rights of defendants (viewed as victimizers by victim advocates) have inspired growing interest in victims using the less restrictive civil courts to bring suits.

Many of these legislative and procedural reforms find support in law schools and law reviews. New claims about victimization often receive sympathetic treatment, as legal scholars recommend ways to modify the law to redress victims' grievances. Though scholars do not agree on all issues (there has, for example, been considerable debate over how to balance the rights of complainants and defendants in sexual abuse trials), many members of law school faculties—and legislatures and courts—accept elements of the ideology of victimization.

The Medical and Therapeutic Professions.   Many advocates medicalize victimization, defining treatment as the appropriate response and assigning therapeutic professionals ownership of these social problems. Medicalization carries scientific authority; claims couched in medical language seem almost beyond questioning or criticism. A diverse set of professionals receive this scientific imprimatur, as the medical model—usually associated with physicians, psychiatrists, and perhaps clinical psychologists—has spread throughout the "helping professions." Those who treat victims may have been trained in various disciplines, including social work, family counseling, education, and health science, and their treatment practices may be guided by various other ideologies, ranging from fundamentalist Christianity to feminism. Some therapists are "professional ex's," individuals with little formal training who, having recovered from victimization, have now begun careers helping others into recovery. Some specialize in identifying and helping particular types of victims (such as helping victims of Satanic ritual abuse to recover those memories), while others address a broad range of problems.

Many of the medical experts who work with victims argue that their principal responsibility is to their patients rather than to abstract principles of inquiry. This rationale justifies therapeutic practices which some critics argue are inconsistent with scientific objectivity or criminal investigations. For example, therapists interviewing children thought to have been sexually abused may use leading questions to elicit acknowledgment of abuse and justify this practice as a necessary therapeutic step, or therapists may urge patients to ignore doubts and ambiguity when acknowledging their victimization. Such practices, justified as therapeutically necessary, distinguish much treatment of victims from traditional medical or scientific inquiry.

Medicalized discussions often focus on the harms experienced by the victims while largely ignoring the victimizers. Whereas earlier psychiatric claims medicalized deviants (such as sexual psychopaths), contemporary claims medicalize victims (such as survivors of sexual abuse). When deviance is deemed extraordinary, we search for explanations in the peculiarities of offenders, but when victimization is seen as commonplace, victimizers seem less remarkable, simply part of an oppressive social system.

Academia. The ideology of victimization also has made significant inroads into education. The need to educate victims, potential victims, and society at large is central to the ideology. Because victimization often occurs during childhood, teachers are encouraged to attend workshops to learn how to teach students to recognize victimization. Within higher education, enthusiasm for the ideology of victimization seems greatest in the helping professions, such as social work, health education, educational counseling, family relations, criminal justice, and child development programs. Students trained in these fields learn to identify and respond to a range of human problems, and claims about victimization are presented as up-to-date knowledge with useful applications. Victims become the subjects of lectures, classes, term papers, theses, and dissertations. Researchers may find foundations and government agencies eager to fund research on victimization, conferences and professional associations emerge as forums for inquiry, and the proliferation of scholarly publishing has produced specialized journals devoted to studying victims (for example, *Dissociation* publishes studies of multiple-personality disorder). Of course, the audience for these conferences and journals largely endorses victimization claims. Concern with victims also appears in more scholarly disciplines, especially in feminist writings, and women's studies programs often provide leadership for on-campus advocacy. Many campuses develop programs to educate or protect students from victimization. Like medicalization, academics' support gives authority to claims about victims.

Mass Media. Most advocates depend upon the mass media to disseminate their claims to the public. In general, claims about victims receive sympathetic coverage in the press, in popular culture, and, most especially, in the talk shows, made-for-TV movies, and other genres that combine news and entertainment. Claims about victims tend to fit the media's template for social problems coverage: They can be typified in dramatic terms (an innocent victim beset by an exploitative villain); they seem relevant (if victimization is widespread, then many people are, might become, or at least have ties to victims); they offer hope (via the intervention of authority figures from law, medicine, or academia); and they lack unacceptable political overtones (so long as the claims focus on the individual victimizer rather than on the social system—for example, patriarchy or the class system—as producing the victimization). Moreover, because most advocates depict victimization as straightforward exploitation and because most claims arouse little organized opposition, the media typically feel no obligation to "balance" their coverage by presenting "both sides" of the issue. Changing media structures also have worked to the advocates' advantage. Cable and satellite delivery have caused television channels to proliferate; broadcasters need relatively inexpensive, relatively popular offerings to fill these channels, and talk shows and "reality shows" (like *America's Most Wanted*) meet these requirements. These genres frequently cover claims about victimization.

The Recovery Movement.   U.S. culture has a long fascination with self-help. In recent years, the self-help movement—and Alcoholics Anonymous in particular—has inspired numerous campaigns to help victims recover. This recovery movement has many facets: twelve-step groups, weekend workshops and conferences, lecture tours, and publishers who generate books, pamphlets, magazines, and audio-and videotapes filled with inspirational advice. During the 1980s, most bookstores opened substantial sections devoted to "Recovery." By 1990, nearly three hundred bookstores sold nothing but recovery movement literature, featuring separate sections devoted to alcoholism, adult children of alcoholics, codependency, and so on. The popularity of recovery movement literature seems to transcend otherwise important ideological divisions: Recovery sections can be found in both women's bookstores and Christian book shops. The recovery movement often provides a grass-roots embodiment of claims about victims; it offers continual socialization for both neophytes and experienced members, links victims to experts, and often inspires media coverage.

Other institutional supports for victims' claims include policies promoted by government agencies, religious bodies, and private industry. Again, these involve many parallel movements, each promoting recognition of a particular type of victim, each seeking particular reforms within particular institutions. Some campaigns have been more successful than others; issues such as sexual abuse, stalking, and sexual harassment have received widespread institutional validation, whereas, aside from the well-publicized claims of Harvard professor John Mack, victims of UFO abductions have found relatively few visible supporters in law, medicine, and academia. But the overall pattern is clear: Several major institutions respond sympathetically to the ideology of victimization.

THE VICTIM INDUSTRY

The ideology of victimization, when coupled with institutional support for that ideology, makes it possible to label large numbers of victims. Studies of witchhunts and political purges speak of social control as an "industry," engaged in the "manufacturing" or the "mass production" of deviants. Analogously, we may speak of a contemporary victim industry mass producing victims. According to Elliott Currie, the great European witchhunt had three key organizational characteristics that fostered the discovery of many thousands of witches: (1) The witchhunters faced few restraints from other social institutions; (2) They had few internal restraints on their powers; and (3) They had a vested interest in identifying witches. Analogous arrangements support the victim industry's campaign to identify large numbers of victims.

Absence of External Restraints.   Because the contemporary ideology of victimization has been accepted and incorporated by key institutions, victim advocates face little external opposition. For instance, individuals being treated for some form of victimization may find that their claims—and the claims of their therapists—are protected by sympathetic laws, ratified by academics, depicted favorably in the mass media, and endorsed by the recovery movement. The ideological prohibition against challenging victims' claims further discourages skepticism. Moreover, because identifying victims is defined as beneficial, both to the individual being identified and to the society at large, there is no obvious source of resistance.

It is significant that advocates often demand support for victims while largely ignoring victimizers. Some victimizers cannot be identified: the stranger-rapist who was never apprehended; the unfamiliar adult Satanists who abused the victim as a child; or even extraterrestrial aliens. But for many forms of victimization rooted in family dynamics, the victimizers' identities are presumably known. Yet so long as advocates do not identify and denounce particular people as victimizers, few people have cause to oppose claims about victimization. Thus, for example, claims about recovered memories of Satanic ritual abuse faced little opposition until victims began bringing suits against their relatives for childhood abuse. At that point, a countermovement, the False Memory Syndrome Foundation, emerged. But this is an exception: Relatively few victims' movements generate well-organized opposition because relatively few specify their opponents. Most movements face few external restraints.

Absence of Internal Restraints. The contemporary ideology of victimization offers many alternative ways of identifying victims: long lists of symptoms indicative of victimization, rationales for doubting individuals' denials of victimization, and so on. Moreover, this ideology is endorsed by people with impressive credentials: therapists, lawyers, academics, and professional ex's. Defined as experts, they can influence discussions of putative victimization. Because victimization is often hidden and because these experts have the means to discover and reveal it, their assessments become authoritative. Moreover, under their ideology, these individuals have a right—even an obligation—to label individuals as victims and guide them into accepting that label. Since advocates see themselves as helping both the victim and the larger society understand the truth, they have little reason to question their own actions. The knowledge and techniques needed to detect otherwise hidden victimization give these advocates extraordinary powers to label others as victims, even when those individuals deny that the labels fit. At the same time, the ideology of victimization offers few internal restraints on such labeling.

Vested Interests. Participants in the victim industry often have a stake in the identification of victims. Advocates' vested interests include enhanced prestige and influence for themselves and their professions, supportive validation from important social institutions, and, at least among those therapists who label on a fee-for-service basis, increased income. In addition, some people benefit from being identified as victims: They become professional ex's, write books, travel on the lecture circuit, appear on talk shows, receive praise and favorable attention, and even get treated as experts in their own right. They may become victim-celebrities (known for their experiences as victims)—some, of course, are also celebrity victims (that is, established celebrities who reveal their victimization, such as Roseanne). In short, both those doing the labeling and those being labeled often benefit from the process.

Obviously, the contemporary concern for victims is not a witchhunt. Yet the organizational features that supported large-scale witchhunting also make the victim industry productive. Problems that psychiatrists considered relatively rare twenty or thirty years ago (such as incest or multiple-personality disorder) have been redefined as relatively common conditions, and those labels are often applied. The net effect of the victim industry has been the identification of many thousands of victims.

WHY VICTIMS?

No doubt many of the similarities among contemporary victim movements reflect advocates' awareness of one another; rhetoric and methods proven effective in one campaign are borrowed and used to draw attention to other forms of victimization. But this begs a larger question: Why do claims about victims strike a responsive chord in contemporary society? Why are so many kinds of victims being identified at this time and in this society?

The contemporary concern for victims began during the 1960s, when established status hierarchies weakened. Challenges from below—from blacks, women, students, homosexuals, and so on—questioned the legitimacy of existing status arrangements. Talking about victims was often an effective way of pressing these claims. Victimization dramatized the illegitimacy of social arrangements that allowed the exploitation of the vulnerable. Advocates used the ideology of victimization not only to draw attention to specific social problems but also to challenge existing hierarchies. What sort of society fostered and then ignored widespread victimization? Calls to protect victims were also bids to raise the status of those vulnerable to victimization, and victim advocacy was often tied to broader social movements, such as the women's movement.

In addition, victim movements offer a contemporary answer to fundamental, primal issues that every culture must address—issues of justice and evil. Social order is society's most basic accomplishment. But in every society, order sometimes breaks down. Some people do the right thing, but they do not get their just rewards. Other people break the rules. Social control attempts to right these wrongs and restore order to the social system.

In most societies during most of recorded history, punishment has been central to social control. Society roots out the rule breakers, the deviants, and the evildoers and dispenses justice by punishing them. But during the twentieth century, we have become increasingly suspicious of these traditional practices. We favor a rational, scientific point of view, and we suspect that evil is a superstitious notion and that punishment is a barbaric method of achieving justice.

The social sciences bear a good deal of responsibility here. They are in the business of explaining social patterns, of identifying causes and their effects, and they have diligently tried to understand the causes of deviance. But the social scientific perspective on deviance doesn't translate terribly well into social policy. The sticking point, of course, is the notion—fundamental to law—of responsibility. If we can point to the causes of deviant behavior, how can we hold the deviant responsible? Is it just to blame deviants for rule breaking when we believe that their deviance is caused by social conditions? Note the term "blame"—it is central to much social control but largely foreign to social science.

This reveals the attractions of talking about victims. Talking about victims can avoid many of the conflicts between the social scientific and social policy perspectives raised in debates over deviants. To social scientists, victims can be understood as the effects of causal processes. But, as advocates continually warn, social policy must sympathize with—support—victims, not blame them. This helps explain why victims movements tend to gloss over the victimizers. Once advocates start identifying victimizers, they're back in the messy, divisive business of trying to both understand and blame deviants. So long as they stay focused on the victims, advocates can hope to win consensus.

This explanation suggests that victim movements may have more than organizational features in common with witchhunting. The victim plays a symbolic role in our society, not unlike the role played by witches during the witch craze. Both allow society to identify evil and injustice. In societies that interpret events in religious terms, witches consorting with the demonic can explain all sorts of problems. Similarly, our contemporary society, which seeks to understand the world in rational, scientific terms, finds processes of victimization useful explanations for all sorts of contemporary ills. In this way, new victims answer old questions.

CULTURE AND THE CASE OF CHILD SEXUAL ABUSE

Katherine Beckett

Beckett studies stages in the media career of child sexual abuse. She analyzed articles in news magazines about child sexual abuse that had appeared over three different five-year periods. She found that different groups predominated as the claimants during each period and that they had different themes about who the "victims" were and what needed to be done about the problem. She found that personnel in the "child abuse industry" were the dominant claimants during the first five-year period, depicting children as victims and proclaiming the need for the public to end its collective denial of the problem. During the second five-year period, professionals and academics became the principal claimants and more often turned on its head the construction of who the offender was—depicting alleged child victims as the actual offenders (through coaching by their elders and false accusations). During the third five-year period, it was adult survivors and celebrities who became dominant as claimants recalling their victimization

From Katherine Beckett, "Culture and the Politics of Signification: The Case of Child Sexual Abuse," *Social Problems*, 43: 57–76. Copyright © 1996. Reprinted by permission of The Society for the Study of Social Problems and the author.

in childhood and urging others to break the silence. Beckett also describes what
it is that makes some claimants more successful than others in promoting their
issue.

Child abuse did not receive a significant degree of attention in the United States
until the 1960s. Private child-protection specialists and the American Humane
Society facilitated this "discovery" by highlighting the problem of child neglect
in the 1950s (Nelson 1984), but it was pediatric radiologists with X-rays documenting extensive damage to children's limbs who catapulted the issue of physical
child abuse to the front pages (Nelson 1984; Pfohl 1977). In the late 1940s
doctors attributed children's broken bones, bruises, and other injuries to "internal
medical causes," but by the early 1960s they were diagnosed as evidence of
"battered child syndrome" (Pfohl 1977).

By 1962 the Children's Bureau was highly involved in the issue of physical
child abuse, and physicians played a leading role in the determination of "steps
which could be taken to control child abuse" (Nelson 1984:42). One of the bureau's first policy recommendations was the development of a model child abuse
reporting law. With the help of the mass media, which paid particular attention
to the most brutal instances of abuse, public concern about abuse grew dramatically (Nelson 1984). Between 1963 and 1967, all states and the District of Columbia passed legislation mandating that teachers, doctors, and other professionals report suspected child abuse to authorities (Nelson 1984). In an effort to
make these laws more consistent, the federal government passed the Child Abuse
Prevention and Treatment Act (CAPTA) in 1974 requiring that states adopt a
uniform definition of abuse in order to qualify for federal monies. Federal authorities specifically mentioned "sexual abuse" when listing the types of behaviors
that constituted abuse. As a result of these reporting laws, the number of cases
of suspected abuse—both physical and sexual—reported to authorities has increased dramatically (Finkelhor 1990; Nelson 1984), and more of these cases
enter the legal system every year (Myers 1993).

As was discussed earlier, advocates of CAPTA quite self-consciously adopted
a narrow construction of child abuse that ignored the social and economic conditions associated with child abuse[1] (Nelson 1984). At the same time, this legislation identified sexual abuse as a category of behavior about which the government was concerned. The inclusion of sexual misconduct in the federal
government's definition of abusive behaviors was largely the result of the activities of feminists, psychologists, and social workers (Weisberg 1984). While feminist concern about child abuse grew out of a larger critique of patriarchal family
arrangements and sexual violence, mental health professionals offered a less political analysis of the issue. These professionals viewed "sexually inappropriate"
behavior as a symptom of a distorted family homeostasis and advocated treatment
and family counseling (Weisberg 1984). These differences aside, the inclusion of
"sexual abuse" as a category of behavior covered by CAPTA undoubtedly contributed to increased reports and was an important precondition for the development of public awareness of the issue (Finkelhor 1990; Myers 1993).

Media coverage of the issue of sexual abuse gradually increased throughout the 1970s, but it was not until the 1980s that significant media attention was accorded this topic. Following the arrests of 24 alleged members of a "sex ring" in Jordan, Minnesota, in late 1983 and the emergence of the McMartin Preschool case in March 1984, media interest in the topic increased dramatically.

METHODS AND ISSUE PACKAGES

In what follows, "frame analysis" techniques are used to identify the culturally available issue frames that shape discussions of child sexual abuse and to trace each of their careers in the mass media. Issue frames consist of discursive elements organized into what William Gamson calls "interpretive packages" (1992; Gamson and Modigliani 1987; Gamson and Lasch 1983). These "packages" consist of linguistic and symbolic resources that make sense of and give meaning to one or more aspects of social issues such as child sexual abuse. This methodology is thus primarily concerned with the cultural images and associations different issue packages create and connote. In addition, by identifying the "signature elements" of all culturally available issue frames and enumerating the frequency with which their components appear in the mass media, the prominence and fate of each package in public discourse may be traced (Gamson 1992; Gamson and Modigliani 1987; Gamson and Lasch 1983). It is important to note that issue packages do not reflect the objective structure of the discourse on child abuse, but are heuristic devices used to describe representations of this issue (Gamson and Modigliani 1987).

Identification of Child Sexual Abuse Issue Packages

In order to identify all culturally available packages, I analyzed a wide range of specialized publications. These included materials produced by various grass-roots associations (such as the North American Man-Boy Love Association. Victims of Child Abuse Laws, the Incest Survivors Network, and the False Memory Syndrome Foundation), as well as articles appearing in specialized journals such as *The Nation*, *Society*, and *The Family Networker* and more mainstream magazines. On the basis of these materials, three main culturally available issue packages were identified.

The "core frame" and "core position" of each culturally available child sexual abuse package are described below, as are the "reasoning devices" that justify each of them. These devices include a causal analysis of the issue in question, appeals to principles contained within the package, and an assessment of policy consequences. Other devices used to suggest a frame include: exemplars (events that illustrate a key point); catchphrases (thematic statements or slogans that suggest a particular frame); and depictions (characterizations of relevant subjects). These signature elements make up the "signature matrix" of the various issue packages (see Gamson and Lasch 1983:399–401).

For two of the three cultural packages, I also identified "sub-packages," or variants of the parent package. These sub-packages share the position and frame of their parent package and are thus largely consistent with its analysis and imagery. Typically, however, these sub-packages identify a different "root" problem, make different (but not incompatible) policy recommendations, and entail somewhat distinct imagery from their parent package. The packages and sub-packages are described and summarized in Table 1.

Child Sexual Abuse Issue Packages[2]

Positive Pedophilia. The hysteria around child abuse is a symptom of an outdated approach to sexuality; our Victorian legacy is what informs opposition to adult-child sexual relations. Children are sexual beings and should "be given the liberty to run their own lives as they choose, including the ability to determine how and with whom they should have sex" (Rhodes 1988:294). Children often seek and initiate sexual relations with adults. Adult-child sexual relations are therefore not necessarily exploitative or traumatic, but may be helpful to or empowering for children: "A childhood sexual experience, such as being the partner of an older person, need not necessarily affect the child adversely" (quoted in *Time*, April 14, 1980:72). Our sexual prudishness does not give the state the right to deprive children of their sexual freedom or to harass those who have unpopular sexual preferences.

Collective Denial. Society denies the reality of child sexual abuse. Children are uniquely vulnerable victims, and, contrary to some claims, are not able to give informed consent. Because recognizing this reality would force us to rethink some of our most cherished institutions and bring us face to face with the dark side of human nature, the truth about child abuse is resisted. The fact that well-respected and socially prominent persons perpetrate this crime threatens our collective sense of security and is therefore particularly disturbing. Claims of abuse have been denied for too long as a result of our unwillingness to face this unpleasant reality. Both children and adults are likely to downplay or hide these painful experiences rather than exaggerate or make up stories of abuse. The problem is therefore under-reporting, not over-reporting. Our unwillingness to face the reality of child abuse means that violations of children rarely make it into the criminal justice system, and when they do, justice is not typically served.

Male Prerogative. This explicitly feminist version of Collective Denial emphasizes the fact that it is overwhelmingly men who are responsible for sexual assaults against children (and women). The widespread nature of child sexual abuse is seen as a consequence of male dominance and socialization: "Men, in learning to become men, learn that they have the right to be sexually and emotionally serviced by women; they learn that their power can ensure that this happens; and that in order to feel like a man, they have to feel powerful" (MacLeod and Saraga 1987:24). Reports of abuse by women and children are easily dismissed as "hysteria" in patriarchal culture. It is only by challenging male dominance both inside and outside the home that the problem of child sexual abuse will be diminished.

Survivors Speak. A second Collective Denial sub-package focuses on the viability of repressed and recovered memories of abuse. Because "the child [often] forgets because remembering is simply too painful" (*Newsweek*, October 7, 1991: 71), memories of abuse often surface during adulthood. The memories of incest, ritual abuse, and all child abuse survivors must be treated respectfully rather than dismissed as the result of suggestion, fantasy, or delusion. Denying their validity and attacking therapists who help to uncover them is simply another means by which the reality of sexual abuse is denied. Because the tragedies of incest and child abuse are perpetuated by silence and denial, it is crucial that adult survivors of abuse speak out and that the reality of their experiences be affirmed.

False Accusations. While no one condones child abuse, concern about child sexual abuse now borders on hysteria. The pendulum has swung too far as panicky parents, intrusive child protective workers, over-zealous therapists, and assorted "victims" cry "abuse." Accusations are made all too easily and cannot be accepted at face value. Both children's and adults' perceptions and memories are fallible and vulnerable to suggestion, and the methods used to uncover these are highly suspect. Furthermore, a "culture of abuse" now exists in which children may use allegations of abuse to gain power over adults and in which adults assume that mental distress must be the consequence of "abuse." The consequences of being wrongly accused have destroyed many innocent people's lives. Protections must be built into the system in order to prevent the harm caused by unfounded accusations.

Official Misconduct. In this False Accusations sub-package, child protective personnel, prosecutors, social workers, and therapists are depicted as part of a "child abuse industry." This industry operates on the basis of the "presumption of guilt" and has eroded parental rights and authority. Most disturbing is the absence of due process and the use of unsound techniques by child welfare personnel. Children will attempt to please social workers and others who "want" to hear that they have been abused. The use of suggestive interviewing techniques has therefore produced a raft of unfounded allegations.[3] False allegations are also common in custody battles; these cases further illustrate the importance of enhancing procedural and legal protections within the child welfare bureaucracy, family courts, and criminal justice system.

False Memories. The focus of this False Accusations sub-package is the falseness of adult survivors' "recovered" memories of abuse, the role of mental health professionals in creating these memories, and on the fallibility of memory/perception in general. "Memories" of incest and abuse recovered during adulthood provide a *raison d'etre* for therapists and a simple explanation for complex problems and symptoms. "Memories" of ritual or satanic abuse are particularly dubious and thus illustrate the fallibility of memory. Laws that allow for the inclusion of "repressed" and "recovered" memories of abuse in civil and criminal trials are unsupported by empirical evidence demonstrating the validity of the concept of repression, and they have led to the unnecessary destruction of many innocent lives.

Content Analysis

While frame analysis techniques seek to elucidate the meaning systems available for talking about social issues, content analysis generates more specific information about the content of media stories. I therefore used content analysis to obtain data regarding the descriptive characteristics of persons involved in inci-

Table 1 Signature Matrix of Child Sexual Abuse Issue Packages

Package	Frame	Position	Roots	Principles	Policies	Exemplars	Catchphrases	Depictions
POSITIVE PEDOPHILIA	The issue is how to liberate children so that they are free to express themselves sexually.	By prohibiting all adult-child sexual contact, we deprive children of their rights.	Much of the concern about "abuse" reflects our prudishness and Victorianism.	Children are entitled to human rights, including the right to express themselves sexually.	Decriminalization of consensual adult-child sexual relations would promote the liberation of children.	Past prohibitions of other, currently tolerated sexual behaviors (such as masturbation)	The New Victorians: children's rights	Opponents are depicted as old-fashioned and prudish.
COLLECTIVE DENIAL	The issue is how to deal with and respond to the problem of sexual abuse.	We deny rather than exaggerate the prevalence and seriousness of sexual abuse.	Our resistance to recognizing and dealing with the problem is what perpetuates it.	Abuse is an immoral misuse of power; our silence makes us all culpable.	Policies that relax restrictions on children's testimony and recovered memories help bring justice to victims.	Stories of victim's pain: statistics indicating the widespread nature of abuse; stories of denial	Denial; epidemic backlash	Opponents are depicted as part of a backlash against the movement to speak out about abuse.
MALE PREROGATIVE (CD sub-package)	Same as CD	Same as CD	Child sexual abuse has its roots in the patriarchal family and male socialization.	The oppression and abuse of women and children is immoral and undemocratic.	We need fundamental social change in order to empower women and kids	Stories of male sexual exploitation and tolerance of it throughout the ages	Woman-blaming; patriarchal family; patriarchy	Opponents are depicted as protectors of male privilege.
SURVIVORS SPEAK (CD sub-package)	Same as CD	Same as CD; By speaking out about abuse we can help to end this tragedy.	Denying the validity of recovered memories of abuse is just another attempt to bury our heads in the sand.	Denying the reality of memories of abuse constitutes revictimization of abuse survivors.	Same as CD; Also: Family members must not be allowed to sue therapists for damages caused by recovered memories.	Stories of confirmed memories of abuse	Same as CD; Also: "False Memory Syndrome."	Same as CD; Also: Survivors and those who work with them are depicted as courageous and under assault.

FALSE ACCUSATIONS	The issue is how to prevent the spread of hysteria about child abuse and protect people from false allegations.	Too many innocent people's lives have been destroyed by false accusations of abuse.	The "culture of abuse" and a witch hunt mentality are the cause of this latest panic.	The rights of the innocent must be protected.	We need policies and procedures that will ensure that the rights of the accused are protected.	The witch hunts, McCarthyism, and other instances in which innocent persons were wrongly persecuted	Witch hunts; lynch mobs; false accusations; false allegations; satanic panic; hysteria	Opponents are depicted as emotional and/or ideological.
OFFICIAL MISCONDUCT (FA subpackage)	Same as FA	Same as FA	The child abuse industry violates the rights of the accused and ignores due process.	Same as FA	We need to reform the child protective system in order to protect the rights of accused parents and better serve truly abused kids.	Same as FA	Due process: presumption of guilt; accountability; child abuse industry	Members of the "child abuse industry" are depicted as overzealous and unprofessional.
FALSE MEMORIES (FA subpackage)	Same as FA	Same as FA	Mental health professionals use unreliable methods to help clients "recover" memories of abuse.	Same as FA	Same as FA; Also: we must enhance the training of mental health professionals and hold them accountable for damage caused by unprofessional practices.	Same as FA	Also: Incest-survivor machine; recovered memory therapists	Same as FA; Therapists who argue for the validity of recovered memories are depicted as misguided and unscientific.

dents of abuse described in the media. Specifically, information regarding perpetrators (age, gender, and identity/occupation) and victims (age and gender) of abuse was recorded. In addition, the identity of persons recounting their personal experience with abuse or accusations of abuse was noted. These data supplement the results of the frame analysis and will be considered in the discussion.

Identifying Relevant Media Items

Four leading news magazines were selected for analysis: *Time, Newsweek, U.S. News and World Report,* and *People Magazine.*[4] The *Reader's Guide to Periodical Literature* was used to identify all stories pertaining to the issue of child sexual abuse. Because the categorization of such stories changed over the past several decades, locating them was somewhat complicated. Before 1976, articles that focused on what might now be called child abuse were indexed under "cruelty to children," and only a very few of these discussed adult-child sexual relations. Between 1976 and 1980, "child abuse" emerged as a separate category: stories about both sexual and physical abuse appeared under this heading. Some stories discussing adult-child sexual relations were also indexed under "incest" during this period. After 1981, most items that focused on child-adult sexual relations appeared in the new category "child molestation," although some continued to be listed under "incest".[5] In 1992, "False Memory Syndrome" appeared as a separate category, and 1994 saw the emergence of "ritual abuse" as a distinct heading, although only one story was indexed here.

In sum, stories that focused on adult-child sexual relations, were indexed under "child molestation," "child abuse," "incest," "False Memory Syndrome," or "ritual abuse," and appeared in any of the four selected magazines between 1970 and 1994 were analyzed. The number and content of such articles is depicted in Table 2. Twenty-nine articles on child sexual abuse were listed in the *Reader's Guide* before 1980, but none of these articles was published in the four newsmagazines selected for analysis. The 103 articles analyzed here appeared in the selected magazines between 1980 and 1994.

Measuring Package Prominence and Sponsorship

The following procedure was used to trace the media careers of the child sexual abuse packages and sub-packages. First, displays of any of the "signature elements" that characterize the packages and sub-packages were identified in the news stories. Next, these signature element displays were coded according to which package they signified. For example, a statement such as "the reality of child sexual abuse has been ignored for too long . . ." would be coded CD (Collective Denial). (A single article might display signature elements of various issue packages and sub-packages). Third, the number of displays of each package and sub-package was enumerated and tabulated by year. The results of this frame analysis thus identify the media career of each of the issue packages and sub-packages, and are presented in Table 3.

The content analysis of the incidents of abuse and testimonials describing experiences of abuse/allegations of abuse proceeded as follows. First, the victims and offenders described in the media stories were categorized according to their

Table 2 Number and Content of Periodical Articles Focusing on Child Sexual Abuse

Year	In All Periodicals	In Selected Periodicals	Package Display	Sexual Abuse Incidents	Experiences of Abuse/ Accusations
1970	0	0	0	0	0
1971	0	0	0	0	0
1972	1	0	0	0	0
1973	1	0	0	0	0
1974	0	0	0	0	0
1975	2	0	0	0	0
1976	4	0	0	0	0
1977	10	0	0	0	0
1978	6	0	0	0	0
1979	5	0	0	0	0
1980	6	2	9	0	0
1981	20	0	0	0	0
1982	7	4	25	10	0
1983	6	0	0	0	0
1984	57	18	75	35	6
1985	32	7	45	10	1
1986	30	5	11	2	2
1987	33	7	27	4	6
1988	24	6	19	6	5
1989	13	6	18	11	6
1990	20	5	20	0	0
1991	36	9	49	11	8
1992	48	9	20	14	7
1993	99	14	77	12	7
1994	69	11	34	9	3

Table 3 Displays of Child Sexual Abuse Issue Packages and Sub-Packages[a]

Package	1980–84		1985–90		1991–94	
Positive Pedophilla Package	7%	(8)	0%	(0)	0%	(0)
Collective Denial Package and Sub-packages	85%	(93)	41%	(54)	42%	(75)
Collective Denial	83%	(90)	44%	(53)	18%	(32)
Male Prerogative	3%	(3)	0%	(0)	0%	(0)
Survivors Speak	0%	(0)	1%	(1)	24%	(44)
False Accusations Package and Sub-packages	7%	(8)	59%	(66)	58%	(105)
False Accusations	7%	(8)	38%	(45)	20%	(36)
Official Misconduct	0%	(0)	18%	(21)	6%	(11)
False Memories	0%	(0)	0%	(0)	32%	(58)
Total Displays	100%	(109)	100%	(120)	100%	(180)

[a] Percentages may not add up to 100 due to rounding.

age (as children, including adolescents, or adults) and their gender (male, female, or both[6]). Data were also compiled regarding the identity/occupation of the offender (stranger, neighbor, religious figure, teacher, babysitter/day care worker, or family member). This information is depicted in Table 4. Second, the identity of persons providing testimonials regarding their personal experience with abuse or allegations of abuse[7] are categorized as one of the following: victim of abuse, relative/sympathizer of victim of abuse, victim of false accusations, perpetrator of abuse (admitting guilt). These results are summarized in Table 5.

THE TRANSFORMATION OF MEDIA DISCOURSE AND CHILD SEXUAL ABUSE

1980–84

Collective Denial was cleary the dominant frame in the 24 articles that appeared between 1980 and 1984. In general, the focus of these stories was on the recent discovery of the "hidden problem" of child sexual abuse, the pain that victims of such abuse endured, and the need to raise our collective consciousness regarding the prevalence of this problem. In May 1984, for example, *Newsweek* ran a cover story titled "A Hidden Epidemic: Sexual Abuse of Children is Much More Common than Most Americans Suspect." The article emphasized the widespread nature of child sexual abuse and lamented that "few offenders will be reported to any authority; fewer still will be punished" (May 14, 1984:30). During this period, claims of abuse were understood as valid indicators of a previously ignored social problem. Despite the prominence of Collective Denial during this period, the feminist version of this package (Male Prerogative) was depicted very rarely.

Positive Pedophilia was also largely absent from articles appearing in the early 1980s, except for a single article analyzing the victims of "sex researchers" who espoused this perspective. Interestingly, though, the *Reader's Guide to Periodical Literature* indicates that this particular item was the last in a series of such articles published in less mainstream magazines and journals. It therefore appears that the few depictions of Positive Pedophilia found in this early sample of media items are indicative of a brief and fairly circumscribed appearance of this cultural package in public discourse. Indeed, many of the early sponsors of Collective Denial specifically sought to refute the notion that adult–child sexual relations could be benign or positive for children by asserting that children cannot give informed consent.

As Table 4 suggests, much of the media coverage during this early period focused on allegations of abuse in day care settings: One-third of all of the offenders described in incidents of abuse were babysitters or day care workers. This focus helps to account for the fact that a relatively high proportion of alleged offenders were female or mixed groups of men and women. A few articles presented the testimonials of adult incest survivors (see Table 5), but the longer and more sensationalistic stories published during this period focused primarily on abuse in day care settings.

Table 4 Victim and Offender Characteristics in Child Sexual Abuse Incidents[a]

	1980–84		1985–90		1991–94	
OFFENDER						
AGE						
child	3%	(1)	0%	(0)	11%	(5)
adult	98%	(44)	0%	(33)	89%	(41)
GENDER						
male	64%	(29)	71%	(24)	92%	(42)
female	19%	(8)	3%	(1)	4%	(2)
both	19%	(8)	26%	(8)	4%	(2)
IDENTITY/OCCUPATION						
stranger	13%	(6)	0%	(0)	20%	(9)
neighbor	7%	(3)	0%	(0)	0%	(0)
religious figure	2%	(1)	0%	(0)	26%	(12)
teacher	2%	(1)	3%	(1)	9%	(4)
babysitter/day care	33%	(15)	35%	(11)	2%	(1)
family member	22%	(10)	55%	(19)	39%	(18)
other/unknown	20%	(9)	6%	(2)	4%	(2)
VICTIM						
AGE						
child	89%	(40)	97%	(32)	70%	(32)
adult[b]	11%	(5)	3%	(1)	30%	(14)
GENDER						
male	17%	(8)	12%	(4)	35%	(16)
female	49%	(22)	51%	(23)	55%	(25)
both	33%	(15)	36%	(12)	11%	(5)
Total Number of Incidents	100%	(45)	100%	(33)	100%	(46)

[a] Percentages may not add up to 100 due to rounding.
[b] While all incidents involved allegations of child sexual abuse, this category refers to such incidents reported by adults victimized as children.

Table 5 Identity of Persons Recounting Experience with Abuse/Allegations of Abuse[a]

Identity of Recounter	1980–84		1985–90		1991–94	
Victims of Abuse	50%	(3)	10%	(1)	56%	(14)
child victim	0%	(0)	5%	(1)	4%	(1)
adult survivor	50%	(3)	5%	(1)	52%	(13)
Relative/Sympathizer of Victim of Abuse	17%	(1)	60%	(12)	0%	(0)
mother	17%	(1)	55%	(11)	0%	(0)
father	0%	(0)	5%	(1)	0%	(0)
other	0%	(0)	0%	(0)	0%	(0)
Victim of False Accusations	17%	(1)	28%	(5)	44%	(11)
father	0%	(0)	22%	(4)	28%	(7)
other relative	0%	(0)	0%	(0)	4%	(1)
day care/teacher	17%	(1)	6%	(1)	8%	(2)
other	0%	(0)	0%	(0)	4%	(1)
Perpetrator of Abuse (guilty)	17%	(1)	0%	(0)	0%	(0)
Total Number of Incidents	100%	(6)	100%	(20)	100%	(25)

[a] Percentages may not add up to 100 due to rounding.

1985–90

The situation changed fairly dramatically after 1984. False Accusations began to appear more frequently in newsmagazine coverage in 1985; between 1985 and 1990 this frame and its sub-package, Official Misconduct displaced Collective Denial as the dominant way of framing discussions of sexual abuse. Thus, only eight months after declaring that child sexual abuse was an under-reported and "hidden epidemic," *Newsweek* provocatively titled another article on the subject: "The Youngest Witnesses: Is There a Witch Hunt Mentality in Sex Abuse Cases?" (February 18, 1985:82). Controversy around day care cases, some of which involved charges of ritual abuse, grew between 1985 and 1990. Increasingly, these allegations and the methods used to elicit them were identified as problematic.

The question of how to understand and interpret children's allegations of abuse was highly contested during this period. Early on, sponsors of Collective Denial argued that "There is no shred of evidence that children lie about sexual assault" (*Newsweek*, February 18, 1985:83) and cited studies that found that "children are telling the truth more than 95% of the time" (*Newsweek*, October 9, 1987:41). Later in this period, these sponsors made somewhat more cautious statements: "Children can lie, but research shows that they do not fabricate detailed descriptions of adult sexual acts . . ." (*People*, January 1990:76).

By contrast, sponsors of False Accusations emphasized children's suggestibility or propensity to lie or fantasize about abuse. One article reported that "the fantasies of some youngsters are causing nightmares for innocent adults" (*U.S. News and World Report*, April 1, 1985:66), while another reported that "children are insidious, practiced liars" (*People*, July 8, 1985:27). Others suggested that children "falsify on purpose to get revenge against a parent or teacher who disciplined them or to support one side in a custody dispute" (*Newsweek*, September 16, 1985:43). Assertions of children's suggestibility, such as the following, were even more common: "Children, particularly those that have been extensively coached, give inaccurate testimony far more often than previously imagined" (*Time*, March 4, 1991:76). Sponsors of Official Misconduct emphasized the role of "the system" in generating false allegations of abuse: "Officials have encouraged suggestible youngsters to tell tales" (*Newsweek*, September 16, 1985: 43), or more dramatically, "the increased determination by authorities to uncover child sexual abuse has had less than wholesome consequences: a raft of false charges that devastate the lives of those accused" (*Time*, May 11, 1987:49). This emphasis on "the system's" role in generating false allegations is a central feature of Official Misconduct and largely accounts for its appearance during this period.

While day care cases continued to be a central focus, the proportion of stories describing incidents of incest increased dramatically in the late '80s (see Table 4). Familial offenders were increasingly common in reported incidents of abuse; most of these were fathers or stepfathers. As Table 5 further indicates, a new, corresponding genre of testimonials appeared during this period: Relatives of victims of abuse (predominantly mothers of girls abused by their fathers) described their frustration at the court's unwillingness to protect children from familial abusers and their consequent decision to take their children "underground."

Testimonials by fathers claiming to have been falsely accused provided a rival interpretation of these accounts, although these were not as numerous as mothers' stories. On the other hand, fathers' reports were supported by expert and media claims that many, if not most, allegations of abuse made in the context of custody disputes were false: "A significant portion of the increase [in the reported number of sex abuse allegations], in fact—and most of the false allegations—come in the vindictive climate of custody battles" (*Newsweek*, November 13, 1989:99). Some further specified that "some wives use false accusations as a weapon of last resort" in custody cases (*Time*, May 11, 1987:49).

In sum, the period from 1985–90 saw the emergence and ascendance of False Accusations and its sub-package, Official Misconduct. These packages were used to signify two dimensions of the child sexual abuse issue. First, claims of abuse in day care settings were increasingly likely to be depicted as the consequence of children's propensity to lie, parents' tendency to panic, or the use of suggestive interviewing techniques. Second, claims of abuse in custody cases became highly controversial during this period. A series of articles presenting the stories of mothers "on the run" depicted the judicial system as insensitive to the reality of familial abuse, while testimonials by fathers challenged the legitimacy of such abuse claims. Assessments of the validity of allegations of abuse were central to both of these discussions, and sponsors of alternative packages offered conflicting interpretations of them.

1991–94

After 1991, familial abusers remained prominent, but the plight of adult incest and abuse survivors became the primary focus. Celebrities such as actress Roseanne Barr, LaToya Jackson, Oprah Winfrey, and former Miss America Marilyn Van Derbur shared their experiences of incest/abuse and urged others to "break the silence." One article representative of this genre was titled "The Pain of the Last Taboo: For Many Survivors of Incest, Struggling With Suppressed Memories is the Hardest Battle of All" (*Newsweek*, October 7, 1991:28). While adult survivors of extra-familial abuse also related their experiences during this period, most of those sharing their stories identified themselves as victims of incest.

Table 6 depicts the careers of the various packages by year for the period from 1991 to 1994. For a short time, Collective Denial and its sub-package, Survivors Speak, dominated the newsmagazine coverage: These packages were depicted in 82 percent of all package displays in 1991. These stories emphasized the horror of incest and the need to speak out about it and treated the assertion that "most often, the child forgets because remembering is too painful . . ." as non-controversial. This emphasis on the validity of once-hidden memories of abuse and the importance of affirming them was central to Survivors Speak.

The relatively uncontested nature of incest-survivor reports, however, was short-lived. Between 1992 and 1994, Collective Denial and Survivors Speak were superseded by False Accusations, and in particular by the emerging False Memories sub-package. From 1992–1994, False Accusations and its sub-packages were

Table 6 Displays of Child Sexual Abuse Issue Packages and Sub-Packages. By Year, 1991–94[a]

Package	1991		1992		1993		1994	
Positive Pedophilia								
Package	0%	(0)	0%	(0)	0%	(0)	0%	(0)
Collective Denial								
Package and Sub-packages	82%	(40)	45%	(9)	27%	(21)	15%	(5)
Collective Denial	22%	(11)	40%	(8)	12%	(9)	9%	(3)
Male Prerogative	0%	(0)	0%	(0)	0%	(0)	0%	(0)
Survivors Speak	59%	(29)	5%	(1)	16%	(12)	6%	(2)
False Accusations								
Package and Sub-packages	18%	(9)	55%	(11)	58%	(56)	85%	(29)
False Accusations	14%	(7)	50%	(10)	16%	(12)	20%	(7)
Official Misconduct	0%	(0)	5%	(1)	13%	(10)	0%	(0)
False Memories	4%	(2)	0%	(0)	39%	(34)	65%	(22)
Total Displays	100%	(49)	100%	(20)	100%	(77)	100%	(34)

[a]Percentages may not add up to 100 due to rounding.

depicted in 73 percent of all package displays. The emergence and ascendance of False Memories during this period was particularly dramatic: While this sub-package was largely absent from the media prior to 1992, it comprised 39 percent of the total package displays in 1993 and 65 percent of all package displays in 1994. This sub-package emphasized the unreliability of repressed memories of abuse, as well as the damage that was done to families and wrongly accused persons as a result of false accusations, and was thus a rebuttal of the key claims of Survivors Speak. Titles of articles depicting these elements include "Lies of the Mind," "Memories Lost and Found," "Misty Watercolored Memories," "Was It Real or Memories?", "Dubious Memories," and "You Must Remember This: How the Brain Forms False Memories."

As Table 4 indicates, the majority of incidents described during the early 1990s involved familial offenders—and for the first time, virtually none involved day care workers. The sharp rise in the proportion of stories involving religious figures reflected increased attention to sexual abuse perpetrated by priests. Offenders mentioned in these incidents were increasingly likely to be male (the focus on fathers and priests helps to account for this). Victims (especially those claiming to have been molested by priests) were also more likely to be male and adult at the same time the article was written. As Table 5 indicates, persons recounting their own experiences were largely adults identifying themselves as survivors of abuse and adults (mostly fathers) claiming to have been falsely accused of abuse.

Summary

The results of this analysis suggest that the framing of media discussions of child sexual abuse changed dramatically over the past 15 years. While Collective Denial dominated the early coverage of this topic, False Accusations and, more recently, False Memories, have emerged as the dominant way of interpreting claims of abuse. Indeed, these packages now clearly overshadow Collective Denial and Survivors Speak. How can the rise and fall of the various issue packages be explained? Following Gamson (1988), three main factors that help to explain the shifting discourse on child sexual abuse are described below. These include the activities of claimsmakers or sponsors of the various packages, media practices, and cultural resonances. In addition, social actors' capacity to create and mobilize new issue packages is analyzed.

ACCOUNTING FOR THE CHANGING IMAGE OF CHILD SEXUAL ABUSE

Sponsor Activities

Collective Denial was largely displaced by False Accusations and Official Misconduct in the mid-1980s, while Survivors Speak was superseded by False Memories in the 1990s. These shifts reflect, in part, the political mobilization of sponsor groups advocating and mobilizing alternative issue frames, for as Gamson and Modigliani (1987:165) point out, "changing culture is the product of enterprise." Sponsors do not merely advocate cultural packages; they often take concrete steps in their efforts to disseminate and legitimate them. These "definitional" or "claimsmaking" activities include making speeches, writing articles and pamphlets, holding news conferences, and lobbying legislators and other policymakers.

One of the first organized sponsor groups, Victims of Child Abuse Laws (VOCAL), was created in 1984 by parents claiming to have been falsely accused of child abuse. VOCAL now has chapters across the country and sits "on many government task forces and committees throughout the United States and Canada" (Wimberly 1994:49). One of the main tasks of this organization is to "put a human face on the falsely accused and to bring about an understanding that false allegations are every bit as damaging . . . as the tyranny of incest" (Wimberly 1994:49). VOCAL's critique centers on the "presumption of guilt" and absence of due process protections in cases involving allegations of abuse, the unprofessional nature of child protective practices, and the fact that "children today know that to cry abuse holds a threat over parents and caretakers. . . . a threat that can be used as a weapon against any adult-contrived structure that they dislike" (Wimberly 1994:56). VOCAL advocates reform of the child protection system in order to protect the rights of the accused, and improvement of the techniques used by child protection personnel. The emergence and mobilization of this organization helps to account for the appearance of Official Misconduct between 1985 and 1990.

The next wave of claimsmaking activity was conducted by high profile celebrities, incest survivors, and domestic violence organizations. As was discussed earlier, these sponsors paid particular attention to intra-familial abuse. They also argued that since repression is a common mechanism by which survivors cope with their abuse, legislation allowing the admission of recovered memories of abuse in civil cases should be adopted. A few identifying themselves as adult survivors sued their alleged perpetrators, and in some states (especially Washington) these cases received a great deal of publicity.

It was in this context that Survivors Speak was largely displaced by False Memories. In 1992, parents claiming to have been falsely accused and assorted "scientific experts" (mainly psychiatrists and psychological researchers) formed a new organization called the False Memory Syndrome Foundation (FMSF). As is suggested by the results presented earlier, this organization has been particularly successful in resignifying the issue of child abuse through the creation and mobilization of False Memories. This success stems, in part, from the fact that the FMSF identified influencing media coverage as its most important objective (Freyd 1994). In sum, the shifting representation of the issue of child sexual abuse can be partially explained in terms of the mobilization of sponsor groups and their definitional activities. Conversely, the absence of (suitable) groups sponsoring either Positive Pedophilia or Male Prerogative contributed to their weak performance in media discourse.

Media Practices

Media practices also have an important impact on public discourse. One of the most important of these for representations of child sexual abuse is journalists' prioritization of drama and novelty. A now-famous memo sent from NBC executive Reuven Frank to his staff gave expression to these values: "Every news story should, without any sacrifice of probity or responsibility, display the attributes of fiction, of drama" (cited in Epstein 1973:271). In the competition to attract media consumers, the dramatic—emotional, conflictual, and human interest—aspects of social problems are crucial (Hilgartner and Bosk 1988). These values undoubtedly heightened the media's interest in both victims of abuse and the wrongly accused. Advocates of the False Memories package, for example, have used testimony to highlight the pain of the falsely accused, and in so doing, have attracted significant media attention to their cause[8]. The fact that Collective Denial and False Accusations typically identify an individual victim (of either abuse or of false accusations) may mean that these packages are more able than Positive Pedophilia to satisfy the media's interest in the dramatic and conflictual. Similarly, Male Prerogative's focus on the systemic causes of abuse may contribute to its disfavor among journalists.[9]

The media's related interest in novelty may also be relevant. The ideal story contains a new angle or twist that helps it retain its dramatic edge. Both sponsors and media personnel constantly seek new ways of presenting issues in order to inject a sense of urgency in their discussions of them (Hilgartner and Bosk 1988). The ebb and flow of the Collective Denial and False Accusations packages and associated sub-packages can be partially explained in terms of the media's attempt to avoid saturation. While this emphasis on novelty would also appear to work in favor of Positive Pedophilia and Male Prerogative, this has not been the case, for several reasons.

The first has to do with the relative status of potential media sources. It is clear that some sponsors are accorded greater legitimacy by media personnel than others. Becker (1967:241) called attention to these "hierarchies of credibility" when he argued that news workers accord those at the top of status hierarchies greater legitimacy and authority. High ranking "moral entrepreneurs" therefore enjoy greater access to the media. This particular media practice helps to account for the ability of celebrities to promote the Collective Denial frame by telling their stories of abuse. Similarly, the dramatic ascendance of the False Memories package between 1992 and 1994 may also have been facilitated by the status and authority of many of the academic and professional sponsors of this frame.

By contrast, advocates of Positive Pedophilia and Male Prerogative are relatively marginal by contemporary cultural standards. While some academic researchers promoted the former sub-package in the 1970s, by the 1980s these sponsors had been largely replaced by "fringe" organizations such as the North American Man–Boy Love Association. And while one might expect domestic violence organizations to promote Male Prerogative, most of these offered more psychological and less political interpretations of the issue; it was primarily "radical" feminist organizations that sponsored this package. Thus, the media's tendency to accord those at the top of the status hierarchies greater legitimacy helps to account for the presence of some issue packages and the absence of others.

Cultural Themes and Resources

Issue packages often resonate with larger cultural themes, and those that do so with relatively salient themes have an advantage over those that do not (Gamson and Modigliani 1987). For example, Collective Denial resonates with the now-prevalent cultural image of the child-victim (see Best 1990). False Accusations accords with discourses that highlight the rights of the accused and the autonomy of the family vis à vis the state. Conversely, Male Prerogative's identification of patriarchy as a cause of sexual abuse does not appear to have much cultural salience in this "post-feminist" era. However, not just the resonance of the themes invoked, but the credibility of their connection to the particular issue at hand is relevant. For example, Positive Pedophilia draws on the quite salient discourses of individual rights and sexual liberation, but in the context of discussions of adult-child sexual encounters these themes do not appear to resonate with many. This may reflect the emergence of the image of the child-as-victim and a cultural consensus regarding children's vulnerability to exploitation by adults[10] (Best 1990).

The extent to which family members are depicted as offenders may also have an impact on the framing of child sexual abuse. It is interesting to note that the rise of False Accusations and its sub-packages since 1985 corresponds with an increased emphasis on familial offenders. While a causal connection between these developments cannot be confirmed, an emphasis on the threat posed to children by dangerous "outsiders" may afford greater opportunities for the solidaristic processes identified by Durkheim. Conversely, to the extent that offenders appear as "insiders," discussions of sexual abuse may become more disruptive of social solidarity and therefore troubling. It is possible, then, that the emerging focus on familial offenders provided VOCAL and FMSF activists with an important set of psycho-social resources and helps to explain the rise of False Accusations and False Memories in media discourse.

In sum, the extent to which frames resonate with salient cultural themes helps to explain the ability or inability of sponsors to contest the signification of child sexual abuse and other social issues. As Gamson points out, however, cultural themes cannot be invoked without also suggesting their "countertheme" (Gamson and Modigliani 1987). The point is not that all cultural themes are equally salient, or that one theme may not be dominant at a given historical moment, but that cultures are profoundly ambivalent (Dirks, Eley, and Ortner 1994). For example, while the cultural image of the "child-victim" is currently quite salient (Best 1990), this image exists alongside a darker, more suspicious view of children as "insidious, practiced liars." As Hall (1988) put it, social objects are always "multi-accentual": They can be discursively rearticulated to construct new meanings, connect with different social practices, and position subjects differently.

It is this cultural complexity that makes the "disarticulation" and "rearticulation" of issue frames possible. These terms refer to the severing, realignment, and recombination of discourses; it is through these processes that ideological transformation occurs (Hall 1988). The emergence of False Memories in the early 1990s illustrates the capacity of social actors to create new discursive syntheses in the course of struggles over signification. The False Memory subpackage, for example, represents a new and creative synthesis of (late) Freudian ideas regarding the impact of fantasy and suggestion on memory,[11] a critique of the lack of professionalism of mental health clinicians, and an emphasis on the rights and plight of the wrongly accused. Advocates of this perspective thus appropriated bits and pieces of pre-existing discourses and reconfigured these in an unprecedented way in their attempt to imbue discussions of child sexual abuse with an alternative and often competing meaning. . . .

Notes

1. Over time, state legislatures reinforce the connection between child abuse and social class, race, and gender by broadening the statutory definitions of abuse/neglect and by adding protective custody clauses. Support for child protection policies waned as these laws led to the adoption of welfare rather than public health programs, and as the issues's link to familial authority relations was highlighted (see Nelson 1984:135–137).

2. My use of the term "child sexual abuse" itself reflects a particular issue package: The use of this term is an implicit rejection of Positive Pedophilia, which holds that only some adult–child sexual encounters are abusive.

3. The coding of assertions of children's suggestibility depended upon its attribution of blame. Statements that attributed children's false claims of abuse to either their propensity to lie/fantasize about abuse or to parental "hysteria"/suggestions were treated as displays of False Accusations. Those that attributed children's false claims to the interviewing techniques of prosecutors, social workers, therapists, and criminal justice personnel—members of the "child abuse industry" or the "system"—were treated as displays of Official Misconduct.

4. Newsmagazine articles were analyzed because "hard news" coverage in newspapers and on television tended to focus on specific cases, and, as a result, displayed fewer signature elements of the various cultural packages. *Time, Newsweek,* and *U.S. News and World*

Report were selected because they are the largest newsmagazines; *People* was also included in the interest of examining a more entertainment-oriented medium.

5. Stories that were indexed under "incest" but focused on intra-familial adult sexual relations were not analyzed.

6. This category was relevant in some cases involving multiple defendants/offenders.

7. These testimonials were distinguished from reported incidents of abuse by the reporter's use of interviewing techniques and the presence of the interviewees own account of the incident. Stories in which more than one descriptive statement came from the participant her—or himself was treated as a "testimonial."

8. According to Pamela Freyd, executive director of the False Memory Syndrome Foundation, the FMSF encouraged parents claiming to have been falsely accused to tell their stories to the media in order to shift attention to the plight of the wrongly accused (Freyd 1994).

9. Indeed, there is evidence that media personnel are more likely to frame social issues in individualistic rather than systemic terms, and that this framing has important consequences for viewers' assessments of these issues (Iyengar 1991).

10. The existence of such consensus—and the dangers of violating it—are revealed by a recent incident involving a member of the False Memory Syndrome Foundation. Ralph Underwager, early supporter and member of the board of directors of FMSF, was encouraged to "resign" from the board after he described pedophilia as a "responsible choice of the individual" in an interview with the Dutch journal *Paidika: The Journal of Paedophilia* (Fried 1994).

11. Advocates of both Survivors Speak and False Memories sometimes invoke Freudian ideas. The former draw on Freud's early work, which relied on the concept of repression and highlighted the widespread and devastating nature of incest. In contrast, advocates of False Memories draw on those writings that followed Freud's renunciation of his view that his female client's reports of incest were descriptions of real events. This "late" Freud reinterpreted these reports as projections of unconscious desires and feelings, and thus highlighted the impact of fantasy on memory. This reversal has itself become the object of much controversy (see Masson 1992).

References

Becker, Howard (1967). "Whose side are we on?" *Social Problems* 14: 239–247.

Best, Joel (1990). *Threatened Children: Rhetoric and Concern about Child Victims*. Chicago: University of Chicago Press.

Dirks, Nicholas B., Geoff Eley, and Sherry Ortner, eds. (1994). *Culture/Power/History: A Reader in Contemporary Social Theory*. Princeton, NJ: Princeton University Press.

Epstein, Edward Jay (1973). *News from Nowhere*. New York: Random House.

Finkelhor, David (1990). "Is child abuse overreported? The data rebuts arguments for less intervention." *Public Welfare* 48: 22–29.

Freyd, Pamela (1994). Interview with the author. August 19, Philadelphia, PA.

Fried, Stephen (1994). "War of remembrance." *Philadelphia*, January: 66–71 and 149–157.

Gamson, William (1988). "Political discourse and collective action." *International Social Movement Research* 1: 219–244.

————(1992). *Talking Politics*. Boston: Cambridge University Press.

Gamson, William, and Kathryn E. Lasch (1983). "The political culture of social welfare policy." *In Evaluating the Welfare State: Social and Political Perspectives*, eds. Shimon E. Spiro and Ephraim Yuchtman-Yaar, 397–416. New York: Academic Press.

Gamson, William A., and Andre Modigliani (1987). "The changing culture of affirmative action." *Research in Political Sociology* 3: 137–177.

Hall, Stuart (1988). *The Hard Road to Renewal: Thatcherism and the Crisis of the Left*. New York: Verso Press.

Hilgartner, Stephen, and Charles L. Bosk (1988). "The rise and fall of social problems: A public arenas model." *American Journal of Sociology* 94: 53–78.

Iyengar, Shanto (1991). *Is Anyone Responsible?* Chicago: University of Chicago Press.

MacLeod, Mary, and Esther Saraga (1987). "Child sexual abuse: A feminist analysis." *Spare Rib* 181: 22–26.

Masson, Jeffrey (1992). *The Assault on the Truth: Freud's Suppression of Seduction Theory*. New York: HarperPerennial.

Myers, John E. B. (1993). "Expert testimony regarding child sexual abuse." *Child Abuse and Neglect* 17: 175–185.

Nelson, Barbara J. (1984). *Making An Issue of Child Abuse: Political Agenda Setting for Social Problems*. Chicago: University of Chicago Press.

Pfohl, Steven (1977). "The discovery of child abuse." *Social Problems* 24: 310–323.

Rhodes, Robert (1988). "Interview with Robert Rhodes." *In The Battle and the Backlash: The Child Sexual Abuse War*, ed. David Hechler, pp. 293–298. Massachusetts: Lexington Books.

Weisberg, Kelly D. (1994). "The 'discovery' of sexual abuse: Experts' role in legal policy formulation." *UC Davis Law Review* 18: 1–54.

Wimberly, Lesley (1994). "The perspective from victims of child abuse laws." In *The Backlash: Child Protection Under Fire*, ed. John Myers, pp. 47–59. Thousand Oaks: Sage Publications.

CONSTRUCTIONISM IN CONTEXT

Joel Best

Best examines criticisms of constructionism, types of constructionists, and practical as well as theoretical uses to which constructionism may be put. Hostile critics say it makes no sense to ignore "objective conditions" which constitute the core of social problems and that constructionists ignore the harms and suffering social problems cause. Sympathetic critics answer that years of studying the objective aspects of problems have yet to alleviate suffering let alone produce a

From Joel Best (ed.), *Images of Issues: Typifying Contemporary Social Problems*, 2nd ed. (New York: Aldine de Gruyter). Copyright 1995 by Walter de Gruyter, Inc., New York. Reprinted with permission.

genuine sociological theory of social problems; furthermore, if no one points to the harms, the situation remains undefined as a social problem.

Still other sympathetic critics argue that constructionists either make assumptions about objective conditions or, worse, believe they know when objective conditions have changed or not. If so, they are unable to fulfill the constructionist imperative, which requires information on the beliefs of the people involved in the social problems process rather than the beliefs of sociologists.

As a result, two schools of thought have emerged within the developing constructionist tradition: strict social constructionists, those who only study the claims-making process, and contextual constructionists, who take into account what is known about objective conditions. Best says people who want to solve problems would do well to study the successful claims-making of others.

The constructionist approach to studying social problems emerged from some sociologists' dissatisfaction with the dominant, objectivist stance. Constructionists argued that defining social problems in terms of objective conditions within society had two key flaws: it ignored the fact that identifying a social condition as a social problem required subjective judgment; and, by labeling conditions with little in common as social problems, objectivism could not serve as a foundation for more general theories of social problems.

In contrast, constructionists define social problems in terms of claims-making; they focus on the subjective judgments (claims that X is a social problem) that the objectivists slighted.[1] And, as the chapters in this book reveal, the constructionist approach offers a basis for developing new theories—about claims, claims-makers, connections among claimsmaking campaigns, and social policies, among other topics.

The constructionist approach to social problems is relatively new, and it remains controversial. Critics attack constructionism from several sides; some sociologists defend objectivism and criticize the constructionist stance, or they argue that objectivism and constructionism can be easily reconciled; others warn that constructionism is inherently inconsistent, that its theoretical assumptions are contradictory; while, even among sociologists who see themselves as working within the constructionist tradition, there are disagreements about what sorts of analysis ought to be called "constructionist."

This afterword offers an introduction to the recent debates over social problems theory. But it is only an introduction to a growing literature. Some readers may want to learn more about those debates by going on to explore some of the references cited in this afterword.[2]

CONSTRUCTIONISM'S CRITICS: ATTACKS FROM OUTSIDE

Constructionism offers a dramatic break from the traditional objectivist approach to studying social problems. Even the term "social problem" has a different meaning when constructionists use it. While the constructionist perspective has inspired a large body of research, it continues to be criticized by sociologists who remain within the objectivist tradition. Most objectivist critiques of construction-ism can be summarized within four general arguments.

1. Constructionism and Objectivism Are Complementary.

Some sociolo-gists who remain more-or-less committed to the objectivist perspective deny that constructionism represents a genuinely different approach. They argue that ob-jectivism and constructionism are merely "two sides of the same coin," that the two theoretical perspectives can be easily reconciled. Most often, these efforts to minimize the differences between objectivism and constructionism give only lip service to constructionist concerns. For instance, many social problems text-books' definitions of social problems mention the role of subjective judgments in identifying problems, but constructionist issues receive no further attention in these books. Such treatments misunderstand the nature of constructionism, which involves more than acknowledging that definitions of social problems are subjective. By defining social problems in terms of claimsmaking, constructionists set a new agenda for those who would study social problems; constructionist research addresses a distinct set of questions about the nature of claims, those who make claims, and so on. Thus, a traditional, objectivist approach to home-lessness might focus on measuring the size of the homeless population, learning why some people become homeless, or otherwise exploring homelessness as a social condition, while a constructionist analysis would ask whose claims brought homelessness to public attention, how those claims typified the homeless, how the public and policy-makers responded to the claims, and so on.

Because the two perspectives define social problems differently and focus on different issues, it is not simple to reconcile objectivism and constructionism in a single, integrated theory. For example, Jones, McFalls, and Gallagher (1989: 344) offer a "unified model" in which "three major factors—visibility (intrinsic and extrinsic), expectations, and values—[interpose] themselves between objec-tive and subjective dimensions." For constructionists, such models depend upon objectivist assumptions about social life and sociology, assumptions that construc-tionist analysis begins by rejecting. As a result, integrated models receive little support from the constructionist camp.

2. Constructionism's Subject Is Relatively Unimportant.

Other objectivist sociologists acknowledge that constructionism has a unique approach—one they deplore. They argue that constructionists' focus on claimsmaking ignores a far more important subject: the harmful social conditions that are the "real" social problems. Thus, an article criticizing constructionist analyses in social work is titled "Reality Exists O.K.?" (Speed 1991). The constructionist response to this call for analysts to return to their traditional subject matter is twofold: (1) while there is nothing wrong with studying particular social conditions, decades of ob-jectivist research on social conditions have failed to lay a foundation for general theories of social problems; and (2) it is important to remember that we recognize social conditions as "really" harmful only because someone made persuasive claims to that effect. Again, objectivism and constructionism ask different ques-tions; the relative value of the two sets of questions depends upon what we want to know.

3. Constructionism Has Moral or Political Biases.

Many sociologists bring moral or political commitments to their work; often, their concerns with social issues led them to study sociology. Typically, sociologists have left-liberal sympathies, and they favor egalitarian social change. Some critics—including some sociologists who identify their approach as constructionist—worry that constructionism may somehow subvert these goals. Usually, this critique argues that because people with less power have a harder time getting heard, the constructionist focus on vocal, visible claimsmaking will overlook the concerns of society's invisible members—those too inarticulate, alienated, or powerless to voice claims. For example, Patricia Hill Collins (1989:90) argues: "Poor Black women face critical issues that merit study, yet they lack the power to make their claims known within current political structures of social problems discourse," while Leslie J. Miller (1993) suggests that analysts often ignore the claimsmaking styles favored by marginalized "underdogs." Concerned that constructionists cannot be counted upon to recognize conditions that afflict those who cannot easily make claims, these critics call for a return to objective definitions of social problems. They offer various bases for such definitions, including "moral imperatives and human needs that are trans-societal and trans-historical" (Eitzen 1984:11), "the knowledge related values of science" (Manis 1985:5), and "an overarching ethical framework" (Collins 1989:90).

The argument that constructionism springs from a particular set of moral or political values is not convincing. Reading between the lines, it is sometimes possible to infer that an analyst has made certain assumptions about how the social world works—or should work. A left-liberal bent is common among sociologists, and it is no surprise that many constructionist works seem to incorporate more-or-less liberal assumptions, yet it is possible to point to particular studies that seem to reflect very different values. Moreover, it is not clear why we ought to suspect that constructionism inevitably draws upon particular values; constructionism is a tool that can be put to many uses.

Nor does it seem probable that constructionists are especially likely to overlook the concerns of the powerless. Certainly many constructionist case studies examine social movements by people who have been marginalized and discredited. In spite of some critics' concerns, there seems to be no shortage of outlets for claims, and many scholars in sociology and other disciplines seem eager to identify and describe claimsmaking by the disadvantaged. No doubt there will always be some concerns that go unstated, unnoticed, and unanalyzed, but it is not clear why we should expect sociologists operating from objectivist assumptions to be any more likely than constructionists to identify these hidden concerns as subjects for research. Again, social conditions become topics for objectivist research only when they have been subjectively constructed as problematic.

4. Constructionism Is Merely Debunking.

Constructionism shifts the analyst's focus from social conditions to members' claims about those conditions. It is the claim, not the condition that is at issue; in fact, some constructionists carefully speak of "putative conditions" that may or may not exist. This has led some critics to equate constructionism with debunking, so that they may ask whether a particular social problem is an objective social condition, or "just" a social construction. This equates social construction with error, and defines constructionist analysis as a method of exposing mistaken or distorted claims. For instance, Forsyth and Oliver (1990:285) state: "Basically the constructionist argument is that there has been no significant change in the activity in question, but that activities which were not previously defined [sic] as problematic, have been defined as a problem."

This criticism reflects a basic misunderstanding: equating social construction with erroneous reasoning. All claims—and all other human knowledge—are socially constructed. It is wrong to assume that analyses of objective conditions deal with what is true, while analyses of socially constructed claims deal with what is false. Again, all our knowledge—including our knowledge of objective conditions—is a product of social interaction, a social construction.[3]

STRICT CONSTRUCTIONISM

The most influential critique of constructionism came not from objectivists, but from two sociologists writing from a subjectivist stance, who charged that constructionists base their analyses on hidden, objectivist assumptions. Steve Woolgar and Dorothy Pawluch (1985a) argue that constructionism is internally inconsistent. They note that while constructionists identify their focus as subjective judgments or claims, constructionist analyses usually assume some knowledge of objective conditions. Thus, a standard constructionist explanation might proceed: although social condition X remained unchanged, X became defined as a social problem when people began making claims about it. Woolgar and Pawluch point to the (sometimes unstated) assumption that X was unchanged. Although constructionists speak of claims about *putative* conditions as the proper subject for social problems analysis, implying that the nature of the social conditions is irrelevant (and perhaps unknowable), they typically assume that they do know the actual status of the social condition (as an unchanging phenomenon). For Woolgar and Pawluch (1985a:216), this contradiction is at the core of constructionism: "The successful [constructionist] social problems explanation depends on making problematic the truth status of certain states of affairs selected for analysis and explanation, while backgrounding or minimizing the possibility that the same problems apply to assumptions upon which the analysis depends." Woolgar and Pawluch call this selective attention to objective conditions "ontological gerrymandering."

Woolgar and Pawluch's critique launched a lively debate among those who saw themselves as constructionists (Gusfield 1985; Hazelrigg 1985, 1986; Pfohl 1985; J. Schneider 1985b; Woolgar and Pawluch 1985b). At issue are the analytic assumptions at the perspective's foundation. What assumptions about the social world are appropriate? Should all such assumptions be avoided, or are some acceptable? What are the consequences of making different assumptions? Constructionists give various answers to these questions.

At one extreme are those sympathetic to Woolgar and Pawluch's critique. These are the *strict constructionists*, who argue that social problems analysts should avoid making assumptions about objective reality. In their view, constructionists should examine the perspectives of claimsmakers, policymakers, and other members of society. The actual social conditions are irrelevant; what matters is what the members say about those conditions. Strict constructionists focus on claimsmaking; they seek to understand, but do not presume to judge the members' claims.

In fact, because they adopt a phenomenological perspective, strict constructionists question the analyst's ability to make judgments about social conditions. Phenomenological sociology argues that all we know about the world is a social construction. This includes the claims members make about social issues, but it also includes the analyses that constructionist sociologists write about claimsmaking. In this view, the sociologist is not specially privileged; he or she is just another actor trying to make sense of the surrounding world. A sociologist who makes statements about social conditions is simply another claimsmaker, one more participant in the claimsmaking process. Strict constructionists, then, find little attraction in reconciling constructionist and objectivist theories, since they view members' claims, rather than the validity of those claims, as the subject matter for the sociology of social problems. On the other hand, strict constructionists find considerable merit in Woolgar and Pawluch's critique, and they strive to avoid making (even implicit) assumptions about objective reality.

Once Woolgar and Pawluch drew attention to the problem of ontological gerrymandering, several leading constructionists rallied around the cause of strict constructionism (Holstein and Miller 1993; Ibarra and Kitsuse 1993; Kitsuse and Schneider 1989; Sarbin and Kitsuse 1994; Spector and Kitsuse 1987; Troyer 1992). They called for constructionist researchers to shun all claims or assumptions about social conditions, to confine their analysis strictly to claims.

The most influential advocate of the strict constructionist position is John I. Kitsuse—co-author of the classic constructionist text, *Constructing Social Problems* (Spector and Kitsuse 1977). It is worth tracing how Kitsuse's interpretation of strict constructionism has evolved. Initially, strict constructionists treated ontological gerrymandering as carelessness on the part of the analyst; a careful constructionist, they argued, could avoid making forbidden assumptions (e.g., J. Schneider 1985a, 1985b). Thus, Kitsuse and Schneider (1989: xii–xiii) insist that the strict constructionist

> does not compete with members as an arbiter of true and accurate knowledge. Instead, the theoretical task is to study how members define, lodge, and press claims; how they publicize their concerns, redefine the issues in question in the face of political obstacles, indifference, or opposition; how they enter into alliances with other claims-makers; and the myriad other activities that constitute subject matter for the study of social problems.

While this seems to imply that constructionists could (carefully) continue studying cases of social problems construction, the issue was not so simple. Even this brief passage raises questions for strict constructionist analysts. For instance, how—without making any assumptions about social conditions—can an analyst identify "political opposition, indifference, or obstacles" or "alliances"? Strict constructionists began to recognize that, in practice, background assumptions about social conditions were far more commonplace in constructionist work than even Woolgar and Pawluch had suggested.

Some strict constructionists responded to this recognition by moving away from case studies. Writing with Peter R. Ibarra, Kitsuse suggested that case studies were analytically troublesome:

> [O]ur position is that the project of developing a theory of *social problems discourse* is a much more coherent way of proceeding with constructionism than, for example, the development of a series of discrete theories on the social construction of X, Y, and Z. To develop a theory about condition X when the ontological status of X is suspended results in "ontological gerrymandering" . . . which is to say flawed theory. (Ibarra and Kitsuse 1993:33—emphasis in original)

Ibarra and Kitsuse's solution was to offer a new classification of claims-making rhetoric, in which the analytic focus was not social conditions, but "condition-categories"—claims about putative conditions. But, upon inspection, even their statement of this abstract theory of social problems discourse incorporated numerous assumptions about social conditions (Best 1993).[4]

Much as earlier generations of sociologists came to question whether sociology could be "value-free," strict constructionists began to recognize that their goal of an "assumption-free" sociology was an illusion. Thus, when Kitsuse and psychologist Theodore R. Sarbin introduce their 1994 collection of constructionist cases studies, they speak of the logical desirability of strict constructionism. (They equate the strict constructionist approach with what they call "contextualism"—"tell[ing] a story about phenomena in their natural contexts" [Sarbin and Kitsuse 1994:7].) But then they confess:

> None of the chapters in this volume is an exemplar of strict constructionism. . . . It is questionable whether researchers can sustain any method that would be consistent with the requirements of strict contextualism. . . . Investigators and analysts in spite of themselves cannot help but import their interests, if not their professional agendas, into their interactions with their informants. (Sarbin and Kitsuse 1994:14)[5]

In other words, strict constructionism is an elusive, unattainable goal. All sociological analysis requires stepping back from the subjects of research, calling at least a portion of the taken-for-granted social world into question. Constructionism requires stepping back a bit further, in order to question the definitions of social conditions as social problems. And the strict constructionists advocate stepping back further still, assuming less and calling still more into question. But, however far analysts distance themselves from their subject matter, they can never jettison all assumptions. Analysis requires the analyst to use language, and a culture's assumptions are built into its language. As a result, all analysts, no matter how far they may distance themselves from their subject matter, can be attacked for ontological gerrymandering.

How should sociologists respond to the strict constructionist critique? Some strict constructionists advocate directing sociological research in new directions. Thus, Woolgar and Pawluch (1985b:12) call for sociologists to "move beyond constructivism" and refocus their analyses on the nature of sociological inquiry, although they concede that the new questions they raise "will not contribute . . . to our understanding of the world as we have traditionally conceived that pursuit." This not only shifts the analytic focus away from the social conditions studied by objectivist sociologists, but also away from the claimsmaking studied by constructionists, so that the analyst's subject becomes how sociologists purport to study others. Other strict constructionists argue that sociologists should re-define their analyses as literary products, understanding that sociology is just another form of narrative, that sociologists are storytellers, and that sociological explanation is merely another genre to be subjected to literary analysis. Of course, these new, introspective research agendas completely abandon studying what most people commonly call "social problems" (see also Holstein and Miller 1993). The strict constructionists seem to have convinced themselves of the impossibility of doing sociological—or at least social scientific—analysis.

CONTEXTUAL CONSTRUCTIONISM

While debate over strict constructionism occupied the attention of a few social problems theorists, many more sociologists tried to use the constructionist per-spective to do research. The years following Woolgar and Pawluch's critique of ontological gerrymandering saw the publication of numerous constructionist stud-ies, including pieces in such prestigious journals as the *American Sociological Review* (Block and Burns 1986), the *American Journal of Sociology* (Gamson and Modigliani 1989; Hilgartner and Bosk 1988), and the *American Political Science Review* (A Schneider and Ingram 1993). Most of this research simply ignored the strict constructionsit critique.

This does not mean that the critique of ontological gerrymandering has no merit. Strict constructionism reminds analysts that they must pay attention to the assumptions they bring to their analyses. Consider, for example, arguments—discussed earlier—that equate constructionism with debunking. We might call this *vulgar constructionism*, in which the analyst argues that social problems claims are "just" social constructions, i.e., that the claims are mistaken. Strict constructionists would argue that such debunking should not be considered a form of constructionism, that it is objectivist sociology, since the debunker pre-sumes to know—and focuses on—the actual nature of social conditions, rather than the claimsmaking process.

But the majority of constructionist research falls somewhere between the two extremes of the strict constructionists' phenomenology, with its impossible de-mand that analysts avoid all assumptions about social conditions, and the vulgar constructionists' debunking, which loses sight of claimsmaking as the focus for social problems analysis. Constructionist work that occupies this middle ground—the chapters in this volume are examples—is called *contextual constructionism*.

Rather than retreating into general theories of condition categories and other abstractions, contextual constructionism seeks to locate claimsmaking within its context. Claims emerge at particular historical moments in particular societies; they are made by particular claimsmakers, who address particular audiences. Claimsmakers have particular reasons for choosing particular rhetoric to address particular problems. Such specific elements form claimsmaking's context, and contextual constructionists argue that understanding social problems claims often depends upon understanding their context.[6]

Consider, for example, John M. Johnson's analysis of child-abuse horror sto-ries. . . . The context for these claims includes many elements: child abuse's emergence as a highly visible social issue during the 1960s and 1970s, the expansion of federal government influence through contingent funding of child protection programs, the women's movement's calls for increased attention to various forms of family violence, widespread cultural acceptance of a sentimental view of children as vulnerable innocents, conventions within the press for using examples to attract and maintain interest in complex stories—the list goes on and on. Johnson explicitly mentions some, but not all, of these. We can imagine that a longer, more complete analysis might explore some of the elements Johnson neglects. Nor is Johnson's chapter in any way exceptional; analogous comments could be made about each of the other chapters and, in fact, about any constructionist analysis. All claims emerge in contexts and, in their efforts to understand claims, analysts inevitably refer to these contexts.

But the key point is that any analysis of the social construction of child abuse—or any other social problem—requires locating claimsmaking within at least part of its context. Contrary to what strict constructionism demands, it is neither possible nor desirable to ignore the context of claims. And, because context has so many elements, the analyst invariably has to make assumptions about some of these elements.

Contextual constructionists, then, acknowledge making various assumptions about the social context of claimsmaking. Some of these assumptions may be explicit—announced by the analyst, others may be implicit—recognized by the analyst but not announced, and still others may never be consciously articulated by the analyst. The issue is not whether an analyst makes assumptions; analysts inevitably make assumptions. Remember that even strict constructionists have come to concede the impossibility of assumption-free analyses. Rather, the issue should be whether particular assumptions somehow damage an analysis.

Consider Woolgar and Pawluch's (1985a) initial example of ontological gerrymandering, their critique of Spector and Kitsuse's (1977) *Constructing Social Problems*. In a passage about changing claims regarding marijuana, Spector and Kitsuse (1977:43) remark: "The nature of marijuana remained constant." After quoting this passage, Woolgar and Pawluch (1985a:217) pounce: "[T]he key assertion is that the actual character of a substance (marijuana), condition, or behavior remained constant." Having been found to have made an assumption about a social condition, Spector and Kitsuse stand convicted of ontological gerrymandering. The strict constructionists accepted this as a legitimate criticism, but contextual constructionists demand something more—evidence that the assumption somehow damaged the analysis.

Was this indeed Spector and Kitsuse's "key assertion"? Was it unreasonable for them to assume that the nature of marijuana had not changed? Of course, Woolgar and Pawluch are not concerned about the marijuana problem's history; they simply use this example to identify what they see as a logical error, an unwarranted assumption bootlegged into Spector and Kitsuse's analysis. But Woolgar and Pawluch do not explain why this assumption was unreasonable; they do not, for example, hypothesize that through genetic mutation or altered cultivation practices, new strains of marijuana became available. In fact, it is not clear how Spector and Kitsuse damaged their analysis by assuming that marijuana had not changed.

In contrast, critics may find it much easier to specify what is wrong with other assumptions. Imagine, for example, an analyst who describes growing concern about illicit drug use and then assumes that "Illicit drug use remained constant." A critic who argues that illicit drug use probably did not remain constant—and who can offer convincing evidence to that effect—can argue that the analysis is flawed, that the assumption has damaged the analysis.

In other words, it is neither necessary nor possible for analysts to avoid all assumptions. But analysts must be prepared to acknowledge and defend the assumptions they do make. Critics should adopt a pragmatic standard: damage caused by an assumption must be demonstrated, rather than presumed. This is, of course, the traditional standard for evaluating social scientific inquiry: analysts report their methods and findings, and invite critics to spot flaws in the reasoning. But making an assumption is not, in and of itself, a logical flaw: making an assumption should not be considered a flaw until a critic can demonstrate why that assumption should be called into question.

It is important to emphasize that contextual constructionism remains focused on claimsmaking as a process. That is, contextual constructionists make assumptions about social conditions in order to better understand how social problems claims emerge and evolve. But this does not mean that strict constructionists are right when they equate contextual constructionism with objectivist sociology. Contextual constructionist analysts continue to ask questions that are very different from the ones asked by traditional objectivist researchers.

Suppose we study a campaign against "increasing crime in the streets." What might account for those claims? A strict constructionist might note claimsmakers' references to higher crime rates or rising fear of crime. But the strict constructionist would view these statements as claims, without making any effort to assess whether there really were increases in crime or the fear of crime. In contrast, a contextual constructionist might also look at official crime statistics or polls measuring the fear of crime—even if claimsmakers never referred to statistics or polls. Suppose, for instance, that claimsmakers campaigned against increasing crime at a time when official statistics showed no increase in the crime rate. A contextual constructionist might well choose to make something of the discrepancy between the claims and other information about social conditions. At a minimum, it seems reasonable to ask what the claimsmakers used as the basis for their claims of increasing crime, and an analyst might also ask what else could account for the timing of those claims.

Here, we see a key difference between strict and contextual constructionism. Obviously, any discussion about social conditions is a social construction. A claim that crime (or the fear of crime) is increasing is just that—a claim. But calling a statement a claim does not discredit it. Contextual constructionists argue that any claim can be evaluated. A claim may be based on various sorts of evidence, such as official criminal justice statistics or public opinion polls, which are in turn social constructions—products of the organizational practices of police departments, polling firms, and so on. Strict constructionists often argue that one set of claims (e.g., statistics about rising crime) cannot be used to assess other claims (e.g., claimsmaking about "crime in the streets"). But contextual constructionists assume that they can know—with reasonable confidence—something about social conditions. They acknowledge the socially constructed nature of crime rates and other information about social conditions, but they assume that such information can still be used to (imperfectly) describe the context within which claimsmaking occurs. Certainly, whether or not official statistics showed a rising crime rate might affect a contextual constructionist's interpretation of claims about rising street crime. Note that analysts can handle official statistics and other information about social conditions in different ways. In debunking, for instance, one simply accepts the official figures as true, accurate representations of reality—an approach more objectivist than constructionist. But a contextual constructionist views official statistics as social constructions, and is more likely to ask how claimsmakers use such statistics. Are claimsmakers familiar with the official data, or do they ignore it, or interpret it selectively in a way consistent with their claims? Treating official statistics as accurate measures of social conditions may move an analyst outside the constructionist tradition, but the error in treating official statistics as part of the claimsmakers' contest—and as claims in their own right—is less obvious.

The distinction between strict and contextual constructionism, then, becomes a matter of degree. Woolgar and Pawluch helped sensitize sociologists to the ways assumptions can creep unnoticed into analyses, but strict constructionism's goal of assumption-free analysis can never be achieved. Moreover, strict constructionism comes at a cost; it constrains analysis and limits what we can learn about the process of constructing social problems. Analysts who hope to understand how and why social problems emerge and evolve must locate claimsmaking within its context. By default, all constructionist analysis becomes a form of contextual constructionism.

USING THE CONSTRUCTIONIST PERSPECTIVE

The debate over the theoretical underpinnings of constructionism may give the impression that this is a dry, academic, ivory-tower perspective of little practical value. It would be a shame to end on that note. Once understood, the constructionist perspective can be useful, both for would-be claimsmakers and would-be social problems analysts.

Constructionism as a Guide to Making Claims.   Relatively few people achieve national recognition as claimsmakers who are invited to testify before Congress, are photographed for news-magazines, and are interviewed on the evening network news. But not all claimsmaking occurs in the national arena. Claimsmaking also takes place in state capitols and city halls, in communities and neighborhoods, at workplaces, and on college campuses—wherever people try to draw attention to what they consider troublesome conditions.

Constructionist research offers valuable lessons for would-be claimsmakers. Claimsmakers face practical obstacles: they must attract attention, enlist support, and shape policy. Constructionist research shows how other claimsmakers have dealt with these obstacles. In a sense, constructionist case studies present guidelines for what works (and what does not), and under what circumstances. Studying sociologists' analyses of successful and unsuccessful claimsmaking can help would-be claimsmakers, plan their own campaigns.

Applying Constructionism to New Topics.   While insights from construction-ist research can be used to help design new claimsmaking campaigns, construc-tionism remains most useful as an analytic tool. Constructionism is a stance, an orientation, a perspective we can apply to better understand the world around us. We live in a world where claimsmaking has become routine. The front page of a typical morning newspaper probably features three or four examples of claimsmaking. Claims account for large shares of the material presented in news-magazines, on news broadcasts, before Congressional hearings, on radio and tele-vision talk shows, and so on. Usually these claims highlight fresh aspects of fa-miliar social problems—say, a report that researchers have identified another cancer-causing substance. Less often, the claimsmakers say they have discovered a brand new problem.

While the media offer a steady supply of contemporary claims, it is also easy to identify historical examples of claimsmaking. American history, for instance, features campaigns for the abolition of slavery, women's suffrage, temperance, and so on. While more often described as political or social movements, these were, obviously, instances of claimsmaking.

Whether contemporary or historical, claims can be studied by adopting the constructionist perspective (see Spector and Kitsuse [1977:159–171] for practical suggestions). This requires focusing on the claims themselves, the claimsmakers, and the claimsmaking process.

Claims. The first task in constructionist analysis is to locate examples of the claims being made. Sources for claims vary, depending upon how and when the claims were made, the claimsmakers' credentials, and so on, but standard sources include (1) press coverage, both print (e.g., newspaper and newsmagazine arti-cles) and electronic (e.g., evening network news, *60 Minutes*), (2) scholarly and professional books and periodical articles, (3) popular treatments, trade books, articles in general-interest magazines, or talk show discussions, (4) testimony before Congressional hearings, (5) pamphlets, flyers, handouts, and other ephem-eral materials, (6) public opinion polls, and (7) interviews with claimsmakers.

Sometimes is it possible to trace the shifting level of interest in a social problem by measuring the frequency with which a particular type of claim ap-pears. Sociologists often use indexes to the mass media (e.g., the *Reader's Guide to Periodical Literature,* the *New York Times Index,* or the *Television News Index and Abstracts*) to measure changing levels of media coverage of social problems.

Once a set of claims has been located, their content can be analyzed. Several questions become important: What is being said about the problem? How is the problem being typified? What is the rhetoric of claimsmaking—how are claims presented so as to persuade their audiences?

Claimsmakers. A second focus for analysis is claimsmakers. To begin, the claimsmakers must be identified. Who actually makes the claims? Whom (if anyone besides themselves) do the claimsmakers say they represent? Are the claims-makers leaders or representatives of particular organizations, social movements, professions, or interest groups? With whom are they allied or linked through previous contacts? Are they experienced claimsmakers, or novices? Do they re-flect a particular ideology? What are their interests—in the issues they raise, in the policies they are promoting, and in the success of the campaign? How does the fact that these are the people making the claims shape the claims that get made?

The Claimsmaking Process. Claims evoke varying responses. Some claims are ignored—the claimsmakers choose not to pursue their campaign and the matter is quickly forgotten. Occasional claimsmakers have dramatic success stories: peo-ple listen to the claims and respond quickly by adopting whatever policies the claimsmakers recommend. Most often, of course, campaigns have mixed success: only prolonged claimsmaking produces results, or the claimsmakers manage to organize an active social movement, but have difficulty changing social policy; or it becomes necessary to mount a series of campaigns, each leading to small policy changes. Obviously, claimsmaking processes are complex, and a good deal of comparative research will be needed before they can be understood. Some basic questions about any claimsmaking campaign might include: Whom did the claimsmakers address? Were other claimsmakers presenting rival claims? What concerns and interests did the claimsmakers' audience bring to the issue, and how did those concerns or interests shape the audience's response to the claims? How did the nature of the claims or the identity of the claimsmakers affect the audience's response?

In addressing the various questions raised by constructionists, it is important to remain focused on claimsmaking, to avoid being distracted by the social con-ditions about which claims are being made. This does not mean—in spite of the strict constructionist's objections—that conditions cannot figure into the analysis, but conditions should never become the focal point. Strict constructionists prefer to ask how claimsmakers perceive and describe social conditions. Contextual con-structionists may also ask how its larger context shapes claimsmaking. But neither form of constructionism treats social conditions as its analytic centerpiece.

In short, constructionism has become a useful, active research tradition—one that promises to lead to general theories of social problems. . . .

ACKNOWLEDGMENTS

Jun Ayukawa, Donna Maurer, and T. Memoree Thibodeau made helpful com-ments on an earlier draft of this chapter.

Notes

1. Spector and Kitsuse's (1977) *Constructing Social Problems* and an earlier article by Herbert Blumer (1971) were the most influential early theoretical statements of the con-

structionist perspective. Joseph Schneider's (1985a) review article lists many early case studies. Holstein and Miller's (1993; Miller and Holstein 1993) recent collections include discussions that approach constructionism from a variety of theoretical orientations. The constructionist approach to social problems is related to recent intellectual movements in other disciplines, including philosophy, anthropology, communications, literary analysis, and political science, that share a concern with understanding how people assign meaning to their worlds.

2. While constructionist research appears in many sociological journals, most articles concerning theoretical issues about constructionism in particular, and social problems theory in general, have appeared in *Social Problems*, the journal of the Society for the Study of Social Problems. In addition, the *SSSP Newsletter* has printed a number of brief but noteworthy contributions to the debate. Anyone can receive both *Social Problems* and the *SSSP Newsletter* by joining the Society (see a current issue of *Social Problems* for details— dues for students are modest).

3. This is not to deny that some constructionist work does debunk claims. There are some "plot lines" that reoccur in many constructionist studies. One standard plot features plucky claimsmakers who draw attention to a neglected social problem. These sympathetic portraits tend to focus on social movements' struggles to bring issues to the fore. When we read between the lines, we may suspect that the analyst approves of the claimsmakers' cause. In these studies, the analytic focus is less often a critical analysis of the claims that a discussion of the practical problems claimsmakers face: how to mobilize supporters, how to generate sympathetic media coverage, how to influence policymakers, and so on. This plot's drama comes from casting the claimsmakers as underdogs, who must struggle to call attention to a neglected, albeit legitimate issue.

A second common constructionist plot line seems more critical of the claimsmakers. Here, the analyst dissects claims, often calling them into question. (It is these analyses that lead some critics to equate constructionism with debunking.) The claimsmakers in these accounts are rarely underdogs: they may be powerful officials, prestigious professionals, influential members of the mass media, or other well-placed elites; if they are activists, they typically have powerful allies. In this plot, the drama comes from the analyst challenging widely accepted claims.

The choice of plot line often seems to depend upon the politics of analysts and their sociological audience. Because sociologists tend to have liberal sympathies, most analysts no doubt find it easier to adopt the first plot line to analyze campaigns for left-liberal causes. Thus, we have numerous sympathetic studies of claimsmaking by feminists, peace activists, and so on. In contrast, analysts who focus on more conservative causes, such as drug wars, tend to subject the claimsmakers' rhetoric to criticism. In contrast, there seem to be relatively fewer critical analyses of, say, the rhetoric of claimsmaking about sexual harassment, just as there are few studies celebrating the struggles of the English-only movement.

But, again, this pattern is not inherent in the constructionist stance. While analysts may seem to favor some politically charged topics and shy away from others, these values are something analysts bring to the perspective. Constructionism is a tool, not an ideology; it orients the analysts to forgo concentrating on the nature of social conditions and, instead, to ask questions about claimsmaking. People with very different values may agree that constructionism's topic—the rise and fall of social problems—is a significant feature of contemporary society and warrants study, and they may find it useful to adopt the constructionist approach.

4. Holstein and Miller (1993) and Miller and Holstein (1993) present some 20 commentaries on Ibarra and Kitsuse's paper, written from a range of theoretical orientations.

5. The final sentence in this passage offers another example of the problem with strict constructionism. Even here, Sarbin and Kitsuse makes assumptions about analysts' intent, interests, and agendas. It is apparently impossible to describe strict constructionism in terms that do not violate its tenets (Best 1993).

6. Some researchers have begun identifying their work as examples of contextual constructionism (Goode and Ben-Yehuda 1994; Hallett and Rogers 1994; Rafter 1992; Sarbin and Kitsuse 1994).

References

Best, J. 1993. "But Seriously Folks." Pp. 129–147 in *Reconsidering Social Constructionism*, edited by J. A. Holstein and G. Miller. Hawthorne, NY: Aldine de Gruyter.

Block, F., and G. A. Burns. 1986. "Productivity as a Social Problem." *American Sociological Review* 51:767–780.

Blumer, H. 1971. "Social Problems as Collective Behavior." *Social Problems* 18:298–306.

Collins, P. H. 1989. "The Social Construction of Invisibility." *Perspectives on Social Problems* 1:77–93.

Eitzen, D. S. 1984. "Teaching Social Problems: Implications of the Objectivist Subjectivist Debate." *SSSP Newsletter* 16 (Fall):10–12.

Forsyth, C. J., and M. D. Oliver. 1990. "The Theoretical Framing of a Social Problem." *Deviant Behavior* 11:281–292.

Gamson, W., and A. Modigliani. 1989. "Media Discourse and Public Opinion on Nuclear Power." *American Journal of Sociology* 95:1–37.

Goode, E., and N. Ben-Yehuda. 1994. *Moral Panics*. Oxford, UK: Blackwell.

Gusfield, J. R. 1985. "Theories and Hobgoblins." *SSSP Newsletter* 17 (Fall):16–18.

Hallett, M. A., and R. Rogers. 1994. "The Push for 'Truth in Sentencing'." *Evaluation and Program and Planning* 17:187–196.

Hazelrigg, L. E. 1985. "Were It Not for Words." *Social Problems* 32:234–237.

———.1986. "Is There a Choice Between 'Constructionism' and 'Objectivism'?" *Social Problems* 33 (October/December):S1–S13.

Hilgartner, S., and C. L. Bosk. 1988. "The Rise and Fall of Social Problems." *American Journal of Sociology* 94:53–78.

Holstein, J. A., and G. Miller (eds.). 1993. *Reconsidering Social Constructionism*. Hawthorne, NY: Aldine de Gruyter.

Ibarra, P. R., and J. I. Kitsuse. 1993. "Vernacular Constituents of Moral Discourse." Pp. 25–58 in *Reconsidering Social Constructionism*, edited by J. A. Holstein and G. Miller. Hawthorne, NY: Aldine de Gruyter.

Jones B. J., J. A. McFalls, Jr., and B. J. Gallagher III. 1989. "Toward a Unified Model for Social Problems Theory." *Journal for the Theory of Social Behavior* 19:337–356.

Kitsuse, J. I., and J. W. Schneider. 1989. "Preface." Pp. xi–xiii in *Images of Issues*, edited by J. Best. Hawthorne, NY: Aldine de Gruyter.

Manis J. G. 1985. "Defining Social Problems." *SSSP Newsletter* 16 (Winter):5.

Miller, G., and J. A. Holstein. 1993. *Constructionist Controversies*. Hawthorne, NY: Aldine de Gruyter.

Miller, L. J. 1993. "Claims-Making from the Underside." Pp. 349–376 in *Reconsidering Social Constructionism,* edited by J. A. Holstein and G. Miller. Hawthorne, NY: Aldine de Gruyter.

Pfohl, S. 1985. "Toward a Sociological Deconstruction of Social Problems." *Social Problems* 32:228–232.

Rafter, N. H. 1992. "Claims-Making and Socio-Cultural Context in the First U.S. Eugenics Gampaign." *Social Problems* 39:17–34.

Sarbin, T. R., and J. I. Kitsuse. 1994. "A Prologue to *Constructing the Social.*" Pp. 1–18 in *Constructing the Social,* edited by T. R. Sarbin and J. I. Kitsuse. Thousand Oaks, CA: Sage.

Schneider, A., and H. Ingram. 1993. "Social Construction of Target Populations," *American Political Science Review* 87:334–347.

Schneider, J. W. 1985a. "Social Problems Theory." *Annual Review of Sociology* 11:209–229.

———. 1985b. "Defining the Definitional Perspective on Social Problems." *Social Problems* 32:232–234.

Spector, M., and J. I. Kitsuse. 1977. *Constructing Social Problems.* Menlo Park, CA: Cummings.

———. 1987. "Preface to the Japanese Edition: Constructing Social Problems." *SSSP Newsletter* 18 (Fall):13–15.

Speed, B. 1991. "Reality Exists O.K.?" *Family Therapy* 13:395–409.

Troyer, R. 1992. "Some Consequences of Contextual Constructionism." *Social Problems* 39:35–37.

Woolgar, S., and D. Pawluch. 1985a. "Ontological Gerrymandering." *Social Problems* 32:214–227.

———. 1985b. "How Shall We Move Beyond Constructionism." *Social Problems* 33:159–162.

Questions for Discussion

1. In what way is Kitsuse and Spector's approach to the study of social problems different from that of Fuller and Myers? How is it different from the focus of labeling theory? Do you think these differences are important ones? If yes, in what ways? If not, why not?

2. Choose an alleged situation that you think needs to be recognized as a social problem. Use Loseke's scheme to design a program that would best be able to reach your goal.

3. How does Beckett's article on child sexual abuse both illustrate and add to Loseke's ideas?

4. What does Best say in his article about "Victimization and the Victim Industry" that fits with the points Wagner makes in his article on "The Universalization of Social Problems" (which is included in Chapter 7 on the Critical Perspective)?

5. What is the social constructionist critique of the objectivist stance? What are the critiques of the constructionist approach? What is your position in this debate?

Selected References

Best, Joel. *Threatened Children*. Chicago: University of Chicago Press, 1990.
  A social constructionist account of how people, groups, and media came to create varieties of child abuse as a social problem.

Best, Joel, ed. *Images of Issues: Typifying Contemporary Social Problems*. 2nd ed. New York: Aldine de Gruyter, 1995.
  This collection examines thirteen social problems from the constructionist perspective. Contains Best's useful distinction of strict and contextual constructionists.

Joel Best, ed. *How Claims Spread: Cross-National Diffusion of Social Problems*. Hawthorne, NY: Aldine de Gruyter, 2001.
  A collection of thirteen papers that employ Kitsuse and Spector's concept of claims making. The authors seek to answer the conditions under which a problem socially constructed in one nation spreads to another. Social contacts as well as mass media turns out to be the most likely agencies of diffusion. However, diffusion varies. Claims that make for social construction in one nation may not be taken over in others.

Chase, Susan E., and Colleen S. Bell. "Ideology, Discourse, and Gender: How Gatekeepers Talk About Women School Superintendents." *Social Problems* 37 (May 1990): 163–77.
  This study shows how institutionalized inequality can be based on the social construction of gender. It investigates the situation in which the majority of public school teachers are women but nearly all the school superintendents are men. In their interview study the gatekeepers (mostly school board members) did not express prejudice toward women; in fact, they praised the competent performances of those women superintendents with whom they were familiar. However, the way they spoke about the demands of the job of superintendent perpetuated the notion that the job requires masculine qualities (authority and rationality) as opposed to feminine qualities (nurturing and patience). Thus, the social construction of gender establishes the conditions of persistent inequality in the American public school system.

Conrad, Peter. "Public Eyes and Private Genes: Historical Frames, News Constructions, and Social Problems." *Social Problems* 44 (May 1997): 139–54.
  Personnel in all the media of communication play a significant role in the social construction of social problems. A case in point is how they translate highly complex scientific findings into simple shorthand terms. Conrad shows how the many findings of the Human Genome Project have been oversimplified and popularized through numerous communications in several media. He points out that findings that tend to support the idea of a "gay gene" get front page coverage whereas studies disproving its role in male homosexuality are buried in the back page. And the same goes for the genetic explanation for alcoholics. Today most people know about scientific findings as they have been translated and popularized in the press. Conrad argues that the widespread publicity accompanying the genetic revolution will probably generate widespread public attitudes favoring biological rather than social solutions to social problems.

Conrad, Peter, and Joseph W. Schneider. *Deviance and Medicalization: From Badness to Sickness*. Philadelphia: Temple University Press, 1994. Expanded Edition with a new afterword by the authors.
  The authors show how alcoholism, child abuse, delinquency, drug addiction, homosexuality, hyperkinesis, and mental illness have been redefined over time by relabeling crimes, habits, or sins as illnesses. An important work in the history of sociological perspectives on social problems. Conrad and Schneider's book helped develop the social constructionist perspective.

Holstein, James A., and Gale Miller, eds. *Perspectives on Social Problems*, vol. 1. Greenwich, CT: JAI. Press, 1989.
  Fifteen papers that deal with different aspects of constructionism.

Glassner, Barry. *The Culture of Fear: Why Americans Are Afraid of the Wrong Things.* New York: Basic Books, 1999.

Glassner advances the constructionist argument that combinations of interested parties, moral reformers, and, perhaps most important of all, the various media of communication have called attention successfully to what they collectively claim to be social problems. Generally, the amount of attention (newspaper, magazine, book coverage, and legislation) is inversely proportional to the severity of the "problem." Like Roman dictators, their successful claimsmaking has, according to Glassner, deflected the public's attention from the really intractable problems confronting American society.

Gubrium, Jason and James Holstein, *Social Problems in Everyday Life: Studies of Social Problems Work.* Greenwich, CT: JAI Press, 1997.

Kitsuse and Spector had suggested in their *Constructing Social Problems* that sociologists might study the process of claimsmaking by approaching it in the same manner that sociologists have studied occupations. Gubrium and Holstein, acting on Kitsuse and Spector's suggestion, examine in a number of social services occupations how workers take action on the very claims that they make about problem clients.

Gusfield, Joseph R. *Contested Meanings: The Social Construction of Alcohol Problems.* Madison, WI: University of Wisconsin Press, 1996.

In this collection of essays, Gusfield examines how specific groups became successful in making claims that alcoholism was a disease, that alcoholics should be treated, not punished, and that problem drinkers caused automobile accidents. His earlier 1981 book, *The Culture of Public Problems*, a pioneering work in constructionist analysis, spells out in great detail how the social response to drinking–driving accidents shifted from educating drivers to apprehending drunken drivers.

Holstein, James A., and Gale Miller, eds. *Reconsidering Social Constructionism: Debates in Social Problems Theory.* New York: Aldine de Gruyter, 1993.

In this wide-ranging collection of original articles, Holstein and Miller have assembled views supporting as well as attacking social constructionism. They have also included a number of pieces applying this perspective to a variety of social problems.

Jenkins, Philip. *Intimate Enemies: Moral Panics in Contemporary Great Britain.* Hawthorne, NY: Aldine de Gruyter, 1992.

Jenkins applies the constructionist perspective to moral panics of the 1980s. He shows how activists, groups, media, and government combine to create social problems of serial killers, child abuse, and satanism.

Kirk, Stuart A., and Herb Kutchins. *The Selling of DSM: The Rhetoric of Scientific Psychiatry.* Hawthorne, NY: Aldine de Gruyter, 1992.

The authors show how the development of a "scientific" classification of mental disorders resolved on paper the problem of uncertainty in diagnosis. Government, mental health professions, and insurance companies quickly adopted DSM-III.

Loseke, Donileen. *Thinking About Social Problems.* New York: Aldine de Gruyter, 1999.

In this slim book, Loseke presents the social constructionist perspective in very readable and understandable prose.

Miller, Gale, and Kathryn J. Fox. "Learning from Sociological Practice: The Case of Applied Constructionism." *The American Sociologist* 80 (Spring, 1999): 54–73.

Miller and Fox carried out constructionist studies of human service organizations. Miller studied a clinic in which practitioners carried out brief therapy with their clients. Fox studied the administrators and the outreach workers in a West Coast AIDS project offering sterile needles to heroin addicts. They argue that "social constructionism is an aspect of the diverse social world in which we live." As a consequence of their separate research experiences, they came to the conclusion that they are "sociological constructionists" whereas the practitioners they studied are "applied constructionists." Clinic therapists focus talk on solutions, not problems, that clients are "competent managers of their own lives" and that they, not the therapists, decide what changes they need to make in their own lives. The therapists say ". . . since social realities are constructed anyway, why not construct realities that are positive and hopeful about the future?" Hence, their designation of applied constructionists. By contrast, administrators at the West Coast AIDS project, familiar with constructionism, took their clients' definitions of reality seriously only to find that their employees, the outreach workers, thought clients were wrong-headed and did not take the risk of AIDS seriously. Conclusions the authors draw from their paper are as follows: More studies in social settings may produce data to solve the argument between strict and contextual constructionists, sociologists should examine how they construct sociological realities, and more constructionist studies in human service organizations may prove fruitful in uniting theory, research, and application.

Miller, Gale, and James A. Holstein, eds. *Constructionist Controversies: Issues in Social Problems Theory.* Hawthorne, NY: Aldine de Gruyter, 1993.

A collection of papers extending, applying, and criticizing the perspective of social constructionism.

Peyrot, Mark. "Cycles of Social Problem Development: The Case of Drug Abuse." *Sociological Quarterly* 25 (Winter 1984): 83–96.

In this example of contextual constructionism, Peyrot develops a model of stages in social problems that involves the interplay of politics and history over time. The cycle, using responses to drug abuse as the case for analysis, consists of five stages: Mobilizing agitation, policy formation, and policy implementation are the first three. In time, the other two stages develop: program modification and reform agitation. After this fifth stage a transition to another cycle follows. The bulk of the paper applies this model to an analysis of how U.S. responses to drug abuse have gone from punishment to treatment and back to punishment over the course of the twentieth century.

Rafter, Nicole Hahn. *Creating Born Criminals.* Urbana: University of Illinois Press, 1997.

A social history of mental retardation in the United States carried out from a contextual constructionist perspective. Rafter describes several phases in the social construction of the mentally retarded. Prior to 1850, they were consigned to the "undifferentiated trash heaps of human misery." Starting in 1850, a movement arose to take those labeled as "idiots" out of poorhouses and prisons and to train them. Prison reform in 1870 brought the Elmira Reformatory, which sought to reward good behavior, use indeterminate sentences, and retrain inmates for life after prison. Criminal anthropology came into being about this time and came to see eugenics as being the solution to criminality. But by the second decade of the twentieth century, a newcomer, psychology, took ownership of mental retardation with its development of the intelligence quotient.

Schneider, Joseph W. "Social Problems Theory: The Constructionist View." *Annual Review of Sociology* 11. Palo Alto, CA: Annual Reviews, 1985, pp. 209–29.

Schneider outlines the social constructionist argument, reviews almost thirty papers published in the journal *Social Problems* that apply this perspective to a diversity of social problems, and notes strong and weak points of this approach.

Schneider, Joseph W., and John I. Kitsuse. *Studies in the Sociology of Social Problems.* Norwood, NJ: Ablex, 1984.

A collection of eight papers that deal with various aspects of the constructionist perspective.

III / THE PROSPECTS

9/A SOCIOLOGICAL REVIEW OF THE PERSPECTIVES

The purpose of this book has been to show the different ways in which American sociologists have viewed social problems from the early twentieth century until the present. In this chapter, we would like to review briefly the central themes of the perspectives, their relative strengths and weaknesses, and how they represent different ways of resolving the dual mandate. (The "dual mandate," it will be recalled, refers to sociology's dual goals of solving social problems and of developing sociology as a discipline.)

THE SEVEN PERSPECTIVES

The study of social problems is entangled as much with changes in American society as with the development of American sociology. A rapid review of the perspectives illustrates the point. (See Table 1.)

Social Pathology. In the early years of American sociology, an optimistic spirit gripped its founders. Committed to a broad social philosophy, they saw their task as the demonstration of how society could grow to fulfill a scheme of natural law and progress. These sociologists became social reformers, and as they focused on the social problems of the day, their work was infused with moral indignation. They formulated this indignation in terms of a medical model, regarding one set of social problems as the work of persons who were "sick"—that is, defective, delinquent, or dependent. At the same time, these early sociologists were also morally indignant at those who occupied command posts in business, industry, and government, attributing many of their actions to vice, greed, corruption, and power.

A revised version of the pathology perspective shows even more concern with institutional arrangements. The moral indignation remains, but now it is the society and its institutions, rather than nonconformity, that those that call themselves social pathologists regard as "sick." At the same time, they continue to advocate the moral education of the individuals involved as the solution to such problems.

Social Disorganization. In the second phase of American sociology, reformism began to give way to a conception of the sociologist as a scientist building a new academic discipline. Sociologists in this period directed their efforts toward devising concepts, developing theories, and producing empirical research rather than making

Table 1 Prime Periods of the Perspectives

Period 1: Establishing a base (1905 to 1918)	Period 2: Forming a scientific policy (1918 to 1935)	Period 3: Integrating theory, research and application (1935 to 1954)	Period 4: Cultivating specialties (1954 to 1970)	Period 5: Reemergence of macro theory (1970 to 1985)	Period 6: Ascendancy of social constructionism (1985 on)
Social pathology	Social disorganization	Value conflict	Deviant behavior	Critical	Social constructionism
			Labeling		

moral, philosophical, or critical pronouncements. Thomas and Znaniecki, for example, argued that sociology must follow in the footsteps of other, more developed, sciences by staking out a special subject matter. In an effort to develop sociology along these lines, sociologists of this period focused on social rules rather than persons in their study of social problems. For them, social disorganization followed from the breakdown of the influence of rules on the individual. When rules were absent, unclear, or in conflict, social problems came into being.

Value Conflict. During the third period of American sociology, most sociologists continued to argue for the development of sociological theory. Nonetheless, a relatively small band of sociologists began to argue against pursuing the development of sociology as a value-free science. Instead, they advocated working for the benefit of society. As this critical band examined social problems, most of them came to feel that such problems are inevitable because people cannot agree on social policies. And usually the reason people disagree is not because they do not know the rules, but because they hold different values or pursue their own interests. Given the turmoil of the Great Depression and World War II, the value conflict perspective made sense. Whereas the social disorganization perspective encouraged sociologists to remain aloof from struggles within the society, the value conflict position encouraged them to integrate theory, research, and application, and to espouse values and take sides on social issues.

Deviant Behavior. Early in the fourth period of American sociology, the deviant behavior perspective came into being. Building on the social disorganization perspective, it continued sociology's orientation as, first and foremost, a science. It assumed that the sociologist's job is testing the implications of theory, rather than solving society's numerous problems. Although people have since drawn on the deviant behavior perspective in efforts to solve problems of crime and delinquency, sociologists in this tradition studied social problems primarily because they had relevance for sociological theory. In the course of specialization, however, these sociologists restricted their attention almost exclusively to the study of deviant behavior, defined as a violation of normative expectations. Thus, this influential perspective on social problems concentrated attention on the causes of deviance, on deviant behavior systems, and on social control.

Labeling. Late in the fourth period of American sociology, the labeling perspective arose, in large part from questions left unanswered by the deviant behavior perspective. For example: How do people and situations come to be defined as problematic or deviant? With what effects? And how are some people able to avoid being so labeled even though they may have done something "deviant"? Thus, while the deviant behavior perspective defines social problems as objective violations of normative expectations, the labeling perspective sees social problems as being whatever people say they are (that is, as subjectively constructed). Like the deviant behavior perspective, the labeling perspective is specialized, focusing primarily on social definitions of and reactions to social problems, with little interest in other facets of social problems.

Critical Perspective. The political nature of the turbulence in the 1970s led to a focus on social problems as created by the ruling class. This focus carried over into sociology. Some sociologists in this period began to ask whether any of the existing perspectives explained the plethora of social problems being identified or suggested workable solutions for them. Others thought that the perspectives neglected the theoretical in their concern for the socially problematic. Thus, adopting a broader, macro, more holistic view, some writers began to look at how various social problems are related to the political-economic structure of society. Drawing on the numerous and complex strands of the European Marxist tradition, they directed their attention to class relations. Individuals, differently situated with respect to the economic market, came to share interests and values. Their effort to maintain, protect, and further these interests makes for the class struggle, which Marx saw as both the basic source of social problems and, ultimately, their solution.

Social Constructionism. Despite years of studying social problems, sociologists have yet to develop a theory of social problems. Spector and Kitsuse said their colleagues failed because either they accepted commonsense definitions of social problems ("what everybody knows") or they as "experts" decided what alleged situations were social problems. Their criticism gave rise to the constructionist perspective. Numerous situations have existed where objective conditions were present, but a subjective definition of a "social problem" was absent. These circumstances gave rise to the constructionists' question, What do people have to do to make an alleged situation a "social problem"? Spector and Kitsuse's answer: people have to work at it. In their words, some people have to come forward and "make claims." Thus, social problems are a social process, they have a natural history, and unless all of the conditions, necessary and sufficient are present, the problem does not "come into being." The necessary condition is the subjective definition while the sufficient condition consists of the actions other people take in response to the "claims-makers' " definition of the situation.

Thus each of seven perspectives has its own emphasis. The social pathology perspective focuses on *persons;* the social disorganization perspective stresses *rules;* the value-conflict perspective looks at *values and interests;* the deviant behavior perspective emphasizes *roles;* the labeling perspective examines *social reactions;* the critical perspective focuses on *class relations;* and the constructionist perspective concentrates on the *claims-making process.*

In addition, each perspective implies its own causal chain by which these elements (persons, rules, values and interests, roles, social reactions, class relations, and claims-making) are linked. For example, both the deviant behavior and the labeling perspectives deal with deviant roles and social reactions. In the deviant behavior perspective, however, deviant roles *precipitate* social reactions, while the labeling perspective regards deviant roles as *consequences of social reactions.* Similarly, in the value-conflict perspective, *values and interests produce roles;* in the critical perspectives *roles produce values and interests.* And, lastly, in the social constructionist perspective *social reactions produce claims-making roles.*

APPLICABILITY

Each perspective has been more powerful in dealing with some types of issues or problems than others, and each seems more likely to be employed in some cases than in others. In this section, we briefly consider the relative strengths and weaknesses of the perspectives.

When notions about the person as an immoral or dehumanized entity are strongly held, the pathology perspective finds fertile ground. Instances of destructiveness to oneself or others are examples.[1] Unless there are clearcut and unambiguous indicators of the "pathological" elements, however, such an analysis is likely to embody merely the analyst's personal prejudice.

The social disorganization approach works best when it is restricted to studying the organization of specific social units and the effects of rapid change on such units.[2] For instance, it is a powerful tool for understanding the disorganizing effects of social change on particular towns (for example, "Northton"). The social disorganization approach has been faulted, however, for its failure to provide objective indicators of social disorganization and, in the absence of such indicators, for using abstract concepts to conceal implicit value judgments.

The value conflict approach has proved particularly useful where issues are sharply defined by polarization and conflict between groups. The history of Prohibition is a good example.[3] Where the conflicting values or interests of opposing groups cannot be clearly identified, however, this perspective is not as applicable.

Deviant behavior analysis has had and can be expected to have continued popularity in the study of deviance. Interestingly enough, the strengths of the labeling perspective are precisely the weaknesses of the deviant behavior approach, and vice versa. Where clearly defined and uniformly supported norms are involved, the deviant behavior perspective is relatively straightforward and useful. But where agreement on norms is lacking, and where norms do not have strong social support, the labeling perspective makes a special contribution by focusing on the situational contingencies and consequences of labeling.[4] Thus, while the social processes surrounding such crimes as armed robbery and burglary are likely to be studied more from the perspective of deviant behavior, the social processes surrounding crimes such as marijuana use, are more likely to be studied from the labeling perspective.

1. See, for example, Viola W. Bernard, Perry Ottenberg, and Fritz Redl, "Dehumanization: A Composite Psychological Defense in Relation to Modern War," in *Behavioral Sciences and Human Survival,* ed. Milton Schwebel (Palo Alto, CA: Science and Behavior Books, 1965), pp. 64–82.

2. See, for example, Robert K. Merton and Robert Nisbet, eds., *Contemporary Social Problems: An Introduction to the Sociology of Deviant Behavior and Social Disorganization,* 3rd ed. (New York: Harcourt Brace Jovanovich, 1971).

3. See Joseph R. Gusfield, *Symbolic Crusade: Status Politics and the American Temperance Movement* (Urbana: University of Illinois Press, 1969).

4. The affinity of labeling theorists for socially ambiguous subject matter is not theoretically necessary. This focus does, however, dramatize the imputational process. See Prudence Rains, "Imputations of Deviance: A Retrospective Essay on the Labeling Perspective," *Social Problems* 23 (October 1975): 1–11.

And when social inequality can be seen to underlie a large-scale problem, the holistic critical perspective may define the problem as the typically expected consequence of capitalist society and culture.

Spector and Kitsuse said sociologists had yet to devise a systematic sociological theory of social problems. All previous perspectives on social problems were unable to account for two anomalous social situations. One was the presence of persistent troublesome situations without there being a collective definition of them as social problems. The second was the absence of recurrent troublesome situations, but with a collective definition of them as basic social problems. They devised the social constructionist perspective to account for these anomalous situations. Thus, this perspective is most applicable when the interest is in how an alleged situation comes to be considered a social problem.

The above, however, are not the only factors that influences which perspective a sociologist will employ. In the next section, we speculate about some of the other factors involved in the selection of perspectives.

THE DUAL MANDATE AND SOCIOLOGICAL PERSPECTIVES

As we see it, the major point of tension for sociologists studying social problems lies in the dual mandate—that is, to solve social problems as well as to develop sociology as a discipline. In responding to this dual mandate, sociologists adopt four predominant roles. Although sociologists may switch roles during the course of their careers or combine all four roles at once, one of the four roles is usually dominant in the work of any particular sociologist. And along with that dominant role goes a preference for one perspective on social problems over another.

The four roles are theorist, researcher, applier, and critic. Both theorists and researchers focus on developing sociology as a discipline. Theorists develop a network of interrelated propositions that they hope will ultimately explain a vast array of seemingly unrelated events. The social disorganization perspective, for example, contains the nucleus of a theory advanced to explain a broad assortment of social problems. And the labeling and constructionist perspectives have elaborated the theoretical framework of symbolic interactionism.[5]

Researchers, however, seek empirical data. They may derive a set of testable hypotheses from a given sociological theory in order to support or disprove it by means of empirical research. The body of studies based on the deviant behavior and labeling perspectives reflects the work of researchers.

For appliers and critics, sociology should work primarily on behalf of society. Appliers draw on the implications of a given sociological theory in order to propose solutions for specific social problems. The deviant behavior perspective has been particularly popular among appliers, and numerous rehabilitation programs have been fashioned along these lines—for example, for juvenile delinquents or drug addicts.[6] The labeling perspective has also proved to be useful in this regard. More

5. See, for example, Earl Rubington and Martin S. Weinberg, eds., *Deviance: The Interactionist Perspective,* 8th ed. (New York: Allyn and Bacon, 2002) and Donileen R. Loecke, *Thinking About Social Problems: An Introduction to Constructionist Perspectives* (New York: Aldine de Gruyter, 1989).

6. Opportunity theory was applied in President Lyndon Johnson's War on Poverty and in the New York community-action agency called Mobilization for Youth. For the source of these programs, see Richard A. Cloward and Lloyd E. Ohlin, *Delinquency and Opportunity: A Theory of Delinquent Gangs* (New York: Free Press, 1960). For an application of sociological theory to the rehabilitation of juvenile delinquents, see Lamar T. Empey and Jerome Rabow, "The Provo Experiment in Delinquency Rehabilitation," *American Sociological Review* 26 (October 1961): 679–95. For an application to the

and more people have become aware of the arbitrariness and negative consequences of labeling certain behaviors as crimes and with this increased awareness
there has been a trend toward decriminalization.[7] For example some states have
changed their laws regarding marijuana use.[8]

Critics tend to protest against the status quo and to seek broader changes in the
structure of society (the most extreme being revolution). Since the work of Karl Marx
has been the major theoretical inspiration for most critics of society, they tend to
draw most heavily from the critical perspective. Prior to the 1970s, though, the critics
tended to draw on the value conflict perspective or the reviving social pathology
perspective.

In responding to the dual mandate, sociologists also adopt different stances in
teaching social problems courses. In the late 1960s and early 1970s, for example,
students clamored for greater "relevance" in their college courses. Thus, many sociologists began to give more attention in their teaching to the concrete problems of
society than they had in the past and to assume the role of applier or critic in their
teaching. This demand was short-lived, however, and today most sociologists have
returned in their teaching to a study of the work of theorists and researchers and to
the development of knowledge in the discipline.

SOCIETY, SOCIOLOGY, AND THE STUDY OF SOCIAL PROBLEMS

In the last third of the twentieth century, society has seen great changes in population, technology, information, and points of view. These same changes have also
affected colleges. Some 15,000,000 students attend college today, and most two-
year and four-year colleges have grown in size, physical plant, and curriculums.
Unlike the nineteenth century, when there were fewer colleges and most faculty and
students came from the upper classes, most colleges today reflect the increasing
diversity of the population. Today's faculty and students come from all social classes.
In ever-increasing numbers, women and members of various ethnic minorities are
represented in the faculty, administration, and student bodies. What has been true
of colleges in general has also been true of sociology departments.

In the 1960s the leading course in all sociology departments was Introductory
Sociology. The next most popular course was Social Problems. And, typically, most
social problems courses dealt with a large number of social problems and used a
textbook in which each chapter covered a single one of these problems (alcoholism,
crime, drug addiction, mental illness, etc.). Today such general social problems
courses continue to exist, but now, diversification and specialization in sociology
courses has extended to a variety of each one dealing with a specific social problem
(alcoholism, crime, drug addiction, mental illness, etc.). Also many colleges today
now have specialized courses dealing with African American Studies, Gay and Lesbian Studies, Latino Studies, Gender Studies, and so on, which are often housed in
departments of sociology. If, in the beginnings of academic sociology, there were

rehabilitation of drug addicts, see Rita Volkman Johnson and Donald R. Cressey, "Differential Association and the Rehabilitation of Drug Addicts," *American Journal of Sociology* 69 (September 1963):
129–42.

7. See, for example, Rubington's study of responses to the repeal of the public drunkenness statute
in Massachusetts: Earl Rubington, "Top and Bottom: How Police Administrators and Public Inebriates
View Decriminalization," *Journal of Drug Issues* 5 (Fall 1975): 412–25.

8. For an example of this approach to juvenile delinquency, see Edwin M. Schur, *Radical Noninter-
vention: Rethinking the Delinquency Problem* (Englewood Cliffs, NJ: Prentice-Hall, 1973).

only six professional journals, now there are more that 200, most of them specialized. Yet another index of diversification and specialization is the more than 60 sections within the American Sociological Association (ASA) and a like number in the Society for the Study of Social Problems (SSSP). Many of these sections in the ASA deal with specific social problems. In the SSSP, most of them do so. For example, both the ASA and the SSSP have sections on Alcohol and Drugs. And just as the ASA has its own Sociological Theory section, the SSSP has its own section devoted solely to Social Problems Theory.

These changes have altered sociologist's roles and their main audiences in the last third of the twentieth century. Theorists, who stand at the top of the discipline's prestige system, are more often found at major research universities, Ivy League Schools, and major state universities. The main audience for theorists are other theorists along with the members of the ASA section on Sociological Theory. Researchers are divided into two categories, methodologists or area specialists, with other sociologists of their bent serving as their main audience. Applied sociologists, a much smaller category, now have several of their own professional journals and have as their audience other appliers, as well as the employers or clients of applied sociologists. Critics concentrate on one of two audiences, the general public and / or students taking courses in social problems. They come in two varieties: teachers of sociology or social reformers (much like many of the early founders of sociology). Teachers of sociology want their students to examine issues about social problems critically, whereas reformers seek to inspire civic activism.

Sociology, like any other academic discipline, has been characterized by intellectual conflict, competition, and its own cyclical movements of social thought. In earlier years, philosophers discussed the conflict between human agency (free will) and determinism. The pathology perspective provided a good example of a moral determinism. When the social disorganization perspective dominated, moralism almost disappeared as sociology became more concerned with attaining the status of a value-free discipline. But people were still objects of outside forces determining their responses to events beyond their control. The rise of the perspective of value conflict signified a turn. While the deterministic view emphasized passive responses to pressures and events outside the individual's control, proponents of the value conflict perspective saw people actively making choices based on core values and self-interests. Later, the deviant behavior perspective vied with the labeling perspective for domination. The deviant behavior perspective relied on determinism while labeling showed how human agency created deviant roles. The critical perspective came to be known as economic determinism. Proponents of the critical perspective held that social problems stemmed from the workings of the capitalist system over which people had little control. Only in the latest period, the sixth (1985 and on), did human agency become more of a dominant focus rather than determinism. In the constructionist perspective, people become the subjects of social problems. Without their efforts at claims-making, "social problems" do not come into being. With those efforts, problems become socially constructed.

Constructionism made clearer the differences between deterministic perspectives and those focusing on human agency. With respect to the study of social problems, the table below classifies the differences from the point of view of the four roles we have delineated.

The ascendancy of constructionism in the study of social problems evinces a more complete conception of the issues between a deterministic and a human agency focus. But it is not likely that a pure human agency focus will ever defeat a

	Focus	
Role	Determinism	Human Agency
Theorist	General theories about whole societies	Local theories about specific social problems
Researcher	Studied people as effected by external forces	Studied people as creating an external force
Applier	Official records basic	Agents' viewpoints that produce the records are more basic
Critic	More apt to criticize the total social system	More apt to criticize a specific social policy

pure deterministic one. Some synthesis of the two perspectives is more likely. And as that happens, yet another perspective on social problems will emerge.

Questions for Discussion

1. Now that you are familiar with all of the perspectives, which one(s) do you prefer for analyzing social problems? Why? Does the usefulness of each perspective depend on what particular issue or problem you are trying to analyze? If so, how? If not, why not?

2. Consider some social problem currently discussed in the mass media or among your acquaintances. Which of the perspectives is reflected in the way the problem is conceptualized by each of the following: you, your parents, experts on the subject, journalists, legislators, the people directly involved in the problem, churches, people of different ages, people of different classes? What might account for differences in the perspectives of these groups?

3. To what extent do the perspectives overlap? Can any of the perspectives be seen as, to some degree, subsuming any of the others? Why or why not?

4. Using a social problem that interests you, analyze it from each of the perspectives. What are the major differences among your analyses? Now provide an eclectic analysis, using elements from a number of the perspectives.

Selected References

Blumer, Herbert. "Social Problems as Collective Behavior." *Social Problems* 18 (Winter 1971): 298–306.
    A useful theoretical article that combines the value conflict and the labeling perspectives and treats social problems as aspects of social movements.

Downes, David, and Paul Rock. *Understanding Deviance: A Guide to the Sociology of Crime and Rule Breaking.* 3rd ed. New York: Oxford University Press, 1998.
    A systematic exposition and critique of social disorganization, deviant behavior, labeling, and critical perspectives that draws heavily on British and American theorists and researchers.

Hilgartner, Stephen, and Charles L. Bosk, "The Rise and Fall of Social Problems: A Public Arenas Model." *American Journal of Sociology* 94 (July 1988): 53–78.

Accepts the Spector and Kitsuse approach to the study of social problems. It goes on to establish a systematic method for establishing the conditions under which some situations attain social problem status whereas others do not.

Horton, John. "Order and Conflict Theories of Social Problems." *American Journal of Sociology* 31 (May 1966): 701–13.

Horton makes a number of points about the conditions under which sociological perspectives on social problems emerge and the ways in which sociologists construct definitions, causes, conditions, consequences, and solutions of social problems. He argues that definitions of social problems ultimately rest on assumptions about values and that radical and more liberal sociologists are more apt to construct value conflict perspectives, whereas less liberal and more conservative sociologists are more apt to construct deviant behavior perspectives.

Horton, Paul B., Gerald R. Leslie, Richard F. Larson, and Robert L. Morton. *The Sociology of Social Problems*. 12th ed. Upper Saddle River, NJ: Prentice-Hall, 1997.

This textbook on social problems has remained in print much longer than any other. Its longevity may rest on the fact that it examines a changing variety of social problems over the years from three perspectives: social disorganization, value conflict, and deviant behavior.

Julian, Joseph, and William Kornblum. *Social Problems*. 5th ed. Englewood Cliffs, NJ: Prentice-Hall, 1986.

A leading text that examines a number of social problems through a variety of perspectives and concludes each chapter with suggestions on social policy.

Liska, Allen E., and Steven E. Messner. *Perspectives on Crime and Deviance*. 3rd ed. Upper Saddle River, NJ: Prentice-Hall, 1999.

A text that systematically examines social disorganization, deviant behavior, labeling, and critical perspectives according to four headings: concepts, empirical support, critique, and implications for policy.

Marris, Peter. "Witnesses, Engineers, or Storytellers? Roles of Sociologists in Social Policy." In *Sociology In America*, ed. Herbert Gans. Newbury Park, CA: Sage, 1990 pp. 75–87.

Marris, drawing on his thirty years of applied social research in Great Britain, the United States, and Africa, argues that sociologists could have more influence on social policy if they paid more attention to a convincing narrative when reporting their findings. Showing that they did systematic social observation awards them the authority of research. Generally, however, they report their conclusions in the foreign language of their trade, thereby losing their lay audience. If they would tell their story presenting the drama involved in their tale, they would be more likely to capture the moral imagination of their readers. In telling the story they would convince their readers with the evidence they have collected and would also persuade them that their findings point the way to rectifying some form of social injustice.

Mauss, Armand L. *Social Problems as Social Movements*. Philadelphia: Lippincott, 1975.

A textbook with a genuinely new approach to social problems. Blending the value conflict perspective with the labeling perspective, Mauss analyzes social problems as a special kind of social movement.

Merton, Robert K., and Robert Nisbet. *Contemporary Social Problems*. 3rd ed. New York: Harcourt Brace Jovanovich, 1971.

A highly influential textbook that examines social problems from both the deviant behavior and the social disorganization perspectives.

Orcutt, James D. *Analyzing Deviance*. Homewood, IL: Dorsey Press, 1983.

Orcutt classifies deviance in four ways, discusses how the various perspectives we described can fit into these categories, and then presents illustrations of how researchers have applied these conceptions to particular cases.

Pfohl, Stephen J. *Images of Deviance and Social Control: A Sociological History.* New York: McGraw-Hill, 1985.

This "text about texts" considers how sociologists and others have looked at social problems over time. Pfohl provides a detailed treatment of the perspectives we discussed.

Rose, Arnold M. "Theory for the Study of Social Problems." *Social Problems* 4 (January 1957): 189–99.

A stimulating attempt to reconcile conflict and disorganization theories as a means of both studying and solving social problems.

Seidman, Steven. *Contested Knowledge: Social Theory in the Postmodern Era.* Cambridge, MA: Blackwell Publishers, 1994.

After tracing the emergence of classical sociology with Comte and Marx up to its present status, Seidman argues that the search for a general scientific theory of society has proven to be futile. The mistaken attempt to make sociology follow in the footsteps of natural science has only made the findings of social research irrelevant for solving the many serious social problems so many people face in their daily lives. Seidman argues for an activist role for sociologists. Rather than studying what is, they should marshal the already existent knowledge to work for a better society. They should enter the marketplace of ideas to contest with others in a democratic struggle to solve social problems. In Seidman's view, sociologists should apply their knowledge to eliminate or reduce social problems rather than to study society solely for the purpose of building the discipline of sociology.

Weinberg, Martin S., Earl Rubington, and Sue Kiefer Hammersmith, eds. *The Solution of Social Problems: Five Perspectives.* 2nd ed. New York: Oxford University Press, 1981.

A text-reader on the application of the first five sociological perspectives to the solution of social problems.